TEACHING SOCIAL STUDIES TO CULTURALLY DIFFERENT CHILDREN

TEACHING
SOCIAL STUDIES
TO CULTURALLY
DIFFERENT CHILDREN

Edited by

JAMES A. BANKS
University of Washington, Seattle

WILLIAM W. JOYCE
Michigan State University

ADDISON-WESLEY PUBLISHING COMPANY
Reading, Massachusetts
Menlo Park, California · London · Don Mills, Ontario

This book is in the
ADDISON-WESLEY SERIES IN EDUCATION

PREFACE

On April 5, 1968, a tall young white teacher looked baffled and bewildered as he stood in front of his all-black social studies class and screamed, "Why aren't you ever interested in anything?" Even his anguished cry failed to elicit the children's response. They had been studying "Children of Other Lands" for three weeks, but on that morning the poignant and stark picture of Martin Luther King, Jr. lying fatally wounded on a Memphis motel balcony the previous evening was vivid in their troubled minds. The teacher later told a social studies consultant that the children had "no interests" because he had been trying unsuccessfully all year to "reach" them.

This young teacher, perhaps like thousands of others throughout the nation, did not realize that the social studies he was trying to teach his students was too remote from their lives and interests to "turn them on." A child with a deflated self-image, who feels that his cultural environment is inferior to that which is depicted in school as ideal and desirable, finds it difficult to become concerned about children of other lands; he is too preoccupied with the crises of daily living. To be relevant to the culturally different child, social studies must help him to identify, clarify, and solve the baffling social problems which permeate his life and environment.

This book is designed to help classroom teachers attain the knowledge, perceptions, attitudes, and teaching strategies they need to make social studies relevant and exciting for Afro-American, Mexican-American, Puerto Rican-American, American Indian, and other children who come from a culture of poverty. Although a number of experimental programs, among them Head Start, Follow-Through, and Upward Bound, have been implemented to help culturally different children learn more in school, they have focused primarily on improving reading and language-arts skills. Social studies has been almost completely neglected. Even a cursory review of social studies literature for culturally different children reveals the tremendous dearth of work in this area. This is a serious shortcoming. Poverty, discrimination, and alienation are *social* problems with which such children are intimately acquainted. Thus no area of the curriculum should be more relevant to their lives and aspirations than social studies.

This book is divided into three major parts. Part One explores the basic problems and issues involved in teaching social studies to culturally different children. It discusses racial prejudice; the social, cultural, and psychological factors of learning; teacher attitudes; and the image of minority groups presented in teaching materials. The emphasis is on the role of the teacher as a *human being* in the learning process. No matter how promising a teaching strategy may be, it is worthless in the hands of a teacher who lacks the necessary perceptions, insights, and attitudes to work effectively with culturally different children. The contributors stress the need for teachers to set high expectations for these children.

Part Two presents promising classroom strategies for teachers of culturally different children. It also emphasizes the need to make social critics of these children, who must be able to delineate and solve critical social problems in order to attain power and contribute to the improvement of their lives. Because alienated children require highly creative teaching strategies, a chapter is devoted to simulation, role-playing, and sociodrama. This section also describes strategies which can be or have been used successfully in teaching different cultural and racial groups. An entire chapter is devoted to the teaching of black history because of the current interest in and debate over this topic. Rather than providing definite answers, the articles in this chapter raise critical questions and suggest alternative and often conflicting ways to teach this highly controversial subject. The reader is encouraged to explore and reflect on the various strategies in order to reach his own conclusions regarding the most effective methods of teaching black history and culture.

The final part of the book discusses and suggests ways of implementing some of the urgent changes in schools and curricula needed to make social studies and other subjects relevant and meaningful for poor and alienated children.

As Lawrence C. Howard suggests in Chapter 10, poor children can teach America much about the nature of freedom, for they are concerned with little else. Some of the more militant black leaders have stated that our oppressed minorities will be our salvation, since perhaps only they can force this nation to create a society consistent with the democratic ethos it verbally extols.

We are immensely grateful to the authors and publishers who permitted us to reprint their material, and to Bernice Goldmark of Sonoma State College for writing an original contribution. We wish to thank our wives, Cherry McGee Banks and Mary Bosser Joyce, for their diligent work in obtaining permissions. They performed a formidable task well.

December 1970   J. A. B.
                                                    W. W. J.

CONTENTS

PART ONE
PROBLEMS
AND ISSUES

The chapters in this section focus primarily on the role of the teacher in the learning process. In exploring the issues relevant to social studies for culturally different children, the contributors emphasize the need for teachers to clarify their attitudes toward racial and cultural minorities, and to question traditional assumptions regarding culture, environment, intelligence, and intellectual honesty.

In the final analysis, teaching is a human endeavor; the most effective teaching strategies are worthless in the hands of a teacher who lacks the perceptions and predispositions needed to work with children from diverse cultural groups. Our behavior is largely a product of the expectations and norms of the social situations in which we find ourselves. Thus a child's self-perceptions, attitudes, and academic performance are primarily determined by the pervasive norms and expectations of the classroom. If we are to make social studies relevant and meaningful for culturally different children, therefore, we must help teachers to attain those attitudes and values that will maximize their ability to work effectively with their students.

CHAPTER 1
RACE, ETHNICITY,
AND PREJUDICE

One of the founding principles of this country was that oppressed peoples from other lands would find in America tolerance and acceptance, if not a utopia for the full development of their potentials. People who were denied religious, economic, and political freedom flocked to the New World in search of a better life. Perhaps more than any other nation in the world, America has succeeded in culturally assimilating its immigrants and providing them with the opportunity to attain a decent human existence. Indeed, the elimination of differences among people of diverse nationalities is the essence of the "melting pot" concept. With the emergence of this idea, however, black men and other minority groups were denied the opportunity to assimilate fully because they differed from other Americans racially and culturally. Thus while the United States has successfully assimilated diverse nationalities, it has systematically excluded its largest minority group from full participation in American life. European and white ancestry have been the primary requisites for full realization of the American dream.

To justify this oppression of the Negro, Americans developed and perpetuated many rationalizations and myths. The image of the Negro as a cruel, ruthless savage who was content in his misery was promulgated by social scientists during the late 19th century. Sociologists produced "proof" of the natural inferiority of the Negro. Lothrop Stoddard, in his *Rising Tide of Color*, developed the thesis that there are higher and lower races, whose intermixture produces a race which reverts to the lower type.[1] He also argued that the downfall of the great civilizations was due to the mixing of higher and lower races.

This chapter is concerned with the conglomeration of attitudes and predispositions that produces and perpetuates racial prejudice and racism in American society. While racism in America is now less blatant than it was

5

in the 19th century, it is more insidious and constitutes one of the critical problems of our times. As the U.S. Advisory Commission on Civil Disorders (Kerner Commission) reported in 1968:

> This is our basic conclusion. Our nation is moving toward two societies, one white, one black—separate and unequal ... the most fundamental [cause of the riots] is the racial attitude and behavior of white Americans toward black Americans ... Race prejudice has shaped our history decisively; it now threatens to affect our future.... White racism is essentially responsible for the explosive mixture which has been accumulating in our cities since the end of World War II.[2]

Charles E. Silberman has also illuminated the extent of racism in American life. He writes, "What we are discovering ... is that the United States—all of it—is a racist society in a sense and to a degree that we have refused so far to admit, much less face."[3]

While it is essential that *all* teachers acquaint themselves with social science concepts and research regarding racial prejudice and racism, teachers of racial and ethnic minorities in particular should study this body of knowledge in order to help their students understand how they have been adversely affected by pervasive racial attitudes. As the research findings reviewed in this chapter by J. Kenneth Morland indicate, black children frequently accept the racial attitudes which permeate our society. Unless these children are made sufficiently aware of both the sociological and historical factors involved in the formation of racial prejudice and its effect on their lives, they will be likely to conclude that the discrimination they experience is morally justified because it results from their innate inferiority.

NOTES

1. Lothrop Stoddard, *The Rising Tide of Color Against White-World Supremacy*, New York: Scribner, 1920, pp. 162–165.

2. Quoted in Bradford Chambers, ed., *Chronicles of Black Protest*, New York: The New American Library, 1968, p. 238.

3. Charles E. Silberman, *Crisis in Black and White*, New York: Vintage Books, 1964, p. 10.

EDUCATORS AND THE RACIAL ISSUE IN EDUCATION

Benjamin Solomon

The time is long overdue for a meaningful dialogue among educators—teachers and officials—on the issue of racism in education. The question may be fairly put: Can we have progress that will reach into the hearts and minds of children unless there first is progress in the hearts and minds of educators? Yet, as things stand today, it is possible to assert that professional personnel, through their inertia and resistance, constitute a major obstacle to educational integration. What might be considered a necessary pre-condition for progress—an active and penetrating dialogue out of which an adequate understanding might emerge—hardly exists among teachers.

There has been much discussion recently of the status of the school integration movement. The Coleman report issued by the Office of Education[1] and the *Racial Isolation* study of the U.S. Commission on Civil Rights[2] differ on the precise benefits of what integration there has been. More important, the cutting edge of the civil rights school integration movement seems blunted as resistance and attrition take their toll of supporting organizations. Despite the broad support for integration in the Negro community, the ensuing frustration has helped Black Nationalists in New York City put forth a program aimed at local control of schools—much to the glee of white anti-integrationists. But the argument of black militants is a serious one: Negro children must be protected from mental and moral destruction by white-controlled educational institutions. Jonathan Kozol's book, *Death at an Early Age*,[3] comes at an opportune time to support this thesis. Its subtitle is *The Destruction of the Hearts and Minds of Negro Children in Boston Public Schools.*

Nevertheless, it is not likely that the issue of school integration will fade away. What has happened so far may be best viewed as merely the opening stages of a fundamental struggle in American education. The largely passive role played by teachers indicates the limited character of the approach to integration up till now. The main protagonists have been elements external to the professional community such as civil rights groups, their opponents in white areas, and in the courts.

Benjamin Solomon, "Educators and the Racial Issue in Education," *Illinois Schools Journal*, **48** (Spring 1968), 25–34. Copyright © 1968 by Chicago State College. Reprinted with permission of the author and publisher.

The general passivity (extending at times to foot-dragging resistance) among teachers and the absence of serious discussion reinforce the notion that most professional personnel view the racial question as one that is external or at best peripheral to education. Implicit in this outlook is identification of the problem with the civil rights movement, whose pressures brought it to the fore, rather than with education. This view appears confirmed by the occasional imposition on schools of certain tasks, such as improved racial balance, as a result of reluctant changes in community social policy stemming from these pressures. Such tasks are seen as similar to other responsibilities, marginal to education, which historically have been thrust on schools by outside groups.

If this is the prevailing, though usually unspoken, opinion in the professional community, it is necessary to ask: Is the racial question, then, one primarily external to education? Or, on the other hand, does it go to the heart of the teaching-learning process and to the core of the role and responsibilities of teachers?

The purpose of this article is to show in a systematic discussion the link between racism and education, to analyze the posture of educators on this question, and to present a concept of integration in education.

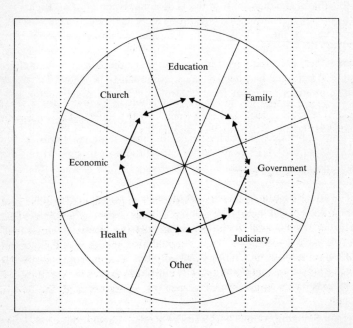

Diagram A. Patterns of racism prevail through the interrelated institutions of society as shown above.

SOCIETY, RACISM, AND SCHOOLS

Diagram A provides our starting point. Three things are shown here:

Society consists of a number of intimately related institutions.

Schools are one of the key institutions of society.

Our society incorporates a deep-rooted pattern of racism, one necessarily reflected in and perpetuated by its key institutions.

If these statements hold, then it is hard to avoid the conclusion that schools share in the overall pattern of racism. To avoid this conclusion, to say that schools are somehow different from the other institutions, we should be able to cite a record of substantial and long-term efforts by public education to resist the basic pattern. In the absence of such a record—and, unfortunately, such a record is lacking—it is inconceivable that our schools should be different from the whole.

What is the historical pattern of *de facto* segregation in our city? We will use the following characterization as a working guide:

A complex set of beliefs and practices for regulating white-Negro relationships (including but not limited to certain types of physical separation), based on explicit or tacit assumption of Negro difference and inferiority.

Superior conditions and consequences for whites.

Inferior conditions and consequences for Negroes.

Degradation of the quality of life for the whole community.

Resistance to change by the dominant group.

Does this racial design for the society as a whole apply to our urban school systems? Let us first look at key elements of the educational process and then consider certain educational consequences.

A COMPREHENSIVE WEB

We can here only briefly delineate the existence of racism in the key elements of the structure and operation of our schools. There is ample evidence available in the relevant literature to support the characterization made respecting each element. The reader should also note that 1) the elements should be considered not only individually but as comprising a mutually supportive and consistent pattern and 2) most have existed in overt form over long periods with apparent acceptance by educators and the general community.

School district gerrymandering, school location, and pupil assignment practices have resulted in more racial separation of pupils than could be accounted for solely by housing concentrations. This history goes back to the

beginnings of public education. Over the years most educators simply col-
laborated with separation, seemingly viewing it as only "natural."

Historically, virtually no Negro teachers were employed in white areas
(though recent pressures are bringing some change here). Negro teachers
learned not to bid for jobs outside the ghetto schools. The rationalization
that Negro teachers imposed the limitation themselves is, of course, trans-
parent.

The traditional, white-supremacist version of American history continues
to be taught in most of our classrooms, although for years now the cry has been
raised that a new, authoritative scholarship has amply exposed it as the
historical version of white supremacy mythology. This traditional history
is a vast attack on the psychological identity of Negro children by robbing
them of their heritage as people of African descent and as citizens of this
country. At the same time it has helped to perpetuate the illusions of racism
among white children.[4]

Materials in other subject areas, from primers used in the first grade on
up, have almost invariably excluded Negroes or only portrayed them in
menial roles.

Since the attitudes and expectations of teachers provide the crucial
dynamic of education, the question arises: Do teachers share the pervasive
orientation toward Negroes? The answer perhaps is that teachers in all parts
of the country were exposed in their early lives as much as other members of
society to prevalent beliefs and practices. There is little to suggest that college
experience typically challenged earlier indoctrination, and the record of
professional activity would hardly bear out any theory that teachers have
strongly opposed the racial system. Kenneth B. Clark, among others, noted the
virtual institutionalization of the viewpoint that a lesser achievement by
black students is normal:

> ... teachers in the New York public school system whom my white
> students have interviewed said that Negro children are inherently in-
> ferior in intelligence and therefore cannot be expected to learn as much
> or as readily as white children. ...[5]

The clinching factor often is the belief that Negroes are, in any case,
destined for menial jobs. Much vocational guidance openly or tacitly has
accepted horizons for Negro youth limited to the narrow range of "Negro
occupations." Trade schools have been historically closed to Negroes by
union fiat, with the acquiescence of school authorities.

The institutionalization of low expectations, commitment, and standards
has been embodied in "difficult schools." Historically these have been schools
with grossly inadequate conditions for learning but nevertheless accepted as a
permanent feature of the educational landscape in ghetto areas—deteriorated
buildings, over-crowded classrooms, insufficient supplies, transient and flee-

ing teachers, inappropriate techniques, abandonment of standards, low morale, and little learning. Both the school system and community appear to have two standards of education—good schools for white children and "difficult" schools for black children.

White children no less than Negro experience the pattern. We have already mentioned physical separation, denial to white children of Afro-American teachers or principals, and bias in the curriculum. Attitudes and practices in all-white schools often directly or indirectly reflect prevalent community biases. Faculties express no mutual professional concern—whether to try to prevent instances of open or subtle bias in the classroom or to consider the value of integration. How many all-white schools have asked for Negro children to fill empty classroom seats or have made sincere efforts to recruit Negro colleagues? The pervasive climate in all-white schools is such as to reinforce the notion that Negro schools are an alien part of the school system and that Negro students are different, inferior and not worthy of association with white students.

EDUCATIONAL CONSEQUENCES

If the key, interrelated aspects of the educational process are indeed infected with society's racial malady, what, then, are the consequences in education?

1. Schools inculate a falsehood. A public school system which has accommodated to segregation becomes a living example of segregation in its structure and operation. Such a system necessarily confirms and supports in the minds and attitudes of its student body the beliefs that 1) segregation is the proper way of life in America and 2) Negroes are racially inferior, the doctrine which underlies segregation. To help perpetuate the falsehood of racial inferiority is to abandon truth as a fundamental striving of education. The falsehood is one of enormous proportions, endangering the very survival of society.

2. The pervasive incorporation of racism in education results in psychological injury to and substandard education for large numbers of Negro children. Much recent history stems from the protest movement finally generated by this fact. Negro children in public schools have been walled off from the rest of society. They have been placed in a system which institutionalizes low expectations, diluted standards, inadequate educational conditions, scandalously little achievement, and psychological attack on black children.

3. Segregated education has deeply dehumanizing effects on white children. Since these are often glossed over, it is worth quoting the eloquent words of Lillian Smith:

I have never been sure that racial segregation has hurt the Negro more than the white. I am not certain that physical lynching of the few is worse than the spiritual lynching of many white children by their own parents and school and church. . . . What segregation has actually done is to destroy spiritually and mentally millions of its children of both races. Arrogance or shame—which do you prefer that your child feel? A mind deadened to knowledge, or a body shut out of a decent school? An indifference to the suffering of others, or suffering itself?[6]

4. The quality of education is degraded throughout the system. White children as well as Negro suffer from *de facto* segregated education in ways additional to inculcation of the premise of racism. Neither white children nor teachers can be insulated from the effects of substandard education in the Negro sector. The new white teacher who suffers through an assignment in a black school until he can transfer out learns meanwhile to accept inferior educational conditions and standards as normal. This experience tends to corrupt those sensibilities which are most important for the learning process—for the white children he will teach as well as for the Negro. For the system as a whole, the average level of attainment, which sets the standard of comparison and challenge, is lowered by the downward pull of the ghetto schools where standards go by the board. This is no small matter, for the intangible factors of expectation and demand by teachers and community have a great effect on what students accomplish. In biracial schools which appear on the moving periphery of the ghetto, track systems and other methods provide microcosms of the segregation in the larger system. Negroes, kept outside of the mainstream of the educational process, can contribute little to the intellectual life of the school and become the source of complaints that the school is deteriorating. The destructive instability in white communities induced by fear of Negro penetration of their schools turns attention away from the real needs of education to defensive measures or flight.

5. Professional values are subverted. Acceptance of segregated education by teachers—where it occurs—damages the commitment, standards, integrity, and unity of the profession. One glaring example, the color line shown by the absence of Negro teachers in schools in white areas, is an outright violation of professional integrity and a disunifying force in the profession. More generally, the educator who accepts, whether consciously or not, racism in education incorporates in his personality and acts in behalf of values antagonistic to education. Teachers who are caught up in the web of racism often become defenders of it when change is demanded. Such hardening of defensive postures entails further compromise of professional values. The question which haunts them in the rapidly-changing city is: "Will Negroes eventually come to my school?" On the other hand, teachers who see the pressing need for integration may find themselves isolated or harassed if they are outspoken and seek to initiate changes with a sense of urgency.

RACISM AND THE POSTURE OF NEUTRALITY

Our analysis so far points to but one conclusion—namely, that the premise of racial difference enters dynamically into every aspect of school processes. The general pattern of segregation in society is fully confirmed as existing in and fostered by education.

Nevertheless, we also see that the racial issue is in every sense one *intrinsic to American public education and a responsibility of educators* (and not merely a civil rights cause imposed on schools). It is best defined as a problem of *truth in education*, since racism is built on the lie of humanly-relevant differences among the so-called races. (This lie provides the fundamental link between the issue in education and the broad civil rights movement.) The problem is not simply a "Negro problem" but applies to everyone—children, parents, teachers—white or black (or any other racial group). Further, the problem is not solely, as many discussions of integration seem to delimit it, one of racial separation of students, but encompasses the entire, interwoven pattern of racism in education.

Particularly salient in education are the attitudes and behavior of professional people. The collaboration of school systems with the prevailing racial pattern has meant, in human terms, that teachers and officials—with few honorable exceptions—geared decisions to the overall pattern. The pattern, after all, had its own logic, its own sense of being natural and fitting, its own support from those who shared its premises, and its own tremendous resistance to change. To try to change even one aspect might bring opposition, simply because any change is a threat to the whole. If a teacher should strive for Negro members on an all-white faculty or raise questions about the social science materials, would he not be inviting trouble and notoriety? If a school official decided that attendance boundaries could be drawn to increase integration, would not this incur outraged cries from certain sources? Better, therefore, to adhere to what was normal, established, and expected. In any case, why try to change one practice in what is clearly an overall pattern, one established not only in tried-and-true practice but also in the ingrained mental and emotional habits of many people? Before the issue was forced by civil rights protests, few educators thought of altering it.

The historic rationale of large numbers of school people on the racial issue in education has been a combination of "neutrality" and "color blindness." According to the first, educators should not take sides on such a controversial issue, one outside the province of education. The second concept, color blindness, has tended to reinforce that of neutrality. In effect, it meant that the problem wasn't there in the first place. Teachers, according to this view, did not make distinctions on the basis of race—they did not "see" color in their classrooms or schools.

But the posture of color blindness, whatever virtues it may have possessed in certain contexts, served mainly as a mask for the continued existence of de facto segregation. The fact is that color blindness never existed in the first place. Virtually every person, including educators, in a city with a racist pattern is intensely aware of color. The common use of the appellations, "Negro schools" or "white schools," is only one example of this awareness.

In short, color blindness and neutrality are false postures: they do not really exist. The racial issue is a real one in society: neutrality in education can only be a pretense for conformity with the *status quo*. The real alternatives before educators are either to strive for a fully integrated educational process or to collaborate with the existing pattern of segregation.

INTEGRATION—AN AFFIRMATIVE POSITION FOR EDUCATORS

We have seen that underlying the racist design is the false premise of racial difference. This lie has operated as an abnormal, a cancerous interference in Negro-white relationships. However, in a segregated society, abnormality has become normal and even "natural." A concept of integration is in a sense undramatic, since removal of the racist premise would mean only that relationships between Afro-Americans and whites would merely be truly normal—i.e., that they would accept each other and work with each other as ordinary and equal human beings in relationships of mutual respect and understanding.

Thus, from this standpoint, school integration would mean making the existing racist pattern abnormal and substituting for it an educational process in which black and white children and teachers learn and work together as a normal condition and with the development of normal relationships. Remove the premise of racism and people can face each other as people, not as stereotypes.

Any pretense of neutrality clearly must be dropped—the cause of integration in education is inseparable from the cause of education.

Further, the primary locale of necessary change is in white sectors and primary responsibility and initiative should be taken by white personnel, since the "abnormal factor" in relationships is one that basically originates in and emanates from white society. As noted earlier, the question of school integration should not be looked at as mainly a "Negro problem."

In view of the historical situation we are in, school integration requires a tremendous affirmative effort, and teachers are crucial to this effort. Most "solutions" so far have ignored the role of teachers and have emphasized racial balance. But a genuine integration program would be comprehensive—i.e., an interrelated attack on all the manifestations of segregation in education—and it would be led by teachers. It would seek at every given moment to attain the maximum possible physical integration of children because educators would realize that a biracial classroom is the best context for education in a biracial city. But it would not be hung up on the practical difficulties of achieving full racial balance immediately. It would do what could be done and at the same time come to grips with every other element of racism, tangible and intangible.

The dynamics of such a program can only emerge from a continuing confrontation and dialogue among all the professional personnel—from each school on up through to the topmost levels of the system.[7] Teachers and school officials must learn, no matter how painful, how racism insinuated itself deeply into every aspect of school operations and the consequences thereof. They must come to confront the painful reality that the existence of racism in education manifests more than anything else its existence in the hearts and minds of professional personnel.

Educators must grasp and make real the concept of a thoroughly integrated school system environment, one which reflects their professional determination to undo every vestige of segregation within their reach. The spirit and practice throughout should become such that the new atmosphere will touch positively the hearts and minds of even those children who for a period may remain in all-white or all-Negro schools. Even these children should be able to feel that they are in an environment which has rejected segregation as a way of life and which in many ways helps them to come into meaningful interaction with the world across the barriers.

Integration is a hard road—but it can lead to a solution, to an educational process that is sound, stable, honest, and effective. In contrast, passivity and "neutrality" mean only longer entrapment with segregation, a sure recipe for endless trouble. Educators should be leaders, not the reluctant followers. School integration would mean not only a great advance in education but also a major contribution towards weakening the grip of segregation on the total community.

NOTES

1. James S. Colman, *et al.*, *Equality of Educational Opportunity*, Report of Survey Submitted to President and Congress under Section 402 of the Civil Rights Act of 1964, U.S. Office of Education, 1966.

2. U.S. Commission on Civil Rights, *Racial Isolation in Public Schools*, Vols. I and II, Washington. D.C.: Government Printing Office, 1967.

3. Boston: Houghton Mifflin, 1967.

4. Beatrice Young and Benjamin Solomon, "Joy and Conscience in Teaching American History," *Changing Education*, I (Fall 1966), 3–7.

5. "Clash of Cultures in the Classroom," *Integrated Education*, I (August 1963), 10.

6. *Integrated Education*, **I** (April 1963), 45.

7. Benjamin Solomon, "An Approach to In-Service Re-education," in Meyer Weinberg, ed., *Techniques for Achieving Racially Desegregated, Superior Quality Education in the Public Schools of Chicago, Illinois*, paper prepared for the National Conference on Equal Educational Opportunity, Washington, D.C.: U.S. Commission on Civil Rights, 1967, pp. 38–45 [mimeographed].

THE CAUSES
OF PREJUDICE*

James A. Banks

We cannot reduce racial prejudice unless we acquire an understanding of its causes. First, however, we shall find it useful to define prejudice.

The literature on racial relations is replete with efforts to define prejudice. While the definitions differ to some extent, most suggest that prejudice is a set of rigid and unfavorable attitudes toward a particular group or groups which is formed in disregard of facts. The prejudiced individual responds to perceived members of these groups on the basis of his preconceptions, tending to disregard behavior or personal characteristics that are inconsistent with his biases. George E. Simpson and J. Milton Yinger have provided a lucid and useful definition of prejudice: "... [P]rejudice is an emotional, rigid attitude (a *predisposition* to respond to a certain stimulus in a certain way) toward a group of people. They may be a group only in the mind of the prejudiced person ... he categorizes them together, although they may have little similarity or interaction. Prejudices are thus attitudes, but not all attitudes are prejudices."[1]

Although social scientists have attempted for years to derive a comprehensive and coherent theory of prejudice, their efforts have not been totally successful. A number of theories explain various components of prejudice, but none sufficiently describes its many dimensions. Social scientists have rejected some of the older, more simplistic theories of prejudice; other theories are too limited in scope to be functional. Still others are extremely useful in explaining certain forms of prejudice directed toward specific groups, but fail to account for its other facets. A serious study of the theories of prejudice reveals the complexity of this configuration of attitudes and pre-

---

* Written especially for this volume.

dispositions; thus simplistic explanations of prejudice only hinder our understanding of it.

Arnold M. Rose has critically reviewed both the older, simpler theories of prejudice and the more complex modern psychological explanations.[2] A summary of his analysis is presented below in order to illuminate the strengths and weaknesses of the various theories.

The racial and cultural difference theory maintains that man has an instinctive fear and dislike of individuals who are physically and culturally different from him.[3] Rose dismisses this theory as untenable, since research indicates that children are tolerant of other races and groups until they acquire the dominant cultural attitudes toward ethnic minorities. Children must be *taught* to dislike different races and ethnic groups. Writes Rose, "[This theory] should be thought of as a rationalization of prejudice rather than as an explanation of it."[4]

The economic competition theory holds that prejudice emanates from antagonism caused by competition between various groups for jobs and other economic rewards.[5] Although this theory sheds light on many historical examples of racial prejudice and discrimination, it has some gross limitations. It fails to explain why a group continues to practice discrimination when it no longer profits economically from doing so. A number of studies document the severe financial losses attributable to discrimination against the black American.

The social control theory maintains that prejudice exists because the individual is forced to conform to society's traditions and norms;[6] thus he dislikes certain groups because he is taught to do so by his culture. While this theory helps to explain why prejudice may be perpetuated when it is no longer functional, it does not consider how it originates.

The traumatic experience theory states that racial prejudice emerges in an individual following a traumatic experience involving a member of a minority group during early childhood.[7] This theory is inadequate because a child does not associate an early unpleasant experience with a particular racial group unless he has already been exposed to the concept of racial differences. In noting another limitation of this theory, Harley writes, "This idea can be discounted because persons can hold extreme prejudice with no contact with persons of the discriminated class, and the traumatic experiences reported by persons as reason for their prejudice are very often found to be either imagined by them or elaborated and embellished beyond recognition."[8]

The frustration-aggression theory is a modern psychological explanation of prejudice.[9] It suggests that prejudice results when individuals become frustrated because they are unable to satisfy real or perceived needs. Frustration leads to aggression, which may then be directed toward minority groups because they are highly visible targets and unable to retaliate. Displacing aggression on stigmatized groups is much safer than attacking the real source of the frustration. Rose illuminates two basic weaknesses in this theory: 1) it fails to explain why certain groups are selected as targets rather than others, and 2) it assumes that all frustration must be expressed.[10] However, a number of writers and researchers have relied heavily on this theory to help explain the emergence and perpetuation of prejudice.

The projection theory states that "people attribute to others motives which they sense in themselves but which they would not wish to acknowledge openly."[11] This theory is severly limited because it fails to explain motives for prejudice or why certain characteristics are attributed to specific groups.

Symbolic theories attempt to explain prejudice as deriving from an individual's ambivalent attitude toward important phenomena.[12] Rose relates writer Lillian Smith's interpretation of anti-Negro prejudice: "The heart of this theory is that Negroes are the objects of the whites' desires for, and yet fear of, uninhibited sex."[13] Symbolic theories are basically weak because they are formulated on the basis of inferences and have not been rigorously tested.

In attempting to derive a conprehensive theory of prejudice, Rose suggests that the modern psychological theories are the most useful explanations. He writes

> The central theories today which seriously attempt to explain prejudice are based on the concepts of frustration-aggression, projection, and symbolic substitution. These theories have a good deal in common despite the differing kinds of evidence which lead to their formation. All of them postulate 1) a need to express antagonism 2) toward something which is not the real object of antagonism. Not only is there an essential similarity among the three theories, but they complement each other at their weakest points. The symbolic theory does most to explain which group is selected for prejudice and why. The frustration-aggression theory does most to explain the strength behind prejudice. The projection theory offers a plausible explanation of the psychological function of prejudice as a cleansing agent to dissolve inner guilt or hurt.[14]

Simpson and Yinger have formulated a comprehensive theory of prejudice "around three highly interactive but analytically distinct factors, each the convergence of several lines of theory and evidence."[15] The first factor is the personality requirements of the individual. As a result of both constitutional and learned needs, some people develop personalities that thrive on prejudices and irrational responses. This theory has been offered by a number of other writers and researchers. Later we will review some of the research on which it is based.

An individual may also develop prejudices based not on personality needs but on the way society is structured.[16] The power structure of society is especially important to this concept, which is similar to the economic competition theory discussed by Rose. Simpson and Yinger write, "It is impossible to interpret individual behavior adequately without careful attention to the social dimension."[17]

The third basic cause of prejudice suggested by Simpson and Yinger is society itself. "In almost every society ... each new generation is taught appropriate beliefs and practices regarding other groups. Prejudices are, in part, simply a portion of the cultural heritage; they are among the folkways."[18] This explanation is identical to the social control theory summarized by Rose.

Simpson and Yinger stress that all three of these factors interact: "Any specific individual, in his pattern of prejudice, almost certainly reflects all of the causes."[19] Both they and Rose emphasize that multiple explanations are needed to account for the complexity of racial prejudice.

In his review of the theories of prejudice, Rose discusses personality explanations. As we have seen, Simpson and Yinger cite the personality needs of the individual as one of the basic causes of prejudice; earlier researchers considered personality *the* most important variable in the formation of bigotry. The latter attributed different types of personalities to differences in child-rearing practices, some of which were thought to produce personalities that were intolerant of different races and groups, while others helped to develop racial tolerance and acceptance in the child. Else Frenkel-Brunswik and her associates conducted the pioneering research on the role of personality in the formation of prejudice.

In one of a series of studies (1948), Frenkel-Brunswik compared the racial attitudes and personality characteristics of 1500 children.[20] Interviews were conducted with the subjects and their parents; both personality and attitude tests were administered. Frenkel-Brunswik concluded that there were significant differences in the personalities of prejudiced and unprejudiced children. She found that prejudiced children evidenced more rejection of outgroups, a blind acceptance of the in group, a greater degree of aggression, and a strong rejection of persons perceived as weak. The more prejudiced children also displayed a greater resentment of the opposite sex and an admiration for strong figures. They were more willing to submit to authority, more compulsive about cleanliness, and more moralistic. The unprejudiced children were "more oriented toward love and less toward power than the ethnocentric child ... and more capable of giving affection."[21] Frenkel-Brunswik notes, in summarizing her study, "It was found that some children tend to reveal a stereotyped and rigid glorification of their own group and an aggressive rejection of outgroups and foreign countries."[22]

Frenkel-Brunswik and her associates also studied the relationship between personality and prejudice in adults.[23] They concluded that certain individuals, because of their early childhood experiences, have insecure personalities and a need to dominate and to feel superior to other individuals. These individuals possess an *authoritarian personality* which is manifested not only in racial prejudice but also in their sexual behavior and religious and political views. The authors write:

> The most crucial result of the present study, as it seems to the authors, is the demonstration of close correspondence in the type of approach and outlook a subject is likely to have in a great variety of areas, ranging from the most intimate features of family and sex adjustment through relationships to other people in general, to religion and to social and political philosophy. Thus a basically hierarchical, authoritarian, exploitive parent-child relationship is apt to carry over into a power-oriented, exploitively dependent attitude toward one's sex partner and one's God and may well culminate in a political philosophy and social outlook which has no room for anything but a desperate clinging to what appears to be strong and a disdainful rejection of whatever is relegated to the bottom.[24]

While the research by Frenkel-Brunswik and her associates contributed greatly to the literature on the origins of prejudice, recent writers have severely criticized it because of its methodological flaws and theoretical base. We will defer a discussion of the theory on which the research is based and review a number of its methodological weaknesses. Simpson and Yinger have written one of the most perceptive critiques.[25] They point out that the inadequate attention given to sampling techniques limits the generability of the findings. The research is also weakened by the heavy reliance on the subjects' memories of childhood, the inadequate control of variables, such as education and group membership, and the low reliability of the measuring instruments. The F Scale used by the researchers measured many variables simultaneously, failing to measure any one variable well. However, Simpson and Yinger conclude that the flaws in the research do not substantially diminish its import. "Despite the seriousness of such methodological problems, they do not refute, in the judgment of most observers, the significance of personality research for the student of prejudice."[26]

Other researchers have also attempted to explain the emergence of racial prejudice as a personality variable. Lindzey (1950) studied the personalities of 22 individuals judged "high in prejudice" and 22 judged "low in prejudice."[27] The subjects were divided into experimental and control groups. After exposing members of the experimental group to a frustration experience, Lindzey concluded that the individuals high in prejudice evidenced more "frustration susceptibility" and "more overt disturbance in response to frustration than those low in minority group prejudice."[28] The subjects high in prejudice also received higher scores on an instrument which measured "conservative nationalistic statements." Writes Lindzey,

We have pointed to certain evidence in our data suggesting that the high in prejudice are more "frustratable," somewhat more aggressive, and more conforming to authority norms than the low in prejudice. Further, we have proposed that early exposure to strict norms is one means by which we might account for the behavior patterns that appeared to characterize the high in prejudice in this study.[29]

Allport and Kramer (1946) found that the more prejudiced persons in a sample of college students maintained closer ties with their families, whereas the least prejudiced students "reacted against" their parents' attitudes.[30] The former also had more negative memories of childhood, were better able to identify racial and ethnic groups, were more religious, and expressed more hostility and aggression. "From all these results," they write, "we conclude *that prejudice is woven into the very fabric of personality*. A style of life is adopted. It proceeds by rule of thumb."[31] (Emphasis added.) The subjects who reported that they had studied "scientific facts about race" in school were more often classified as "less prejudiced." However, only 8% of the subjects could recall studying racial facts in school.

Like Frenkel-Brunswik, Allport and Kramer believe that prejudice can be explained largely as a product of personality. However, both research teams compared extreme bigots with individuals who manifested few negative racial attitudes, whereas most white Americans exhibit only an average amount of racial prejudice and do not have seriously disorganized personalities. Thus there are severe limitations implicit in an exclusive *personality* approach to the study of prejudice.

Herbert Blumer seriously questions attempts to attribute prejudice and discrimination to personality variables. He almost completely dismisses the role of attitudes in influencing behavior. Blumer asserts that the social setting rather than racial attitudes is the "prime determinant of behavior."[32] In trying to understand discrimination against minority groups, he contends, we should analyze social settings and norms instead of the personal attitudes of the individual. Blumer reviews a number of studies which indicate that there is frequently a discrepancy between an individual's verbalized attitudes and his actual behavior. Saenger and Gilbert found that prejudiced individuals will patronize a racially mixed store when their desire to shop exceeds their antipathy toward blacks.[33] Research by Blalock suggests that discrimination is not always a correlate of racial prejudice.[34] That is, in certain situations, prejudiced individuals may not discriminate, since the prevailing norms may affect their behavior more than their personal attitudes do. Blumer summarizes an important study by Lohman and Reitzes:

> . . . in a study of race relations in a large city . . . the same set of whites behaved entirely differently toward Negroes in three situations—working

establishment, residential neighborhood and shopping center; no prejudice or discrimination was shown in the working establishment where the whites and Negroes belonged to the same labor union, whereas prejudice and discrimination toward Negroes by the same whites was pronounced in the case of residential neighborhood.[35]

Blumer seriously underestimates the role of attitudes and personality as determinants of racial discrimination and prejudice. An adequate theory of prejudice must take into account both personality variables and the social setting. Explaining prejudice and discrimination as totally a product of a disorganized personality ignores the fact that humans are social beings, and that their reactions in a social setting reflect not only their individual idiosyncrasies and biases but also the prevailing norms and expectations. Thus a bigoted teacher will be less inclined to manifest her true attitudes toward black children when black parents are visiting her room than she is when she and the children are alone.

However, social setting alone cannot completely explain racial discrimination, nor can it, as Blumer implies, totally diminish the importance of racial attitudes. If the same bigoted teacher were transferred to an all-black school in which there was little tolerance for racial discrimination, her behavior would probably become more consistent with the dominant norms of the new setting, but her *attitudes* would be revealed to her students in subtle ways, and perhaps affect them just as profoundly. *The most equalitarian social setting cannot cause an intense bigot to exhibit behavior identical to that of a person free of racial prejudice.*

Much of the research that Blumer relies on to support his hypothesis is subject to serious criticism, particularly the study by Lohman and Reitzes. These authors found that their white subjects behaved "*entirely differently toward Negroes in different social settings*" and showed "no prejudice" toward them at work.[36] (Emphasis added.) However, this writer seriously questions whether the black factory workers would have endorsed these conclusions, believing instead that they could have cited numerous examples of discrimination directed against them by their white co-workers. It is inconceivable that persons who are so bigoted that they would exclude blacks from their neighborhoods could treat them with full equality at work or indeed in any other setting.

The *social setting* explanation of prejudice and discrimination presents other difficulties. In trying to explain an individual's reactions in a given situation, we must consider not only the group norms but the importance the individual attaches to the group and setting. Research suggests that a group or situation must be important to an individual before he accepts its norms and values. Pearlin (1954) classified a random sample of 383 college students into "acceptors" and "rejectors" on the basis of their attitudes toward blacks.[37] A majority of the subjects who accepted blacks in different situations had broken their close family ties and developed identifications with campus groups. The more prejudiced individuals indicated that they had maintained close ties with their families and developed few associations with campus groups. Students who became more racially liberal as a result of their college experience considered college group norms more important than their parents' attitudes, while the more prejudiced subjects deemed family norms more important. Thus simply placing individuals in new settings with different norms and values does not necessarily change their behavior and attitudes. Pearlin writes:

> These findings indicate that when a person holds membership in groups having conflicting views on an issue, his own attitudes will be influenced by the relative importance of the groups to him. Generally, in such a situation the attitudes of the individual will approximate most nearly the norms of the groups to which he most closely refers himself ... attitude change cannot be reckoned solely in terms of exposure to new ideas. Whether or not an individual will undergo modification of his attitude depends in large part on the nature of his relationship to groups holding the opposing sentiments and opinions.[38]

The social setting hypothesis also fails to take into account the fact that individuals collectively determine the group norm. Whether a group sanctions racial discrimination or racial tolerance thus depends on the attitudes of its members. Clearly, then, we must consider both individual attitudes and social norms when attempting to explain the genesis and perpetuation of racial discrimination and prejudice. The most important variables that affect the formation of racial prejudice are summarized in Chart I.

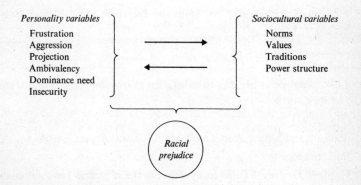

Chart I. Variables that cause racial prejudice.

NOTES

1. George Eaton Simpson and J. Milton Yinger, *Racial and Cultural Minorities*, New York: Harper and Row, 1965, p. 10.

2. Arnold M. Rose, "The Causes of Prejudice," in Milton L. Barron, ed., *American Cultural Minorities: A Textbook of Readings in Intergroup Relations*, New York: Alfred A. Knopf, 1962.

3. *Ibid.*, pp. 77–80.

4. *Ibid.*, p. 78.

5. *Ibid.*, pp. 79–80.

6. *Ibid.*, pp. 80–81.

7. *Ibid.*, pp. 77–78.

8. David Harley, "Prejudice in Whites," unpublished paper, Michigan State University, 1968.

9. Rose, "The Causes of Prejudice," pp. 82–83.

10. *Ibid.*, pp. 82–83.

11. *Ibid.*, p. 83.

12. *Ibid.*, pp. 83–87.

13. *Ibid.*, p. 86.

14. *Ibid.*, pp. 92–93.

15. Simpson and Yinger, *Racial and Cultural Minorities*, p. 49.

16. *Ibid.*, p. 50.

17. *Ibid.*

18. *Ibid.*

19. *Ibid.*

20. Else Frenkel-Brunswik, "A Study of Prejudice in Children," *Human Relations*, 1 (1948), 295–306.

21. *Ibid.*, p. 305.

22. *Ibid.*, p. 296.

23. T. W. Adorno, *et al.*, *The Authoritarian Personality*, New York: Harper and Row, 1950.

24. *Ibid.*, p. 971.

25. Simpson and Yinger, *Racial and Cultural Minorities*, pp. 65–66.

26. *Ibid.*, p. 66.

27. Gardner Lindzey, "Differences Between the High and Low in Prejudice and Their Implications for a Theory of Prejudice," *Personality*, 19 (1950), 16–40.

28. *Ibid.*, p. 39.

29. *Ibid.*, p. 33.

30. Gordon W. Allport and Bernard M. Kramer, "Some Roots of Prejudice," *The Journal of Psychology*, **22** (1946), 9–39.

31. *Ibid.*, p. 35.

32. Herbert Blumer, "United States of America," in *Research on Racial Relations*, New York: UNESCO, 1966, pp. 87–133.

33. Reported in *Ibid.*, p. 112.

34. *Ibid.*

35. *Ibid.*, pp. 112–113.

36. *Ibid.*, p. 112.

37. Leonard I. Pearlin, "Shifting Group Attachments and Attitudes Toward Negroes," *Social Forces*, **33** (1954), 41–47.

38. *Ibid.*, p. 50.

THE DEVELOPMENT
OF RACIAL BIAS
IN YOUNG CHILDREN

J. Kenneth Morland

In a sense, American society educates for prejudice. Studies in both Northern and Southern communities in the United States show that Negro as well as white children develop a bias for the white race at an early age. This bias is indicated by both a preference for and an identification with whites rather than with Negroes. While racial bias does not necessarily imply rejection because of race, and is therefore somewhat different from racial prejudice, it is a foundation upon which racial prejudice can be erected. These studies show, further, that American society itself lays this foundation, because children learn their biases through contact with attitudes of racial prejudice and with overt results of racial discrimination.

J. Kenneth Morland, "The Development of Racial Bias in Children," *Theory Into Practice*, **2** (June 1963), 120–127. Reprinted with permission of the author and publisher.

RACIAL PREFERENCE

While investigations of racial attitudes of young children have varied in methods, the results have generally been consistent in showing racial preference. This is not to imply, however, that there are no regional differences in racial attitudes. One study has suggested that within each race there is significant regional variation in the age at which preschool children learn to recognize race differences. This study found that white children in segregated Southern nursery schools learned to make correct racial designations at an earlier age than Negro children.[1] This is in direct contrast to what has been found in integrated nursery schools in the North.[2] But in all regions where studies have been made, young children have shown a preference for whites over Negroes. Thus, the Clarks found that a majority of 253 Negro children in Massachusetts and in Arkansas who were asked to choose between white and colored dolls showed a preference for white dolls.[3] Furthermore, the children were more likely to characterize the colored dolls as looking "bad," while the white dolls were more likely to be described as "nice" and as having "a nice color." In another study, which used a picture test, Horowitz found the same preference among white children in New York, Georgia, and Tennessee.[4]

In a study of 407 Negro and white nursery-school children in Lynchburg, Virginia, the author also found a preference for whites.[5] Subjects were shown a set of pictures of Negroes and whites and were asked several questions concerning the ones with whom they would rather play. A strong preference for white playmates was indicated by a large majority of both Negro and white children in each of the age categories tested, regardless of whether or not they could use racial terms to differentiate those in the pictures.

RACIAL SELF-IDENTIFICATION

Most of the studies of racial attitudes in young children agree that Negroes are less likely than whites to make correct racial self-identification. Thus, when the Clarks, in the study cited earlier, asked Negro children to "Give me the doll that looks like you" (the subjects could choose from Negro and white dolls), far fewer chose a Negro doll than had demonstrated the ability to distinguish between white and Negro dolls. Awareness of race differences on the part of these Negro children did not lead to accuracy of racial self-identification.

In the Lynchburg study, the author also found that Negro children tended to make incorrect racial self-identification.[6] When shown a set of pictures and asked which children (Negro or white) they looked more like, a majority of Negro subjects identified themselves with white children. White subjects, on the other hand, identified themselves with children of their own race. Similar results were found regardless of the age or racial recognition ability of the subjects.

In their study of prejudice among young school children in Philadelphia, Trager and Yarrow asked Negro and white subjects indirectly about racial self-identification. These investigators showed their respondents a picture containing both a white and a colored child and asked whether the white child was glad he was white and if he sometimes wanted to be colored, and whether the colored child was glad he was colored and if he sometimes wanted to be white. A majority of both Negro and white subjects stated that the white child was glad he was white and did not want to be colored, but the colored child was not glad he was colored and that he sometimes wished he were white. It is logical to assume that these subjects were projecting their own feelings about racial self-identification.[7]

SOURCE OF BIAS

How can we account for these persistent findings indicating a bias for whites by both Negro and white children? Some argue that there may be a "natural" preference for light skin. They point out that *black* is frequently associated with darkness and evil, as in expressions like "black magic," "black lies," "blacklisted," and the like. In contrast, *white* often suggests purity, cleanliness, brightness, and hope. But the assumption that it is the nature of things that dictates the superiority of white over black is open to serious question. When cross-cultural comparisons are made, little doubt remains that the use of colors to designate approval or disapproval is culture-based, rather than being "natural" or in any way inevitable. A Cherokee creation myth tells of how God succeeded in making the Indian a rich, lovely brown color, after failing with the "overdone," burnt black man and the "underdone," sick-looking white man. The Honorable R. S. Garfield Todd, former prime minister of Southern Rhodesia, tells of the following complimentary introduction by a Negro African school prefect. The prefect told his Negro audience that although Mr. Todd had a white skin, "his heart is as black as ours."

In the author's opinion, the most logical explanation of the preference for and identification with whites by both Negro and white children is the result of the higher status of the white in American society. Children of both races see the superior positions of whites—in books, in magazines, on television, in movies, and in pictures on the walls of their schools. Whites live in better houses, have more money, and are in positions of power. It seems reasonable to believe that this bias for whites reflects a desire to be associated with the more privileged race.

Results of the Lynchburg study support this explanation in several ways. As indicated earlier, a clear majority of the children of both races showed a preference for and identification with whites before they had developed the ability to recognize race differences or even to use the terms *white* and *colored*. This suggests that learning to prefer and to identify with whites is not simply a matter of direct verbal instruction, but may well be the result of indirect teaching of the environment itself. Other writers have also questioned the importance of direct inculcation in the development of racial attitudes in young children. Quinn, for example, reports that among the white Southerners she studied, verbal instruction was rarely resorted to in transmitting racial attitudes. In the rare instances when such instruction was used, it was justified in other than racial terms.[8]

The Lynchburg study also shows that racial bias develops early, for a majority of even the three-year-olds of both races, as well as most of the four- and five-year-olds, preferred and identified with whites. It is likely that these reactions at such a young age reflect indirect learning from the environment rather than direct teaching of parents and nursery-school teachers.

Finally, the Lynchburg and other comparable studies indicate that bias is not developed from direct contact with members of the other race. Rather, it is the result of contact with other attitudes and with the results of racial discrimination itself. In the Lynchburg study, it was noted that contact between Negro and white children was rare, but by nursery-school age, both had learned to prefer white to Negro playmates and to identify with whites rather than with Negroes.

Radke, Trager, and Davis explain the basis of such learning in the following way:

> The child entering school already has a long past of social learning. He brings with him perceptions of the self and differentiations of his social environment. . . .

> The social learning in these early years has taken place mainly within the family and play groups of children. Through these agents the child becomes aware of and reacts to social forces which constitute culture; through them content, structuring, and attitudes concerning his social-psychological environment are conveyed to him; and cultural standards and mores begin to have consequences for his personality and behavior.

> In this process of socialization, one of the important components of the culture which the child takes over, and one of the important determinants of his needs and his social and self perceptions is the factor of social groups in society. Even while the child's experience is within the bounds of his family, values of class and group enter into his world as they are part of the family life and customs, and as they affect the goals and anxieties of his parents. As the child's experience extends to neighbor-

hood and school, there is greater opportunity for cultural values with respect to groups to affect his outlook on life.[9]

In a society characterized by racial prejudice and discrimination, it follows that the child will acquire attitudes and modes of behavior appropriate in such a society, just as he acquires other responses demanded by the society.

IMPLICATIONS OF RACIAL BIAS

The preceding discussion has sought to show that racial bias develops very early in the life of the American child and that the chief factor in this development is the prevalence of racial prejudice and discrimination in American society. It is apparent that the child does not acquire knowledge about race and develop attitudes toward race differences from any particular institution. He "absorbs" ideas and attitudes about race from those nearest him and from the way in which society itself is structured. Unless some institution takes the responsibility for teaching accurate information about race and helps to develop a learning situation in which democratic values may be practiced between children of different races, it is likely that most young children will develop racial biases.

When white children realize that being a member of the white race is an advantage, they are likely to develop positive attitudes toward being white and negative attitudes toward being Negro. Bias for whites will probably grow into prejudice against Negroes, especially as white adults begin to insist on it. When Negro children find, through experience, that membership in their race is a handicap, they are apt to develop negative reactions toward their race as they take on the evaluation of those dominant in the society. James Baldwin, a Negro writer, has expressed the basis of self-rejection in the following way: "Negroes in this country—and Negroes do not, strictly or legally speaking, exist in any other—are taught really to despise themselves from the moment their eyes open on the world. The world is white, and they're black. . . ."[10] At the same time, Negroes are likely to develop ambivalent attitudes toward those imposing racial discrimination. Members of the dominant race are resented because they enforce unequal treatment, but they are also envied because of their advantages.

THE SCHOOL AND RACIAL KNOWLEDGE

One way to reduce racial bias and consequent racial prejudice is to present accurate information about race and race differences, for false notions of racial superiority can undergird such bias and prejudice. The school, in my opinion, is the most appropriate organization to take the responsibility for developing democratic attitudes, just as it takes the responsibility for imparting valid knowledge about other important fields.[11] We need to realize, however, that although sound knowledge is necessary to combat false information, it is not sufficient to change attitudes. Facts do not speak for themselves; rather, they are interpreted through the experience and biases of those hearing them. At the same time, accurate information can challenge incorrect beliefs that support bias and prejudice and can at least make such support shift to other grounds.

An obvious difficulty in expecting public schools to teach scientifically valid knowldege about race is the fact that in the states where this knowledge is most lacking there is strong racial prejudice among those in political authority. At least three Southern states have given official support to books purporting to prove the racial superiority of whites.[12]

It may be a long time before school boards in some states are willing to have their schools deal objectively with race, but many boards, unhindered by a racist policy, could begin at once. Colleges could also make this a part of their programs of teacher preparation.

THE SCHOOL AND RACIAL ATTITUDES

While the school cannot be expected to deal with the extreme prejudice resulting from deep-seated personality disturbances, it can modify milder forms of prejudice. The present paper assumes that the racial bias and prejudice that characterize the majority of children in America are "normal" and relatively mild. The author believes that both the child who is virtually without prejudice and the one who is highly prejudiced are deviants from the American norm.[13] The racial attitudes that might be altered by the school are those developed by most children in the course of growing up. More hostile and authoritarian children, whose personalities "require" prejudice, are not likely to be affected.

The school can help to lessen "normal" prejudice by providing a setting in which children of different races can associate on a basis of equality. Studies have shown that racial bias and prejudice can be modified by experiences that take place in such a setting. For example, in a one-year period changes have been reported in attitudes of racially prejudiced white students in newly integrated schools of Atlanta and New Orleans. Martin Coles, a psychiatrist, has spent the last year and a half interviewing Negro and white pupils in these two cities to find out the effects of attending integrated schools. The following portion of an interview tells of the change that occurred in a white high-school student after a year of integration:

> I've changed a lot of my ideas. You can't help having respect for them [the Negro pupils], the way they've gone through the year so well. They're nice kids, that's what you find out after a while. They speak

well, and are more intelligent than a lot of my friends.... I sneered a few times the first few weeks, but I just couldn't keep it up, and I felt kind of bad and kind of sorry for them.... Next thing I knew I was quiet when some of my friends were calling them all the old names.... I felt that I never again would look at them the way I did last September and before.... I can't really describe any time or episode.... No, it was just a kind of gradual feeling.[14]

Such direct contact is probably a necessary condition for changing feelings of prejudice, but it is not often a sufficient condition. Coles found that some of the white children who had strong feelings of rejection for Negroes did not change.

In their study of young children in Philadelphia, Trager and Yarrow concluded that children learn prejudices not only from the larger social environment of adult values and behavior patterns but also from the content of the curriculum and its values. They contend that "If democratic attitudes are to be learned they must be specifically taught and experienced."[15] The experiment that they conducted in Philadelphia schools demonstrated that democratic attitudes can be taught to young children if the teachers are properly prepared and are willing to make a deliberate effort.

Educators, then, are faced with a great challenge. At present, little is being done to counter the biased and prejudiced racial attitudes that develop among American children; valid information on race differences is very rarely given to them. This failure to provide opportunities for learning about race differences inhibits a child's understanding of others; and, perhaps more important, such silence about race differences may be interpreted as agreement with the evaluation of the larger society. Admittedly the task of changing racial bias and prejudice is a difficult one, but it is none the less essential for the maintenance and development of a democracy.

NOTES

1. J. Kenneth Morland, "Racial Recognition by Nursery School Children in Lynchburg, Virginia," *Social Forces*, **37** (December 1958) 134.

2. See, for example, Mary Ellen Goodman, *Race Awareness in Young Children*, New York: Macmillan, 1952, pp. 178–179, 223.

3. Kenneth B. and Mamie P. Clark, "Racial Identification and Preference in Negro Children," in Theodore M. Newcomb and Eugene L. Hartley, eds., *Readings in Social Psychology*, New York: Henry Holt, 1947, pp. 169–178.

4. Eugene L. Horowitz, "The Development of Attitudes Toward the Negro," *Archives of Psychology*, **194** (January 1936).

5. J. Kenneth Morland, "Racial Acceptance and Preference of Nursery School Children in a Southern City," *Merrill-Palmer Quarterly of Behavior and Development*, **8** (1962), 271–280.

6. J. Kenneth Morland, "Racial Self-Identification: A Study of Nursery School Children." Paper presented to the American Catholic Sociological Society, Washington, D.C., September 1962.

7. Helen G. Trager and Marian Radke Yarrow, *They Learn What They Live: Prejudice in Young Children*, New York: Harper and Brothers, 1952, pp. 121–144.

8. Olive Westbrooke Quinn, "The Transmission of Racial Attitudes Among White Southerners," *Social Forces*, **33** (October 1954), 42.

9. Marian Radke, Helen G. Trager, and Hadassah Davis, "Social Perceptions and Attitudes of Children," *Genetic Psychology Monographs*, **40** (1949), 331.

10. "Letter from a Region in My Mind," *New Yorker*, **38** (Nov. 17, 1962), 65.

11. Cyril Bibby, in *Race, Prejudice and Education* (London: William Heineman, Ltd., 1959), suggests ways in which teachers can deal with race differences. The book is clear, readable, and anthropologically sound.

12. The Louisiana State Board of Education adopted a resolution on July 25, 1961, urging administrators, teachers, and "mature" students to read the book *Race and Reason: A Yankee View*, by Carleton Putnam (Washington, D.C.: Public Affairs Press, 1961), which advocates the inferiority of the Negro race. The governor of Mississippi proclaimed Oct. 26, 1961, as "Race and Reason Day" to give special honor to this book. The state of Alabama authorized the writing of a book designed to prove "that the white race, intellectually, is superior to the Negro...."—*Southern School News* (December 1961), 1.

13. See Miriam Reimann, "How Children Become Prejudiced," in Milton L. Barron, ed., *American Minorities: A Textbook of Readings in Intergroup Relations*, New York: Alfred A. Knopf, 1957, pp. 94–104.

14. Martin Robert Coles, *Children under Desegregation: A Preliminary Psychiatric Report*, Atlanta: Southern Regional Council, 1962, p. 24.

15. Trager and Yarrow, *They Learn What They Live*, p. 341. See also Radke, Trager, and Davis, "Social Perceptions of Children," pp. 332–333.

THE WORLD
THROUGH
MARK'S EYES

Cynthia N. Shepard

I would like you to know my son Mark, who is now five years old. Although he has not yet attended kindergarten, he can both read and write, and can accurately identify colors and forms with an acuity beyond his years. He collects American flags, and pictures and ceramics of our national emblem, the eagle. He learned from somewhere on his own initiative the Pledge of Allegiance, which he recites with deep fervor. He only asked me the definitions of those difficult words: *indivisible, liberty, justice.* My precious, precocious Mark is very proud of his white, Anglo-Saxon heritage. But, he's black: a beautifully carved and polished piece of black American earth.

You may debate with me whether I should have taught him from birth that he is black. Instead, I invite you to see the world through Mark's eyes. Mark learned to read when he was three years old—books based on the white American style of life with pictures of blond, blue-eyed suburbia, with decent interspersing of browns and brunets—but no blacks. He watched the "educational" newsreels on television, which for him reinforced the rightness of whiteness. The man in the white hat—beating the black man with a billy club and then kicking him into insensibility—was the good guy. He was the protector of our individual rights. The books said so.

Black is the night which Mark fears, vanquished by the white of day. White is the knight on the white horse charging the black stains of daily living, and they all vanish. Black is unwanted; black is weak and easily defeated; black is bad.

I took Mark South with me and placed him in an all black nursery school while I taught during the day. The first evening, when I brought him home, he was in tears, writhing and retching in painful confusion. "Why did you make me go to school with all those Negroes?"

Then, just like NOW, I dig! Intellectuality had blocked my insight, creating of me a blind broad and of my black son a white racist. In his innocence—or highest sophistry, you see—he had intuitively perceived race not as a color, but as an attitude that he did not exemplify. My arguments to the contrary were completely hushed by his own words: "You said I could be anything I choose, and I choose to be white. I am white."

I returned North and searched both public and university libraries for literature with both pictures and narrative with which he might relate. *Little Black Sambo*? Oh no, dear God! Where are the black men of history, the Nat Turners, the Veseys, the Prossers? The uncompromising, unprecedented, unheralded warriors for true democracy?

I found a book about John Henry, with all the usual legendary verbiage. But it had pictures—pictures of John Henry as a big, black and beautiful baby; pictures of a handsome, adventurous black youth; and then, a picture of a dynamic, virile, muscle-bound black man. John Henry, the steel-driving man: a beautiful portrayal of black maleness, bared to the waist, swinging that hammer with all his might. It is with *that* picture that my son finally identified: an uncompromising image of black masculinity. That's what it's all about, baby.

I doubled my search for books that pictured black and white children running and laughing together, while black and white mothers shopped and lunched together, while black and white fathers worked and played together. I found a few. Mark had no difficulty identifying me in the pictures, but only recently could he find himself. Eventually, I overheard him speak of himself as a little brown boy, and I rejoiced—deeply, I say—that he was finding his way out.

Now, I have brought him East and have enrolled him in a kindergarten where all the other children are white. But I have not yet been able to send him to that school, although soon legally I will have to send him. What can be done to save my child from a plunge into utter confusion? What can be done to help my little black boy?

What can the world of education do to alleviate his pain—and mine? Must he grow like Topsy: confused, angry, alienated, lighting chaotic fires from the burning bitterness within? By America's guilt-ridden permissiveness, will he be ignored to become a black-helmeted, black-booted, black-bigoted replica of the swastika? Will my son see the necessity of asserting his blackness, his maleness, militantly and insensitively, riding roughshod over all who might in any manner oppose? Or, can the world of education, with all its demonstrated expertise, utilize the precociousness of my little black boy for the building of a better world for all people? How? When? *Now* is the answer.

Today Mark told me he is going to be an eagle and fly high above the earth where nobody will be able to stop him. That speaks to me. I gaze into Mark's face as he lies peacefully sleeping. With all the normal pains of growing, what utter, needless trauma I know he must also face tomorrow—unless change is *made* to happen.

Bitterness wells up within me, too, and I wretchedly whisper into his unheeding ear the words of a writer who must also have known deep human agony over the inhumanity of man to man:

O pardon me, thou bleeding piece of earth,
That I am meek and gentle with these butchers.

WHAT SHALL I TELL MY CHILDREN
WHO ARE BLACK

Margaret Burroughs

What shall I tell my children who are black
Of what it means to be a captive in this dark skin?
What shall I tell my dear one, fruit of my womb,
Of how beautiful they are when everywhere they turn
They are faced with abhorrence of everything that is black.
The night is black and so is the boogyman.
Villains are black with black hearts.
A black cow gives no milk. A black hen lays no eggs.
Bad news comes bordered in black, mourning clothes black,
Storm clouds, black, black is evil
And evil is black and devils food is black ...

What shall I tell my dear ones raised in a white world
A place where white has been made to represent
All that is good and pure and fine and decent,
Where clouds are white and dolls, and heaven
Surely is a white, white place with angels
Robed in white, and cotton candy and ice cream
And milk and ruffled Sunday dresses
And dream houses and long sleek Cadillacs
And angel's food is white ... all, all ... white.

What can I say therefore, when my child
Comes home in tears because a playmate
Has called him black, big lipped, flatnosed
And nappy headed? What will he think
When I dry his tears and whisper, "Yes, that's true.
But no less beautiful and dear."
How shall I lift up his head, get him to square
His shoulders, look his adversaries in the eye,

Confident in the knowledge of his worth,
Serene under his sable skin and proud of his own beauty?

What can I do to give him strength
That he may come through life's adversities
As a whole human being unwarped and human in a world
Of biased laws and inhuman practices, that he might
Survive. And survive he must! For who knows?
Perhaps this black child here bears the genius
To discover the cure for . . . cancer
Or to chart the course for exploration of the universe.
So, he must survive for the good of all humanity.
He must and will survive.
I have drunk deeply of late from the fountain
Of my black culture, sat at the knee and learned
From Mother Africa, discovered the truth of my heritage,
The truth, so often obscured and omitted.
And I find I have much to say to my black children.

I will lift up their heads in proud blackness
With the story of their fathers and their fathers
Fathers. And I shall take them into a way back time
Of Kings and Queens who ruled the Nile,
And measured the stars and discovered the
Laws of mathematics. Upon whose backs have been built
The wealth of two continents. I will tell him
This and more. And his heritage shall be his weapon
And his armor; will make him strong enough to win
Any battle he may face. And since this story is
Often obscured, I must sacrifice to find it
For my children, even as I sacrificed to feed,
Clothe and shelter them. So this I will do for them
If I love them. None will do it for me.
I must find the truth of heritage for myself
And pass it on to them. In years to come, I believe
Because I have armed them with the truth, my children
And their children's children will venerate me.
For it is the truth that will make us free!

STUDY QUESTIONS

1. Solomon contends that our society, including the schools, "incorporates a deep-rooted pattern of racism." What school practices would
   Solomon regard as racist? What effects do they have on culturally
   different children? What steps might the school take to eliminate such
   practices?

2. Assuming that Solomon accurately describes the public schools, what

problems might a classroom teacher face in teaching the democratic ideology? How might he attempt to resolve them?

3. For a number of years social scientists have been attempting with varying degrees of success, to derive a comprehensive and coherent theory of prejudice. In his selection, Banks discusses the attempts by various social scientists to derive such a theory and offers his own explanation. Which theories does Rose consider most important in explaining the origin of prejudice? How do they compare with the explanations offered by Simpson and Yinger? According to Banks, what are the most important variables contributing to the formation and perpetuation of racial prejudice? What are the limitations of current theories of prejudice? What are their implications, as discussed by Banks, for formulating and implementing a program to reduce racial prejudice in the school?

4. Morland maintains that our society "educates for prejudice." What research does he cite to support his argument? Why do young children develop a bias for the white race at an early age? How might the school help children to develop more positive racial attitudes?

5. Research by Kenneth and Mamie P. Clark, Trager and Yarrow, Morland, and others suggests that black as well as white children prefer white to black dolls. Black children also tend to make more incorrect racial self-identifications than do white children. Why is it especially important for the school to help culturally different children to clarify their racial attitudes and predispositions?

6. In her selection, Shepard contends that her black son Mark became a "white racist." How is it possible for a black child to develop racial attitudes which are highly similar or identical to those of a white racist? What kind of dilemma did Mark face? How might his teacher help him to feel better about his race and his culture?

7. In her powerful poem, Burroughs suggests, as do other writers in this volume, that the black child can better his self-image by learning the "truth" of his black heritage. What are some of the difficulties involved in ascertaining historical truths? What are the values as well as the limitations of attempting to improve the self-images of black children by exposing them to black history and culture? What other approaches to this problem are promising?

8. A social studies teacher cannot work effectively with culturally different children until he can perceive them, their culture, and their people more positively and realistically. Do you agree or disagree with this statement? If you agree, think of ways in which teachers might clarify their racial attitudes. If you disagree, explain why.

SUGGESTED READINGS

Allport, Gordon W., *The Nature of Prejudice*. Reading, Mass.: Addison-Wesley, 1958

Bibby, Cyril, *Race, Prejudice and Education*. New York: Frederick A. Praeger, 1960

Block, Charles Y., and Ellen Siegelman (Editors), *Prejudice U.S.A.* New York: Praeger Publishers, 1969

Clark, Kenneth B., *Prejudice and Your Child*. Boston: Beacon Press, 1968.

Bentler, Robert A., Bernard Mackler, and Mary Ellen Warshauer, *The Urban R's: Race Relations as the Problem in Urban Education*. New York: Frederick A. Praeger, 1967

Gibson, John S., *The Intergroup Relations Curriculum: A Program for Elementary School Education, Volumes I and II*. Medford, Mass.: Lincoln Filene Center for Citizenship and Public Affairs, 1969

Goodman, Mary Ellen, *Race Awareness in Young Children*. New York: Collier Books, 1968

Kopp, M. Audrey, *The Myth of Race*. Techny, Illinois: Divine Word Publications, 1967

Marden, Charles F., and Gladys Meyer, *Minorities in American Society*. New York: American Book Company, 1968

Report of the National Advisory Commission on Civil Disorders. New York: Bantam Books, 1968

Research on Racial Relations. New York: UNESCO, 1966

Rose, Arnold M., *The Roots of Prejudice*. Paris, France: UNESCO, 1958

Rose, Arnold M., "The Causes of Prejudice," in F. E. Merrill, H. W. Dunham, A. M. Rose and Paul W. Tappan, *Social Problems*. New York: Alfred A. Knopf, 1950

Rose, Arnold M., and Caroline B. Rose (Editors), *Minority Problems: A Textbook of Readings in Intergroup Relations*. Chapter 16, New York: Harper and Row, 1965

Rose, Peter I., *They and We: Racial and Ethnic Relations in the United States*. New York: Random House, 1965

Simpson, George E., and J. Milton Yinger, *Racial and Cultural Minorities: An Analysis of Prejudice and Discrimination*. New York: Harper and Row, 1965.

Trager, Helen G., and Marian Radke Yarrow, *They Learn What They Live*. New York: Harper and Brothers Publishers, 1952

The United States Commission on Civil Rights, *Racism in America and How To Combat It*. Washington, D.C.: U.S. Government Printing Office, 1970

CHAPTER 2
SOCIAL AND CULTURAL
FACTORS OF LEARNING

When educators first focused their attention on the instruction of cultural and ethnic minorities a few years ago, they stressed the devastating effects of poverty on a child's social and cognitive development. They attributed the poor child's massive failure in school to his economic condition, over which they had little control. Rarely did educators question their assumptions or goals; their main objective was to mold poor and minority-group children so that they could more easily adapt to the dominant middle-class culture of our society. Rarely, too, did educators discuss the need to encourage the existence of multiethnicity or suggest that culturally different children failed in school because of curricular and instructional shortcomings.

The articles in this chapter delineate both the environment of poverty from which many children emanate and the unique cultural components of various racial and ethnic groups. The dominant theme of the chapter is *cultural conflict*—the dilemma children from minority groups face when they are forced to reject their own cultures and accept the school's middle-class values. This conflict results in high dropout rates, low educational aspirations, and degraded self-images.

While most of the writers in this chapter feel that all children should learn the ways of the dominant culture of their society, they also stress the need for the school to *respect* and *accept* cultural and ethnic diversity. The school must become truly multicultural if it is to create an effective learning environment for all of its pupils. Chapters 3 and 4 illuminate the need for teachers and administrators to re-evaluate and question their *assumptions* regarding the deficient cognitive development of poor children as a factor contributing to their failure in school. These chapters suggest that the attitudes and expectations of teachers may be the most significant variables determining academic success or failure.

THE SOCIAL WORLD OF
THE URBAN SLUM CHILD:
SOME EARLY FINDINGS

Suzanne Keller

Throughout its history, this country has been settled largely, though not exclusively, by men and women seeking to escape the stings of poverty, unemployment, overcrowding in rapidly expanding cities, poor hygiene and social discrimination and turmoil. Many came to make their fortunes and many succeeded. But after a century or two it turned out that even the "land of opportunity" had room for poverty and for slums and knew unemployment, ignorance and failure. Periodically, the awareness that there are millions of city poor in the richest industrial society in the world comes as a shock only to be displaced by more immediate concerns. The prosperity since World War II, the rising standard of living and extensive social and geographical mobility among large segments of the population are chiefly responsible for this relative neglect.

But the poor survive. In a metropolis like New York about 25 per cent of the families would be considered poor by any standards—underfed, under-employed, ill-educated and socially and economically marginal. Children continue to be born in Negro ghettoes; mothers are deserted; families are on relief in a society that has put self-reliance and self-support among its cardinal virtues. And social and economic deprivation go hand in hand with other frightening problems—with crime and delinquency, with illiteracy and ill health. It is the poorest children who do least well in school, who care least about learning, and who swell the ranks of youthful delinquents, drug addicts and the mentally and emotionally disabled. Poverty has always had its cost and its price. Its victims are many. Its most innocent victims are the children raised under its influence.

This paper describes some aspects of the lives of underprivileged New York City public school children. Though the numbers involved are small, a general pattern may be discerned which, rather than any statistical uniformities, is of interest here. I will describe the social and family backgrounds of these children, their ambitions, achievements and activities and their perceptions of themselves and their future. And since I had access to both

Suzanne Keller, "The Social World of the Urban Slum Child: Some Early Findings," *American Journal of Orthopsychiatry*, **33**, 5 (October 1963), 823–831. Copyright © 1963 by the American Orthopsychiatric Association. Reprinted with permission of the publisher.

Negro and white children I will also describe their discernible similarities and differences.

The data are drawn from a larger study of the verbal and intellectual development of some 250 school children from various social and cultural backgrounds. The purpose of this study, carried out by the Institute for Developmental Studies, was to ascertain the influence of social and familial factors on the development of basic cognitive and verbal skills in young children. It arose out of a concern for the hundreds of thousands of children who annually fail to benefit from instruction in the city's public schools by failing to learn their three Rs, which are considered a part of their birthright. Failure in the first grade is usually only a prelude to failure in the fifth, and failure in school is all too often a forerunner of failure in life.

As is well known, most of the standard achievement and intelligence tests, the school curricula and the children's books are based on the capacities and problems of middle-class children, who are used as a yardstick for all children. It is also known, however, that these children are by no means typical of all in their life experiences, family relationships and socioeconomic opportunities. Numerically, at any rate, the lower-class children outnumber them. And if the middle-class child were an "ideal type" of child for our society, then, by definition, the majority of children fall far short of this ideal.

Educators, psychologists, psychiatrists and, of course, parents have long been aware of this fact and attempts are being made to take the differential experiences, motivations and life chances into account when preparing and evaluating programs for teaching children from underprivileged back-grounds. But in order to do so systematically, it is necessary to know what the typical life experiences of underprivileged children are. This paper is an attempt to provide some relevant information.

The children studied are 46 first- and fifth-grade children currently living and attending public school in the poorer sections of New York City. Both colored and white children are included, though in view of the incompleteness of the larger study from which they are drawn, they are not equally represented. By means of an Index of Social Class developed at the Institute, based on occupational and educational level of the main support of the family and on a Crowding Index, these children were all classified as Level IV on a ten-level stratification continuum, which might be considered as somewhere at the top of the lower-lower class stratum or at the bottom of the upper-lower class stratum.

The children were seen in the schools for several hours, during which they took a number of tests tapping their verbal, intellectual and conceptual abilities. Their parents received questionnaires by mail and the children themselves gave accounts of their typical weekend activities and their life at home. It must be pointed out that the major purpose of the larger study was to compare test performances on various measures, and not to obtain full and comprehensive information on socioeconomic backgrounds. The background measures, in fact, permit at best only a rough classification of the socioeconomic levels of the children. But, although these measures are gross, they do depict some aspects of life in the slums of Harlem and in some of the poorer white sections in the changing neighborhoods of Brooklyn and Manhattan. One-fifth of the families were interviewed in their own homes.

The following summary is divided into two parts: an over-all comparison, and a comparison of Negroes and whites separately. Four areas are discussed: (1) social and economic characteristics of the families, such as size, available space, regional origins of the parents and educational and occupational attainments; (2) the children's after-school and weekend activities; (3) the children's self-perceptions; and (4) parental aspirations for the children.

SOCIAL AND ECONOMIC BACKGROUNDS

The children were selected so as to be roughly comparable in the educational and occupational attainments of the main support of the family and a Crowding Index. On all three of these they fell on the lower end of a socioeconomic continuum, although gross measures such as these hardly tap more than a fraction of the characteristics associated with lower-class life. The breadwinners in these families were employed as porters, short-order cooks, unskilled and semiskilled factory workers and maintenance and service workers. A few were bus or taxi drivers, clerks and self-employed. The somewhat higher occupational positions of the self-employed were offset by overcrowded living conditions and conspicuously low educational attainments. One out of six of the bread-winners was unemployed at the time of the study and these families were receiving welfare assistance. On the average, the parents of these children had not gone beyond the first year of high school, and the mothers had somewhat more schooling than the fathers.

Family size, nativity and family composition showed some important variations within the group. Less than three-fifths of these families conformed to the modal American type of two parents with between two and three children; more than two-fifths were large families with six to ten members. The average number of persons per room in the household was 1.2; this went as high as 1.5 persons per room for the larger families.

These families are not by and large the poor immigrant of half a century ago. These poor are Americanized, the majority born and raised on native ground. They also have been poor for a long time—two-thirds have held their current low-level jobs for six years or more, one-third for as long as ten years or more. Nor have they experienced extensive job mobility—one-half have had no other job during the past ten years, and none more than three jobs during that time. If either rapid horizontal or vertical mobility is characteristic of workers at higher levels and at the lowest levels, it does not, apparently, characterize these.

These, then, are among the poorest elements of the population, they hold low-level jobs, they have had such jobs for a number of years, and they typically have not finished high school. Their actual chances for upward mobility are therefore objectively low. Thus their own subjective appraisals for such mobility are interesting. When asked to classify themselves in one of three groups, those going up, those going down in the world, and those doing neither, fully two-thirds felt they were going up in the world, three-tenths felt they were at a standstill, and only 2 per cent stated that they were going downhill: The ethic of success is very much in evidence.

LIFE OUTSIDE OF SCHOOL

All 46 children live in homes that contain both radio and television sets and all utilize both media regularly and frequently. Three-fourths had spent at least two hours (a sizable proportion as many as five) before their television sets the previous day watching a variety of entertainment programs—cartoons, the fights, Westerns, a few adult shows such as "I Love Lucy" and "Hitchcock Presents," and some of the better known comedians. The larger society seems to come to these children via entertainment and escapist stories on television. The children are familiar, even in the first grade, with the names of programs and of leading characters—a fact which might be used in school instruction.

This emphasis on peer-group entertainment also runs through their accounts of typical weekend activities. These children are between the ages of five and 13, years crucial for the acquisition of skills and information and the development of any talents they may possess. Life is not yet as serious as it will one day be, responsibilities are at a minimum, and the mind is receptive to new experiences and to the exploration of the natural and the social world. Yet hardly any of these children mention using their time to prepare themselves for something—they play, they watch television, they see films and they listen to music on the radio. Sometimes they visit relatives and go to Church on Sundays. They do not read, they do not study, they do not take lessons, they do not get instruction in any of the things that interest many children at these ages.

There is clearly a lack of sustained interaction with adult members of their families—a fact corroborating the findings of studies by Esther Milner, Walter B. Miller and others. Only about one-half, for example, regularly eat one meal with one or both parents, the rest either eat alone or with brothers and sisters only. This robs them of one of the important socializing and intellectually stimulating experiences of childhood. According to Bossard and Boll,[1] the family meal is a focus for a number of important emotional, cultural and educational experiences. Participation and interaction with significant others in an organized way helps shape the personality and sensitizes the participants to each other's needs and inclinations. Organized conversation helps shape vocabulary, influences the development of verbal facility and subtlety and determines a whole set of complex attitudes and feelings about the use of language. The family meal also serves as an acculturating agency, for, in their interaction, the members teach each other and develop a way of seeing themselves and the world in which they live. The family meal has been described as a forum, as a clearing house for information, as a school for life and as an opportunity to act out deeper personality needs. Such experiences were absent in the lives of at least one-half of the lower-class children here discussed.

SELF-PERCEPTIONS

Compared to middle-class children these children are evidently handicapped, both in their objective living conditions and in their opportunities for learning outside of school, either from their parents and other family members through sustained relationships and contacts, or through organized activities other than play or passive response to the mass media. Presumably, this will affect their self-perceptions and their school performance.

The Self-Concept and Motivation Test of the Institute contains ten incompleted sentences, each relating to some wish, judgment or evaluation of the child. One in particular seems to tap the self-image of the child by comparison with other children: "When I look at other boys and girls, and then look at myself, I feel. . . ." In all, 28 of 46 responses (or 60 per cent) were unfavorable to the child, and only 14 of the 46 (30 per cent) were favorable. The favorable responses read: "I feel good, happy, the same." The unfavorable ones read: "I feel ashamed, sad, heartbroken." The proportion of unfavorable self-references, moreover, increases from 55 per cent in the first grade to 65 per cent in the fifth. These children, then, typically express a low self-esteem, drawing unfavorable comparisons between themselves and their school mates. If such self-deprecation is representative of the feelings of most young children from lower socioeconomic backgrounds, it suggests one potential source for early school failure.

PARENTAL ASPIRATIONS FOR THEIR CHILDREN

A number of studies have shown that parents may abandon their hopes for conspicuous achievements only to project them the more intensely onto their children.[2] These parents, too, conform to this pattern. When they were asked to indicate a first and a second choice of possible future occupations, although they could have nothing but vague hopes and expectation about the occupational future of their young children, their replies provide some insight into their ambitions and hopes. In their choices for the boys, fully two-thirds of the parents currently engaged in unskilled and semiskilled labor or unemployed hoped that their sons would become professional men such as doctors, lawyers, engineers or business executives. Parents of girls most frequently mentioned such traditional feminine callings as nursing and teaching.

As to the amount of schooling they would like their children to obtain, here again, aspirations were high. Eight-tenths of the parents wish their children to acquire a college degree. Only one-tenth would be satisfied with a high school diploma.

These responses compare interestingly with those given in private interviews in the homes of the ten families who had not answered the mail questionnaire. When asked what they considered the best sort of job to have, security and steady work, rather than prestige, power or riches, received greatest emphasis. Ideally, then, on the fantasy level perhaps, these parents would like to see their sons get to the top. More realistically, they will be satisfied if their children manage to do what they themselves have failed to do—get a steady and secure job.

In sum, the children described in this paper come from large families living in relatively crowded quarters in the midst or on the edge of poverty. Only two out of three are being supported solely by their father's earning in low-level jobs, and one out of six are currently exposed to the stings of their parents' unemployment and the mixed blessings of public assistance. The majority of the parents, most of whom are native born, have been in this relatively deprived status for a long time—two-thirds for more than six years, one-third for more then ten. Nor has there been the sort of rapid job mobility one has come to expect from the official statistics on national trends, for, most of these people had held at most two other jobs at similar levels during the previous ten years.

All of this might lead to a pervasive sense of discouragement among them—and well it may, for we have no data to tap these feelings directly. Such discouragement is not, however, translated into resignation or indifference toward upward mobility. For, fully two-thirds of the group believe that they are on the way up in the world and a bare 2 per cent feel that things are going downhill. These great expectations are further reflected in the high hopes they have for their children, whom they would like to see graduating from college and entering one of the professions. Whether these desires reflect concrete plans or unrealistic fantasies about the future cannot be assessed.

What else do we know about these children, most of whom do poorly in school about which they care very little? Television seems to be a rather persistent influence. They like to play and they have friends. But they have little sustained contact with adults, they have few organized conversations with other adults the way middle-class children do, and few participate in shared family activities. Even at meal times, one-half of these children are alone or in the company of their brothers and sisters. It is interesting that, although these children are poor, they are not starving—the foods typically eaten at breakfast and dinner include a considerable variety of nutritionally adequate foods although amounts were not indicated. Poverty, today, probably extends more to housing, to lack of spending money, to lack of comforts and to a constricted milieu for learning and exploring the world. A city, especially a metropolis, would seem to be a fascinating place in which to grow up, but one would not believe this from these accounts of restricted movement and the monotonous repetitiveness of activities—TV and more TV, play with other children, movies and, as the single organized activity besides school, Church on Sunday for one-half of the group. Their world seems to be small and monotonous, though not necessarily unhappy.

This constriction of experience and the poverty of spirit it engenders may account for the below normal IQ scores of this group of poor children by the time of the fifth grade (mean IQ is 88.57 on Lorge Thorndike nonverbal IQ test; in first grade, Lorge Thorndike IQ mean scores were 96.56), confirming countless other studies that have shown a similar scholastic and verbal inferiority for children from underprivileged environments. It may also account for the high degree of negative self-evaluations already discussed.

In recent years there has been talk of the existence of a lower-class culture that performs much the same function for its members as any culture does: It defines the world, structures perceptions and habitual reactions, sets goals and standards and permits people to evaluate and approve each other's conduct. This means that lower-class culture patterns, while substantially different from middle-class patterns, nevertheless provide a web of shared meanings for those subject to its rewards and penalties. Still, cultural relativism ignores the fact that schools and industry are middle-class in organization and outlook. If lower-class children conform to the "focal concerns"[3] of their milieu they will typically be misfits in the schools they attend. Short of adapting the public school to the cultural milieu of different groups, the children of this background will be at a disadvantage.

Clearly these children have a profound initial handicap in the scholastic competition with middle-class children. This initial disadvantage rarely turns to later advantage—instead, they become negativistic or bored and fail to learn the rudiments of the verbal and intellectual skills expected of adults in an industrial society.

The discrepancy in preschool orientation by social class is duplicated within the lower class by race. Using the same index of socioeconomic status, we find that even when gross socioeconomic factors are controlled, Negroes and whites do not live in comparable social environments.

For one thing, lower-class Negro (Level IV on the Index) children come from larger families than white children (nearly one-half as compared to one-third among the white children have at least three brothers and sisters). Thus an already low income must stretch farther for one group than for the other. More significantly, only one-half the Negro children were supported solely by the earnings of their fathers, whereas fully nine-tenths of the white children had fathers who could assume the traditional male role of chief breadwinner. In addition, three times as many Negro as white children at the same socioeconomic level live in families where the adults are currently unemployed and receiving welfare and other types of aid for the indigent. In educational attainment, too, the white families were somewhat at an advantage, the fathers of the white children having on the average one more year of schooling than the Negro fathers, and the white mothers having one-half a year more. In each group, however, the mothers were somewhat better educated than the fathers.

One of the striking differences occurs with regard to place of birth. Three-fourths of the Negro parents were geographically mobile, two-thirds having been born in the South and one-tenth outside the United States. None of the white children came from mobile families—all had parents both of whom had been born in the North.

As regards occupational mobility, however, Negro families were more likely to have held their present low-level jobs for a long time. In fact, whereas more than half the white families were at this low level for less than six years, more than half the Negro families had been there for six years or more. Thus, whereas Negro families at this level were more mobile geographically, they were less mobile occupationally. This does not, apparently, diminish their belief in their own success. Fully three-fourths of the Negro families, as against only one-third of the white families, felt that they were going up in the world. Only one-fifth of the Negro families felt that they were at a standstill, but three-fifths of the white felt this way. Negro lower-class children are thus raised in objectively inferior homes in which subjective appraisals of life's chances are much higher than among a comparable group of white families. Without more extensive data it is impossible to account for this discrepancy, although two possibilities suggest themselves. One relates to the differential geographical mobility of Negro families, which may lead them to expect other types of mobility as well. That is, they may have migrated to New York in the hope of improving their standing. The other relates to the relative standing of two equally low-level socioeconomic groups in the larger world. Level IV has been described as somewhere at the top of the lowest and most underprivileged stratum, or at the bottom of the upper-lower stratum. But, while the two groups were objectively at the same socioeconomic level, their status relative to most others of their rate is quite different. The majority of white persons in this country are above the lower-lower class level but the same does not hold true for Negroes. This means, then, that the top of the lower-lower class is an exceedingly low status for most of the white families but perhaps a relatively high one for the Negro families. In other words, the white families may feel relatively deprived by comparison with others, whereas the Negro families may feel relatively favored. Further exploration on a larger sample should clarify this. It would be interesting, for example, to see whether this expressed optimism is also characteristic of the very lowest socioeconomic group among Negroes.

The most striking finding regarding the children themselves concerns the self-perceptions of the fifth graders. Negro children definitely exhibit more negative self-evaluations than do white children; 30 per cent of the white children but fully 80 per cent of the Negro children draw unfavorable self-other comparisons, paralleling findings from a number of other studies.[4]

These fifth-grade Negro children had also been evaluated by their teachers and some of their observations are relevant. More than half were judged to have little motivation for school work, to be typically sad or pre-occupied, and to be working below capacity in school. The interplay between self-perception and school achievement must be explored further, particularly in view of the fact that the parents of the Negro children were very much concerned about their children's work, for, whereas nearly all the white families were satisfied with their children's school work, only one-half of the Negro families were. This may be yet another indication of the greater ambitiousness of the Negro families already noted.

These preliminary results reveal rather striking differences between Negro and white school children at the same socioeconomic level in their objective living conditions, parental aspirations, and their self-evaluations. Similarly, by inference, lower-class children, irrespective of race, differ sharply in their preparation for school from the ideal middle-class children with whom they must compete. Presumably, in both instances, this will exert a negative effect on intellectual interests and ambitions and may thus help account for the long-demonstrated correlation between socioeconomic deprivation and school failure.

NOTES

1. J. H. S. Bossard and E. S. Boll, *The Sociology of Child Development,* New York: Harper and Brothers, 1960.

2. E. Chinoy, *Automobile Workers and the American Dream*, New York: Random House, 1955; S. M. Lipset and R. Bendix, *Social Mobility in Industrial Society*, Berkeley and Los Angeles: University of California

Press, 1962; F. Zweig, *The Worker in an Affluent Society*, New York: Free Press of Glencoe, 1961, p. 21.

3. W. B. Miller, "Lower Class Culture as a Generating Milieu of Gang Delinquency," *Journal of Social Issues*, **14**, (1958), 5–19.

4. For a summary of such studies, see R. M. Drager and K. S. Miller, "Comparative Psychological Studies of Negroes and Whites in the United States," *Psychological Bulletin*, **57**, 5 (1960), 382–383.

THE CULTURAL
DILEMMA OF
AMERICAN INDIANS

Lorraine Misiaszek

American Indian culture is unique in this nation today because it has endured almost five hundred years of exposure to the predominant Euro-American culture. It has resisted, to some degree, all the philosophic socio-economic pressures to change and to conform to white, middle-class American standards.

Since the durability of any culture lies in the strength of its value system, it may be enlightening to examine why Indian people are still influenced in varying degrees today by their culture, and why they have not assimilated into the "mainstream of American life" as quickly as other ethnic groups who have immigrated to this country.

INDIAN STANDARDS AND VALUES

The philosophy of American Indians was profound. In comparison with current philosophies, it was relatively uncomplicated. Indians lived their beliefs spiritually and physically. Although the numerous Indian tribes inhabiting what is now the United States have different religious, economic and social structures to some extent, there exists a common thread running

Lorraine Misiaszek, "The Cultural Dilemma of American Indians," *Social Education*, **33** (April 1969), 438–439, ff. 446. Revised by the author and reprinted with permission of the author and the National Council for the Social Studies.

through their philosophy that is reflected today in the beliefs, attitudes and feelings that they experience. This is termed "Indianness".

I will attempt to sketch briefly the significant aspects of their way of life which should provide some insight into the foundation of contemporary Indian beliefs and attitudes.

As naturally as the air we breathe, their belief in the goodness and justice of a great Spirit permeated their thoughts and actions. They lived in very close harmony with nature and with themselves. Each moment of their lives was highly valued; time was not measured by seconds, minutes, or hours, but Indians lived on a "here and now" basis.

The economy of any society will determine greatly the kinds of rules that have to be developed and maintained if that society is to survive. Tribal communal living meant that each member shared mutually all the hardships along with the good times when food was plentiful and the climate favorable. Because the tribe members had to rely upon one another, the qualities they valued most highly were personal integrity, individual autonomy, and a demonstrated concern for the community.

For centuries, the survival of American Indian tribes in the mountainous region of the Northwest depended upon their ability to hunt, fish, gather roots and plants for food and medicinal purposes. The young men of the tribe developed keen hunting instincts, tough physiques, and courageous hearts to endure the rigors of hunting wild game in the rugged terrain. Extremely cold or hot weather contributed to the challenge of a successful hunt as they utilized the hand-fashioned spears or bows and arrows. Salmon fishing in the deep, swift rivers and turbulent waterfalls required precise timing and superior skill.

These brave and courageous acts, the constant tests of physical stamina and endurance, and the highly developed skills demonstrated almost daily by the fathers, uncles, and brothers of the young children provided them a living example of the admirable traits they were expected and encouraged to follow and internalize as a necessary part of their education.

Tasks patiently undertaken by the womenfolk of the tribe included dressing out the game. They prepared the food for the long winter months ahead by smoking and drying the meat of deer, elk, bear, and the salmon. Certain roots were dug and baked. Huckleberries and strawberries were picked and sun dried for storage. The long tedious job of tanning deer hides for use as clothing and to cover family dwellings was an important occupation of the older women.

Traditions were followed religiously and tribal values were taught the children by the elders, usually grandparents, who passed their wisdom and knowledge along through songs and legends. Age was respected, because to be old was accepted as synonymous with being wise. The older people supervised the young in their work and play. They were responsible for shaping the characters of these children in a non-coercive way that allowed a high degree of freedom for individual choice.

The tribe to which one belonged was considered in terms of an "extended family". In fact, cousins, however distant, are today referred to as one's brother or sister. Many Indian languages have no words or expressions to make the distinction between very distant or close relatives. Strong family ties were maintained and reinforced through the values that the tribe placed on sharing, individual autonomy, and the use they made of the talents possessed by all age groups for the continuance of the tribe.

Communal living required a cooperative spirit vital to the well-being of the tribe. It was essential that each person realized his own individual value in relation to the interdependence of the group—how his growth and development of character evolved from the tribal culture, and in turn, what his contribution could be to the group. Therefore, personal qualities that were considered most important centered around honesty, integrity and generosity. High spirits and good humor were always appreciated and welcome in any gathering.

Just as positive virtues were rewarded by admiration, the negative ones were punished through ridicule primarily. More stern measures were applied such as forced exile and even death if the offense was serious. The traits that were discouraged included boasting of one's accomplishments, loud or immodest behavior, stinginess, stealing and lying. Promises that were made and broken were considered the same as lying because a person's word, once given, was as good as that person. His reputation was on trial when he had made a promise.

THE INDIAN IN TODAY'S SOCIETY

Today the American Indians find themselves in a society based on an economy calling for highly competitive ability with the ultimate goals being financial success and upward social mobility. It follows that an entirely new set of standards and values is imposed on Indian people today. There is some question in their minds, however, whether or not they want to accept these new standards since it means they must repudiate all the deeply ingrained values of their culture if they are to conform to the new. It is safe to state that many are going through the motions outwardly, but they have not really accepted or internalized these modern values. As a result, many Indian people have developed a deep hostility toward society as a whole.

Consequently, a serious conflict exists for the Indian—a conflict manifested by a growing alcoholism problem and an increasing suicide rate amongst the youth. Disrupted family life from broken marriages compounded by poor education opportunities is an element that contributes to the poverty cycle. It appears that there is not an easy or immediate solution in sight for this troubled people.

Because the values of a given culture are often unconsciously accepted and applied, today's Indian is not aware of what is taking place in his own situation or what is causing the conflict within himself. At no time in his educational experience has he been taught anything about his past rich culture. He is unaware of how deeply he is influenced by his cultural values that conflict with the work day world concept of 8 A.M. to 5 P.M. schedule that he must function in daily. Traditionally, he followed the "present" oriented way of his tribe, and today the Indian does not concern himself too seriously with tomorrow, next week, or next year. Furthermore, he does not see anything wrong in sharing whatever he has with others of his "extended family" if he has more than they have. He can see little merit in boasting about his abilities or talents in order to impress a prospective employer. Because Indian people do not easily adopt a competitive spirit in the employment area, they have been labeled "lazy."

On the other hand, the individual Indian who has established himself economically through his own efforts finds that he must repudiate the tribal value of sharing with others. Because he is seen by his friends and relatives as not being generous and even as stingy, he is alienated from them. As a consequence, this person tends to reject his race and his ethnic identity entirely. I cite this as an example of the common pressures confronting the American Indian in his daily life as he attempts to earn a livelihood and provide for his basic needs.

HELPING THE INDIAN CHILD TO ADJUST

The American Indian can be assisted in making an adjustment to today's society through education. A good adjustment can be made if the changes are implemented on the basis of what the child believes and follows of tribal values. Therefore, emphasis ought to be placed on the kind of pre-school educational experiences offered the Indian child. Because the early part of his development takes place in the home, he is apt to absorb his basic cultural values long before he enters the classroom. The difficult task facing the teacher will be to build on the foundation already established. If that foundation is destroyed in the process of introducing the new values, the Indian child will experience great difficulty in making a good adjustment and is likely to fail scholastically. Ultimately, he will drop out of school. This has already happened far too often as evidenced by the high drop-out rate in the public schools amongst Indian children throughout the nation. Reports show an average 50 percent drop-out rate. Some schools have an 80 percent rate, and a few reflect a 100 percent drop-out ratio for Indian children.

It is obvious that the Indian child will be confronted with a cultural conflict when he begins to associate with his peer group and the teacher in the classroom. It is at this point in the child's life experience that the teacher can make the most progress in introducing new concepts. It would be valuable if the teacher knew what kind of a home environment the child came from. In view of the cultural conflict experienced by most adult Indians, one or both of the child's parents may suffer from an alcoholic problem, and the family income may be unsteady and frequently non-existent.

Often a grandparent, an aunt, or another relative is raising the child. The child is usually treated permissively and is loved by his parents and relatives. The trait of respecting an individual's autonomy is applied to the child at an early age, so he does very much as he pleases with little regulation of his activities. In reference to my own childhood, punishment or displeasure was expressed by my parents in a frown and a scolding for unacceptable behavior, but never was I given a sound spanking, which I would have preferred to a scolding. Physical punishment for Indian children was not a part of their cultural pattern.

People in the role of authority such as law enforcement officers, doctors, or nurses usually appear to the child in an unpleasant or unfavorable light because of an experience with some member of the family. Instead of considering these people as friends, he sees them as enemies who should be avoided whenever possible. The teacher may easily be placed in this category if the child's first contact with the teacher appears to him as a negative experience. Although the teacher may act in an impersonal manner, the child may define this as unfriendly and not respond readily to friendly gestures at a later time.

Most Indian children are taught to be seen but not heard when adults are present. This training is likely to affect the child's behavior in the classroom, and if this happens, he will not respond easily unless he is specifically asked to answer a question or give his opinion. Many teachers regard such behavior as sullen, but more often than not, the child is really quite shy and exhibiting the cultural trait he has learned at home.

Experienced teachers of Indian children relate that it is not uncommon to ask a pupil a question in class, and if he doesn't know the answer, the other Indian children will declare that they do not know it either, even though they might. This reaction relates to the non-competitive aspect of Indian culture and concern for the individual by not causing him to lose self-esteem. However, this is not the only behavior pattern that Indian children demonstrate today. There are some who exhibit and express hostility by being a show-off, using shocking language, or being a bully. In these ways they are attempting to compensate for feelings of inferiority and frustration in an unstable, changing environment. The child's shyness or hostility can be overcome easily by praise and admiration for somthing he has done.

Indian children do respond well to programs emphasizing art, music, nature studies, and athletic activities. Traditionally, there has not been a great deal of verbalizing in the Indian home and, as a result, the child will develop his ability to perceive meanings that underlie facial expressions, gestures, or tone of voice. Programs that relate to perceptive ability often prompt successful achievement more rapidly than do the academically oriented subjects. The Indian pupil will profit from special language and reading helps to assist him in developing verbal expression.

If an understanding teacher-pupil relationship can be established successfully early in the school experience of the Indian child, the chances are immeasurably improved that this child will achieve scholastic success at a level comparable to non-Indian children.

As the teacher strives to gain a better understanding of the response behavior of the culturally different, his efforts will be facilitated by first examining his own responses and attitudes. He must question the basis of his expectations relative to pupil achievement and evaluate his classroom practices in an objective way. By recognizing the degree to which his own culture has conditioned him, the non-Indian teacher can begin to understand the problem in clearer perspective. He is better prepared to commence building on the cultural foundation that has shaped this child prior to enrollment in school.

I have endeavored to present, from the American Indian's point of view, the stronger values of a native minority culture as they are manifested in the behavior and feelings of Indian children, while these children attempt to find a place in the system developed by a dominant non-Indian middle-class society. These enduring cultural values have offered many strengths to the individual while at the same time have caused a conflict that frequently leads to self-destructive behavior. Such behavior lends credence to the negative stereotyped image of the contemporary American Indian as he is viewed by his fellow Americans, and so the cycle continues. I trust that one day soon American society will see that its strength lies in the differences of its multi-racial membership and that respect for individual differences will become the rule rather than the exception.

ACCULTURATION AND
LEARNING PROBLEMS OF
PUERTO RICAN CHILDREN

Sophie L. Elam

Many studies have been made and much has been said about the Puerto Rican child in cities. Although there are characteristics common to Puerto Rican children, these are by no means very different from those of other minority and emigrant children in the lower economic range. Problems of acculturation of emigrant groups are not new in our society, but invariably there is an urgency about them which is reflected in the many problems in the school and the community.

Perhaps as we look back at other migrations and note how these have been assimilated it is possible to reflect that people who, like the Puerto Ricans, have recently come out of a rural peasant cultural pattern of living find acculturation more difficult than those who come from an urban center. It may well be that rural peoples tend to be tradition-oriented while those from metropolitan communities are more other-directed so that they more readily respond to the cues available to them in our culture.

Acculturation is basically a problem of accommodation to a whole new set of patterns and being. It is actually the change-over from one culture to another. Culture is primarily a learning which is begun at birth and which provides the base for living. It permeates all behavior, from the simple fundamentals of eating and dressing and talking to the more complex and involved patterns of communication, use of symbols, and the development of a value system. Culture is also considered to be a determinant of the way one perceives oneself and others. It involves the totality of living from the biological to the social and intellectual. And the greatest complexity of the adjustment lies largely in the social sphere. " . . . under situations of stress or strain, of rapid change and consequent disorientation there is likely to be an increase in manifest ill health."[1]

Despite the vast network of our communications in mass media each emigrant group maintains almost intact its social constructs. For the adult who is already completely oriented to a way of life and whose whole gamut of responses is organized around the expected cues in his culture, the transition is difficult enough. He must select from the new what has resemblance

Sophie L. Elam, "Acculturation and Learning Problems of Puerto Rican Children," *Teachers College Record*, **61** (February 1960), 258–264. Reprinted with permission of the author and publisher.

to the familiar and add to this repertoire by trial and error the new learnings as they are needed. He tends to remain in his own ethnic and cultural clusters, both in industry and in neighborhood living, as witness the conclaves of Puerto Ricans in our cities.

But for the child who is still in the process of learning his social role and inherent responses, the transition—often in only a few hours from the known to the unknown; from the simple to the complex environment; from rural areas to the cosmopolitan city—creates an even greater problem. It is the children who manifest the greatest degree of maladjustment.[2]

When the culture process is interrupted or suddenly changed, learning seems to cease. The new setting often destroys the foundations of security. It is, therefore, little wonder that the child who is an emigrant has not completely learned the culture of the land of origin before he is thrust into the new world with a brand-new set of learning conditions to deal with. He is also usually the child of a family that is socially and economically disadvantaged and is therefore heir to all the insecurity, fears, and instabilities of our society to a larger degree than others. Both he and the adults in his family pursue a day-to-day existence with the attendant problems of inadequate housing, clothing, and nourishment. His parents too are caught in the crosscurrents of adjustment: to find jobs though they may be unskilled; to find housing at a cost they can afford when there is little available; to hold onto their own culture in a setting which neither understands nor is able to accept this.

The Puerto Rican child is thus caught between the two cultures, that of his people and the one which he must meet every day in the school. Sometimes he must respond to one that contradicts his own. The little girl who has been compliant is now expected to be active and responsive, to take the initiative, to face new people and situations on her own. In the schoolroom she is expected to talk and play with boys and to socialize more freely with her peers. There are rewards in our culture for this, but when she goes home she is forbidden to go out on the street to play. At home there is no reward for enterprising deeds, but rather the awaited and expected punishment. The emigrant child's age and sex roles and his developmental tasks are not the same as ours. If he adjusts to one, he negates the other, and as a result may lose his sense of identity with his family. The rewards we offer for these "disloyalties" are perhaps not as satisfying, nor can they be easily integrated into the patterns of the home and the other culture. We do, in fact, tend to create "culture conflict"—the battle of the supremacy of cultures in the family and the clash of roles between parents and children.[3]

Parents play the primary role in transmitting culture to the child. This is part of the socialization process. The child identifies with the parent and internalizes the learnings. In the new environment the parent is no longer in tune with the prevalent culture. He cannot command his child's involvement, since the new society does not value his contribution to the socialization of his own child. The dichotomies and dualisms we create tend to whip the dog we taught to eat.

I

Such a situation is evident in the story of Ana, the sixth of eight children in a family.* She was eight years old when she came to the mainland. Ana's mother is the strong and managing figure in the family—a traditional Puerto Rican mother who holds her daughters in rigid control. They are not allowed out on the street; they must not talk to other people, particularly boys. Even the older girls are kept in this strict regimen. Ana could perhaps have developed some ease in interchange, but the mother's restrictions were so forceful that the girl's only recourse was to deny all contact. As a result, no one was able to reach out to Ana. She went on to junior high school, where she is barely passing. In addition, she has developed even more reticence and isolates herself. She has frequent headaches and stomach upsets, and is absent from school very often.

This is a rather extreme example of the frequently found conflict in social roles particularly in reference to the upbringing of girls. Since the neighborhoods in which these families settle are often socially disorganized, there is a kind of justification for the fears of the parents which further constricts the life of the girls and the younger children. It is important in working with Puerto Rican parents to help them find ways to protect their children without completely depriving them of social interchange. However, the traditions are so firmly imbedded in the structure of their living that this is difficult to achieve. It is equally difficult to help growing children find the channel between outright rebellion and complete submission, hence they live in an atmosphere of conflict and indecision. It is at this point that they either compliantly submit and lose the ability to relate to their own peer group, or completely leave their families and join the peer group, thereby losing the support which they still need so much.

The language disability which pervades all these problems is very real. It is also a measure of the emotional stability of the person at this time of pressure. The differential rates of language learning are not only the result of age differentials and intelligence levels (the younger child learning more rapidly than the older and the brighter child learning faster than

---

* The cases described below are derived from the operation of a training program for undergraduates in Education at the City College of New York. Students serve as leaders for groups of children in a community group work program. The names of all cases described here are fictitious.

the duller) but also cues to the general level of the individual's emotional adjustment and the resolution of cultural identification and conflicts. Language is one of the tools for learning which the emigrant child lacks. He is left with only the cues he can obtain from nonverbal communication; the expressive gestures which may convey some meaning for him. Here too, however, a facial expression or a gesture may mean something else to him, since gestures are also a language and are richly colored by each culture with specific meanings. Meanwhile he must manage without the necessary cues for directing his behavior.

As a result of these handicaps the child begins to feel inadequate. He cannot solve all the problems of adjustment to a new land, new language, new living, and new culture. He cannot seek support from his parents since they too are faced with the identical problems and with the added responsibility of founding their families in this new land. Therefore, if the child fails he suffers further indignity. He may reason that it is better not to try. Then one has not failed. Or better still, it is possible to remain so indifferent, uninvolved, and apathetic that one evades all responsibility for functioning in a setting fraught with failure and with many demands that one cannot meet.[4] This kind of "culture shock" is frequently found in great or small degree in many of our children and families.

The school is brought face to face with all these problems. There may be some variation in the nature of these difficulties in different families or individuals, but the total problem is present in every child the school works with who has recently arrived from Puerto Rico. Neither the school nor the teacher has been trained to see behavior in the light of these causes. Rather, they tend to meet each situation separately either as a discipline question or as an education problem. Our training practices in education have dealt chiefly with the child who is native to our land and has no outstanding language problem. The child of the lower economic and social strata is also rarely dealt with in our academic courses. Most of our textbooks are written by middle-class professors for middle-class teachers of middle-class children. We tend to think of education as primarily establishing literacy and the ability to deal with the daily technics of middle-class living in urban centers.

Education, although drawn from many other disciplines, for a long time tended to ignore the findings in anthropology, social psychology, and clinical psychology. Or at least it has not found a way to integrate these findings into the educational and developmental sequence usually taught in the teacher-preparation courses. We tend to divide sharply our disciplines at the college level, thus making it more difficult to provide an interdisciplinary approach to problems that the school faces. It seems hardly necessary to point out that if we are to work with a large number of children from a given culture we must, at the very least, learn something of the specifics of that culture, and of how it pervades the entire personality and its perceptions in new situations.

Learning how Puerto Rican children dance or play ball or count in Spanish will not make the teacher aware of how Puerto Rican children view their inadequacy in learning the fundamentals of arithmetic or how and why it is so difficult for them to retain the fact that three and four are seven or remember that our *j* does not sound like *h*. There needs to be rather the concept of *"fundamental education* to cover the whole of living; to teach not only new ways but the need and the incentive for new ways."[5]

How does it feel to be unable to comprehend the cues in this new setting? How does it feel not to understand what people are saying? How do anxiety and insecurity affect a child's readiness to learn? How do people acquire a new culture without stress and destruction to their sense of well-being? The findings and skills of anthropology, sociology, and social and clinical psychology will help us interpret this kind of defeat and better still to learn to look for these problems. They will perhaps also sharpen our focus and help us find the educational methods which are best employed for reaching these children who really so desperately want to achieve. The individual caught in the maelstrom of conflicting cultures and feelings can be helped to move from inadequacy and near panic (as in "culture shock") to independence and courage.

II

In our work we encounter many children who reflect these problems. Rafael, a boy of two, saw his father migrate to the states. His mother left when he was three. When he was four his younger sister was sent to the mainland to join the family. He and his grandmother lived in Puerto Rico until he was seven. All these years of separation seemed to have given him the feeling of being unwanted. When he arrived here his mother was again unavailable to him, since she worked long hours away from home. During his first two years in this country he made few friends, and seemed to his teacher unable to learn. Carmen, his younger sister, was much more competent than he, and carried on much of the interchange for him and other members of the family with the new and strange world. Rafael was frequently sick and remained at home with his old grandmother to care for him. In the third year of his stay he seemed able to come to terms with his new country—to emerge from his chrysalis. Now he is lively and takes an interest in what goes on around him. He greets adults and children alike with warmth and friendliness, and his work at school has begun to show the real potential that he possesses.

Elsa is another child who experienced the privation of her mother's departure. When Elsa was two, her mother left for the United States, leaving her children to the care of their maternal grandmother. At three Elsa was brought to the mainland, but since her mother was working the children were left in the care of a woman living in the same apartment house. Elsa's initial adjustment to school was so poor that when she was in the second grade the school notified the mother that something had to be done. The child was hyperactive, inattentive, and created too much distraction in the classroom. The mother sent Elsa back to Puerto Rico to live with an aunt for a year. When Elsa returned, her adjustment to school, and her learning achievement were no better. At this time Elsa is being referred to a child guidance clinic.

These are only two cases among the many which we encounter in the schools. The pattern of emigration here depicted is usual in the Puerto Rican family. Early deprivation of the mother creates social and emotional problems which are very difficult to overcome, even with care and concern by the school and other agencies.

Many Puerto Rican children arrive after a period of separation from their mothers or both parents. Thus the emotional concomitants are disabling before the schools in this country even begin to work with the children. Exploration of conditions in each of the new families might alert the schools to the problems and perhaps gear the school situation to help these children. The syndrome of this difficulty has already been fully described by such writers in this field as John Bowlby and Lauretta Bender. It includes a range of behavior: apathy, lack of social responsiveness, depressed intellectual functioning (discussed by William Goldfarb), inability to form meaningful relationships, hyperactivity, aggression, and lowered intellectual potential.

III

The Alvarez family presents a different picture, yet it also has within it all the problems of adjustment to a new environment. There were four children in this family, who lived originally in a rural community on the island. The father worked in the sugar cane fields; they had a small house, a cow, and chickens. Miguel, the father, migrated to the United States eight years ago. Two years later, Rosa, the mother, leaving the children on the island, came to set up the new home. After a few months of separation all the children were brought to the mainland.

The father had no skills, but he found employment as a dishwasher and has remained in that work. He is always employed but does not earn enough to care fully for his growing family. Two children were born here and the entire family lives in a partly furnished apartment (they have never been able to save enough to buy the requisite furniture). The Department of Public Welfare helps to subsidize the family, but even with this help the budget is too small to provide adequate bed linen, blankets, and warm winter clothing. All the children are slender and the school records indicate poor nutrition for all the school-age children.

Frequently the members of the family are prey to the upper respiratory illnesses so common to Puerto Rican families. Maria, the thirteen-year-old daughter must then remain at home to help care for the mother and children. She had so many absences from school that the teachers complained they could not really help her.

Maria is a tall, stoop-shouldered girl with large dark eyes, pale olive skin, and a slow, hesitant manner. She attended an after-school club program for three years but always remained on the outskirts of the group, although nearly all the club members are of Puerto Rican background. She uttered hardly a word. When she was ten Maria had the first of a series of minor epileptic attacks and is now attending the Seizure Clinic regularly. (This is another common ailment among newly emigrant families, who refer to this illness as "attaques." It may be another manifestation of the somatic effects of the stress in adjustment.)

Maria has repeated the sixth grade and even now has achieved a reading level of only third grade. Her ability in mathematics is even lower than her reading level. This girl saw herself as completely inadequate in every aspect of her living. She never undertook anything for fear of failure. It was only after a year of intensive work with Maria and her family, using nearly every resource in the community, that Maria gained any sense of competence.

There were many health problems in the family for which nursing, nutritional guidance, and hospital care had to be obtained. Fortunately, though the mother speaks no English and is completely illiterate, she is deeply concerned for her children, has much warmth and affection to give, and is eager to help her family adjust to the new environment. She is able to overcome the traditional patterns and encourages Irma [Maria?] to participate in clubs and activities.

The problem of family finances was partially solved by additional funds allotted for special diets for several of the children. The family was encouraged to make application for public housing. The social service resources were made available for Maria by the Catholic Big Sisters, and Maria is now assured of a permanent relationship to meet her emotional needs.

A special program was set up to give Maria opportunities for relationships with children in the group club program, and a special worker was assigned to act in a supportive role for the child as she began to make the transition to active participation. A remedial program in reading was also arranged. From the start it was felt that Maria had much more potential than her low IQ indicated. She seemed quite creative with art materials. As all this enrichment was made available she bagan to wake from her long passive role and to look out and see people. She clamored for help in her school work; she wanted to achieve. She began to take a more active role with her peers. Even her slow, hesitant manner and walk changed. She ran now and jumped; she had a close friend; and she had abandoned her role on the periphery of the group.

Although there are still many problems in the Alvarez family and Maria has a long way to go, we have already some sense of the potential of the child and the possibility that she can move more rapidly now toward the achievement of a large part of that potential. She will probably never achieve all that is possible for her. But having studied Maria we can continue with the other children and help each one of them. They are younger and there may be a better chance to bring to fruition more of their potential. Perhaps the second generation of this family will achieve greater self-actualization.

The school has to meet the needs of many children. Now it is the Puerto Rican child, as it was once the Irish, the Italian, the Jewish groups in other tides of emigration. In each child there will be problems which stand in the way of learning. It is only as the school and the community come to know the family and its needs that these newcomers can be helped. It will be through the school, together with many other agencies and with a view to the totality of the child and his family, that the acculturation will come about.

NOTES

1. Margaret Mead, *Cultural Patterns and Technological Change*, New York: Mentor Books, 1955.

2. *Ibid.*, p. 281.

3. *Ibid.*, p. 254.

4. A. Anastasi and F. A. Cordova, "Some Effects of Bilingualism upon the Intelligence Test Performance of Puerto Rican Children in New York City," *Journal of Educational Psychology*, **44**, 1–19.

5. Margaret Mead, *Cultural Patterns*, p. 253.

A MINORITY
NOBODY KNOWS

Helen Rowan

There are some five million Americans of Mexican descent or birth. About four and a half million live in five Southwestern states: Arizona, California, Colorado, New Mexico, and Texas. Between them, California and Texas account for 82 percent of the Southwest's total, with California holding the edge.

Census statistics and other studies show the Mexican-Americans in the Southwest to be worse off in every respect than the nonwhites (Negroes, Indians, and Orientals), not to mention the dominant Anglos (everybody else). They are poorer, their housing is more crowded and more dilapidated, their unemployment rate is higher, their average educational level is lower (two years below nonwhite, four below Anglo).

What is extraordinary about the situation is not so much that it exists as that it is so little known. In California, Mexican-Americans outnumber Negroes by almost two to one, but probably not one Californian in ten thousand knows that simple fact. It is an easy one to overlook if you measure a minority's importance by the obvious signs: poverty programs, education, and job-training activities geared to its situation, the elected and appointed officials it can number, the attention directed to it by the press, politicians, and even textbooks, and the help given it by do-good organizations. By all these measures, the Mexican-Americans have been slighted.

The Johnson Administration is beginning to pay them some attention, though in a fitful and nervous manner. Mexican-Americans have been demanding such baubles as jobs, federal appointments, and Great Society programs tailored to their needs. Since they justifiably consider themselves to be the nation's best-kept secret, they would like some national visibility, preferably through the lens of a White House Conference focused on their many problems. This the Administration has been loath to give them, though it has tried to appease them for a couple of years by holding out the possibility of such a meeting. Still, there are signs that the *federales* are thinking of some programs specifically designed for Mexican-Americans. While their first needs are the same as those of a lot of other people—money and jobs— there are certain issues which clearly affect them in a special way.

The Mexican-American birthrate is 50 percent higher than that of the

Helen Rowan, "A Minority Nobody Knows," *Atlantic*, **219** (June 1967), 47–52. Copyright © 1967 by the Atlantic Monthly Company, Boston. Reprinted with permission.

general population; the community's average age is already ten years younger than that of the total population. The school dropout rate is higher than that of any other group, and very few of those who do graduate from high school move on to college. Even in California, with its vaunted and supposedly inclusive system of higher education, only about 2 percent of the four-year college enrollment is Mexican-American, while Mexican-Americans constitute about 10 percent of the total population and a much higher percentage of the school-age population. Delinquency and drug addiction rates are high. Residential segregation is increasing. As far as jobs go, the old devil, overt discrimination, has been largely replaced by the new devil, automation, and by more subtle "cultural discrimination" in the form of tests which penalize the Mexican-American first as a student and then as a prospective employee. Finally, there are signs of increasing family change. In the Spanish-speaking ghetto of east Los Angeles, for instance, 26 percent of all children under eighteen are not living with both parents (the figure is only 13 percent for Los Angeles as a whole). This is a particularly serious development for the Mexican-American community, which springs from a culture in which the family is the strongest of all institutions.

If they think of them at all, Easterners are likely to think of Mexican-Americans in terms of wetbacks who cross the border to fester in farm shacks for the miserly wages paid to migratory workers. In fact, Mexican-Americans are heavily urbanized. Almost 80 percent in the Southwest live in cities and towns, a proportion fully as high as the Anglo concentration and considerably higher than the nonwhite. For every Mexican-American picking fruit in California's Central Valley there are scores working as hod carriers and busboys in Los Angeles. For every stereotypical migrant who follows the crops, there are dozens crowded into the *colonias* and *barrios* that cling to the fringes of innumerable Southwest towns. The recent urbanization of such a group, given its low educational level and other characteristics, must represent social, economic, educational—and potentially political—significance of a high order.

But the Mexican-Americans' few successes in bringing themselves to national attention have had to do with the farm-labor issue, which is appropriate yet somewhat ironic. The farm workers, with an average annual income of about $1500 and generally unspeakable living and working conditions, are worse off than anybody else. In the past two years, Cesar Chavez managed to organize and sustain a successful strike of grape pickers. The strike was dramatic, colorful, and immensely appealing, and it drew the support of activist Anglos from all over. Pilgrimages to the Central Valley were undertaken by Bobby Kennedy and youngsters from SNCC, by correspondents of the New York *Times* and television crews from national networks. Bay area liberals who had never set foot in San Francisco's Mission

District or in east San Jose made the 550-mile round trip to Delano, the strike headquarters, carrying money, food, and clothing. And many middle-of-the-road Californians did not eat so much as one grape for months, so as not to risk patronizing a struck vineyard.

The condition of the farm workers is obvious and desperate. But Chavez himself is said to have urged urban leaders not to allow the farm-labor issue to deflect their attention from the more complex problems of the *barrios*, which are bound to grow worse as the ghettos continue to receive steady influxes of Mexican immigrants (almost a thousand a week) and displaced domestic farm workers.

East Los Angeles is one of those areas that Eastern eyes would never recognize as being poor. The low dwellings (though there may be as many as three on a tiny lot) have yards around them, and flowers, and on smogless days the nearby mountains stand out beautifully. There is a color that is heightened by the left-over symbols of other peoples for whom the area earlier served as a port of entry: Orientals, Italians, and then Russian Jews. Mexicatessens offer kosher *burritos* and Okie *frijoles*, and Winchell's Do-Nut House features a Taco Fiesta. Youngsters cruise around in beat-up cars for which they buy gas by the quarter's worth. An "Operator Wanted" sign in a curtained storefront window signifies that yet another small sweatshop has opened where the illiterate (and perhaps illegal) immigrant or school dropout may find a few days' work sewing blouses or shirts.

Following the riots in nearby Watts, a special census was made of that area and east L. A. What attention the survey got was mainly directed to the part on Watts, but those who read the rest of the report could find that in east L.A., too, between 1960 and 1965 real income slipped by 8 to 10 percent, housing deteriorated, home ownership declined.

Of the two courses that Mexican-Americans might follow to bring themselves helpful attention, one they have been unable to take and the other they have been unwilling to take. They have not been able to organize into an effective political bloc, and they have not been willing to riot and burn. One federal official describes them as "the most disorganized ethnic group in the country." The federal establishment, according to some officials, is so desperate to find a real leader to treat with that it would even welcome the emergence of a Mexican-American Stokely Carmichael.

There are good reasons for the Mexican-Americans' lack of political clout, but they escape anyone who tries to understand the Mexican-American experience in terms of other ethnic groups. Ernesto Galarza, a distinguished scholar and writer, points out that historically Mexican-Americans have not been seen as a great constitutional and moral issue, as were the Negroes, nor as an ordinary immigrant group to be acculturated or assimilated. They have been looked on simply as an ever replenishing supply of cheap and docile labor.

The Mexican-Americans do have in common with the Negroes a long history of discrimination, but they were never enslaved and no war was ever fought over them, though one was fought over their land. Harsh as the discrimination was, including lynchings and segregation in schools and other public facilities, it was spotty (you could get into a swimming pool if you weren't too swarthy) and varied from place to place and from time to time.

The somewhat nebulous quality of the discrimination—and the concomitant fact that a lucky Mexican-American could "make it" into the middle class—helps explain why the Mexican-Americans have not yet produced the spontaneous leadership or found the unifying force of the civil rights movement. And the very institutions which have been expected to recognize the condition and champion the cause of the Mexican-American—the Roman Catholic Church, labor, the Democratic Party, liberal groups, educational institutions, and the Eastern philanthropic and press establishment—have been by and large deaf, dumb, and blind on the subject. "For the Mexican-American," says a college professor, "there are no liberals."

This is not literally true, of course. Some individuals such as Carey McWilliams have for years written and spoken vigorously on the problem, and twenty years ago Fred Ross, supported by Saul Alinsky's Industrial Areas Foundation, began community organization efforts in Mexican-American sections of California. Other individuals and groups have done effective work on a small scale, and a few priests (though often at the cost of being silenced or sent away by their superiors) have been fairly militant spokesmen for the Mexican-Americans.

But there has been no wide-scale involvement. The white liberals who at one time helped to lead and to bankroll the Negro movement had few Anglo counterparts working with and speaking out on behalf of the Mexican-Americans. Many Southwestern Anglos supported the Negro movement, however, and even some Mexican-American college students confessed to me that they became active in the Negro cause before they caught on that there was work to be done closer to home.

The lack of outside interest and help (spelled m-o-n-e-y), combined with the fact that until recently the group was overwhelmingly rural and had very few educated members, has given the Mexican-Americans of today very little political leverage. Social, fraternal, and thinly disguised political organizations appear and disappear with startling rapidity, but there has never been a Mexican-American equivalent of the NAACP or Urban League, let alone SNCC or CORE. Even the sturdiest and longest-lived of the organizations have very little in the way of paid staffs. If you want to see the head of some group, you phone his place of business or his house, because it is quite likely that there isn't any headquarters. There is no effective clearinghouse or information center, and communications within the community are weak—

among the leaders, and also between them and the poverty-stricken of town and country.

Chavez is the most authentic leader in the traditional sense: a charismatic man sprung from a rural proletariat whose understanding and loyalty, he commands. What is questionable is whether the basis of his appeal—a combination of religious pageantry, evocation of the heroes of the Mexican Revolution, and nonviolent civil rights techniques—could successfully be transferred from the fields to the city streets.

"There are dozens of Chavezes hidden in the *barrios*," a city spokesman said sadly, but presumably these buried Chavezes will have to find new ways to rally the new urban proleteriat. For whatever the culture of the *barrios* may be, it is certainly a hybrid one, neither classical Mexican nor traditional Anglo urban.

"It's always my parents telling me to be proud I'm Mexican and the school telling me to be American," a junior high school student cried out. For the city youngsters (50 percent of the Mexican-American population is under twenty), the goodies offered by the industrialized society are all too visible and unavailable. "The thing to do is learn how the *gringos* keep you down," they say. And the residents of the *barrios* are sophisticated enough to recognize that it is the future they have to fear more than the present.

"They are teaching my boy nothing in that school, *nothing*," a mother said to me with a despair that is impossible to convey in writing. "What will happen to him? What will he do?"

Considering their numbers in California (now estimated at nearly two million), the Mexican-Americans have a singular dearth of elected representation. There is one congressman of Mexican descent, Edward R. Roybal, a Democrat from Los Angeles. No Mexican-American sits in either house of the California legislature, or on the city council, or elected board of education in L.A. Roybal became the first of his community since 1881 to serve on the city council when he was elected in 1949, but when he left for Congress in 1962 his seat was contested by four Mexican-Americans and one Negro, with the result one might expect.

What the Mexican-Americans have lacked in elective political muscle they have tried to make up for by extracting promises and appointments from Anglo politicians. Here again they are handicapped: the Democrats have taken them for granted (traditionally, about 90 percent of the relatively small registration votes Democratic), and the Republicans haven't bothered much until recently. Most Mexican-Americans agree that Democratic Governor Pat Brown did more for the group than any previous governor. Still, it wasn't enough.

During the last campaign the Reagan forces made some successful overtures to the community, and the Republicans made some electoral inroads, notably around Los Angeles, but the Democrats believe that overall they managed to hold on to about 75 percent of the Mexican-American vote. The defections in California and the rest of the Southwest, however, apparently worried the Democrats (they hastily appointed a Mexican-American to the National Committee), and they should be worried; while they may have no place else to go now, the Mexican-Americans are looking around. A mutually satisfactory political marriage will not easily be achieved. The one thing that Anglos and Mexican-Americans do most certainly for each other is to provide inexhaustible sources of frustration. The Anglo litany of complaints about Mexican-American political behavior, to abbreviate it drastically, runs like this:

They can't get organized, they can't agree among themselves, there aren't any real leaders, and the so-called leaders can't deliver. ("They'd come to us with talk about 400,000 votes," one of Governor Brown's campaign managers said aggrievedly, "but some of those guys couldn't deliver their own families.") The community is uninvolved, and it is difficult to find out what it wants. An assistant to a southern California congressman says that when he sends out invitations to a meeting with the congressman—say 250 to the Negro community and 250 to the Mexican-American—about 150 Negroes usually turn up, and about 30 Mexican-Americans. "And the first question, sometimes the only question, they ask is: 'How many Mexican-Americans on your staff?' If it was 100 percent it still wouldn't be enough," he adds glumly.

This leads to another Anglo complaint: that many Mexican-Americans view the American political process with an eye to appointments and that politics for them becomes a superficial numbers game, with little attention paid either to the potential importance of the jobs or the ability and effectiveness of the appointees.

Finally, Anglos complain that many Mexican-American spokesmen prefer to compete among themselves for elective or appointive jobs instead of working out ways and means for achieving at least a show of unity, a drive for a cause. All too often four or five Mexican-Americans insist on running for an office thus dividing the vote.

Beyond the Anglos politicos, who have special and self-centered interests in view, others who are highly sympathetic and have no political axes to grind are appalled by the amount and ferocity of infighting that goes on and the fact that it is so often caused not by ideological but by purely personal differences. So strong is the role of *personalismo* in Mexican-American politics that, as one sympathetic observer commented: "They wouldn't even vote to establish a postal system unless they knew who would be the mailman on the block."

Although there is much evidence to support these complaints, they do not take into account a number of relevant factors, including the Anglo role in perpetuating disunity and ineffectiveness within the group, whether intentionally or heedlessly. The Anglos politicians who criticize the lack of Mexican-American political organization make the very decisions that render such organization nearly impossible. In California, the Democrats, apparently thinking they knew a safe thing when they saw it, gerrymandered the Spanish surname sections of Los Angeles and San Francisco so as to make Spanish-speaking voters the pivotal but never the controlling factors in their various districts. This makes it difficult for Mexican-Americans to vote as a block and cuts off incipient leadership.

While the Democrats complain that they have to deal with leaders who have no followers, they have not financed the kind of block-to-block canvassing and voter registration that would produce organized constituencies. In search of votes, they woo the heads of the Mexican-American organizations and other community leaders in the hope that the leaders can exert personal influence over the community; it has to be personal, since the organizations themselves lack the money or manpower to organize real constituencies.

In making appointments, too, Anglos seem to set up situations which inevitably cause trouble in and for the Mexican-American community. Because they want to get the maximum political mileage from the few appointments they are willing to make, Anglo officials undertake elaborate though clandestine efforts to procure the perfect all-purpose Mexican-American than assert that no man can be found to meet the wildly urealistic qualifications established for the job.

Anglo officials make incessant demands for unity among Mexican-Americans, the implication being that the Anglos are unable to do anything until they can discern an unmistakably clear picture of exactly what the community wants. While there are real frustrations involved in dealing with a group as fragmented as the Mexican-Americans there is also real cynicism involved in the way so many Anglo officials in positions of power at all levels seize on the condition as an excuse to do nothing. It should not be necessary to identify genuine leaders or take a poll of the grass roots to guess, for instance, that no group "wants" to have urban renewal accomplished at the price of its own removal (in at least one border town the Mexican-Americans were renewed right over into Mexico); that no community "wants" to be slashed into chunks by hideous freeways (as has happened in east Los Angeles); that few people "want" their children to attend a school run by someone who could remark, as the former principal of an east Los Angeles high school did in the presence of an Anglo friend of mine, "We couldn't run this school without the dropout rate. They don't belong here anyway—they belong in the fields."

The truth is that the endless jockeying, delaying, rumormongering, and playing of the cat-and-mouse game simply elicit and intensify the very kind of behavior the Anglos deplore: dissension and a flying off in all directions.

The entire protracted handling of the on-again, off-again White House Conference is a perfect case in point.

In the fall of 1965, some Mexican-Americans, having heard of plans for a major civil rights conference in Washington, asked to be included. They were given to understand, in writing, that a separate conference would be held for Mexican-Americans or possibly all Spanish-speaking Americans. From then on there were unanswered telegrams from this group, unanswered letters from that one, understandings and misunderstandings, and joint attempts by the leaders of Mexican-American groups to apply pressure. A year ago the President had a few spokesmen to dinner and left them with the impression that there would be a conference. Others of a group that considered itself the prime negotiating committee were not invited. Their exclusion, of course, strained relations among the Mexican-Americans as well as between them and the *federales*.

No more was heard of the much-wanted conference until late October of 1966, when high officials of the Administraton found time, despite, or because of, the imminence of the elections, to meet with about sixty Mexican-American spokesmen in "preplanning" discussions of the real conference. Since then official silence has been accompanied by comic-opera goings-on. A small group with Labor Department leadership and the use of White House stationery—but with offices in neither place—is known to be "doing something" about Mexican-Americans and other Spanish-speaking Americans. A receptionist answers its phone "National Conference" but is unable to say on what, or where, or when, or for whom any conferring is being or is going to be done. So rumors fly, consternation and frustration increase among the Mexican-Americans, and much of their attention, time, and energy, and that of a number of federal officials, is diverted from the real problems, which continue to grow more malignant.

"The school systems of the Southwest have totally failed the Mexican-American community," says Dr. Miguel Montes of California's state board of education. The cold statistics alone make his case.

What is striking is that so little has been done or said until recently, despite the fact that a few educators such as Dr. George Sanchez of the University of Texas have for years been urging bilingual instruction, a revision of the curriculum and text books to appeal to the interests and to strengthen the sense of cultural identity of Mexican-American students, decent counseling and guidance, and teacher training that might produce instructors capable of reaching and educating Mexican-American children.

In most of the states, among them California, it is against the law to use any language but English as the medium of instruction, though the law is openly flouted by the few teachers who can speak Spanish. The psychological and educational implications of such a policy are clear. By denying the child the right to speak his own language (in some places children are still punished for speaking Spanish even on the playground), the system is telling him, in effect, that his language, his culture, and by extension he himself, are inferior. And he rapidly becomes truly inferior in achievement, since the teachers must perforce water down the subject matter, such as arithmetic or social studies, for use as a vehicle for teaching English rather than the subject itself.

Counseling in the schools is notoriously bad, and constitutes a special source of bitterness for the Mexican-Americans who have survived it—that is, defied it. "Realistic" counselors say, in effect: college costs too much; besides, you couldn't make it anyway; besides, you couldn't get a good job when you finished. Congressman Roybal was advised to become an electrician on the strength of an A in his ninth-grade algebra class (he was lucky to get into algebra; "general math" is usually considered sufficient). Julian Nava, a young professor at San Fernando Valley State College with a Ph.D. in history from Harvard, was advised to take, and did take, body and fender courses in high school in east Los Angeles. There are plenty of current stories of this sort.

The inadequacy of ability tests when applied to many groups is also notorious; the question is how, when the fact is so well known, school officials can summon the arrogance to brand young children as mentally deficient when it is the tests and the schools that are deficient. In California, Negro and Mexican-American children are overwhelmingly overrepresented proportionally in classes for the "mentally retarded." A former education official (an angry Anglo) told me of visiting a school in the San Joaquin Valley where he saw records listing one child as having an I.Q. of 46. Wanting to learn more about how such a mental basket case could function at all, he inquired around and found that the child, a boy of eleven, has a paper route, takes care of his four younger brothers and sisters after school, and prepares the evening meal for the family. He also speaks no English.

Many Anglo educators claim that they cannot make headway against the problems of language, culture, and parents. The stereotype has it that Mexican-Americans are not interested in having their children get an education, though every bit of evidence I found suggested just the reverse. In fact, many Mexican-American adults have an entirely unwarranted respect for the wisdom of teachers and principals, which is one reason why they have allowed their children to be pushed around for so long. There are problems, but they are by no means insurmountable. Actually, they have been used as a mask, and not a very effective one at that, for the real attitudes of the Anglo community at large.

"The schools are the places where Anglos and Mexican-Americans come to learn and act out the roles they will later play," says Theodore W. Parsons; an anthropologist at the University of California. He recently spent months studying the schools in a California town where the population is about 57 percent Mexican-American; practices similar to the ones he observed there are followed in many schools all over the feudal Southwest. The children —Anglos are called "Americans" and Mexican-Americans are called "Mexicans"—are conditioned for their respective roles in the adult world from their first day in school to their final one, when at graduation the Mexicans march in last and sit at the back of the platform. "This makes for a better-looking stage," a teacher explained to Parsons, adding that it allows the Americans, who have all the parts in the program, to get to the front more easily.

"Once we did let a Mexican girl give a little talk of some kind," Parsons was told, "and all she did was mumble around. She had quite an accent, too. Afterwards we had several complaints from other parents, so we haven't done anything like that since. That was about twelve years ago."

The Negro revolution has stimulated, but by its great drama has also obscured, already existing ferment within the Mexican-American community. Spokesmen have had increasingly stormy sessions (and nonsessions—the walkout is becoming something of a fad) with federal, state, and local officials.

Many Anglos seem to dismiss the volubly expressed anger of Mexican-American leaders as not being "representative" of the feelings of the masses, but it is foolish to do so. No Mexican-American I know of has ever threatened that blood will run in the streets if conditions continue to grow worse, but thoughtful spokesmen acknowledge that no one can predict what outlet the growing hostility will find, a hostility that may be the more malignant because it has been so long suppressed.

"Man, if east L.A. ever blows, it will *really blow*," one said, and Herman Gallegos of San Francisco, a highly responsible leader, reports that some Mexican-Americans decline to join picket lines or other peaceful demonstrations because they fear they could not remain nonviolent. There is undeniable resentment of not only Anglos but Negroes: "If they don't move over, they're going to find footprints on their backs," one temperate Mexican-American said. He and other sophisticated Mexican-Americans realize that it is not the Negroes' "fault" that they are getting a little bit more of not enough, but there is the dangerous tension that always exists when poor people are set to scrambling for the few crumbs tossed out by the affluent society.

The fuel that could set off a Watts-type explosion is present in ample supply. Perhaps one day it will be ignited by some incident. Or perhaps the youthful population will simply retreat into increasing withdrawal, alienation, and addiction.

There is also, of course, a third possibility: that Anglos will give up their cynical game of divide and rule, listen to the growing number of articulate Mexican-American spokesmen as they define the community's problems, and allow Mexican-Americans the tools they can use to carry themselves into the mainstream of American life.

STUDY QUESTIONS

1. In her selection, Keller illuminates the devastating affects of the urban child's social and cultural environment on his cognitive development and academic achievement, and assumes that the urban child's failure to achieve results primarily from his cognitive deficiencies. To what critical factors in the child's learning environment does Keller fail to give adequate attention? (The article by Donald H. Smith in Chapter 10 raises some serious questions that Keller ignores.)

2. How is the Indian child caught between cultures? How might the public school help him to resolve his dilemma? What problems result when children face a cultural dilemma?

3. How is the cultural dilemma faced by American Indians similar to that experienced by Afro-Americans, Mexican-Americans, Puerto Rican-Americans, and other children who emanate from a culture of poverty?

4. What school practices compound the culturally different child's dilemma? What can classroom teachers do to help such a child adjust to school?

5. What can the classroom teacher do to help children realize that there are many acceptable life styles, and that the value accorded a way of life is culturally and situationally determined?

6. Rowan, in the final selection in this chapter, describes the political powerlessness and alienation experienced by Mexican-Americans. How can social studies help Mexican-Americans attain the political power and influence they need to improve their condition in American society?

7. What school practices help deflate the self-concepts of minority group children? How can these practices be eliminated?

SUGGESTED READINGS

Bernstein, Abraham, *The Education of Urban Populations*. New York: Random House, 1967

Barron, Milton L. (Editor), *American Minorities: A Textbook of Readings In Intergroup Relations*. New York: Alfred A. Knopf, 1957

Glazer, Nathan, and Daniel P. Moynihan, *Beyond the Melting Pot*. Cambridge. Mass.: Harvard University Press, 1963

Green, Robert L., *Racial Crisis in American Education*. Chicago: Follett Educational Corporation, 1969

Harrington, Michael, *The Other America*. New York: Macmillan, 1962

Miller, Harry A., and Majorie B. Smiley, *Education in the Metropolis*. New York: The Free Press, 1967

Miller, Harry L., and Roger R. Woock, *Social Foundations of Urban Education*. Hinsdale, Illinois: The Dryden Press, 1970

Passow, A. Harry (Editor), *Education in Depressed Areas*. New York: Teachers College Press, 1963

Roberts, Joan I., *School Children in The Urban School*. New York: The Free Press, 1967

CHAPTER 3
PSYCHOLOGICAL FACTORS
OF LEARNING

Many culturally different children are placed in low academic tracks, classified as mentally retarded, and exposed to an unstimulating educational environment because they perform poorly on I.Q. and other standardized tests. The public schools operate on the assumption that there are individual differences in innate intelligence which can be ascertained by the appropriate tests. Much of the ability grouping done in schools is designed to "individualize" instruction: children of supposedly similar intellectual capacities are placed together. Such grouping, it is assumed, maximizes student achievement.

The readings in this chapter indicate that our concept of intelligence has changed drastically. They suggest that new assumptions regarding individual differences and I.Q. are urgently needed if we are to help all children meet the increasing intellectual demands of our highly technological society.

BLACK GENES—
WHITE ENVIRONMENT

J. McVicker Hunt

What determines human intelligence? What determines the competence of people? Is it fixed and immutable at a child's birth? Or does it change with time and circumstance? If it does, then what circumstances will best foster its maximum growth?

These questions once agitated only a small group of scholars and scientists. No longer. Today they have acquired urgent social and political significance. The fates of vast programs and many a career may hinge on the conclusions of the most recondite social-psychological study. A scholarly paper, a thicket of statistical tables, becomes an object of burning interest for journalists, politicians, and others concerned to find "the" answer to why the children of the poor don't seem to learn as much in school as their own children do.

I had thought, though, that at least in the years since World War II we had learned something about most of these matters. I had thought we had learned that it was no longer tenable to conceive of intelligence tests as indicators of fixed capacity or innate potential in children. I had thought we had learned that it was quite wrong to think we could predict an adult's intellectual competence from his score on a test taken as a child without specifying the circumstances he would encounter in the interim.

In fact our political and educational leaders do seem to have gotten this message. The circumstances that affect a child's experiences in the course of growing up *are* believed to play an important role in affecting intelligence and the motivation for achievement and competence. This notion has been used in formulating solutions to the crisis of the cities created by the heavy migration of the poor from the South. Only a little imagination and goodwill has been needed to infer that the children of lower socioeconomic backgrounds, once very widely considered to be innately stupid and lazy, may instead be viewed as children who have been cheated of that equality of opportunity which our forefathers considered to be the birthright of all.

Unfortunately, however, these changing conceptions of intelligence and growth appear to have reached the leaders even before they have been fully appreciated among those of us trained in the psychological sciences.

J. McVicker Hunt, "Black Genes—White Environment," *Transaction*, **6** (June 1969), 12–22. Copyright © 1969 by *Trans-Action*, New Brunswick, N.J. Reprinted with permission of the author and publisher.

I say "unfortunately" because the newer conceptions may have led to exc[
sive hopes among politicians and the administrators of our educational
systems. Too many of them have a tendency to confuse the perfectly justifiable
expectation that there can be significant improvement in the competence of
the children of the poor with the basic scientific know-how required to carry
out, or even to plan, the broad educational programs needed to do the
job. What I am worried about is that the confusion and excessive hopes
may have created an "oversell" that will now be followed by an "overkill"
of support for the efforts to develop and deploy effective educational programs. One has only to recall the recent vicissitudes of the Head Start
program.

Moreover, the possibility of an overkill is made all the more dangerous
by the revival of interest and belief in the notion that races differ in inherited potential for competence. People so persuaded are far from extinct.
We all witnessed the great flurry of attention given by the national press to
Arthur Jensen's recent paper on the relative immutability of the I.Q. Although
one cannot with certainty rule out the possibility of racial differences in
potential for competence, the whole issue is of very little import so long as
the great majority of black, Puerto Rican, and Indian children grow up in
poverty with extremely limited opportunities to acquire the language and
number abilities and the motivation that underlie full participation in our
society.

But I am no less fearful that the failure of some of our most expensive
and publicized efforts to improve dramatically the learning potential of poor
children may lead to an unjustified discouragement on the part not only of
politicians but of the public that must pay for these efforts. I am afraid
that our ignorance of how to proceed effectively may now deprive us, for an
indefinite period, of the opportunity to do what I am confident ultimately can
be done to meet these challenges. What we need is the opportunity to innovate
and evaluate, to fail, to correct our misinterpretations and our failures, and
gradually to develop programs of educational technology, beginning even at
birth, that *are* effective in fostering development.

It is these concerns that have prompted me to review here the evidence
for the crucial importance of life's circumstances for the development of the
cognitive skills and the attitudes that comprise competence.

INTELLIGENCE TEST SCORES NOT INDICATORS OF CAPACITY OR POTENTIAL

It should have been obvious from the beginning that scores on tests of intelligence could not possibly serve as indicators of hereditary capacity or
potential. It is a truism to say that one's genetic endowment sets limits on
intellectual potential and also that it greatly influences what happens when

we encounter any given series of circumstances. As a scientific statement, however, this is basically meaningless, as Alfred Binet, the developer of the most widely used I.Q. test, recognized as early as 1909 when he struck out against

> ... some recent philosophers [who] appear to have given their moral support to this deplorable verdict that the intelligence of an individual is a fixed quantity ... we must protest and act against this brutal pessimism ... (for) a child's mind is like a field for which an expert farmer has advised a change in the methods of cultivation, with the result that in the place of a desert land, we now have a harvest. It is in this particular sense, the one which is significant, that we say that the intelligence of children may be increased. One increases that which constitutes the intelligence of a school child, namely the capacity to learn, to improve with instruction.

Although the complex tests of Binet and Theodore Simon remained pre-eminent in the intelligence-testing movement, the conceptual framework built up around their use was developed by the students of Francis Galton and G. Stanley Hall, rather than by Binet. This framework emphasized from the beginning the role of heredity as a fixer of intelligence and a pre-determinant of development in the interpretation of test scores.

Moreover, throughout more than the first four decades of this century, American textbooks on genetics tended to emphasize the work of Gregor Mendel on the hereditary transmission of traits and to neglect the work of Walter Johannsen on the crucial role of the interaction of the *genotype* (the constellation of genes received by an organism from its progenitors) with the environment in determining the *phenotype* (the observable characteristics of an organism).

To be sure, some of the early evidence did seem to confirm the notion of intelligence tests as indicators of adult capacity. For instance, the I.Q.s of groups of children showed great constancy (which was a consequence of the way the tests were constructed) and also considerable individual constancy once a child got into school. Moreover, efforts at training children directly on the intellectual functions tested turned out to have but short-lived effects. Furthermore, the I.Q.s of persons closely related to a child proved to be more similar than the I.Q.s of persons less closely related or unrelated.

Since World War II, however, evidence has been accumulated that is so out of keeping with the belief that the tests indicate fixed innate capacity or potential that the belief is no longer tenable.

Perhaps the most incontrovertible of this evidence is that of rising intelligence in the face of predicted deterioration. The prediction of deterioration came from combining two observations. First, it has been obvious since the 17th century that poor families have more children than families of the middle and upper classes. Second, many studies have shown that people from low socio-economic background typically average about 20 points of I.Q. below people in the upper-middle class. In 1937, R. B. Cattell multiplied the number of people at each I.Q. level by the reproduction rate at that level and computed the new mean to estimate the I.Q. of the next generation. From this procedure, he estimated a drop of a little over three points a generation, or about one point a decade. This he characterized as a "galloping plunge toward intellectual bankruptcy."

But Cattell's dire prediction has been repeatedly contradicted by rising I.Q.s in those populations where the children of a given age have been tested and retested after intervals of a decade or more. Thirteen years after his own forecast, Cattell himself published a study comparing ten-year-old children living in the city of Leicester, England in 1949 with the ten-year-old children living in that same city in 1936. In the place of the predicted drop of something slightly more than one point in I.Q., Cattell actually found an increase of 1.28 points. Although small, this increase was highly significant from the statistical standpoint.

In other studies, the predicted drop in I.Q. has been proven wrong by gains substantially larger than these. S. Smith reported a growth of around 20 points between the scores of children in various Honolulu schools in 1924, and the scores of children in those same schools in 1938. Lester Wheeler reported a 10-point increase in the mean I.Q. of children from a single group of families in the ten-year period before and after the great changes brought about in that community by the Tennessee Valley Authority. When Frank Finch compared the I.Q.s of all students in a sample of high schools in the 1920's and again in those same high schools in the 1940's, he found the average gains ranging between 10 and 15 points. But perhaps the most dramatic evidence of an upward shift came when the test performances of soldiers in World War II were compared with those of World War I soldiers. Clearly, if the tests measure fixed intellectual capacity or innate potential, and if the majority of each new generation comes from parents in the lowest third in tested intelligence, something very, very strange is happening.

I.Q. TESTS ARE LIKE ACHIEVEMENT TESTS

It has long been customary to differentiate intelligence tests from achievement tests. Some differences do exist. All are differences in degree, however, rather than in kind.

First, intelligence tests tend to tap a wider variety of experience, both in and out of school than do achievement tests. Most achievement tests are closely tied to specific courses of study. Intelligence tests are not. School experience still contributes, however, to performance on more broadly based tests of intelligence. Moreover, experiences in the home and in social groups contribute to performance on achievement tests. Second, achievement tests are aimed at relatively new learning, while intelligence tests depend typically on older learning.

Intelligence tests and achievement tests, then, are measures of current capacity depending directly upon previously acquired skills and information and motivation. Binet saw this at the turn of the century, but he had escaped the "advantages" of the tutelage of men with strong theoretical beliefs in intelligence fixed by heredity.

A CASE OF MISPLACED CONCRETENESS

Semantics can often have unfortunate consequences. The terms "dimension" and "scale" when applied to such matters as intelligence are a case in point. These terms were borrowed from measurement in the physical world where scales are instruments for measuring unvarying dimensions. When these terms are applied to the behavior of people. we tend also to apply notions of concreteness and constancy derived from the world of physical objects. Thus, calling intelligence a *dimension* of behavior and speaking of tests as *scales* tends to obscure reality. This becomes especially unfortunate when the semantics sap the motivation of teachers to change their approaches to promote increased development in children who resist their standard approaches and curricula.

DEVELOPMENT

Let me turn next to those propositions concerning development that I believe are no longer tenable and that I believe are highly unfortunate in their influence upon those working in programs of early childhood education.

Fallacy: the rate of development is predetermined.

I am confident that belief in a predetermined rate of human development is quite untenable. In the history of our thinking about psychological development, the constant I.Q. was the epitome of this notion. But it got support from the widely cited work of G. E. Coghill in the 1920's which related developmental sequences in the behavior of salamander larvae from head to tail and from trunk to limbs to microscopic histological evidences of neuromuscular maturation. Support also came from various other observations that I cannot take time to review here. Suffice it to say that maturation and learning were seen as two distinctly separate processes with maturation predetermined by heredity and learning controlled by the circumstances encountered.

Evidence contradicting the notion of a predetermined rate of development also appeared. Wendell Cruze reported that chicks allowed to peck for only 15 minutes a day failed to improve in the accuracy of their pecking. Moreover, the early longitudinal studies of intellectual development in children uncovered individual growth curves with changes in I.Q. as large as 60 points. Several students in the 1930's found increases in the I.Q.s of young children associated with nursery schooling.

At the time, however, the credibility of these observations of change in the rate of development was questioned by other observers who posited differing inherited patterns of growth or found methodological weaknesses in the studies. Differences of more than 20 points of I.Q. were found between identical twins reared apart under differing kinds of circumstances, but, because such instances were rare, they were considered to be merely examples of errors of measurement.

One of the most impressive of the early studies to cast doubt on the notion of a predetermined rate of development is that of Harold M. Skeels and Murlon H. Dye. This study was prompted by a "clinical surprise." Two residents of a state orphanage, one aged 13 months with a Kühlmann I.Q. of 46 and the other aged 16 months with an I.Q. of 35, were committed to an institution for the retarded. After six months there, where the mentally retarded women doted on them, these two children showed a remarkably rapid rate of development. Coupled with change from apathy to liveliness was an improvement of 31 points of I.Q. in one and 52 points in the other. After this, a group of 13 infants—ranging in age from 7 months to 30 months and in I.Q.s from 36 to 89, with a mean of 64—were transferred from the orphanage (but not committed) to these wards for moron women. After being there for periods ranging from 6 months for the seven-month-old child to 52 months for the 30-month-old child, every one of these infants showed a gain in I.Q. The minimum gain was 7 points; the maximum was 58 points, and all but four showed gains of over 20 points.

On the other hand, 12 other infants—ranging in age from 12 to 22 months and in I.Q. from 50 to 103, with a mean I.Q. of 87—were left in the orphanage. When these infants were retested after periods varying from 20 to 43 months, all but one of them showed decreases in I.Q. that ranged from eight to 45 points, and five of the decreases exceeded 35 points. These findings suggested strongly that the effects of these two institutional environments differed greatly, but the idea that children's I.Q.s had been improved by moving them from an orphanage to a school for the mentally retarded was merely ridiculed, and the ridicule deprived the findings of their highly suggestive import.

In the light of the evidence accumulated since World War II, this study of Skeels and Dye has acquired the status of a classic, and the notion of a predetermined rate of development has become almost incredible.

Fallacy: maturation is independent of circumstances.

Locomotor development has long been considered to be predetermined, but in 1957 Wayne Dennis discovered an orphanage in Tehran where 60 percent of those infants in their second year were still not sitting up alone and where 84 percent of those in their fourth year were still not walking. When one considers that nearly all family-reared infants are sitting alone at eight months and nearly all such infants are walking alone by 20 months of age, it becomes clear that locomotor development cannot be independent of circumstances.

In the 1940's, the theorizing of Donald Hebb prompted investigators to rear animals under circumstances varying in complexity, especially in perceptual complexity. In the first such study, Hebb himself found the adult ability of rats reared as pets to be superior in solving maze problems to that of litter-mates reared in laboratory cages. Other investigators have found that dogs reared freely in complex environments are better as adults at learning mazes than their litter-mates reared in the monotony of laboratory cages.

The neuropsychological theorizing of Hebb and the theorizing of Holger Hydén, a Swedish biochemist, have prompted investigators to rear animals in the dark and in environments of various levels of complexity to determine the effects of such variations in rearing on both behavioral development and neuroanatomical maturation. Dark-reared chimpanzees, cats, rabbits, rats and mice have all shown deficiencies of both nerve cells and glial cells of their retinal ganglia when compared with animals or litter-mates reared in the light of laboratory cages. More recent investigations have extended these neuroanatomical deficiencies associated with dark-rearing to the appropriate nuclei of the thalamus and even to the striate area of the occipital lobe of the brain. These highly exciting finds indicate that even neuroanatomical maturation can no longer be considered to be independent of the circumstances in which animals develop.

Fallacy: longitudinal prediction is possible.

Despite such an accumulation of evidence as I have indicated (and there is much more), the belief in a constant I.Q. has given us the habit of thinking of the validity of tests in longitudinal terms. We have used and still use the scores based on the performances of children on tests administered at one age to predict what their school or test performances will be at later ages.

Yet, if even neuroanatomic maturation can be influenced by circumstances, and if psychological development is as plastic as this evidence implies, *longitudinal prediction is impossible from test scores alone.* The plasticity that appears to exist in the rate at which human organisms develop renders longitudinal prediction basically impossible unless one specifies the circumstances under which this development is to take place. In fact, trying to predict what a person's I.Q. will be at 20 on the basis of his I.Q. at age one or two is like trying to predict how heavy a two-week-old calf will be when he is a two-year-old without knowing whether he will be reared in a dry pasture, in an irrigated pasture, or in a feed lot.

To be sure, longitudinal prediction improves with age. This results from the fact that test-retest validities involve part-whole relationships. Thus, if one is predicting I.Q. at 20, the older the child is at the time of the initial test, the larger becomes the predictor part of the criterion *whole*. Moreover, in actual situations, individuals tend to remain within sets of social, economic, and educational circumstances that are relatively stable. Thus, a very large share of whatever constancy individual I.Q.s have had can be attributed to a combination of the increasingly congruent part-whole relationship and with the sameness of circumstances.

Belief in a predetermined rate of development and in the possibility of predicting performance over time has had very unfortunate consequences for educational practice. When children fail to learn and are found to have low scores on intelligence tests, teachers are prompt to feel that "these children are doing as well as can be expected." Such an attitude dampens any inclination teachers may have to alter their approach to such children. Consequence? The tutelage that the child encounters remains essentially stable, and the child continues in his rut of failure.

An important corollary of the finding that the rate of development depends upon the circumstances encountered is a needed change in the conception of "readiness." The notion that children are ready for certain kinds of experiences and not for others has validity. On the other hand, the notion that this "readiness" is a matter of predetermined maturation, as distinct from learning or past encounters with circumstances, is basically wrong and potentially damaging. What is involved is what I have been calling "the problem of the match." If encountering a given set of circumstances is to induce psychological development in the child, these circumstances must have an appropriate relationship to the information and skills already accumulated by the child. This is no easy matter. Ordinarily, the best indicators of an appropriate match are to be found, I now believe, in emotional behavior. They are evidences of interest and of mild surprise. If the circumstances are too simple and too familiar, the child will fail to develop and he is likely to withdraw into boredom. If the circumstances demand too much of a child, he will withdraw in fear or explode in anger. So long as the child can withdraw from the circumstances without facing punishment, loss of love, fear of disapproval, or what-not, I believe it is impossible to over-stimulate him. The challenge in such a conception of "readiness" as that involved in the "problem of the match" is basically the problem of preparing the environment to foster development. We are a long way from solid knowledge of how to do this, but I believe we do have some sensible suggestions about how to proceed.

DEVELOPMENTAL ORDER AND PREDETERMINISM

One more point about development and its implications. Order has always been obvious in behavioral development. In locomotor development, for instance, it is obvious that the infant is at first rooted to a given spot, that he learns to wheel and twist even before he sits up, that he sits up alone before he can creep, that he creeps or scoots before he stands, that he stands before he cruises, that he cruises while holding on to things before he toddles, that he toddles before he walks, and that he walks before he runs. Arnold Gesell and his collaborators at Yale devoted their total normative enterprise to describing the order in the various domains of behavioral development that take place with advancing age. Jean Piaget and his collaborators have also been concerned with describing the order in intelligence and in the construction of such aspects of reality as object permanence, as constancy of quantity, of shape, and of color, and causality, space, and time. Ina Uzgiris and I have been using these orderly landmarks in development as a basis for our ordinal scales of psychological development in infancy. In short, order in development is an obvious fact.

Although Gesell gave occasional lip service to the interaction between child and environment in behavioral development, all but one of his various principles of growth (that of "individuating maturation") described predetermined processes. Moreover, in 1954 Gesell explicitly said that "the so-called environment, whether internal or external, does not generate the progressions of development. Environmental factors support, inflect, and specify; but they do not engender the basic forms and sequences of ontogenesis."

Similarly, Mary Shirley saw evidence of Coghill's head-to-tail principle when she wrote that "motor control begins headward and travels toward the feet beginning with the eye muscle and progressing through stages in which the head and neck muscles are mastered, arms, and upper trunk come under control . . . the baby at last achieves mastery of his whole body. . . ."

Yet such an interpretation is not a necessary implication of the observed fact of orderliness in development. While Piaget, like Gesell, has found order in psychological development, he, unlike Gesell, has emphasized the role of interaction. According to Piaget, development occurs in the course of adaptive interaction between the child and the environment. This interaction involves two complimentary and invariant processes: *assimilation* and *accommodation*. Piaget conceives these processes as basically common to the physiological as well as the psychological domain. Assimilation occurs whenever an organism utilizes something from the environment and incorporates it into its own structures. Accommodation, the complement of assimilation, operates when-ever encounters with the environment evoke a change in the existing struc-ture of the central processes that mediate the interpretation of events and control action. Thus, accommodation is another term for adaptive learning.

Although I cannot here go into Piaget's ideas, they have definitely in-fluenced my own thinking about learning. Attempting to understand them has opened my own eyes to the fact that circumstances influence development in ways quite other than those within the traditional rubrics under which we have studied learning.

IMPLICATIONS

Learning in poverty As I have already noted, the factors controlling the development of competence in early childhood are no longer purely an academic topic. These factors have acquired both social and political signifi-cance from the fact that our advancing technology is rapidly decreasing the economic opportunities for those without linguistic and mathematical abilities, the motivation to solve problems, and the inclination to carry social responsibility, and from the fact that a large number of black people, coming from a background of poverty and limited opportunity, lack these skills and motives. In the light of these challenges, what are the implications of the foregoing argument?

The intellectual capacity that underlies competence in substantial part is not fixed. In this connection, various lines of evidence suggest strongly that being reared in conditions of poverty and cultural deprivation deprives a child of opportunities to learn. The children in poor families have typically encountered many fewer kinds of objects than children of the middle class. As infants, the children of poverty often have inadequate diets and they live in crowded circumstances which expose them to a continuous vocal racket to which they become habituated. This habituation may account for the in-adequacies in hearing other people speak that was found by Cynthia Deutsch and by Deutsch and Brown. Too often, the verbal interaction of children of the poor with their elders is limited to commands to stop whatever the child is doing without explanations as to why. Seldom are these children invited to note what is going on around them or to formulate their observa-tions in their own language. These children are especially unlikely to learn the syntactical rules of the standard language. Seldom is their ingenuity rewarded except when they learn to avoid the punishment that comes when they get caught at something arbitrarily prohibited. In such circumstances, the low test scores repeatedly observed in the children of poverty are to be expected.

With respect to motivation, moreover, the children of poverty, black or white, have little opportunity to learn to take initiative, to give up present satisfactions for larger satisfactions in the future, or to take pride in problem-solving achievement. Seldom have the poor acquired such motives. Thus, their response to their children's demands are dictated largely by their own immediate impulses and needs, not the children's. To these parents, a good child is typically a quiet child who does not bother them.

Regarding conduct, finally, these children of the poor are exposed to circumstances and standards that are hardly those prescribed by the demands of the dominant society. The models of behavior for these children often make them unfit for adaptation to either schools or marketplace. So long as a large percentage of black people are reared in poverty under these conditions of childrearing it is not tenable to attribute to race the existing deficiency in competence as measured by intelligence tests.

From such evidence as has been accumulating on the matter of class differences in child-rearing, it is becoming clearer and clearer that the accident of being born in poverty serves to deprive children of that equality of opportunity which our founding fathers considered to be the right of all Americans.

What is to be done?   These relatively new findings concerning the role of circumstances in the development of competence suggest that corrective efforts should be focused upon the young, and preferably upon the very young—even beginning with birth. These findings suggest that early childhood education can have tremendous social significance if we learn how to do it effectively. It is a long step, however, from justifiable hopes to the development of the educational technology in workable form and to its broad-scale deployment in America. The question is, can we extend these findings into programs of early childhood education fast enough?

Project Head Start was a fine step in the right direction. The danger is that it may have been taken with hopes too high before an adequately effective technology of early childhood education for the children of the poor had been developed. All too often, the Head-Start programs have merely supplied poor children with an opportunity to play in traditional nursery schools that were designed chiefly to exercise large muscles and to enable middle-class children to escape from their overly strict and solicitous mothers. Such opportunities are unlikely to be very effective in overcoming the deficient skills and motives to be found in the children of the poor.

Nursery schools were invented originally for the purposes of compensatory education. Shortly after the turn of the century, Maria Montessori developed a program for the poor children of the San Lorenzo district of Rome which appeared to be highly successful. She provided a practical solution to what I am calling the "problem of the match" by breaking the lock-step in education and permitting each child to follow his own interests in working with a variety of materials that she had found to be stimulating to children. She arranged these materials in sequences that would lead to conceptual skills. Moreover, in her classes she combined children ranging in age from three to six and thereby provided the younger with a graded series of models for imitation and the older ones with opportunities to learn by helping to teach the younger. Somewhat later, Margaret McMillan established her nursery schools in the slums of England to give these children, whom she considered to be environmentally handicapped, an opportunity to learn many of the abilities and motives that children of the middle class learn spontaneously. When the nursery schools were brought to the United States, however, it was only the well-to-do who could pay for them. Our traditional belief that class differences in ability are the inevitable consequence of heredity left Americans with little inclination to provide nursery schools for children of the poor. Thus, the schools got adapted to what were conceived to be the needs of the middle-class children. When the decision to mount Project Head Start was made, only these programs were widely available for deployment on a large scale. It should be no surprise, then, if the success of Project Head Start in improving the future academic success of children of the poor is highly limited.

In consequence of this unfortunate history, we have no ready-made technology of compensatory early childhood education designed to foster in children of the poor those abilities and motives underlying competence in the dominant society which circumstances prevented their acquiring.

This is beginning to be recognized. With the recognition is coming a tremendous explosion in new curricula for young children. My impression is that these achieve little unless they focus on the fostering of the ability to handle language and number concepts, and, with regard to motivation, on extending the time interval in which these children operate psychologically, and on developing pride in achievement. I see no substitute for a painstaking investigation of what works and what does not work coupled with a theoretical synthesis calculated to give us a more accurate picture of the various kinds of deficits to be found in children of the slums and more effective ways either to compensate for these deficits or to prevent them.

I am inclined to believe that we shall have to extend our programs to include children of ages less than four. I believe we shall have to involve the help of parents in these programs. Attempts to influence the child-rearing of parents of the lowest socioeconomic status by means of psychotherapy-like counseling have regularly failed. On the other hand, involving parents first as observers and then as aids in nursery schools, where they get an opportunity to see the effects of new (to them) ways of dealing with children and where these techniques are explained and tried out first in school and then in home demonstrations, all this appears to be highly promising. Here the investigations of Rupert Klaus and Susan Gray and their colleagues at the George Peabody College for teachers in Nashville, Tennessee, of Ira Gordon at the University of Florida, of Professor Merle Karnes at the University of Illinois, and of David Weikart at Ypsilanti, Michigan appear to be showing the way. In a summer nursery school for children of poverty in Nashville, for instance, Klaus and Gray have developed a curriculum that aimed at teaching language and number skills and the attitudes and motives required to cope with elementary schools. Home visitors brought each mother to observe and later to participate in the teaching at the nursery school. The home visitors interpreted for the mothers what they saw the teachers doing. Then, during the period between summer sessions of the nursery school, the home visitors saw each of the mothers every other week. During these visits, they demonstrated for the mothers such matters as how to read a story with enthusiasm, how to reinforce children for new abilities, and how to talk with children about such homemaking operations as peeling potatoes while in the process.

This effort has been evaluated by means of gains in scores on standard tests of intelligence and will be evaluated in terms of the later progress of these children in the schools. Tests given before and after the summer nursery school have shown spurts in scores of the nursery schoolers that do not appear in the test performances of the children who did not go to the nursery school.

The test results of this program also show two other highly promising phenomena. First, the younger siblings of the children going to nursery school whose mothers saw the home visitors regularly have turned out to be significantly superior in test performance to the younger siblings of four-year-old children in two contrast groups who got neither nursery school nor the home visits. This finding suggests that the mothers must have been learning something about child-rearing that generalized to their management of their younger children.

Second, the younger children of the mothers in the contrast group who lived in the same neighborhood as those receiving the home visits got higher test scores than did the children of mothers in a contrast group living some 60 miles away. This finding suggests that mothers who learn new child-rearing practices from their observations at the nursery school and from the home visitor were somehow communicating them to their neighbors with whom they had face-to-face relationships.

The evidence is highly promising from these new efforts in compensatory education. But after Head Start we should beware of the flush of too-high hopes. I fear that the very limited success to be expected from the deployment of nursery schools designed chiefly for the children of the middle class may lead to an unjustified discouragement on the part of both political leaders and the public. I fear a fading out of support for efforts in the domain of early childhood education. At this stage of history, it is extremely important that both political leaders and voters understand the limited nature of our knowledge about how to foster competence in the young, that they understand the basis for our justified hopes, and that they comprehend the need for the continued support of fundamental research and of the process of developing an adequate technology of early childhood education. Only with continued support for research and development in this domain can we expect to create effective means of compensating for and/or preventing the deficiencies of early experience required to meet the twin challenges of racial discrimination and poverty.

SUGGESTED READINGS

Deutsch, Martin, *The Disadvantaged Child: Studies of the Social Environment and the Learning Process*, New York: Basic Books, 1967. An anthology of many of the pioneering developments in early childhood education

Elkind, David, and John H. Flavell, eds., *Studies in Cognitive Development: Essays in the Honor of Jean Piaget*, New York: Oxford University Press, 1969. This new anthology is primarily concerned with the investigations and theorizing of Piaget, whose work has inspired at least in part many of the recent developments

Harvey, O. J., ed., *Experience, Structure, and Adaptability*, New York: Springer Publishing Co., 1966. Includes a variety of investigations of the role of early experience in the development of flexibility and adaptability

Pines, Maya, *Revolution in Learning: The Years from Birth to Six*, New York: Harper and Row, 1967. This nontechnical survey presented many of the developments in early childhood education before the investigators themselves had published their findings

INNATE INTELLIGENCE:
AN INSIDIOUS MYTH?

William H. Boyer and Paul A. Walsh

In societies where power and privilege are not equally distributed, it has always been consoling to those with favored positions to assume that nature has caused the disparity. When man himself creates unequal opportunity, he can be obliged or even forced to change his social system. But if nature creates inequality, man need only bow to supreme forces beyond his control, and the less fortunate must resign themselves to their inevitable disadvantage.

The metaphysics of natural inequality has served aristocracies well. The Greeks had wealth and leisure as a result of the labor of slaves. Plato expressed the wisdom of the established order with the claim that nature produces a hierarchy of superiority in which philosophers, such as himself, emerge at the top. Aristotle's belief that all men possess a rational faculty had more heretical potential, but it was not difficult to believe that some men are more rational than others.

In later periods, nations that possessed economic superiority explained their advantages on the basis of innate superiority. Sir Francis Galton was convinced that the English were superior and that the propertied classes were even more superior than the general population. They were the repository of what was the most biologically precious in mankind.

The democracies of the new world shattered many elements of the old order, and brought a new, radical, equalitarian outlook. In principle, if not always in practice, man became equal before the law, and the idea of "the worth of the individual" established a principle of moral equality. Yet legal and moral equalitarianism did not necesarily mean that men were intellectually equal. So the assumption upon which American schools and the American market place developed was that democracy should mean *equal opportunity for competition among people who are genetically unequal*. This creed has satisfied the requirements of modern wisdom even for the more liberal founding fathers such as Thomas Jefferson, and it equally fit into the social Darwinism of an emerging industrial society.

In contemporary American education many of these assumptions remain. People are usually assumed to be not only different in appearance, but also innately unequal in intellectual capacity and therefore unequal in capacity to learn. The contemporary creed urges that schools do all they can to develop *individual* capacities, but it is usually assumed that such capacities vary among individuals. Ability grouping is standard practice and begins in the earliest grades. Intelligence tests and the burgeoning armory of psychometric techniques increasingly facilitate ability tracking, and therefore the potentially prosperous American can usually be identified at an early age. If it is true that people have inherently unequal capacities to learn; the American educational system is built on theoretical bedrock, and it helps construct a social order based on natural superiority. But if people actually have inherently equal capacities, the system is grounded in quicksand and reinforces a system of arbitrary privilege.

Four types of evidence are typically offered to prove that people are innately different in their capacity to learn. The first is self-evidential, the second is observational, the third is logical-theoretical, and the fourth is statistical.

The self-evidential position is based on high levels of certainty which include a strong belief in the obviousness of a conclusion. Many people are very certain that there is an innate difference between people in intellectual capacity. However, such tenacity of feeling is not itself a sufficient basis for evidence, for it offers no method of cross-verification. The mere certainty of a point of view regarding the nature of intelligence must be discounted as an adequate basis for verification.

The observation of individual differences in learning capacity cannot be dismissed as a basis for evidence; useful information for hypotheses requiring further verification can be obtained in this way. For instance, parents may notice different rates of learning among their children. People from different social classes learn and perform at different levels. The city child may learn particular skills more rapidly than the rural child. Observations require some care if they are to produce reliable evidence, but it is possible to observe carefully, and such observation can be cross-verified by other careful observers.

But if people learn particular tasks at different rates, does it follow that people must therefore be *innately* different in their learning capacity? It does *not* necessarily follow. Increasingly, as we know more about the role of environment, we see that there are not only differences between cultures, but also differences within cultures. Even within families, no child has the same environment as the others. Being born first, for instance, makes that child different; he is always the oldest sibling. A whole host of variables operates so that the environment as perceived by an individual child has elements of uniqueness (and similarity) with other children raised in proximity.

Observational evidence can be a useful part of the process of understanding when it raises questions that can be subjected to more conclusive evidence, but it is often used as a way of selectively verifying preconceived notions which are endemic in the culture. Western culture is strongly rooted in the belief in a natural intellectual hierarchy. Few observers have been taught to make observations based on assumptions of natural intellectual equality. Observational evidence must be carefully questioned, for it is often based on a metaphysic of differential capacity which encourages selective perception and a priori categories of explanation. Yet these preconceptions are rarely admitted as an interpretive bias of the observer.

Theories based on carefully obtained data provide a more adequate basis for reaching a defensible position on the nature-nurture controversy than either of the previous procedures. A general theory in the field of genetics or psychology which fits available information would be a relevant instrument for making a deduction about the nature of intelligence. If a logical deduction could be made from a more general theory about heredity and environment to the more specific question of innate intellectual capacity, the conclusion would be as strong as the theory. Such deduction is a commonly used procedure.

Both genetic and psychological theories have often been used to support the belief in inherited intelligence. Genetic connections between physical characteristics such as eye color, hair color, and bodily stature are now clearly established. Certain disease propensity has a genetic basis, yet the best established research is now between single genes and specific physical traits. It is commonplace to assume that if a hereditary basis for differential physical traits has been established, there is a similar connection between genes and intelligence. The conclusion, however, does *not* necessarily follow. Intelligence defined as the capacity to profit by experience or as the ability to solve problems is not a function of a single gene. Whatever the particular polygenetic basis for learning, it does not follow that intellectual capacity is variable because physical traits are variable. Current genetic theory does not provide an adequate basis for deducing a theory of abilities.

Similarly, the Darwinian theory of natural selection is often used to ascribe superiority to those in the upper strata of a hierarchical society. Yet a system of individual economic competition for survival is actually a very recent phenomenon in human history, characteristic of only a few societies, primarily in the eighteenth, nineteenth, and early twentieth centuries. It is very likely that it is irrelevant to genetic natural selection because of its recent origin. American immigration came largely from the lower classes, a fact which could condemn America to national inferiority if the Darwinian theory were used. In the long span of human history, most societies have relied mainly on cooperative systems or autocratic systems for their survival, and individual competition is an untypical example drawn largely from the unique conditions of Western, particularly American experience.

Psychological theories which emphasize individual difference have often assumed that the descriptive differences in physical characteristics, personality, and demonstrated ability are all due largely to heredity. Psychology has had strong historical roots in physiology, but as social psychologists and students of culture have provided new understanding of the role of experience, hereditarian explanation has shifted toward environmentalism. Even the chemical and anatomical characteristics of the brain are now known to be modifiable by experience. Psychologists such as Ann Anastasi point out that, "In view of available genetic knowledge, it appears improbable that social differentiation in physical traits was accompanied by differentiation with regard to genes affecting intellectual or personality development."

Anthropologists, with their awareness of the effects of culture, are the least likely to place credence in the genetic hypothesis. Claude Levi-Strauss, a social anthropologist, claims that all men have equal intellectual potentiality, and have been equal for about a million years. Whether or not this is true, it is clear that the best-supported general genetic or psychological theory does not validate the conclusion that individual intellectual capacity is innately unequal.

Statistical studies under controlled conditions, on the other hand, can provide some of the most reliable information. For instance, when animals are genetically the same, there is the possibility of inferring genetic characteristics through experimental studies. Identical twins develop from the separation of a single egg and have identical genetic inheritance. If human twins could be raised under controlled experimental conditions, much could be learned about the respective role of heredity and environment. Many studies have been made of twins, but none under sufficiently controlled experimental conditions. The results, therefore, permit only speculative conclusions. Most twins are so similar that unless they are separated they are likely to be treated alike. When they are separated, in most cases, one twin is moved to a family of the same social class as the other twin. And people of similar appearance tend to be treated similarly—a large, handsome child is not usually treated the same as a short, unattractive child. The resultant similarity of IQ scores of separate twins has not been surprising.

Even if particular identical twins were to show marked differences in ability when they live in substantially different environments, as they occasionally do, the evidence does not prove the *environmentalist* thesis unless a significantly large number of random cases is compared with a similarly random selection of non-identical twins. In a small sample, difference could be due to the experience deprivation of one twin. It is possible to stultify any type of development, and so the variation between identical twins, identified in some studies up to forty points, by no means disproves the hereditarian position. Consequently, current studies do not provide conclusive statistical evidence to support either position over the other.

The second most commonly used statistical evidence to show the hereditary basis of intelligence is the constancy of IQ scores at different age periods. Usually, IQ scores do not change appreciably, but occasionally the changes are dramatic. It is now understood that a standard IQ test is culturally loaded toward middle-class values, and so the general constancy of most IQ scores can be explained as the expected result of limited mobility between social class and the resultant constancy of sub-cultural experiences. So even the statistical "evidence," so often used to support a belief in innate intelligence, is really not conclusive.

Studies of innate intelligence, then, have not produced conclusive evidence to justify the claim for an innate difference in individual intellectual capacity. Equally, there has not been conclusive evidence that the innate potential between people is equal. The research is heavily marked by the self-serving beliefs of the researchers. Psychologists have usually created "intelligence" tests which reflect their own values, predetermining that their own scores will be high. When they have discovered they are high, they have often proclaimed such tests to be indicators of innate superiority.

Many studies are built on simple-minded assumptions about the nature of environment. Psychological environment is related to the subject. A researcher who says that two children live in the "same" environment is quite wrong, for the environment that each child perceives may be quite different from that perceived by the researcher.

Also, it is often assumed that environment is only postnatal, but evidence is now available on the role of prenatal environment, both psychologically and nutritionally. Malnutrition of a pregnant mother can, and often does, have permanent debilitating psychological and physiological effects on her child. Certain diseases contracted by the mother (measles, for example) and certain drugs (thalidomide, for instance) can produce destructive "environmental" effects which limit intellectual capacities. Clearly, people do demonstrate varying capacities to learn, but they have had varying prenatal and postnatal opportunities. If they are female, they are generally treated differently than if they are male. Negroes are treated different from whites—one social class is treated different from another. The *kind* of employment people engage in has a profound effect on what they become. They probably become different through different treatment and different experience, yet our institutions, reflecting our culture, usually operate on the assumption that such differences in ability are innate.

There are at least three ability models which can be supported by current evidence. Each is based on different assumptions about human nature and therefore provides a basis for different social philosophies and different conceptions of government and education.

The first model assumes a great variety of innate ability and a high level of intellectual demand on the average person. In this model, there are hereditary geniuses and idiots, while most people have an intellectual capacity about equal to the demands of their society.

The second model assumes that the innate ability potential of everyone (who has not been injured pre- or postnatally) is equal and far exceeds the normal demand level. (The actual opportunities a person has may produce differential *performance* similar to model No. 1.)

The third model assumes the possibility of some variation, but since all of the ability potential is well beyond the normal demand level, the variation makes virtually no operational difference.

In an economic or educational system, model No. 1 would justify the usual culling, sorting, and excluding through screening devices to create a "natural" hierarchy of ability. It would also justify the common belief in "equal opportunity for competition between unequals," where sorting is achieved through competition.

Both models two and three would justify maximum social effort to develop the abilities of all people, and the failure to achieve high levels of ability in all people would constitute social failure rather than individual failure. American society, with its considerable disparity of wealth and power, is largely a success based on the inequality assumed in the first of the three models. It is largely a failure based on the equality assumed in the second and third models.

Schools make little effort to develop the kind of equal ability assumed in models two and three. IQ tests are widely used to identify presumed differences in innate ability so that culling and grouping can make the management of the school easier and more efficient. The disastrous effects of the schools on lower-class children are now finally becoming known. The "compensatory" concept has gained some headway, but most educators are so overloaded with work and so traditional in outlook that the schools have become partners with the economic system in reinforcing a system of privilege that usually panders to the children of those in power and finds metaphysical excuses to make only minor gestures toward the less fortunate. The "special programs for the gifted" would be more accurately labeled "special programs for the privileged," for the gifted are primarily the children from socio-economic classes which provide the most opportunities. The less fortunate (usually lower class children) are ordinarily neglected or convinced that they are innately inferior. Once they become convinced, the prophesy is soon realized.

Part of the problem is the way "intelligence" is defined. It can be defined in many different ways, each leading to a somewhat different educational direction. We can view it as environmental adaptation, as ability to solve problems, as ability to use logical convergent thinking, or it can emphasize divergent thinking and the creation of ideas and problems. When intelligence is defined as abstract verbal-conceptual ability drawing on the modal experiences of middle class environment, as it is in most IQ tests, a selection has been made which excludes many other plausible and often more useful definitions.

The capacity to become intelligent does, of course, have a genetic basis. A cat is not capable of becoming a psychologist. But this does not mean that demonstrated differences in intelligence among psychologists are innate. What is particularly important is whether intelligence is defined primarily as the input or the output. The input is not subject to control, but the output depends on experience; so it is intelligence as output that should be the central concern of the educator.

Until the particular beliefs, which are endemic in many cultures, including American culture, are seen to be part of the heritage of an ancient, anachronistic, elitist tradition, there is little likelihood that the official liberal and equalitarian goals of many modern nations are likely to be realized, even though the wealth of modern technology gives every promise that they are capable of being achieved. Government, industry, education, and virtually all other institutions are now part of the problem, hobbled by a metaphysics of innate inequality. Elitist assumptions about the meaning of ability permeate all fields of education. When teachers of music, mathematics, art, or physical education find that a student doesn't demonstrate the requisite ability, they often reject him (low grades can be a form of rejection). Then counselors shuttle the student to courses when he shows "ability." All this assumes that the school should not develop abilities, but only grant them opportunity to be expressed. The Rousseauian belief in the pre-existing self is widespread.

The environmental hypothesis may be wrong, but if it is, it should be shown to be wrong only after a society has done everything possible to develop the abilities of people. We should begin with prenatal care, and should eliminate the experience of economic deprivation, ghettoized living, and elitist schools and businesses. *Lacking definitive scientific evidence about human potentialities, social policy should be based on moral considerations.* We should base our policy on the most generous and promising assumptions about human nature rather than the most niggardly and pessimistic. Men will do their best only when they assume they are capable. Liberal assumptions and conservative assumptions about human nature create their own self-fulfilling prophesies. We now create millions of people who think of themselves as failures—as social rejects. Their sense of frustration and despair is a travesty on the potentialities of an affluent nation.

Poor teaching is protected in the American educational system through the assumption that the child doesn't have the ability. An American environmentalist commitment (toward liberal rather than totalitarian goals) would aim at *creating* ability, at *increasing* intelligence, at *developing* interests. The meaning of "education" would need to be broader than merely institutional schooling. It should also include community responsibility, especially for business and the mass media, which must supplement the work of the school if Americans are to receive more equal educational opportunity. This requires more social planning and more public responsibility than Americans have previously been willing to undertake.

Most American institutions, including the schools, still base their policy largely on the old conservative ideology. This outlook resists change and condemns many to inferiority. Ideological rigidity is not exclusive to the United States; in fact, many other nations are even more rigid. Yet the expanding wealth produced by modern technology is beginning to encourage the have-nots within the United States and throughout the world to demand their share by force and violence if necessary. Violence is likely to be an increasingly common road to social change unless a new public morality based on new assumptions about human potentiality is translated into both foreign and domestic policy. It is not merely racism which bogs down American progress, but also the more pervasive belief in intellectual inequality. The failure to develop the abilities of people was useful to the early American aristocracy and to the power elite of an industrial-scarcity economy. But modern economies of abundance flourish through the maximum development of the abilities of people. There is potentially plenty for all. More widespread development of the capabilities of people would not only add greatly to the wealth of nations, but it can also permit people to participate in a social and cultural renaissance.

Aside from the compelling moral obligation to create equal opportunities within nations and even between nations, the excluded millions in the world are starting to force the changes which should have occurred long ago. Some of them don't believe they are inferior, and they are understandably impatient about changing the old processes of exclusion. All institutions, including the schools, will either need to re-examine their self-consoling elitist beliefs and create real and equal opportunity, or else risk that violence and revolution will increasingly become the dominant instruments of social change.

I.Q.:
GOD-GIVEN
OR MAN-MADE?

Gilbert Voyat

Who would have believed that in the declining decades of the twentieth century the antique psychological argument between environment and heredity would garner headlines and rub academic tempers raw? The older, progressive educators scolded each other about the primacy of nurture over nature. The practicing pragmatists insisted that, "You are what you grow up as, not merely what you are born with." The environmentalists declared that slums produce children with more limited intelligence than generous suburbs do. Not so, asserted the genetically persuaded; poor performance in intellectual matters is the result of a shallow gene-pool.

And so the argument continues. In this past winter's issue of the *Harvard Educational Review*, Dr. Arthur R. Jensen, professor of educational psychology at the University of California at Berkeley, suggests that intelligence is a trait not unlike eye color and hardly more susceptible to change. This study presents an interesting renewal of the genetic argument. Although many of the ideas defended have the aura of statistical, scientific work, they are neither new, self-evident, nor irrefutable. The fact that Dr. Jensen's findings are corroborated by statistical evidence does not make them true. It makes them misleading.

His central thesis is simple: Intelligence is a natural trait, inscribed in the genetic pool and unequally distributed among individuals. Theoretically, genius can be found anywhere, regardless of race or social milieu. In practice, however, Jensen insists that in terms of the average I.Q., whites are more intelligent than blacks. The average I.Q. for blacks is, according to his calculation, approximately 15 points below the average for whites. Furthermore, only 15 per cent of the Negro population exceeds the white average. This has been shown, for instance, in a study (cited by Jensen) by Dr. A. M. Shuey, author of *The Testing of Negro Intelligence*, who reviewed 382 previous studies of I.Q. Here we have a typical case of validation by quantification. It is impressive, precise, and wrongheaded. The difference in intelligence between whites and blacks is also noticeable among privileged children; upper-status Negro children average 2.6 I.Q. points below the low-status whites. Jensen makes the further assertion that Indians, who are even more disadvantaged than Negroes, are nevertheless more intelligent. Jensen is very cautious about this differential intelligence. Negro infants, he claims, are more precocious in sensory-motor development in their first year or two than are Caucasian infants. The same holds for motor skills. But, he believes, what is crucially missing among Negroes is what constitutes genuine formal intelligence: conceptual learning and problem-solving ability.

Jensen offers a description of the respective roles of genetic and environmental factors as he defines intelligence. His strategy in demonstrating the roles of inheritance and environment is to utilize exclusively statistical evidence. He discusses extensively the notion of "heritability," which for him is a statistical mean allowing him to state the extent to which individual differences in a trait such as intelligence can be accounted for by genetic factors. He comes to the conclusion that this heritability is quite high in the human species, which means that genetic factors are much more important than environmental factors in producing I.Q. differences. And *this* relationship is almost entirely displayed in achievement on I.Q. tests which Jensen sees as related to genetic differences.

These analyses lead Jensen to the further conclusion that genetic factors are strongly implicated in the average Negro-white intelligence differences. Given these conclusions, Jensen ascribes the failure of compensatory education and other educational enrichment programs to genetic differences, because any attempt to raise intelligence per se probably lies more in the province of the biological sciences than in that of psychology and education. For example, the magnitude of I.Q. and scholastic achievment gains resulting from enrichment and cognitive stimulation programs range between 5 and 20 I.Q. points. But Jensen is inclined to doubt "that I.Q. gains up to 8 to 10 points in young disadvantaged children have much of anything to do with changes in ability. They are largely the result of getting a more accurate I.Q. by testing under more optimal conditions."

Nevertheless, Jensen has some positive recommendations. He distinguishes between two genotypically distinct processes underlying a continuum ranging from "simple" associative learning which he calls Level I, to complex conceptual learning which he calls Level II. Level I involves a relatively high correspondence between the stimulus input and the form of the stimulus output. For example, a child will be able to recite, and perhaps remember, a succession of numbers. Object memory, serial rote learning, and selective trial and error learning are other good examples of Level I. In Level II, a child will be able to classify objects according to their similarities. Thus, Level II involves transforming a stimulus before it becomes an overt response. Concept learning and problem-solving in a whole range of experiences are good examples of Level II. Jensen believes that schooling maximizes the importance of Level II. But schools must also be able to find ways of utilizing other strengths in children whose abilities are not of the conceptual variety. In other words, the ideal educational world of Dr. Jensen would provide two types of education: one directed toward the acquisition of basic skills and simple associative learning, which is training rather than education. Given such training, children with only Level I skills will "perfectly" adapt to any society.

Such is Jensen's thesis. It is based mainly upon the validity of I.Q. tests. What, in fact, do they measure? The crucial question which must be asked concerns the value of I.Q. tests themselves. Not that Jensen does not discuss their value. He defines intelligence too narrowly as what I.Q. tests measure: "a capacity for abstract reasoning and problem-solving." How should we define intelligence? Is it useful to define it at all? In short, the very basis of Jensen's findings must be questioned in the light of what experimental psychology can tell us today about the nature of cognitive development and operations.

For example, fifty years ago any textbook of biology would begin by giving a definition of the word "life." Today, such a procedure is not possible because a definition of life is never adequate. The reason probably lies in the dynamic aspects of the concept, which is incompatible with a static and fixed definition. In a like manner, I.Q. tests essentially quantify static definitions. Therefore, as in biology it is no longer possible to define life statically, so, too, in psychology a static definition of intelligence is impossible. To understand the limitations of Jensen's basic assumptions, it is helpful to consider the point of view of the Swiss psychologist, Dr. Jean Piaget. A brief summary of the Piagetian approach allows us to differentiate between what is measured by standard intelligence tests and what is discovered through the Piagetian technique.

During more than forty years of experimentation, Dr. Piaget has arrived at a formal description of cognitive development and has divided it into four stages. The first one, before the development of language (symbolic function) in the child, deals with the construction of the logic of actions. This has been called "the period of sensory-motor intelligence." Primarily, the process involves the organization of actions into operational patterns, or "schemata of actions," whose main characteristics are to allow the child to differentiate in his actions, between means and goals. Some conditions are necessary in order to achieve this: Space must become organized as a general container; objects must remain permanent; and, in order to anticipate goals, one must assume some acquisition of practical causal processes.

The main consequence of the appearance of the symbolic function is the reorganization of sensory-motor intelligence. This enables the child to integrate symbols, allowing him to expand the range of his operations. The next stage is called "pre-operational," or "the period of egocentric thinking." Thus, from a response to an event, intelligence is mediated through language, but the child is not yet able to maintain in his mind symbols (abstractions) that lead to ideas whose meanings are constant. Those constancies have to do with those aspects of the "real world," such as measure, mass, motion, and logical categories. In this pre-operational world everything appears to be related to an egocentric point of view. This is a limitation as much as a source of enrichment during this level of intellectual functioning.

The following stage is characterized by the development of concrete operations. From what is essentially a subjective orientation, intellectual functioning moves toward more objectivity in elaborating mental constancies. The child no longer thinks only in terms of himself, but also takes into account the limitations that the external, physical world places upon him. For example, the child no longer believes that the moon follows him down the street. For Piaget, this type of intelligence is called "concrete," because essentially the child is only able to deal with tangible, manipulatable objects. That is, his world is concerned with *necessary* relations among objects.

The final stage of intellectual development deals with the development of formal thinking which permits the formation not only of necessary relations but also *possible* and *impossible* ones. In short, he can "play" with his mind. The child, now an adolescent, can dream things that never were and ask "Why not?" The adolescent is able to make exact deductions, to extract all combinations from a potential or a real situation. He is no longer directed only by concrete relations. He can make hypotheses and elaborate theories. He is able to dissociate the form of his thinking from its content.

Piaget's approach strongly contrasts with Jensen's point of view. In particular, Piagetian "tests" clearly differ from typical I.Q. tests. Among the major differences, I.Q. tests are essentially an additive progression of acquired skills. They give a state, a global or overall result for a specific population; their quantitative aspect allows one to place a child among children of his age and development. Piagetian tests, on the other hand, are hierarchical; they describe a progressive organization and individual potentialities. They provide a detailed analysis of the functioning of thinking. In short, they qualify thinking; they do not quantify it. They always respect the intelligence of a specific child.

These differences are important because, given Piaget's theory, we can describe intelligence functionally; we can formalize its structural development. We cannot assign to intelligence a specific, static definition, in terms of properties, for this directly contradicts the idea of development itself. Any static definition reduces intelligence either to exclusively environmental factors or to almost exclusively genetic factors without implying the necessary *equilibrated* interaction between them.

Consider the distinction between Level I and Level II as proposed by Jensen. At First glance, this argument is appealing; transformations are not involved in the process of decoding and understanding information at Level I, whereas transformations are a necessity at Level II.

But what is a transformation? In a fundamental sense, the understanding of *any* transformation is a necessity at both levels of learning. Without distinguishing a transformation in the real world, we would be unable to differentiate one state from another. For instance, we can present to a child glass A of particular width and height and glass B thinner but taller than A. We call the state in which A is filled up and B is empty S-1, and the state in which B is filled and A is empty S-2. We call transformations (T) the pathway from one state to another, that is, in this particular case, the pouring from A to B, as well as the change of level in S-2 since the level of the liquid is higher than in S-1. For the child to understand these two aspects of the transformation, he must be able to understand the operation of conservation because it is this operation which has produced the transformation from one state to another. In other words, the child "makes the discovery" that the amount of water in the short, fat glass is exactly the same when it is poured into the tall, thin glass. Knowledge of the states themselves, however, is only a description of the observable. This point is fundamental. The fact that conservation is achieved by a child around the age of six or seven clearly implies the necessity of mastering invariancies even in order to understand Level I. But, to grasp any invariancy requires the ability to think, even at a very low level, in operational terms.

Thus, the two levels proposed by Jensen are inadequate to provide a clear idea of the development of intelligence itself.

Piaget, on the other hand, never gives a static definition of intelligence; essentially, he gives a functional one. The two functions of intelligence are to understand the external world and to build or discover new structures within it. Therefore, Piaget's experiments would always be culture-fair, because they are involved with a description of a progressive organization directed by logic and not greatly influenced by culture. For example, a whole set of Piagetian experiments have been carried out in Africa, Algeria, Iran, and elsewhere.

The main result is that sequential development, in comparable terms, is observed irrespective of the culture or the race. In other words, the stages are respected in their succession and do not permit, even in a theoretical continuum, division into the type of level differences that Jensen describes, and they most strongly suggest the irrelevance of these genotypically distinct basic processes.

In contrast, I.Q. tests have been designed by whites for Western culture. Thus, their value is limited to the culture within which they were designed. They can never be culture-fair. Therefore, in any testing procedure of intelligence, relativity, not absolutism, should be the criterion, and even the correction of I.Q. tests for other populations is not valid. Furthermore, I.Q. tests are simply not adequate to measure processes of thinking. They provide results, they do not lead to an understanding of how intelligence functions. Piaget's approach not only allows an understanding of intellectual functioning but describes it. Furthermore, Piaget's tests allow one to make reliable, individual prognostications. Since their interests lie in a description of the mechanism of thinking, they permit an individual, personalized appraisal of further potentialities independent of the culture. This point is important primarily because it is neglected in I.Q. tests where the global population is assessed rather than individual potentialities estimated.

If one accepts the premises on which I.Q. tests are based, then Jensen's point of view could be valid for what concerns the differences in Negro-white performances, and nevertheless remain questionable for ethnic differences based on genetic facts. His approach produces logical fallacies: first, he criticizes and compares the results of I.Q. tests; next, given differences, he sorts out the environmental and genetic factors; then he minimizes the influence of the milieu, analyzes the remainder in terms of biological implications, and finally compares two ethnic groups and ascribes their differences to genetic factors.

Although Jensen's methodology may have its merits, the problem is that the point of departure is wrong. To decide whether compensatory and other educational programs are failures is an important and responsible act. But, to base a judgment on I.Q. gains or lack of gains is questionable. Of course, one must have a way to judge such programs. But to decide that the I.Q. gains are so small that they do not justify the amount of money poured into such educational enterprises, can give people the impression that psychologists and educators know what they are talking about concerning processes of learning. In reality, many factors make it difficult to assess success and failure in educational programs. Of course, any program must be globally appraised and must work for a reasonably large number of children. But one of the problems of education is that very little is known about the underlying processes of learning. *Furthermore, pedagogy provides generalized techniques for what must be individualized teaching.* Not much is known about how the child grasps and achieves important notions such as conservation, seriation, number, movement, mass, motion, measure, speed, time, and logical categories. This is true regardless of race, color, or creed. Judging educational programs in terms of I.Q. does not settle the learning problem. On the contrary, psychologists who place their confidence in I.Q. tests tend to forget the real issue, which is the critical problem of how the child learns.

The tragedy of education lies in the fact that we are still lacking knowledge about learning processes. This situation should make us modest, and we should accept the fact that the nature of cognitive learning remains an open question for experimental and developmental psychology.

One of the major aims in education is to create openness to cognitive contradictions. One does not learn without confusion. One does not learn without feeling some discrepancy between the actual outlook and an imaginable one. One of the major conditions for cognitive development is the resolution of conflicts which leads to adaptation. Therefore, when Jensen states that we should let those who cannot attain his second level of intellectual functioning develop their capabilities within the limitations of his Level I, his position is a dangerous one strictly on cognitive grounds. It prescribes a limitation on experience for the four- or five-year-old who already has an egocentric view of his world. If learning is to take place in the often confusing circumstances of childhood, then the purpose of teaching is precisely to exploit such circumstances, not to limit them.

Briefly stated, the process of cognitive development in logico-mathematical knowledge is a gradual structuring from inside the child rather than a generalization from repeated external events. Dr. C. Kamii from the Ypsilanti Public Schools makes the point relative to her experience in teaching, following Piaget's model, that if we really want children to learn it is the *process* of interacting with the environment which must be emphasized rather than a specific response already decided upon by the teacher. This idea of process is never considered in Jensen's approach to the problem, either in his theoretical position or in his pedagogical evaluation. In Piaget's conception of process, the idea of emphasizing logical conflicts is naturally involved. Jensen's view of process excludes it.

A primary role of the teacher is to be able to follow the process and to provide creative conflicts at appropriate moments. In the long run, the imposition of rules is a less efficient way to teach than influencing the development of underlying cognitive processes that will eventually enable the child to construct his own rules, which will square with physical reality. Thus, teaching must provide methods whereby the child can make his own discoveries. As stated by the Harvard psychologist, Dr. Lawrence Kohlberg, the cognitive developmental view of teaching aims at building broad, irreversible structures rather than the achievement of immediate gains, which may be short-term. Immediate gains, and very specific abilities, measured through I.Q. increments seem to be the only concern of Jensen. But as Piaget states: "The goal in education is not to increase the amount of knowledge, but to create possibilities for a child to invent and discover. . . . When we teach too fast, we keep the child from inventing and discovering himself. Teaching means creating situations where structures can be discovered; it does not mean transmitting structures which may be assimilated at nothing other than a verbal level."

The whole creative aspect of learning and teaching is completely lost in Jensen's point of view. The child is reduced to a ratio. The teaching act becomes a mechanical adjustment of narrowly identified capacities to severely limited learning goals. Education must be more generous than this.

SELF-CONCEPT
OF ABILITY AND
SCHOOL ACHIEVEMENT

Wilbur B. Brookover, Edsel Erickson, and Lee Joiner

The research reported in the previous chapters was designed to test several hypotheses and explore a number of questions relevant to a social psychological theory of school achievement. These studies have been based on data obtained from a single secondary school class in a mid-western city each year during the 7th through 12th grade. The basic theory postulates that human behavior is a function of the expectations and evaluations of others who are significant to the actor as perceived by him and as internalized in a self-conception of what is appropriate and proper for him to do and what he is able to do. In this research the primary focus has been on the individual's self-concept of academic ability. Self-concept of academic ability refers to the evaluating definitions an individual holds of his ability to achieve in academic tasks as compared with others in his school class.

The basic propositions of this theory assert that a student's self-concept of academic ability results from his perceptions of the evaluations significant others hold of his ability. The student's self-concept of academic ability in turn functions to limit the level of academic achievement attempted. Self-concept of academic ability is therefore hypothesized as an intervening variable between the expectations and evaluations of significant others and school achievement. The relationship of perceived evaluations of significant others is conceptualized as a necessary and sufficient condition, i.e., a change in the perceived evaluations of others will be reflected in a change in self-concept. The relationship of self-concept of academic ability to academic achievement, on the other hand, is hypothesized as a necessary but not a sufficient condition for the occurrence of a particular level of academic performance.

Self-concept of academic ability as used in this research should not be confused with other definitions of self or self-concept. It has not been our

From Wilbur B. Brookover, Edsel Erickson and Lee Joiner, *Self-Concept of Ability and School Achievement III* (Chapter 6, "Summary") Cooperative Research Project 2831, Bureau of Publication Services (East Lansing: Michigan State University, 1967). Used with permission of the authors.

intention to measure or infer a self as a subjective phenomenon. Rather, self-concept of academic ability refers to a category of symbolic behaviors, and as such, to empirical events.

SIGNIFICANT OTHERS

Since it is postulated that not all others with whom an individual interacts are equally relevant or important to a person in the definition of his behavior, it was necessary to identify those persons who were important or significant to the students. The data obtained for this purpose over the six year period reveals that parents are identified by nearly all students each year. Contrary to assumptions frequently made, this evidence indicates that parents and other family members are more likely than any other category to be "significant others" for adolescents during the junior and senior high school years.

Although the proportion of the students naming their friends as significant others is much lower than that naming parents, it increases somewhat during the six year period. Furthermore, analysis of the impact of others' evaluations on students' self-concept of ability indicates that the influence of friends increases somewhat in later years.

Less than half of the students identify teachers and other school personnel as significant others in the junior high school years, and this proportion declines during the later years. Although teachers may exert considerable influence on some students, there is no evidence from this study that teachers are important others for the major portion of the secondary school group.

RELATION OF PERCEIVED EVALUATION BY OTHERS
TO SELF-CONCEPT OF ABILITY

The evaluations which students perceive parents, friends and teachers hold for them are consistently correlated with self-concept of academic ability. The correlations range from .50 to .77 over the period of this study. Although all three perceived evaluations are significantly correlated with self-concept of ability, partial correlation analysis reveals that perceived parents' evaluation is more likely to affect self-concept than the evaluations of the peers or teachers. As noted, however, the impact of friends' evaluations on self-concept of ability increases in later years.

Changes in perceived evaluations are significantly related to changes in self-concept of ability over one and two year periods. This relationship between changes in the two variables and the reasonably high correlation between them supports the hypothesis that perceived evaluations of others are necessary and sufficient conditions for explaining variation in self-concept of ability.

RELATION OF SELF-CONCEPT OF ABILITY TO ACHIEVEMENT

The correlation between self-concept of ability and grade point average ranges from .48 to .63 over the six years. It falls below .50 only among the boys in the 12th grade. Such evidence supports the basic theory involved in this research. In addition, the higher correlation between perceived evaluations and self-concepts tends to support the theory that perceived evaluations are a necessary and sufficient condition for self-concept of ability but self-concept of ability is only a necessary but *not* sufficient condition for achievement. The latter is further supported by the analysis of the achievement of students with high and low self-concepts of ability. This revealed that although a significant proportion of students with high self-concepts of ability achieved at a relatively lower level, practically none of the students with lower self-concepts of ability achieved at a high level.

Change in self-concept of ability over two year periods is significantly related to parallel change in grade point average. Although changes over one year tend in the same direction, the relationship is not significant at the five percent level of probability. Since self-concept of ability is hypothesized as a necessary but *not* sufficient condition in school achievement, a high association between changes in the two variables was not anticipated. The results, therefore, tend to confirm the hypothesized relationship.

SELF-CONCEPT OF ABILITY AS AN INTERVENING VARIABLE

The hypothesis that self-concept of ability intervenes between the independent variable, perceived evaluations, and the dependent one, school achievement, was generally supported by the analysis. The correlation between perceived evaluation and grade point average is generally less than the correlations between each of these variables and self-concept of ability. The partial correlations also substantiate the intervening variable proposition. In this the correlations between perceived evaluations and grade point average are significantly reduced by partialling out the effect of self-concept of ability; the correlation between self-concept of ability and grade point average is not, however, significantly reduced by partialling out the effect of variation in perceived evaluations. Furthermore, changes in perceived evaluations are not directly associated with changes in grade point average over various periods; but changes in self-concept of ability are associated with both changes in perceived evaluations and changes in grade point average over two year periods.

It seems quite clear from these analyses that self-concept of ability makes a significant contribution to the explanation of school achievement as a means through which the evaluations of others are translated into school achievement behavior.

EFFECT OF I.Q. AND SOCIO-ECONOMIC STATUS ON THE RELATIONS AMONG PERCEIVED EVALUATIONS? SELF-VONVEPT, AND ACHIEVEMENT

Both individual and social environment factors are related to the social psychological factors which are the primary focus of this research. Measured intelligence and socio-economic status, among other variables of both types, are known to be related to grade point average. Our research revealed that these variables are also correlated with self-concept of ability. It was, therefore, essential to determine whether or not either of these, measured intelligence or socio-economic status, accounted for the relationship among perceived evaluations, self-concept of ability, and grade point average. Neither does.

The correlations between perceived evaluations and self-concept of ability are only slightly reduced by partialling out the effect of variation in either measured intelligence or socio-economic status. Similarly, control for either of these variables reduces the correlation between self-concept of ability and grade point average to only a limited extent. In contrast, however, the correlations between measured intelligence and grade point average and that between socio-economic status and grades are both greatly reduced by partialling out the effect of variation in self-concept of ability.

The relationships supporting the social psychological theory of school learning presented here are not therefore greatly affected by variation in either measured intelligence or socio-economic status. Rather, the evidence indicates that much of the correlation between these variables and school achievement is accounted for by variation in self-concept of ability.

RELATION OF SELF-CONCEPT OF ABILITY TO OTHER CONCEPTIONS OF SELF

Much recent research has sought to increase our understanding of various conceptions of self and the relation of self to the performance of school children. A number of these studies are based on a general or unitary conception of self which may encompass several dimensions or aspects. Since self-concept of ability, as used here, is more narrowly defined as the student's concept of his academic ability, we examined its relation to a more general self scale and the correlation of each with school achievement.

The correlation between the general self-esteem scale and self-concept of ability was .31. Although the more general index is significantly correlated with school achievement nearly all of this is accounted for by variation in self-concept of academic ability. The latter is therefore apparently a more relevant variable in school performance.

EXPERIMENTS DESIGNED TO ENHANCE SELF-CONCEPT OF ABILITY AND ACHIEVEMENT

In order to assess possible delayed reaction to experiments designed to enhance self-concept of ability and through this school achievement, a follow-up study of available students was carried out. Unfortunately, transfers and drop-outs reduced the number of students who had been involved in the experimental, placebo and control groups during the ninth grade so much that it was not feasible to make a definitive analysis of the impact of experimental treatments during the 11th and 12th grades. There is, however, no evidence of any significant delayed reaction to the experiments.

CONCLUSION

It seems safe to conclude from this longitudinal study and the related research that there is substantial support for the basic hypotheses derived from the more general social psychological theory of school learning. Although the evidence is not always as definitive as one would like to base a theory upon, this extensive research program has not provided any basis for rejecting the theory. Rather, substantial support has been produced.

Much remains to be done before the general theory is substantiated satisfactorily. For example, we have contributed little to our knowledge about how the social norms or the expectations of significant others affect school achievement. Our research indicates that others' evaluations affect the student's conception of his academic ability and thus sets limits on his school achievement, but many students who have high self-concepts of ability do not have commensurate achievement. The analysis of the social psychological process by which those who conceive of themselves as able to learn are motivated or stimulated to do so remains to be investigated.

Although one treatment in the earlier experiments showed some promise of success, we have little knowledge about what social environments will produce either changes in self-concept of ability or the motivation to behave in accord with the maximum limits of that ability. The creation of social environments which will result in maximum levels of learning is a major challenge to contemporary educators and behavioral scientists.

STUDY QUESTIONS

1. According to Hunt, what do I.Q. tests measure? What research does he cite to support his thesis? What implications does his article have for structuring effective learning environments for children from minority groups?

2. How does Hunt distinguish between *achievement* and *intelligence* tests? Why is this distinction important?

3. Hunt argues that the culturally different child's *restricted* environment accounts for his poor academic achievement in school. However, American cultural minorities have rich and diverse cultures. What concept may better explain the urban child's academic failure? Why?

4. According to Boyer and Walsh, we must change our basic assumptions about human intelligence if we are to meet the intellectual demands of our highly technological society. How might the new assumptions they set forth especially benefit culturally different children? What difficulties arise when new assumptions conflict with older and accepted ones? How might these difficulties be overcome?

5. Arthur R. Jensen posits a conception of human intelligence that conflicts with those of Hunt and Boyer and Walsh. Jensen argues that intelligence is basically genetically determined, that human beings differ in innate intellectual potential, and that whites are innately more intelligent than blacks. In his article, Voyat severely attacks Jensen's argument. What important questions does Voyat raise? What are the strengths and weaknesses of his rebuttal?

6. What does the concept of "significant others" suggest regarding the role of the classroom teacher in improving the self-concepts and increasing the academic achievement of culturally different children?

SUGGESTED READINGS

Faris, Robert, "The Ability Dimension in Human Society," *American Sociological Review*, **26**, 835–42, 1961

Brookover, Wilbur B., "A Social-Psychological Conception of Learning," *School and Society*, **87**, 84–87, 1959

Brookover, Wilbur B., "A Social-Psychological Conception of Learning," Boston: Allyn and Bacon, 1969

Green, Robert L., and William F. Farquhar, "Negro Academic Motivation and Scholastic Achievement," *Journal of Educational Psychology*, **56**, 241–243, 1965

Hunt, J. McVicker, "How Children Develop Intellectually," *Children*, pp. 83–91, May-June 1964

Jensen, Arthur R., "How Much Can We Boost I.Q. and Scholastic Achievement," *Harvard Educational Review*, **39**, 1–123, 1969

Kagan, Jerome, J. McVicker Hunt, James F. Crow, Carl Bereiter, David Elkind, Lee J. Cronbach, and William Brazziel, "How Much Can We Boost

I.Q. and Scholastic Achievement: A Discussion," *Harvard Educational Review*, 39, 273–356, 1969. [The authors react to the controversial Jensen research on black-white differences in intelligence.]

Pettigrew, Thomas F., *A Profile of the Negro American*. Princeton, N.J.: Van Nostrand, 1964, Chapter 5.

Pettigrew, Thomas F., "Negro American Intelligence: A New Look At an Old Controversy," *Journal of Negro Education*, pp. 6–25, Winter 1964

CHAPTER 4
TEACHER ATTITUDES
AND EXPECTATIONS

The underlying philosophy of the American public school is to help each child realize his highest academic potential. There is increasing evidence that we rarely, if ever, achieve this elusive goal, especially in working with culturally different children. Many teachers cannot accept and respect the diverse cultural characteristics of these children, who frequently find the school's culture alien. The "cultural clash" in the classroom is by now a cliché. As Schueler points out in this chapter, culturally different pupils need more help from school than any others. However, research indicates that our schools only aggravate the personality problems of children from minority groups (as we saw in Chapter 2) and do little to encourage their academic achievement; some evidence, in fact, suggests that these pupils fall further behind scholastically each year.*

Most educators realize the importance of the teacher in the learning process. The articles in this chapter emphasize the impact of teacher attitudes and expectations on student behavior and perceptions, and describe the personal characteristics that an effective teacher of culturally different children must possess.

---

* Catherine Brunner, "Project Help," *Education Digest*, **29** (March 1954), 22–25.

CHILDREN'S PERCEPTIONS OF THEIR TEACHERS' FEELINGS TOWARD THEM RELATED TO SELF-PERCEPTION, SCHOOL ACHIEVEMENT, AND BEHAVIOR

Helen H. Davidson and Gerhard Lang

INTRODUCTION

The child's self-concept arises and develops in an interpersonal setting.[30] Feelings about the self are established early in life and are modified by subsequent experiences. Among the significant people believed to affect the child's feelings about himself are first, his parents, and, later his teachers. Ausubel[2] and Jourard and Remy[16] are among the few investigators who have reported results which support these theoretical contentions.

Rogers,[24] Snygg and Combs,[27] among others, assign the self-concept a central place in their personality theories and suggest that the individual's self-concept is a major factor influencing his behavior. Vigorous research in this area by Martire[17] and Steiner[28] has produced corroborative evidence for these views.

Only recently has the concept of the self been introduced into the school setting. Typical studies are those by Jersild,[15] Reeder,[23] and Stevens.[29] Jersild demonstrated the value of the self-concept theory in making the educative process more valuable. Reeder, using grade school children, and Stevens, working with college students, explored the relation between self-concept and school achievement. Both of these investigators found that positive feelings about the self are associated with good academic achievement.

A series of studies dealing with teacher-pupil relations have sought to determine (a) how children see and feel about their teachers;[11] (b) how teachers see and feel about their pupils,[5,20] and (c) how teachers think their pupils see themselves.[22]

It has been widely recognized that teachers influence the personality

Helen H. Davidson and Gerhard Lang, "Children's Perceptions of Their Teachers' Feelings Toward Them Related to Self-Perception, School Achievement, and Behavior," *Journal of Experimental Education*, **29** (1960), 107–118. Reprinted with permission of Dembar Educational Research Services, Inc. and the Authors. This study was supported by a grant from the James McKeen Cattell Fund.

development of their pupils.[21] Perkins, for example, found that teachers who had completed several years of child study were able to promote healthier personality growth in children, defined in terms of congruency between the self and the ideal self. For this reason, many researchers, among them Barr and Jones[3] and Symonds,[31] are engaged in the study of personality development of the teacher herself.

Despite the abundance of research on these aspects of the school setting, an important dimension, not previously investigated, is how the child perceives his teacher's feelings toward him. In an investigation of this interaction, we not only may gain insight into the question of what qualities make for an effective teacher, but also an understanding of how the child's perception of this teacher's feelings, irrespective of its accuracy, relates to his self-concept, school achievement, and classroom behavior.

It is the purpose of this investigation to determine what the relation is between children's perception of their teachers' feelings toward them and the variables: self-perception, academic achievement, and classroom behavior.

Specifically, three hypotheses were tested:

1. There exists a positive correlation between children's perception of their teachers' feelings toward them and children's perception of themselves. In behavioral terms it is predicted that the more favorable the child's perception of himself, the more positive will be his perception of teachers' feelings toward him.

2. There exists a positive relationship between favorable perception of teachers' feelings and good academic achievement.

3. There exists a positive relationship between favorable perception of teachers' feelings and desirable classroom behavior.

THE INSTRUMENT

To test the hypotheses proposed, it was necessary to develop an instrument to measure self-perception and the perception of the feelings of others. It was decided to use an adjective checking method, since it is direct and simple. Adjective check lists have been used to measure adjustment,[18] self-acceptance,[4] empathy,[9] character traits,[13] and to distinguish the self-perceptions of persons classified according to some social and psychological variables.[26] In the main, these lists have been used with adults.

In developing the check list with children, words and phrases to be included were selected on the basis of the following three criteria:

1. The words should be those commonly used to describe how people feel toward and how people think of others, especially how teachers feel toward and think of children. An attempt was made to cover varied

aspects of behavior and personality. For this purpose, lists already developed, like those of Allport,[1] Gough,[12] and Hartshorne and May,[13] were scanned for appropriate words.

2. The words should be easy enough for children in approximately the 10–16 year age range to read and comprehend. The Thorndike-Lorge Frequency Count[33] was used to eliminate words which would be too difficult.

3. The list should contain about an equal number of words connoting positive and negative feelings.

From an initial pool of 200 trait names, 135 remained after the application of criteria 1 and 2. The next step was to determine the feeling tone of the 135 words. Each of the words was then rated by 35 teachers and 50 junior high school pupils as *favorable*, *unfavorable*, or *neutral*. Only those words were retained which were judged by more than 80 percent of the teachers and 80 percent of the pupils as being favorable or unfavorable. The words judged neutral were eliminated.

Fifty words remained after the teachers and students judged them as favorable or unfavorable. The 35 words finally used are listed below along with the F or U rating received. Fifteen words were dropped either because of the level of difficulty or because of some duplication in meaning.

Fair	(F)	A hard worker	(F)
A nuisance	(U)	Bad	(U)
Afraid	(U)	A good sport	(F)
Cheerful	(F)	Considerate	(F)
A time waster	(U)	Not eager to study	(U)
Neat	(F)	Helpful	(F)
Not eager to learn	(U)	Careless	(U)
A leader	(F)	Sociable	(F)
Unhappy	(U)	Clever	(F)
Loving	(F)	Not alert	(U)
Outstanding	(F)	Smart	(F)
Loud	(U)	Silly	(U)
Generous	(F)	Kind	(F)
Nervous	(U)	Shy	(U)
Sensible	(F)	A sloppy worker	(U)
Polite	(F)	Dependable	(F)
Lazy	(U)	A day dreamer	(U)
Forgetful	(U)		

Administration and scoring of the check list The children are instructed to decide how the teacher feels toward them with respect to each trait name, and then to rate it on a three-point rating scale: *most of the time, half of the* *time, seldom or almost never*. A favorable word is assigned a score of 3 when it is checked in the most-of-the-time column, a score of 2 for half of the time, and 1 for seldom or almost never. For an unfavorable word the scoring is reversed.

The total score, the Index of Favorability, is obtained by adding the scores of all the words and dividing the total by the number of words checked. The higher the index, the more favorable is the child's perception of the teacher's feelings toward him. Theoretically, the index can range from 1.00 to 3.00.

Reliability and validity   The Check List of Trait Names was administered twice to four classes comprising 105 junior high school children. The interval between the two administrations was from four to six weeks. A correlation of .85 was obtained (rank difference, $p < .001$).

The check list may be considered to have logical validity. However, it was desired to obtain a measure of empirical and concurrent validity. This was done by correlating the child's own perception of his teacher's appraisal of him with his classmates' perceptions of the teachers' feelings toward him. For this purpose, a modified version of the de Groat and Thompson *Teacher Approval and Disapproval Scale*[7] was administered along with check list to 93 children (3 classes). The de Groat and Thompson scale, as modified, consisted of 8 positive statements, such as, "Here is someone whom the teacher praises for trying hard," and 8 negative statements, such as, "Here is someone whom the teacher often points out as wasting too much time." For each statement, pupils were asked to name one to four of their classmates to whom these characteristics applied. They could also name themselves, if they so desired. Of the 93 children, 56 received 5 or more votes on one of the teacher approval and disapproval statements. For these 56 children, a teacher-approval score was determined by subtracting the number of unfavorable statements on which five or more votes were received from the number of favorable statements on which five or more votes were received. A correlation of .51 was obtained (rank difference, $p < .001$) between the Index of Favorability and the teacher-approval score.

The check list developed to assess children's perception of their teachers' feelings toward them appears to have satisfactory reliability and validity. Although the estimate of reliability and validity was based on a sample of junior high school students, the list was considered appropriate also for the upper grades of the elementary school because of the way the words were chosen.

EXPERIMENTAL DESIGN

Subjects   The subjects of this study were 89 boys and 114 girls, attending fourth, fifth, and sixth grades of a New York City public school. These children were distributed in 10 different classrooms. In terms of reading ability, the classes selected were in the upper half of their respective grade level. Originally, it was planned to test all fourth-, fifth-, and sixth-grade children, but after preliminary experimentation, it was found that several words were too difficult for children of limited language ability. It was therefore decided to test children in those classes which were known to have the better readers.

The children represented a wide range in socioeconomic status. It was possible to divide them into three distinct groups on the basis of their fathers' and mothers' occupation. The upper group, consisting of 63 children, came from families of professional people, white-collar workers and businessmen; the middle social class group of 57 children had parents who were skilled workers, policemen, and firemen; the low group contained 83 children of semiskilled and unskilled workers and a number of unemployed.

Table 1 presents the background information for the 203 children involved in the study.

Table 1 Distribution of Subjects in the Ten Classrooms by Sex and Social Class Status

| | Socioeconomic Status | | | | | | | |
| | Upper | | Middle | | Lower | | Total | |
Classroom	Boys	Girls	Boys	Girls	Boys	Girls	Boys	Girls
4–1	8	5	3	8	—	2	11	15
5–1	1	—	—	2	7	8	8	10
5–2	—	—	—	—	3	5	3	5
5–3	7	10	7	2	—	1	14	13
5–4	—	2	3	1	9	8	12	11
5–5	2	4	6	3	3	7	11	14
6–1	5	5	4	3	—	—	9	8
6–2	2	5	4	2	1	6	7	13
6–3	3	3	5	3	—	9	8	15
6–4	—	1	—	1	6	8	6	10
Total	28	35	32	25	29	54	89	114

Procedure The Check List of Trait Names was administered twice to the children. At the first administration, the children were instructed to respond to the 35 adjectives comprising the list in terms of "My teacher thinks I am," and at the second testing, in terms of "I think I am." The first testing was done in the morning, the second in the afternoon. The "My teacher thinks I am" scale yields a measure of perceived teacher feelings, referred to henceforth as the Index of Favorability; the "I think I am" scale yields a measure of self-perception.

The teachers, nine women and one man, rated their pupils on academic achievement, on a four-point scale: Very Well, Adequately, Below Average, and Very Poorly. In the analysis of data, the last two categories were combined due to the paucity of cases in the category Very Poorly. At the same time, the teacher also rated each child on 10 behavioral or personality character-istics. A weight of + 1 was assigned to each of the traits judged to be desirable. The four desirable traits were: eager, obedient, cooperative, assertive. A weight of − 1 was given to the characteristics judged to be undesirable: dis-orderly, destructive, hostile, defiant, unfriendly, and troublesome. The sum of the weights yielded a behavior rating score ranging theoretically, from + 4 (very desirable) to − 6 (very undesirable). Subjects who received the 0 and minus behavioral ratings were combined into one group due to the small number of cases in these categories.

RESULTS AND DISCUSSION

Hypothesis 1 There exists a positive correlation between children's per-ception of their teachers' feelings toward them and children's perception of themselves.

The two perceptual favorability indexes correlated .82 (product-moment, $p < .001$). The children who had a more favorable or a more adequate self-concept, that is, those who achieved a higher self-perception score also perceived their teachers' feelings toward them more favorably.

The finding of a significant correlation between the two kinds of per-ception lends support to the view that a child's assessment of himself is related to the assessment "significant people" make of him.[30] In two previous research investigations, a close relationship was found between self-appraisal and children's perception of their parents' feelings toward them.[2,16] The present study for the first time has shown that a child's self-appraisal is significantly related to his perception of his teacher's feelings as well. Such a finding was anticipated in view of the fact that one role of the teacher, at least at the elementary level, is that of a "parent substitute." Several interesting questions may be raised: To what extent does a child's perception of his teacher's feelings resemble his perception of his mother's or father's feelings toward him? Does the child's perception of his present teacher differ from his perception of his previous teacher? Does favorability or perception decrease or increase with years in school?

Hypothesis 2 There exists a positive relationship between favorable per-ception of teachers' feelings and academic achievement. Table 2 presents the mean favorability scores and their standard deviations for the three levels

Table 2 Index of Favorability as Related to Three Levels of Estimated Achievement

	Achievement category		
Measure	Very well	Adequately	Below average
Mean favorability score	2.68*	2.57	2.40
	N = 53	N = 111	N = 39
S. D.	.22	.24	.25

* The higher the score, the more favorable the child's perception of his teacher's feelings toward him.

of estimated achievement. The *F* ratio of 15.61 was significant at less than the .001 level. The three *t* tests were also significant at better than the .01 level.

Hypothesis 3 There exists a positive relationship between favorable perception of teachers' feelings and desirable classroom behavior. The findings pertaining to the relationship between children's perception and their classroom behavior are shown in Table 3.

The over-all *F* ratio of 7.38 was significant at less than the .001 level. The only significant *t* tests were those between the lowest category (0 and less) and all the other categories. In other words, the children who were rated as being disorderly, defiant, unfriendly, or troublesome, perceived their teachers' feelings toward them as being less favorable than the children who were rated as being eager, cooperative, assertive, and the like.

One of the axioms of educational psychology is the statement that a child learns only when he is motivated to learn. Furthermore, the basic incentives which a teacher can furnish are her acceptance of the child on the one hand, and approval on the other. The findings of the present study furnish support-

Table 3 Index of Favorability as Related to Five Levels of Rated Behavior

	Behavior rating category				
	Very desirable		Desirable		Undesirable
Measure	(+4	+3)	(+2	+1)	(0 and minus scores)
Mean favorability score	2.62*	2.65	2.58	2.53	2.39
	N = 40	N = 54	N = 46	N = 23	N = 40
S. D.	.26	.19	.27	.27	.28

* These percentages are based on the *N's* of the achievement and behavior categories.

ing evidence. The teacher's feelings of acceptance and approval are communicated to the child and perceived by him as positive appraisals. It is likely that these appraisals encourage the child to seek further teacher approval by achieving well and behaving in a manner acceptable to his teacher. We may also begin this cycle with the child's behavior. The child who achieves well and behaves satisfactorily is bound to please his teacher. She, in turn, communicates positive feelings toward the child, thus reinforcing his desire to be a good pupil. Which of these variables serves as the primary determiner is a fact difficult to ascertain. It seems rather that they reinforce each other. The implication is clear. It is essential that teachers communicate positive feelings to their children and thus not only strengthen their positive self-appraisals but stimulate their growth, academically as well as interpersonally.

It should be emphasized that these findings do not imply causality but rather suggest that certain pupil characteristics, such as self-perception, perceived teacher feelings, achievement, and behavior in school are interrelated.

In addition to the results relevant to the tested hypotheses, other findings will now be reported.

Sex differences Sex differences were observed with regard to the three variables studied: Index of Favorability,* achievement, and behavior in school. Girls perceived their teachers' feelings toward them more favorably than did the boys (girls' mean $= 2.60$; boys' mean $= 2.52$; $t = 2.41, p < .02$). The behavior ratings of the girls were more favorable than those of the boys ($x^2 = 10.72$, df $= 4$, $p < .05$); the girls were likewise rated more favorably in achievement, although this difference was not significant ($x^2 = 3.41$, df $= 2$, $.10 < p < .20$).

Past research has consistently shown that teachers report more problem behavior among boys.[32] One explanation, though not widely accepted, is that boys are naturally more aggressive. Another view, more plausible, holds that our society encourages aggressive behavior in men (and men to be) and submissive behavior in women. Teachers, most of whom are women, especially in the primary grades, therefore regard boys' classroom behavior as disturbingly different from the norms of behavior appropriate to their own female sex. The temptation is great to reward children of one's own sex. Meyer and Thompson's study[19] is pertinent here. Teacher-pupil interaction of sixth-grade pupils was studied over a one-year period and analyzed in terms of "approval" and "disapproval" contacts. In addition, children were asked to nominate by the "Guess Who" technique which of their classmates receive

---

*   The index used in this and subsequent analyses is based on the check list score of the child's perception of his teacher's feelings toward him.

their teacher's approval and disapproval. Both approaches yielded the same finding. Classroom observers, as well as the children themselves, noted that teachers expressed greater approval of girls and greater disapproval of boys. The findings of the present investigation, which ascertained directly children's perceptions of their teachers' feelings, are in accord with the results of prior research. The suggestion has been frequently made that more men should be urged to teach at the primary level. Findings such as those discussed above suggest the urgency to establish a sexual balance in the teaching staff at the primary grades. Not only is it desirable for boys to have a male model with whom to identify, but conditions may then be created which may assure greater teacher approval for boys and reduce teacher disapproval for behavior which is, to a large extent, culturally instigated.

Social class differences Because of the distinct differences found in social class status in this group of children, it was decided to investigate the relation of social class to the Index of Favorability, achievement, and behavior in school. All three variables are related to social class in the direction one would predict. These data are shown in Table 4.

It may be observed from Table 4 that there is a decline in mean favorability index from the upper to the lower social class. Two of the three t tests

Table 4 Social Class Status Related to Favorability Index, Achievement, and Behavior

Variable	Upper social class N = 63	Middle social class N = 57	Lower social class N = 83
Mean favorability index	2.63	2.60	2.49
S. D.	.26	.22	.26
Achievement rating category:			
Very well N = 53	43% *	34%	23%
Adequately N = 111	31%	22%	47%
Below average N = 39	15%	36%	49%
Behavioral rating category:			
Very desirable N = 94	41%	29%	30%
Desirable N = 69	23%	30%	46%
Undesirable N = 40	20%	22%	58%

* These percentages are based on the N's of the achievement and behavior categories.

were significant at better than the .01 level; t was not significant between the upper and middle social class groups. Children in the two advantaged social class groups perceive their teachers' feelings toward them more favorably than do the children in the lower class group.

Social class and achievement in school are significantly related ($x^2 = 18.38$, 4df, $p < .01$). The differences in the percentage of children in the several categories may be pointed out, especially the difference between the two extremes; in the upper social class 43 per cent of the children were rated by their teachers as doing very well in school while only 15 per cent were rated as doing below average work.

Social class and behavior in school as rated by the teachers were not significantly related ($x^2 = 14.97$, 8df, $.05 < p < .10$). However, the distribution of children in the several categories reveal interesting differences. While the great majority of the children in the group were rated favorably by their teachers, there were 58 per cent of the children in the lower class whose behavior was rated as undesirable while only 20 per cent of the upper class children were so rated.

It has been suggested that teachers, as surrogates of middle class values, tend to give preferential treatment to the middle and upper socioeconomic class pupils, and to withhold rewards from pupils who belong to the lower socioeconomic class.[6,8] Furthermore, previous research has shown that lower class children do not achieve as well as middle and upper class children[10,14] in part due to lower motivation.[25] The data obtained in the present study corroborate these observations.

The interrelations found between children's perception of teachers' feelings, school achievement, behavior, and socioeconomic status are particularly significant since the majority of children in the public schools throughout the country come from families of low social class status. It is therefore likely that a lower class child, especially if he is not doing well in school, will have a negative perception of his teachers' feelings toward him. These negative perceptions will in turn tend to lower his efforts to achieve in school and/or increase the probability that he will misbehave. His poor school achievement will aggravate the negative attitudes of his teachers toward him, which in turn will affect his self-confidence, and so on. This vicious entanglement must be interrupted at some point. The point of attack may well be the teacher whose capacity to reflect feelings conducive to the child's growth should be of concern to educators.

Analysis of variance of favorability scores It was found that the Index of Favorability was positively related to achievement in school as well as to social class position. It is also evident from this and other studies that achievement in school is correlated with social class position. In order to study

Table 5   Mean Indexes of Favorability for the Three Achievement Categories
and for the Three Social Class Groups

| | Achievement category | | |
Social class groups	Very well	Adequately	Below average
Upper social class	2.71*	2.61	2.51
	N = 23	N = 34	N = 6
Middle social class	2.71	2.60	2.44
	N = 18	N = 25	N = 14
Lower social class	2.59	2.52	2.34
	N = 12	N = 52	N = 19

* The higher the score, the more favorable the child's perception of his teacher's feelings toward him.

the influence of each of these factors on Index of Favorability, the favorability scores were reanalyzed first, for the three achievement levels within each social class and second, for the three social class groups within each achievement category. The mean favorability indexes for these separate groups are presented in Table 5.

Reading Table 5 vertically, it may be observed that the mean favorability score declines from the upper social class to the lowest social class for each of the achievement categories; this decline is most noticeable between the two highest social class groups and the lowest social class group. It is apparent that the social class variable plays a part in the way a child perceives his teacher's feelings toward him regardless of his achievement in school. Similarly, reading Table 5 horizontally, the mean favorability score is observed to decrease from the highest achievement level to the lowest within each social class group. The evidence here suggests that achievement in school colors the child's perception of his teacher's feelings, regardless of his social class position. Analysis of variance of the data yielded two significant F ratios. These results indicate that both the factors of social class position and achievement are operating independently in affecting the way a child will perceive his teacher's feelings toward him.

These findings should arouse the educator for they imply that a teacher's reaction to a child is not solely influenced by the individuality of the child but also by his social class and achievement characteristics.

Differences among teachers   It may be assumed that teachers reflect a variety of feelings toward children, either because of their own personality needs, or because of the way they use punishment or praise or for any other reason. These differences from teacher to teacher should be observable in the

Table 6 The Index of Favorability for the Ten Classrooms

Class	N	Mean	S. D.
4–1	26	2.61*	.26
5–1	18	2.25	.21
5–2	8	2.45	.29
5–3	27	2.62	.17
5–4	23	2.45	.23
5–5	25	2.62	.22
6–1	17	2.57	.08
6–2	20	2.64	.23
6–3	23	2.64	.19
6–4	16	2.70	.10

* The higher the score, the more favorable the child's perception of his teacher's feelings toward him.

perceptions of the children affected by them. Table 6 presents the mean favorability indexes for the 10 teachers in this study.

It may be observed that the range in mean favorability score is from 2.25 to 2.70. Although the children generally perceived their teachers' feelings more favorably than otherwise, and the actual differences among the classrooms were not large, there were 3 or 4 classrooms with markedly low mean scores. The over-all F ratio of 2.95 is significant at less than the .01 level. It should be remembered, at this point, that the classes were selected for better than average ability in reading, which makes the findings of significant differences even more compelling. Teachers do seem to vary in their inclination and/or their capacity to communicate favorable feelings. It seems urgent that teachers be helped to recognize the significance of the feelings which they express toward children, consciously or unconsciously. Some teachers, in addition, may need the help which can only come through a process of self-understanding, in order to avoid or to minimize the expression of negatively toned feelings toward children, because of their sex, their socioeconomic status, their behavior or achievement in school.

Possible uses of the check list The Check List of Trait Names, in addition to its use as a research tool, may be adapted to practical school situations. Conceivably, it can be employed for the purpose of teacher selection and guidance. For instance, a principal might wish to select a teacher for a class comprised of underprivileged or troublesome children who are very much in need of acceptance and approval. A good candidate for such a class would be a teacher who can easily project positive feelings. Supervisors of student teachers may find the check list useful in evaluating the quality of teacher-student relatons.

Teachers who are found to communicate largely negative feelings may be advised to participate in some kind of counseling or therapy. Similarly, children whose perceptions are primarily negative and/or distorted can be identified for personality diagnosis and thus be helped in self-understanding or in obtaining a more accurate perception of reality.

SUMMARY

The purpose of the study was to relate children's perception of their teachers' feelings toward them to self-perception, academic achievement, and class-room behavior. A Check List of Trait Names, consisting of 35 descriptive terms, was administered to 89 boys and 114 girls in grades 4, 5, and 6 in a New York City public school. The children were rated by their teachers for achievement and on a number of behavioral characteristics.

The major findings were:

1.   The children's perception of their teachers' feelings toward them corre-lated positively and significantly with self-perception. The child with the more favorable self image was the one who more likely than not perceived his teacher's feelings toward him more favorably.

2.   The more positive the children's perception of their teachers' feelings, the better was their academic achievement, and the more desirable their classroom behavior as rated by the teachers.

3.   Further, children in the upper and middle social class groups perceived their teachers' feelings toward them more favorably than did the children in the lower social class group.

4.   Social class position was also found to be positively related with achieve-ment in school.

5.   However, even when the favorability index data were reanalyzed sepa-rately for each social class and for each achievement category, the mean favorability index declined with decline in achievement level, regardless of social class position and, similarly, the mean favorability index declined with social class regardless of achievement level.

6.   Girls generally perceived their teachers' feelings more favorably than did the boys.

7.   Finally, there were some significant classroom differences in the favor-ability of the children's perception of their teachers' feelings. These findings must be considered in light of the nonrandom selection of the sample. Never-theless, it is reasonable to assume that these subjects are representative of the population of New York City elementary school children at these grades levels. . . .

NOTES

1. Allport, G., and H. Odbert, "Trait Names: A Psycho-Lexical Study," *Psychological Monographs*, **47** (1936).

2. Ausubel, D. P., *et al.*, "Perceived Parental Attitudes as Determinants of Children's Ego Structure," *Child Development*, **25** (1954), 173–183.

3. Barr, A. S., and R. E. Jones, "The Measurement and Prediction of Teacher Efficiency," *Review of Educational Research*, **28** (1958), 256–264.

4. Bills, R. E., *et al.*, "An Index of Adjustment and Values," *Journal of Consulting Psychology*, **15** (1951), 257–261.

5. Cook, W. W., "Significant Factors in Teachers' Classroom Attitudes," *Journal of Education*, **7** (1956), 274–279.

6. Davis, A., *Social Class Influences Upon Learning*, Cambridge, Mass.: Harvard University Press, 1952.

7. De Groat, A. F., and G. G. Thompson, "A Study of the Distribution of Teacher Approval and Disapproval Among Sixth-Grade Pupils," *Journal of Experimental Education*, **18** (1949), 57–75.

8. Dixon, N. R., "Social Class and Education," *Harvard Educational Review*, **23** (1953), 330–338.

9. Dymod, Rosalind F., "A Scale for Measurement of Empathic Ability," *Journal of Consulting Psychology*, **13** (1949), 127–133.

10. Friedhoff, W. H., "Relationship Among Various Measures of Socio-Economic Status, Social Class Identification, Intelligence, and School Achievement," *Dissertation Abstract*, **15** (1955), 2098.

11. Gage, N. L., *et al.*, "Teachers' Understanding of Their Pupils and Pupils' Ratings of Their Teachers," *Psychological Monographs*, **69** (1955).

12. Gough, H. G., *Reference Handbook for the Gough Adjective Check List*, Berkeley: University of California Institute of Personality Assessment and Research, 1955 [mimeographed].

13. Hartshorne, H., and H. A. May, *Studies in the Nature of Character, III: Studies in the Organization of Character*, New York: Macmillan, 1930.

14. Heimann, R. A., and A. F. Schenk, "Relations of Social Class and Sex Differences to High School Achievement," *School Review*, **62** (1954), 213–221.

15. Jersild, A. T., *In Search of Self*, New York: Teachers College, 1952.

16. Jourard, S. M., and R. M. Remy, "Perceived Parental Attitudes, the Self, and Security," *Journal of Consulting Psychology*, **19** (1955), 364–366.

17. Martire, J. G., "Relationship Between the Self Concept and Differences

in the Strength and Generality of Achievement Motivation," *Journal of Personality*, **24** (1956), 364–375.

18. Merrill, R. M., and L. B. Heathers, "The Use of an Adjective Check List as a Measure of Adjustment," *Journal of Consulting Psychology*, **1** (1954), 137–143.

19. Meyer, W. J., and G. G. Thompson, "Sex Differences in the Distribution of Teacher Approval and Disapproval Among Sixth-Grade Children," *Journal of Educational Psychology*, **47** (1956), 285–296.

20. National Education Association, Research Division, "Teacher Opinion on Pupil Behavior," *Research Bulletin*, **34** (1956), 51–107.

21. Perkins, H. V., "Factors Influencing Change in Children's Self-Concepts," *Child Development*, **29** (1958), 221–230.

22. ———, "Teachers' and Peers' Perceptions of Children's Self-Concepts," *Child Development*, **29** (1958), 203–220.

23. Reeder, T. A., "A Study of Some Relationships Between Level of Self-Concept, Academic Achievement, and Classroom Adjustment," *Dissertation Abstract*, **15** (1955), 2472.

24. Rogers, C. R., *Client-Centered Therapy*, Boston: Houghton Mifflin, 1951.

25. Rosen, B. C., "The Achievement Syndrome: A Psychocultural Dimension of Social Stratification," *American Sociological Review*, **21** (1956), 203–211.

26. Sarbin, T. R., and B. C. Rosenberg, "Contributions to Role-Taking Theory: IV. A Method for Obtaining a Qualitative Estimate of the Self," *Journal of Social Psychology*, **42** (1955), 71–81.

27. Snygg, D., and A. W. Combs, *Individual Behavior*, New York: Harper & Brothers, 1949.

28. Steiner, I. D., "Self-Perception and Goal-Setting Behavior," *Journal of Personality*, **25** (1957), 344–355.

29. Stevens, P. H., "An Investigation of the Relationship Between Certain Aspects of Self-Concept Behavior and Students' Academic Achievement," *Dissertation Abstract*, **16** (1956), 2531–2532.

30. Sullivan, H. S., *Conceptions of Modern Psychiatry*, Washington, D.C.: W. A. White Psychiatric Foundation, 1947.

31. Symonds, P. M., "Characteristics of the Effective Teacher Based on Pupil Evaluation," *Journal of Experimental Education*, **23** (1955), 289–310.

32. Terman, L. M., and L. E. Tyler, "Psychological Sex Differences," in L. Carmichael, ed., *Manual of Child Psychology*, 2nd ed., New York: John Wiley & Sons, 1954.

33. Thorndike, E. L., and I. Lorge, *The Teacher's Word Book of 30,000 Words*, New York: Teachers College, 1944.

THE TEACHER AND
THE NEGRO CHILD:
"INVISIBILITY" IN THE SCHOOL

Maxine Greene

In a fundamental sense, the civil rights struggle is a struggle for dignity, for what Martin Luther King calls "somebodiness." The goal may not be so defined by the rank and file of activists; nor may the mass of Negro people articulate it in such terms. But this is the note sounded most often in literature by and about the Negro since the Civil War. It is one of the aspects of the Negro Revolt with which teachers must be concerned.

The acknowledged purpose of the public school today is to teach all children to think as intelligently as they can, to conceptualize, to form their worlds. No classroom teacher, however, can ignore the difficulties due to the "degenerating sense of 'nobodiness' " which, we are told by Dr. King,[1] afflicts every Negro, adult as well as child. To feel, in James Baldwin's language, "faceless" is often to feel indifferent to the demands made by the world. In the classroom, this may result in failure to master elementary skills; it may affect an individual's attitude towards any sort of work and make him "play it cool" when asked to feel responsible for what he does or does not do. If this happens, the effects of early impoverishment are confirmed. The disabilities most obvious to employers—unreliability, poor work habits, lack of skills[2]—are built into character and style. And the vicious circle that supports so much discrimination is tightened once again.

This is not, of course, to say that the predicament of the Negro is the "fault" of those who have taught him in the school. It is to suggest that one of the contributing factors may be dealt with in the school if teachers can be brought to see the meaning and somehow feel the pain of "facelessness." As the widow of Willy Loman says in *Death of a Salesman*, "Attention must be paid."

One way to see and to feel is through imaginative engagement in presentations like Ralph Ellison's exemplary novel, entitled—all too relevantly—*Invisible Man*. The nameless hero of that work suffers from what he calls "invisibility," a condition not of his own making but due to a "peculiar disposition in the eyes"[3] of others. Those others are white people; and it

---

Maxine Greene, "The Teacher and the Negro Child: 'Invisibility' in the school," *Educational Forum*, **29** (March 1965), 275–280. Reprinted with permission of the author and Kappa Delta Pi, an honor society in education, owners of the copyright.

makes little difference if they are benevolent or malign. The disposition in their eyes enables then *not* to see the Negro as a living human being, a creature of "substance, of flesh and bone, fibre and liquids,"—of mind. They see him, rather, as an object, an abstraction: "Negro," "member of a sub-culture," "culturally deprived."

Ironically, it is the humanitarian concern for the poor and underprivileged that has led to teaching teachers terms and categories like these. They are obviously useful if linked to understanding of special circumstances influencing learning in the school. But they are also potentially dangerous. They may lead some teachers to regard their pupils as "cases," even "causes,"—to forget that they are individuals, to impose on them (with the best of intentions) a new invisibility.

This is important because of the duality of the work the classroom teacher is asked to perform. The teaching act is, on the one hand, a behavioral affair, rationally conducted, and guided (hopefully) by theory. On the other hand, it is an affair of face-to-face encounters, dependent for their validity on the teacher's own authenticity, on his ability to identify imaginatively.

If he has been recently educated in the art of teaching, he is likely to be familiar with the structure of his subject matter. He is probably equipped to organize the materials of his teaching in accord with the logic of the subject and, at once, with the conceptual level of the learners concerned. There is no question but that he *knows* more and communicates more effectively than some of those who were taught to teach "not the subject, but the child."

If the teacher is a fairly recent graduate, he is also likely to be committed to a subject matter specialty which he finds exciting, complex, "real." He may be exposed, therefore, to a frustration unknown to some of his older colleagues; and this may make it even harder for him to engage in encounters with youngsters innocent of the joys of learning, pupils who "couldn't care less."

When we link such frustration and estrangement to the increasing professionalism and precision of instruction in the schools, we can easily envisage the consequences for the nurture of identity. Yet neutrality and, perhaps, impersonality may be a function of the cognitive orientation becoming characteristic of the schools.

This orientation has been accounted for by Sputnik I and the subsequent panic over "mediocrity." More significant, however, is the general acknowledgement that it is the only appropriate educational response to a society growing more organized, automated, and intricate each day. The person adequately prepared for the jobs to be done requires more than rudimentary literacy. The citizen equipped to make a choice in an election or in a local controversy must be able to conceptualize, to form the world about him in a variety of cognitive ways. We have only to recall some of the recent battles over school desegregation or housing exclusion laws, or the issues raised in the Presidential campaign. Far more than factual information is needed in each case. The individual asked to take a stand must know how to reason, how to visualize alternatives, how to evaluate—how to think. The recent innovations in the fields of curriculum construction and subject matter organization have been responses to these necessities.

Further research, further experience in programming teaching machines, for instance, may increase our understanding of the slow learner and his requirements; but the special problem of the Negro child in the slum school may still remain. This is in part because of the ineradicable effects of deprivation in early life. It is also because of the larger problem of the Negro in America, and the uncertainty regarding his identity. Although—theoretically— every child can be taught any subject, the actuality of the Negro child's expectations is not yet fully understood.

There is a growing consensus that severe impoverishment in early childhood makes "normal" concept development impossible.[4] If a child is deprived of a range of sensory stimulations, of linguistic experiences, individualized care, security, and continuities, he is likely to be doomed to perpetual "underachievement" when measured against the cultural norms. The only hope is said to be compensatory pre-kindergarten education as in the experimental programs developed by Martin Deutsch and his associates at the Institute of Development Studies in New York. The focus there is on preschool enrichment, "to reduce the attenuating influence of the socially marginal environment."[5] Because the pupils are three- and four-year olds, the teachers can devote themselves to cultivating the sense of individual personhood, enriching sensory experiences, cultivating curiosity, teaching the children to know their names. The work done already gives evidence of releasing some children from the limitations of impoverishment, of enabling them to learn to learn.

But there are thousands of equally impoverished youngsters moving through the grades and into high schools. If not helped before the age of six, we are told, the influence of the early environment cannot be reduced. In any case, the Deutsch program—*qua* program—can scarcely be adapted to grades where skills and subject matter must be taught. It holds clues, nonetheless. Something must be done to nurture child identity, even if it is too late for him to be "saved."

The teacher, then, confronts ambiguities and perplexities of all sorts when he takes the responsibility for a Negro child. He realizes that he will be hard put to motivate and teach if there is little feeling of self-regard or worth. He may realize, too, that there is little hope of the child's becoming cognitively excellent if he has not been helped when very young. To complicate his task, he may find that his own view of worth—because of his commitment to subject matter and to learning in general—is linked to his prime regard for capacity to learn.

The very terminology of his trade, "cultural deprivation" and the rest, may intensify this difficulty. A majority or middle-class bias is implied; and, although it may be pragmatically warranted, it is potentially hurtful as far as certain patterns of individuality are concerned. The bias may be reinforced by the teacher's own middle-class values, which often interact with commitment to his discipline to form a kind of screen in front of him. And the screen, once again, obscures his vision of the Negro child as creature "of substance, of flesh and bone. . . ."

He no longer is made to feel guilty about being middle class, as he might have been ten or fifteen years ago. With the exception of those public school people who romanticize the working class and the values they ascribe to it (lack of hypocrisy, delinquent "chivalry"), most teachers tend now to acknowledge at least the expediency of middle-class restraints, aspirations, codes.

Even if he has no feeling of guilt or shame at being middle class and intellectual too, the teacher must still break through the barrier his loyalties tend to raise. If he does not, he will not succeed in "fascinating" children, as Frank Riessman puts it,[6] with what there is to be known. If he cannot reach his pupils, he will be unable to discern the variety of "learning styles" that may be used. If he is unable to individualize the members of his class, he will be unable to adapt the strategies at hand, the techniques that might involve them, *as* individuals, in the struggle to learn. Clearly, he must do all he can to promote the cause of rationality—using flexible time schemes, allowing for alternative ways of framing material and responding to it, being permissive with some children and structured with others. But as he attempts to promote the cause in diverse ways, he must also try to enlarge his own conception of worth. He cannot exclude the life styles which seem to him to be non-rational, frivolous, shallow, "low"; because, if he does, he excludes individuals from his category of the worthy—and, perhaps, from his category of the human. And he cannot teach those he excludes.

If he succeeds in diversifying, in enlarging his conception of worth, if he succeeds in distinguishing among individual youngsters—his task has only begun. He cannot be "color-blind" when he considers his pupils; since this is often to become unintentionally discriminatory. He cannot treat his Negro pupils and his middle-class white pupils equally; since that would lead to thrusting the children of the poor into fixed positions of inequality. He needs to make distinctions and to be non-discriminatory as well. He needs to find a way of permitting every child to express his own uniqueness visibly, to "become" in his own authentic way.

What is authenticity for a Negro child? And how is the white teacher to know? If he cannot know, if he cannot empathize, it will be difficult to move a child to trust—to trust in a way that builds what Erik Erikson calls "fidelity," one of the building stones of personal identity. How can the white teacher find out how it is with his Negro pupils, what it is like to yearn (as a Single One who is deprived and Negro) to become someone—to *be*?

He is told by some articulate Negroes that he can never know, not if he is the Man, "Mister Charlie," white. Le Roi Jones, in his play called *Dutchman*, suggests that no white man can conceivably know, that no white man can even comprehend Negro jazz or Negro blues. When Robert Kennedy met with Dr. Kenneth Clark and James Baldwin, the estrangement between Negro and well-meaning white was dramatized in the public eye. Kennedy, taken unaware, was told that he could not possibly understand. John Oliver Killens, the novelist, explains this with talk of a difference in "psyche"[7] and in emotional chemistries. Yet all stress the importance of respect and regard; all speak of integration; all give voice to the need for a recognition of identity.

The teacher, with his unique responsibility, cannot expect clear directives from the side of his profession or from the Negro people themselves. Day after day—unless he chooses to remain "scientific" and impersonal—he will find himself asked to make particular choices, urgent choices; and no one, in or outside his school, will be able to tell him with certainty that his choices are right or wrong. If he is fortunate, he will have contact with the parents or with other people from his students' neighborhood. It may be that some of them will be equipped to mediate, somehow, between his professional function and the particularities of life on the streets and in tenement rooms. It may be that he will come in touch with the fabric of puzzlements on which his Negro pupils are trying to work with their new cognitive skills. Or he may become acquainted with the jobs that are open—and the jobs that are not. He may learn to help them develop a conception of work for work's own sake, for the sake of meanings in their lives.

It is important for him to try. It is important for his professional effectiveness to consider the significance of encounters, of what Martin Buber (and Martin Luther King) called the "I-Thou." His own humanity may deepen if he reaches out and tries to see; since he could not even begin to reach without becoming open to himself.

Again, literature may play a part. There is not only the possibility of vicarious participation when he reads; there is also engagement on his own terms, engagement in a fundamental human quest for meaning, identity, "somebodiness." He will find no final answers, certainly not to questions about the crippled and the illiterate and the poor; but he will, among all the ambiguities in what he reads, experience the power of possibility.

In *Invisible Man*, there is the question: "Yes, but what *is* the next phase?" There is the perception of diversity and oneness in America; there is the fruitful decision "to put it down," to refuse to "file and forget." And there is, just before the end:

I denounce because though implicated and partially responsible, I have been hurt to the point of abysmal pain, hurt to the point of invisibility.

And I defend because in spite of all I find that I love. In order to get some of it down I *have* to love. I sell you no phony forgiveness, I'm a desperate man—but too much of your life will be lost, its meaning lost, unless you approach it as much through love as through hate.

Through encounter, through the search for meaning—the forms can be imposed and the children can be taught to make sense of it too, to try to learn in their own terms, "to put it down."

The teacher can do no more than explore and pay heed and try to see. He can act *as if* understanding were possible, *as if* youngsters will become visible once he chooses to open his eyes. And he is likely, after a time, to discover that nothing is lost where mastery is concerned—that he has it in him to be a Teacher when he becomes a man.

NOTES

1. "Letter from a Birmingham Jail," in *Why We Can't Wait*, New York: Harper and Row, p. 84.

2. Abram L. Harris, "Education and the Economic Status of the Negro," in Robert A. Goldwin, ed., *100 Years of Emancipation*, Chicago: Rand McNally, 1964, pp. 152–153.

3. Ralph Ellison, *Invisible Man*, Signet edition, p. 7.

4. See, for example, Bruno Bettelheim's review of Benjamin Bloom's *Stability and Change in Human Characteristics* in *The New York Review of Books,* Sept. 10, 1964.

5. Martin Deutsch, "The Disadvantaged Child and the Learning Process," in A. Harry Passow, ed., *Education in Depressed Areas*, New York: Teachers College, 1962, pp. 163–179.

6. *The Culturally Deprived Child*, New York: Harper and Row, 1962, p. 94.

7. "Explanation of the 'Black Psyche'," *The New York Times Magazine*, June 7, 1964.

THE TEACHER OF
THE DISADVANTAGED

Herbert Schueler

The threat to our cherished way of life of a growing, permanently disadvantaged lower class, and its consequent weakening of the possibility of democratic social mobility, has become a major domestic issue of our time. Its political, economic, social and cultural, and ethical implications and consequences are fast becoming a major preoccupation of leadership in all facets of our society, the lowest included. It is an undeniable fact that, in spite of the widespread availability—certainly at the childhood and adolescent level—of public facilities for schooling, it has become the lot of all but a pitifully small minority of the children of our urban and rural centers of disadvantage and deprivation never to be able to look forward to developing the personal, intellectual, and psychological equipment needed to find a way out of the depths to which they were doomed by birth and circumstance. This is not only an unhealthy state for the lowest levels of our society but also a dangerous one for those above. No modern democratic civilization can afford to allow a permanent cementing of lower classes. It is not only contrary to the ethos of democracy but dangerous to the maintenance of law, order, and the social well-being of all classes.

While it may sound like a cliché to affirm the ideal of equal opportunity for all, the undeniable fact is emerging at last to those with responsible social consciences that deprivation is breeding further deprivation and that the rate is increasing, particularly among the young; and this in a society of unparalleled and evidently growing wealth. This is our greatest national debt, our shame, which, unless checked, may well prove to be our undoing.

Of all agencies in society, the school has the greatest latent potential in providing the means for the restoration of social mobility to our deprived lower classes. It cannot bear the whole burden, of course, nor the whole blame for failure, for it will take much more than the influence of the schools to break down the walls of our ghettoes, but it is undeniable that little can be done without the school. The institution of the public school is already there, its attendance by children and youth mandated by law, its facilities by and large adequate, its support through public funds established by custom. It just has to be made effective, and its potential as an agent of desirable social change developed and strengthened. It is no accident that so much

Herbert Schueler, "The Teacher of the Disadvantaged," *Journal of Teacher Education*, **16** (June 1965), 174–180. Reprinted with permission of the author and publisher.

attention is being given to the school by groups seeking to elevate the lot of the disadvantaged (and by those seeking to keep them where they now are).

The time, hopefully, is past when the school's function was limited to reflecting and perpetuating the mores of the community it was expected to serve. A slum, a ghetto, or a despond of poverty and deprivation is no possible standard for perpetuation in a progressive society. Every responsible leader of so-called minority groups (the minorities that are fast becoming majorities in our major population centers) views the school as a major agent for achieving social mobility among the disadvantaged peoples he represents, for only through the proper development and training of the talent that lies latent in all levels of society—the lowest included—can true equality of opportunity and that core of the democratic ideal, an upper mobile society, be achieved.

With this renewed emphasis on the school, some old truths have become manifest—truths that had gone somewhat out of fashion in a more complacent era of academic self-satisfaction—that effective learning requires effective teaching; that knowledge of the student is a primary requisite for effective teaching; that the teaching-learning community in the organized setting of the school is a human enterprise subject to all the potentials for gain and debit characteristic of all arranged social settings; that so-called subject matter has no viable existence per se in a school except as it provides the vehicle for the development of the learner; that living is learning and learning is living; and that the direction, substance, and method of schooling cannot safely be left to the workings of chance, particularly in a disadvantaged society. But above all, this preoccupation with the function of the school as an instrument of social change has helped the enlightened professional and his counterpart in the community to rediscover the student and to appreciate anew the potential function of his mentor, the teacher. None of this is the exclusive province of the disadvantaged society, to be sure, but at no level of society is the need so desperate, the proper education of the young so dependent on the school. A school, with a poor teaching staff and general disregard of individual student development, serving a middle-class community is as ineffective as the same type of school serving a lower-class population, but its effect can never be so devastating or its shortcomings so tragic in their effect, for its meagre resources can more easily be supplemented through family and other private means. It is the fate of the disadvantaged child to have the limits of his horizon dependent largely upon just one agency, the public school; hence, the key role that only the teacher can fill, the importance of the day-by-day contact of child and teacher, and the fashioning of this contact into learning experiences directed to the optimum development of the child.

The development of children to function within and for a nondisadvantaged society makes much of the virtue of emulation and perpetuation of prevailing values and customs, sometimes even to the point of complacency.

But what is worthy to perpetuate, what is safe to emulate in a society of social, economic, and cultural deprivation? Therefore the sights of the school serving the disadvantaged must focus not just toward but beyond the horizon limited by poverty and deprivation that spawned its students, and to which few would want or should have to return. It is surely the depths of misguided sentimentality to consider poverty, whether economic, social, cultural, or spiritual, anything but degrading in a civilized society. Those who find ennobling qualities in the disadvantaged state usually do so from the perspective of their own comfort. Certainly no product of schooling properly conceived in its social mandates should be complacent about, nor satisfied with, a disadvantaged lot. Basically, education for the disadvantaged should not nurture conformity but discontent with the disadvantaged state, and develop the power and the will to rise beyond it.

This is admittedly no simple task, for there are limits to what the school can do with the complex conditions and causes that contribute to the massive deprivation that is threatening to undermine the dynamics once taken for granted in our social structure. Substandard housing, patterns of extremely mobile in-migration, widespread unemployment—particularly among young people—and the cancerous incursions of organized crime and overpopulation all add their festering rot to the disease of poverty. But insofar as the school deals with humanity particularly, the ultimate inheritors of what men and their society have wrought, its mission toward building a better society through the optimum development of each member becames an inescapable mandate, for by being a major part of each individual's life, particularly in the formative years of childhood and early adolescence, it is the only social agency with the means, the opportunity, and if it will only accept it, the power to do so.

Has the school been effective, in degree and kind, in fulfilling this function? By and large it has not, although it is also true that it has not received sufficient credit for what it had done. Many reasons can be found for this failure. The crisis, while of long germination, did not really become acute until the decades of the post-World War II era. The complementary and causally intertwined social phenomena of accelerated population growth; of intensified industrial growth and change through automation, relocation, and the twin forces of development of new industry and processes and the abandonment of the obsolescent and old; and of in-migration of minorities and displaced poor to urban centers of population, with the accompanying blighting of growing areas of older urban housing, have all wrought new conditions upon our society with a suddenness that is terrifying in its impact. The school, in turn, found itself at the same time beset by a teacher shortage of unprecedented proportions, lack of sufficient facilities to house a growing pupil population, and escalating costs, with the inevitably accompanying demands by taxpayer groups to economize. All contributed to a growing helplessness to cope with a changing, unfamiliar pupil population in a community that seemed to be sliding inexorably down the road of multiple deprivation. With the depreciation of the community served by the school, teachers become more and more reluctant to teach there, and many either fled to the more advantaged professional conditions of the middle-class suburban school, left the profession altogether, or descended into the stultifying regimen of the type of teaching that is just above the level of bare custodial care.

Fortunately, many of the dedicated remained, as witness the many heartening contributions by teachers of the disadvantaged to this collection of articles. But to a much greater degree than ever before, schools serving largely disadvantaged populations were, and predominantly still are, beset by the greatest difficulty in attracting and retaining effective teachers. Add to this the unreasoned, degrading, destructive attacks on the schools by self-appointed critics, expert in just about any field but education, together with their varying effects—all bad—of putting teachers and schools on the defensive, of uncritical quick acceptance of nostrums, of bandwagon-inspired educational quackery, of retreating behind "safe," old practices and curricula distinguished by nothing but a greying obsolescence, and it is a wonder that so much that is good, effective, and dedicated still remains.

The speed of change has been unprecedented. The schools have not kept up to a level even approaching that necessary to fulfill their proper function. Nor, it must be said, have the institutions traditionally relied upon to train teachers; their lag has been as great as that of the schools. Certainly in the case of the disadvantaged they have been even slower; for they have not, unfortunately, had much opportunity to deal with them. In the case of the lower schools, facilities and mandated attendance at least assure such contact. American colleges and universities remain and are increasingly becoming more closed to the disadvantaged by the inexorable twin barriers acting separately or in combination of cost and qualifications for admission.

Therefore, the colleges and universities, particularly those engaged in teacher education, are faced with the necessity of rediscovering the school, particularly the one serving the disadvantaged. The time is long past when a university could get by with models of teaching and student behavior as exhibited in middle-class, comfortably safe communities or in campus schools dominated by faculty children. The need is for teachers in schools serving the teeming tenements; and before they can be prepared and served properly, the universities must include these communities and their schools among their laboratories for research, study, and training.

As one reads many of these articles, particularly those written by teachers in service, one is struck by their preoccupation with the day-to-day process of teaching and with their student-centered view. This is heartening and a fitting reminder to university professors engaged in teacher education that the whole process of training stands or falls by the specific everyday effects it has on the work of student and teacher in the classroom. The study of the child in a course in child development has little use unless it assists in the understanding and proper guidance of John, Mary, and Joe in a particular school, in a particular class, in a particular neighborhood. Similarly, no course in curriculum theory will be of much avail unless it finds application in the work of a specific teacher, with specific children, in a specific setting. And it is precisely this imperative specificity of application to specific conditions as they exist (not as they hopefully might be and are not) that has created such major problems for teachers and trainers and supervisors of teachers. It is fast becoming inescapable and devastatingly clear that the Joe and Mary we remember, and of whom our textbooks speak, are not the same as the José and Maria we find in our classes; that the neighborhood we once knew and felt comfortable in has become alien, and to our standards, shabby; that the life-styles, the language, the customs of the community served by our school and the children in our classes have become foreign, at times even threatening and frightening. In sum, the clientele of the school and the human and physical environment of the school have changed, and we have not sufficiently understood these changes nor taken them into sufficient account in our teaching and teaching resources and our programs of teacher education.

As one becomes familiar with the disadvantaged community and its children, particularly through the eyes of its teachers (in part revealed through many of these articles), certain requisites for proper teaching stand out. The first of these and possibly the most obvious, though too often observed in the breach, is a thorough knowledge of the student, his background, his aspirations, fears, habits, his talents, shortcomings, his life-style. The teacher, for example, who considers a child of Puerto Rican origin sneaky because he drops his eyes when being talked to is obviously in ignorance of the fact that in the Latin-American culture this is expected in children as a mark of respect for their elders.

This becomes particularly pressing as a problem for teachers who are not themselves products of the culture and class of their students, a condition that will continue to prevail for some time, since the children of the disadvantaged cultures have not and probably will not in the foreseeable future (not until their schooling enables them to realize their full potentiality) aspire or be admitted to universities for teacher education in sufficiently representative numbers to form more than a small minority of the public school teaching staff serving the disadvantaged. Quite often, a major cause of difficulty of teachers in understanding, and therefore working with, children of disadvantaged circumstances is that they are in ignorance of the life these children lead outside school, except insofar as they may read or hear about it in its more sordid aspects through press reports of local crime and delinquency. After all, the teacher of the disadvantaged, himself of middle-class aspirations, rarely lives in the slum that holds claim to the everyday squalor and deprivation dominating the existence of his students. For him the school neighbor-hood is a road to be traversed hurriedly on the way to and from school and not a human society to be known through firsthand personal contact and experience. Yet this is where his students live, play, laugh, weep, fight, eat, and sleep; here are their parents, their siblings, their pals, their enemies; here are the influences—good, warm, evil, fearsome—that help shape their behavior; here they live among their kind, subject to all the black, grey, and white influences that shape the culture of the slums. All this must be known and understood by the teacher (not just by the social worker) before proper communication based on knowledge and confidence can be developed with the student to form the basis for the proper influence, direction, and motivation of his development. In addition, the school must know and develop working relationships with allies serving similar and complementary ends—the churches, social service agencies, law enforcement, civic and fraternal groups which deal with the same population. The school can make common cause with the positive community agencies and their leadership and receive from and give to them much mutually advantageous assistance. The knowledge of the student and his environment, then, is the first requisite for teaching the disadvantaged.

The second requisite for teaching is the knowledge of ways to order and guide the learning of the disadvantaged child. Teachers have always been enjoined by university departments of education not to become textbook slaves and have been encouraged in the opposite direction by publishers of colorful and durable texts and workbooks. There is no such conflict with the teacher of the disadvantaged. It has been proved abundantly that the standard textbook conceived for and within the traditionally middle-class white society falls far short of reaching and communicating with the child of the disadvantaged and culturally different levels of lower-class society. And while some effective attempts have been made to create materials that do speak to such students, the need is not so much to develop standard material of a widespread market among schools serving the disadvantaged, helpful though such material may be, as to equip each teacher with the adaptive skills to devise his own materials, created anew or adapted and modified from what already exists, tailor-made to fit the particular needs of his own students. The basis for curriculum is all around us; it must be so fashioned as to touch the life of the learner, whatever it may be; it must begin where he is, not where some outside agent assumes he should be; and having begun where he is, it can then begin the process of enlarging, enriching, and broadening the basis of his experience and his development. This cannot be done without a sufficient knowledge of the learner and his environment nor without highly sophisticated skills of cirriculum development, manipulation, and adaptation. With the middle-class population, a teacher without such skills, though ineffective, may still have his shortcomings somewhat ameliorated by the use of good, established text- and workbook materials; but with the teacher of the disadvantaged, this convenient crutch collapses under its own burden of ineffectiveness. In several of these teacher contributions are examples of this highly necessary requisite for teaching.

A third requisite, perhaps the most pervasive of all, is the skill of the teacher in human relations, particularly as they affect the attitudes and behaviors of his students. All children need support, security, understanding, empathy, but those who are products of deprivation need them most of all. The need to develop inner controls and habits of positive interpersonal behavior is an imperative for children of all levels of society, but at no level is it of greater urgency than among the disadvantaged, and at no level is the potential influence of the teacher so great or his failure so tragic in its consequences.

The problem is complicated by the inevitable gulf between the society of which the teacher is a part and the social environment to which the students belong. The values, habits, and life-style of the middle-class professional may have little in common with those of the lower-class slum tenement dweller. Even the professional who is himself a product of the environment of deprivation experiences this gulf, perhaps even more poignantly than his colleague of middle-class origins. The teacher of the disadvantaged, therefore, is faced with the complex human problem of devoting himself to students who are not of his own kind and who return every day to environments basically alien to his own. No matter how close his relationships, how intimate his understanding, how empathic his dealings, the teacher remains basically above and apart from his students, for he is not really one of their kind. This condition adds measurably to the complexities of human interaction between teacher and students and makes all the more difficult the ordering of the human climate in the class group and its effect on the students.

Primary requisites for his effectiveness in human relations are the teacher's ability to see himself as his students see him and to understand the effect of his actions on them. Which of his actions engender resentment, indifference, fear, withdrawal? Which inspire confidence, a measure of respect, affection, friendliness? This requires a high degree of sensitivity to his students as human beings and the ability to order the human climate within which he operates so as to make for the best possible positive effect on their behavior, attitudes, and feelings. This sensitizing of the teacher to his function and effect within the human environment of his classroom requires as well his becoming sensitized to himself as a human being. A teacher to be effective in human relations must know, understand, come to terms with, and alter, if needed and possible, his own feelings and prejudices toward the student people he is dealing with. His function as a teacher is constructive, supportive, positive, and sometimes corrective. If his feelings are largely negative and unsympathetic toward his students, he will find teaching a misery and his effect miserable. This does not mean that he must learn to love them all, but at the very least, he must feel a measure of empathic personal self-satisfaction in their company and seek to inspire similar feelings in them toward himself and toward each other. Teaching is after all a human enterprise, and the human environment in the classroom has its inevitable effect on the development of its members as human beings. At what point does control become repression? When does permissive freedom engender asocial behavior? When does insistence on quiet cause withdrawal? How can one distinguish between harmless mischief and vicious behavior? Are the conventions of discipline and housekeeping characteristic of the school and the classroom more appropriate to a prison than to a school? To these and the myriads of similar questions there are no simple answers that apply to all schools, not even all schools serving disadvantaged populations. They will vary with the human characteristics of the people—students and teacher—involved, and with the human and social requirements demanded by the specific situation. Suffice it to say, however, that no requisite for the teacher of the disadvantaged is so crucial to his function as his ability to affect positively the human climate of his classroom.

What are the implications of the foregoing on preservice, in-service, and continuing education for teachers? There are so many that they may well force the education of teachers into patterns and practices quite different from those that have been held as sufficient in the ignorance of accelerating social change. Universities will have to evaluate their programs in full knowledge of the conditions and circumstances within which teachers must operate, the peoples and communities they are expected to serve, and the aspirations of a democratic society to provide the means for optimum development of each individual in keeping with his potential. In the foundational training for future teachers in preservice programs, they will seek the aid of the disciplines of urban sociology, social psychology, and cultural anthropology to complement the contributions of the familiar disciplines of psychology, philosophy, and the history of education. They will provide, through field visitation, observation, participation, and apprentice or student teaching, increased, intensified opportunities for future teachers to experience, become familiar with, and begin functioning in the schools and neighborhoods that will be their future professional homes. As beginning teachers, the newly licensed professionals will continue their training on an in-service basis in both school- and university-centered seminars and workshops and will receive help through them and through the aid of specially trained supervisory and university personnel in the day-by-day conduct of their classes. A significant portion of this in-service training will be built into the regular work load of the teacher through regularly scheduled time released for participation in courses, seminars, workshops, and conferences, and will not consist as at present of requirements to be fulfilled on an over-time basis. Industry has long recognized the need for further training as part of a skilled worker's work load; it is time that teacher education followed suit. Finally, the continuing development of the career teacher will receive more and more emphasis through intensive summer institutes designed to keep the teacher continually abreast of new knowledge, new procedures, and new resources for teaching. In sum, teacher education will become more intensive, make use of a broader spectrum of disciplines, require more direct experience with school and community (particularly those schools and communities in which the teacher will likely be functioning), and continue far beyond the training for permanent licensure. The universities will discover the need for making the school and community as it exists (not just as it is fashioned in the model campus school) its laboratory for training, experimentation, and research. And the schools, in turn, in cooperation with the universities, will develop more and more as locales for training of present and future teachers, much as the teaching hospital functions for the training of physicians and nurses. Intensive, lifelong teacher education, adaptive to reality and change for service to the disadvantaged, will require a newer, more intimate working relationship among school, university, and community; greater human and material resources; knowledgeable and effective school supervisors and university professors; and the most dedicated, determined, idealistic human kind out of which to fashion the most important professional of them all—the teacher.

But aren't these implications valid for the proper training of all teachers, not just those concerned with the disadvantaged? True, our more favored populations would benefit as well by this extension, intensification, and enrichment of training; but they can make do with less. The teacher of the disadvantaged cannot and still fulfill his mission as the major, often the only, effective force for the human betterment of his students. Our society cannot afford to do less.

STUDY QUESTIONS

1. What is the relationship between a child's conception of himself and his perceptions of his teacher's feelings? What kinds of teacher attitudes foster high academic achievement and desirable classroom behavior?

2. Why is it especially important for culturally different children to have teachers with positive attitudes and high expectations?

3. Green contends that black people are "invisible" in American society. What does she mean? In what ways do teachers make black children feel "invisible?" How can the classroom teacher help the black child to experience a sense of visibility?

4. How can a teacher "enlarge his conception of worth and accept cultures

different from his own?" How can we tell if a person *accepts* different cultures?

5. What three characteristics does Schueler believe the successful teacher of culturally different children must possess? How might a teacher attain these characteristics?

6. Is it possible for a teacher to "see himself as his students see him"? Explain.

SUGGESTED READINGS

Becker, Howard S., "Career Patterns of Public School Teachers," *Journal of Sociology*, **57** 470–477, 1952

Bernstein, Abraham, *The Education of Urban Populations*. New York: Random House, 1967

Chesler, Mark A., "Teacher Training Designs for Improving Instructions in Interracial Classrooms," in *Papers Prepared for National Conference on Equal Educational Opportunity in America's Cities*, pp. 163–198. Washington, D.C.: U.S. Commission on Civil Rights, 1967

Brookover, Wilbur B., and Edsel L. Erickson, *Society, Schools and Learning*. Boston: Allyn and Bacon, Inc., 1969

Fantini, Mario D., and Gerald Weinstein, *The Disadvantaged: Challenge to Education*. New York: Harper and Row, 1968

Gottlieb, David, "Teaching and Students: The Views of Negro and White Teachers," *Sociology of Education*, **27** 245–353, 1964

Green, Robert L., "Crisis in American Education: A Racial Dilemma," in *Papers Prepared for National Conference on Equal Educational Opportunity in America's Cities*, pp. 405–434. Washington, D.C.: U.S. Commission on Civil Rights, 1967

Green, Robert L., (Editor), *Racial Crisis in American Education*. Chicago: Follett Educational Corporation, 1969

Havighurst, Robert J., *Education in Metropolitan Areas*. Boston: Allyn and Bacon, 1968

Herriott, Robert E., and Nancy Hoyt St. John, *Social Class and the Urban School: The Impact of Pupil Background on Teachers and Principals*. New York: John Wiley & Sons, 1966

Kohl, Herbert, *36 Children*. New York: Signet Books, 1968

Kozol, Jonathan, *Death at an Early Age: The Destruction of the Hearts and Minds of Negro Children in the Boston Public Schools*. New York: Bantam Books, 1967.

Miller, Harry L., and Roger Woock, *Social Foundations of Urban Education*. Hinsdale, Illinois: The Dryden Press, 1970

Rosenthal, Robert, and Lenore F. Jacobson, *Pygmalion in the Classroom*. New York: Holt, Rinehart and Winston, 1968

Rosenthal, Robert, and Lenore F. Jacobson, "Teacher Expectations for the Disadvantaged," *Scientific American*, **218** 19–23, 1968

Wisniewski, Richard, *New Teachers in Urban Schools: An Inside View*. New York: Random House, 1968

CHAPTER 5
TEXTBOOKS, TRADEBOOKS
AND INTELLECTUAL HONESTY

In recent years, concern for the treatment of minority groups in textbooks has been evidenced in popular and professional journals, by the publication of "multi-ethnic" and "integrated" readers, and by the actions of state legislatures. The California State Legislature enacted a law in 1965 which stipulates that "the role and contributions of American Negroes and other ethnic groups" be adequately taught.[1] In 1966, the Michigan Legislature passed the Social Studies Textbook Act, which requires an annual evaluation of the treatment of racial and ethnic groups in the social studies textbooks used in the state.[2]

Large city boards of education, including those of New York City and Detroit, have issued mandates to publishers establishing minimum requirements for the adequate treatment of racial and cultural minorities in textbooks. In 1962, the Superintendent of Schools in New York City issued a policy statement urging publishers to present a "comprehensive and satisfactory picture of the status of minority groups in our culture."[3] The Detroit Board of Education discontinued the use of an American history textbook published by Laidlaw Brothers after concluding that it did not adequately treat racial and ethnic minorities.[4] The ban was removed when the publisher revised the book.

Such actions by state legislatures, school superintendents, and boards

This chapter is based on Chapter Two of the senior editor's Ph.D. dissertation, "A Content Analysis of Elementary American History Textbooks: The Treatment of the Negro and Race Relations," Michigan State University. Copyright © 1969 by James A. Banks.

of education emanated largely in response to pressure from civil rights groups for more comprehensive and balanced treatment of the Negro and other minority groups in textbooks.[5] Civil rights groups pressured public school educators and legislators, who in turn pressured publishers.

Publishers have been reluctant to respond to pressure for more comprehensive coverage of minority groups in textbooks because they believe that textbooks that depart drastically from traditional ones will result in severe profit loss. However, they have also felt that it would be economically unwise to ignore completely demands to change the image of minority groups in textbooks because of their desire to secure adoptions in dense urban areas with large ethnic group populations. Black writes,

> . . . He [the publisher] will censor his own books if he thinks the offending passages may hurt sales [or] submit to censorship from outside sources if the potential market is big enough.[6]

Publishers have used various tactics to resolve their dilemma and to create a nationwide market for their textbooks. One strategy has involved publishing two editions of a text, one that is multi-ethnic and one that is all white. Abramowitz (1969) investigated the extent of the practice of using "star edition" texts.[7] He sent a five-item questionnaire to 31 leading textbook publishers, 27 of whom responded. Only seven publishers stated that they issued "star edition" texts. The author concludes, "From the information received in this study, it would seem that the 'star edition' is no longer a major problem."[8] While the results of this study are impressive, they should not be considered conclusive because the researcher used the "self-reporting" technique to gather his data. It is possible that publishers responded to the questionnaire in a way that they perceived as socially acceptable, regardless of their companies' policies regarding "star edition" textbooks.

It is especially important that we focus attention on the image of minority groups in textbooks because of the urgent racial crisis in our nation. Teaching materials influence children's racial attitudes, as the research reviewed by Banks in this chapter indicates. Books should help all children develop positive racial attitudes toward ethnic and cultural minorities. They should help culturally different children feel better about themselves and their cultures. However, as most of the readings in this chapter indicate, textbooks and trade books frequently either stereotype minority groups or ignore them, thus augmenting the culturally different child's already deflated self-image and confused racial attitudes. Similarly, such books tend to inflate the white child's tenuous and false sense of superiority.

The readings in this chapter describe the treatment of minority groups in textbooks and tradebooks and suggest the urgent need for intellectual honesty and realism in teaching materials.

NOTES

1. *Land of the Free and Its Critics*, Burlingame: California Teachers Association, 1967, p. 4.

2. Department of Public Instruction, *A Report on the Treatment of Minorities in American History Textbooks*, Lansing: Michigan Department of Education, 1968.

3. *The Negro in American History*, New York: Board of Education, 1964, p. iv.

4. Hillel Black, *The American Schoolbook*, New York: William Morrow, 1967, pp. 108–114.

5. *Ibid.*, pp. 112–113.

6. Cited in William W. Joyce, "Minority Groups in American Society: Imperatives for Educators," *Social Education*, **33** (April 1969), 429–433.

7. Jack Abramowitz, "Textbooks and Negro History," *Social Education* **33** (March 1969), 306–309.

8. *Ibid.*, p. 309.

THE BLACK AMERICAN
IN AMERICAN
HISTORY TEXTBOOKS

Robert L. Trezise

For a number of years—since the beginning of the Civil Rights Revolution—educators have been aware that textbooks and other school materials have almost totally neglected black Americans. As Ralph Ellison said, the Negro has been the Invisible Man in America, and nowhere has this neglect been more insidiously reflected than in the white world of school textbooks. For generations, about the only black face the Negro schoolboy could find in his textbooks was the stereotyped picture of the "contented" slave, and virtually never could he find a story in his books about other Negro children. Textbooks told him America is white.

In the past few years, the situation has improved somewhat. Not only

Robert L. Trezise, "The Black American in American History Textbooks," *Social Studies*, **60** (April 1969), 164–167. Reprinted with permission of the author and publisher.

have textbook companies made an effort to include black Americans in their most recent standard publications (although this effort can only be called spurious when publishers have simply darkened previously white faces), but a sizable number of excellent supplementary materials on the Negro American have been made available to teachers. However, the question must still be asked: To what extent are the materials that reflect the multi-ethnic, multi-racial character of our society *in actual use* in the schoolrooms across the country?

Recently the Department of Education in the State of Michigan made an attempt to answer this question, at least in regard to American history textbooks; and in July (1968) it issued a report on an investigation it conducted of the twelve American history textbooks that are in greatest use in the state in regard to their treatment of Negroes and other minorities. (The report is now available from the Department in Lansing.) For the purposes of the study, the Department obtained the services of a group of historians from universities throughout the country, and each was asked to review at least two of these widely used texts. Far from being an encouraging indication that the treatment of minorities in textbooks has significantly improved, the report based on the judgment of these historians was a severe indictment of textual materials in current use.

The twelve American history textbooks included in this study, which ranged from high elementary to secondary reading level, were not, of course, judged to be equally inadequate. As a matter of fact, some of the books were highly praised for their "rich illustrations," "splendid assortment of maps," and "clear and simply written prose." But over all, the descriptive phrases that appeared throughout the historians' reviews of these books were anything but complimentary—"misleading," "shockingly casual," "a disembodied abstraction," "incredible statement," "very bad, indeed," "infuriating," "glaring omission," "gross distortion," "travesty on history," "superficial," "bland oversimplification," "grossly deficient," "abysmal failure," and so forth.

Perhaps the most frequent criticism of the textbooks made by the historians was that they create false impressions through errors of omission. For example, one book devotes more space to the New England fishing industry than it does to the establishment of the slave trade in the colonies, and other books fail to mention slave trade in the colonies at all. One book manages to discuss the Civil War without once mentioning slavery—a remarkable feat; and another mentions the Emancipation Proclamation only in passing, but finds space enough to discuss at considerable length the work of Matthew Brady. Even the books that do discuss slavery were found by the historians to be inadequate, and scarcely ever are the harsh realities of slavery described. For instance, one historian says that in the few paragraphs that describe slavery, "the student would never learn that slaves were not taught to read and that they were bought and sold like cattle, that they often suffered corporal punishment."

The historians found that following the Civil War, the Negro largely disappears and does not appear in the texts again until mention of the current Civil Rights Movement. But typical discussions of this most momentous development on the contemporary scene are woefully inadequate. One reviewer notes that "the oversimplification and inadequacy of the Civil Rights Movement is more than misleading—it is simply incorrect." Another historian says that although one book he examined did present some material on Civil Rights, "the discussion lacks an important dimension because the student is never given a full explanation of what Negroes are fighting against."

Besides errors of omission, the historians also found that these very widely used textbooks almost completely avoid all topics that could be considered controversial, which results in a history that is not only bland and tedious, but a distortion of our past. As one of the reviewers said, "The glaring omissions in this book make it a gross distortion of the American past. By ignoring everything that was unfair, unpleasant, exploitative, it falls incredibly short. . . ." There may be those who feel that the American history presented to young people should avoid the controversial and highlight instead the glorious achievements of our past. But as one historian said, "Perhaps if the authors were not so uncritical and were not such pollyannas, young people would feel less complacent when they left school."

The historians found, too, that the textbooks almost completely dehumanize history, and the personal dilemma of the Negro caught in the tragedy of slavery or in the web of prejudice that was re-inforced by every social institution of his country—is not at all suggested. Further, there is an absence of any kind of moral stand in regard to the treatment of the Negro in this country. While some may say that historians should not take moral stands, but should simply present the facts, still, on some issues, the writers of these textbooks do take a moral position—such as in the case of American opposition to the English during the Revolution, Texas' opposition to Santa Anna, and the American position on World War I and in the cold war. But there is no moral position taken in regard to slavery. The textbooks simply say, in effect, "There were arguments both for and against slavery." Period.

Although the focus of the report was the textbooks' treatment of black Americans, the reviewers dealt to some extent with the inadequacy of the treatment of other minorities as well. For example, all immigrant groups are neglected, and the whole immigrant movement greatly under-discussed. The development of the labor movement receives similar scanty and superficial treatment, and religious intolerance in America is—as one might expect— never mentioned. Nothing like an adequate picture of the shocking conditions under which Indians live in modern America is given, and in several of the books, the word "Jew" does not even appear.

In short, in the judgment of this group of historians, these twelve widely used textbooks in American history—and there is no reason to believe these books are not representative of most texts—are clearly inadequate in giving readers any kind of indication that America is a multi-racial, multi-ethnic, and pluralistic society. Too often young people think of minorities almost synonymously with problem groups, rather than as vital and creative contributors to our society; and these textbooks that so studiously avoid minorities and, indeed, strain away from their historical accounts anything that might be controversial and finish with a history that is no better than Pablum—do little to foster the more positive (and more genuinely American) view.

It is important to point out to educators in general and to teachers of American history in particular that the textbooks they are using are inadequate. However, the state of Michigan was not interested in banning twelve books. Indeed, the Department of Education in Michigan does not recommend or ban any textbooks, nor does it follow a policy of state adoptions. The local districts are free to choose the books they feel are best suited to their purposes. Thus, in order to assist these districts in making judgments in choosing books, the report also included a set of guidelines.

Rather than a check list, the guidelines are composed of items that discuss the elements that can be used as the criteria for judging the adequacy or inadequacy of an American history textbook in regard to its treatment of minorities. Four general criteria are included:

First, an American history textbook must above all else be historically accurate. This means that the basic facts themselves must be correct and verifiable. But the bare facts are not history—history must be an interpretation of the facts. In other words, the guidelines indicate that the facts must be interpreted fairly and in the light of current historical research. Further, the interpretations of the facts should be in keeping with the perceptions, attitudes, and concerns of the times. And if it can be said that our contemporary society is deeply concerned with the problems of ensuring human rights for all people, then history textbooks should reflect this paramount social concern.

Second, the textbook should present realistically the accomplishments and contributions of minorities in the past and today. In terms of the Negro American, this means specifically that the black American's historical backgrounds should be discussed; this should include an adequate account of the highly developed culture from which he came in Africa, a description of the harsh realities of the slave trade, a realistic picture of the life of a slave, and a discussion of the establishment of Jim Crow in both the northern and southern sections of the United States. Also, realistic treatment should include coverage of outstanding Negro contributors and a discussion of the struggle minorities have had in America against overwhelming social forces that have opposed their freedom, human rights, and equality of opportunity. In addition, the textbook should discuss racism in contemporary urban society and the significance of social reform for peoples not only in America, but throughout the world.

Third, the textbook should show great caution in its use of the term "race." The word is often used promiscuously, and in many cases, it is used for socially destructive purposes. Whatever scientific meaning it may have had has clearly been greatly obscured. Thus, students must not be encouraged to think of it as a scientifically sound term, and textbooks must be very much aware of the possible misinterpretations that may result from the use of this term.

And fourth, the total tone of the textbook must convey to the reader that certain basic values are intrinsically a part of the American system— values such as a belief in the dignity and worth of the individual, the belief in justice and equality of opportunity, and the belief that the pluralistic nature of our society is good and worthy of perpetuation. Everything in the book— the illustrations, the balance of materials, even the phraseologies—all of these must reflect these American values. A textbook writer who does not see to it that his work is permeated with these values and who writes a "valueless" text in the name of so-called objectivity, derogates one of his responsibilities as a textbook writer—that is, to attempt to not only teach subject matter, but to teach values for citizenship.

At present, it is doubtful that any American history textbook fully meets the criteria defined in the report, and local social studies textbook-selection committees may very well defend their selection of an inadequate textbook by asserting that better ones are not available. However, textbook publishing companies are eager to supply districts with the kinds of textbooks the local educators want. Therefore, it is imperative that social studies teachers demand textbooks that give full and adequate treatment to black Americans and other minorities. By this means, textbooks that more completely meet the criteria will become available, and a situation that at present is lamentable will become ameliorated.

A CONTENT ANALYSIS
OF THE BLACK AMERICAN
IN TEXTBOOKS

James A. Banks

INTRODUCTION

The urgent racial crisis in our nation has evoked considerable concern among educators about the roles of the school and teaching materials in intergroup education. Research indicates that teaching materials *do* affect youngsters' racial attitudes. Trager and Yarrow found that a curriculum which emphasized cultural diversity had a positive influence on children's racial attitudes.[1] Research by Johnson indicated that courses in black history could help black children feel better about themselves and their race.[2] Litcher and Johnson investigated the effects of multiethnic readers on the racial attitudes of second-grade white pupils and concluded that ". . . use of multiethnic readers resulted in marked positive change in the subjects' attitudes toward Negroes."[3] Since textbooks, which comprise the core of the social studies curriculum, can influence racial attitudes, it becomes imperative to evaluate carefully the content of textbooks with a view toward ascertaining the contributions which they might be making toward helping youngsters clarify their racial attitudes, self-perceptions, and value orientations. The careful study of textbooks is especially urgent in this time of high racial tension and polarization.

THE PROBLEM

The purpose of this study was to analyze the content of a selected sample of elementary American history textbooks in terms of major themes used to discuss the Negro and race relations. A review of the literature revealed the need for a current, scientific, and comprehensive study of the black American in textbooks.

James A. Banks, "A Content Analysis of the Black American in Textbooks," *Social Education*, **33** (December 1969), 954–957 ff. Published with permission of the National Council for the Social Studies. This article is based on "A Content Analysis of Elementary American History Textbooks; The Treatment of the Negro and Race Relations," unpublished Ph.D. dissertation, Michigan State University. Copyright © 1969 by James A. Banks.

In recent years, a number of researchers have studied the image of the black American and other minority groups in textbooks. While these studies are significant contributions to the literature on race relations,[4] none utilized a content analysis technique which met the criteria of scientific content analysis as promulgated by researchers such as Berelson, Budd, Thorp and Donohew, Kerlinger, and Borg. These writers maintain that a scientific content analysis must be *objective, systematic*, and *quantitative*.[5] To satisfy these criteria, a study must have well delineated categories, a measure of reliability, clearly formulated data gathering procedures, and research hypotheses which can be tested by analyzing the data gathered during the investigation.

The study reported here was designed to utilize a scientific content analysis technique to illuminate the dominant themes (major ideas) used to discuss the Negro and race relations in a sample of 36 American history books for use in grades 4, 5, 6, 7, and 8. A sub-sample of six books was used to compare the frequency of selected theme units in books published in 1964 and in 1968.[6]

PROCEDURES

Unit of analysis A technique called *thematic analysis* was used in this study. According to Budd, Thorp, and Donohew, a theme is a major idea or single thought unit. A sentence may contain one or more theme units. The sentence, "John is handsome and intelligent," contains *two* themes or ideas. They are, "John is handsome," and "John is intelligent."[7] The total number of themes in *each* sentence analyzed were ascertained and reported in this study.

Formulation of categories and coding sheet Theme units were classified under one of eleven categories (described below). Initially, theme units were selected from a sample of elementary American history textbooks, and the categories developed on the basis of the content of these theme units, recommendations made by social scientists and educators (studies on minority groups in textbooks were analyzed for the major ideas which were recommended for inclusion in textbooks by these researchers), and reading in black history by the investigator. Sample theme units were added and some minor modifications made in category definitions during the analysis, since as Budd, Thorp, and Donohew noted ". . . because it is virtually impossible to anticipate every situation that will arise during the coding, each category definition should allow for expansion. . . ."[8]

Validity of the coding sheet The "jury method" was used to ascertain the validity of the procedures in this study. In this method, ". . . experts are asked to judge relevant parts of the methodology . . . or measuring instruments.''[9] Four experts in the teaching of black history, one historian and three social studies educators, were identified and asked to serve on the panel of jurors to validate the instrument.[10] These individuals were selected because of their publications and reputations in the area of race relations and black history. Each juror was asked to judge whether the theme units from the initial sample of books were *appropriately* or *inappropriately* categorized. All four jurors judged 89% of the theme units to be *appropriately* categorized. *All* theme units were judged appropriately categorized by at least two jurors.

Reliability of the procedures The reliability of the coding procedure was established by having two coders independently code the theme units in five books randomly selected from the total sample.[11] The coder proportion of agreement was .64.

Formulation of hypotheses Each hypothesis stated a predicated relationship between the frequencies of two theme categories. *The investigator assumed that the categories selected for comparison had a high degree of comparability, importance, and the greatest potential for yielding meaningful information.* For example, the theme unit frequencies in the categories "Racial Harmony" and "Racial Violence and Conflict" were compared because they had contrasting definitions and because previous researchers had reported that authors frequently employ units in the former category and rarely in the latter. "Racial Harmony" and "Principal Discrimination" theme unit frequencies were compared for similar reasons. The purpose and scope of this study did not warrant that all possible comparisons between categories be made.

All hypotheses were stated in the null form. The hypotheses stated that there was no difference in the frequencies of theme units in the categories compared. The .05 level of significance was selected as sufficient to reject the null hypothesis. Chi-square was used in the analysis.

Categories and examples

Explained discrimination. Theme units which state reasons for differential treatment based on race but make no attempt to distinguish moral issues and causal issues. Such theme units are susceptible to being interpreted as *justifications* for discrimination.

Example: Negroes could withstand the hot Southern climate much better than whites.

Principal discrimination. Theme units which describe deliberate differential treatment based on race in which no attempt is made by the writer to explain the discriminatory practices depicted.

Example: The Plessy vs. Ferguson Decision upheld segregation.

Nonviolent resistance to discrimination. Theme units which describe acts or words which *did not* involve violence but were designed primarily to resist discriminatory practices based on race.

Example: The NAACP worked to end discrimination.

Deliberate desegregation. Theme units which describe deliberate behavior on the part of majority groups or established institutions which ended or intended to end racial discrimination or segregation.

Example: The Brown Decision of 1954 prohibited segregation in the public schools.

Expedient desegregation. Theme units which describe behavior by majority groups or established institutions which resulted in ending segregation or discrimination but had other dominant objectives, such as political or social advancement of individuals, groups or a nation.

Example: Lincoln freed the slaves to weaken the Confederacy.

Racial violence and conflict. Theme units which describe acts of violence which were caused in part or whole by factors involving racial confrontation and racial antagonism.

Example: The Ku Klux Klan committed violent acts against Negroes.

Deprivation. Theme units which describe the physical and psychological poverty of black Americans.

Example: Slaves were poorly fed.

Stereotypes. Theme units which describe conventional, fixed, and unverified characteristics of Negroes.

Example: Slaves were happy.

Prejudice. Theme units which describe unfavorable racial attitudes which are held or were held in disregard of facts.

Example: Southern whites felt that the Negro was innately inferior.

Racial harmony. Theme units which describe peaceful and friendly relations between Negroes and whites, or events or acts which contributed to good race relations.

Example: Some masters freed their slaves.

Achievements. Theme units which describe the accomplishments of Negroes in literature, music, art, science, industry, sports, entertainment, education and in other fields.

Example: Booker T. Washington was a famous scientist.

SUMMARY OF MAJOR FINDINGS

Theme units to be classified in the eleven categories were selected from the 36 American history textbooks used in the main analysis by checking the table of contents and index of each book and reading those parts of the book which discussed the Negro or race relations. The following comparisons of the resulting frequencies of theme units are of particular interest:

"Principal Discrimination" theme units had a higher frequency than "Racial Violence and Conflict" theme units.

"Explained Discrimination" theme units had a higher frequency than "Racial Violence and Conflict" theme units.

"Principal Discrimination" theme units had a higher frequency than "Racial Harmony" theme units.

"Racial Harmony" theme units and "Racial Violence and Conflict" theme units had equal frequencies.

"Achievement" theme units had a higher frequency than "Deprivation" theme units.

"Non-Violent Resistance to Discrimination" theme units and "Racial Violence and Conflict" theme units had equal frequencies.

"Principal Discrimination" and "Deliberate Desegretation" theme units had equal frequencies.

"Deliberate Desegregation" theme units had a higher frequency than "Expedient Desegregation" theme units.

"Racial Harmony" theme units had a higher frequency than "Prejudice" theme units.

Table 1. Total Unit Frequencies by Category

Theme category	Total unit frequency
Achievements	367
Principal Discrimination	279
Deliberate Desegregation	261
Explained Discrimination	206
Non-Violent Resistance to Discrimination	165
Racial Harmony	164
Racial Violence and Conflict	140
Deprivation	82
Prejudice	25
Stereotypes	19
Expedient Desegregation	14

"Stereotypes" and "Prejudice" theme units had equal frequencies.

Theme units which referred to achievements, racial violence and conflict, peaceful resistance to discrimination, and deliberate acts of discrimination occurred more frequently in books published in 1968 than in 1964.

DISCUSSION OF FINDINGS

While textbook authors often attempt to explain or rationalize racial discrimination, they more frequently discuss discrimination without either explaining or condemning it. This finding supports that of other researchers who have suggested that textbook writers "avoid taking a moral stand."[12]

The authors of elementary history textbooks do not frequently depict racial violence. They seek to explain discrimination more frequently than they mention incidents of racial violence and conflict. However, authors refer to racial violence as often as they relate peaceful and friendly relations between blacks and whites. This finding conflicts with those of Stampp[13] and other writers who suggest that authors emphasize harmonious race relations and neglect discussion of racial conflict. The authors in this study also mentioned racial violence as frequently as they referred to peaceful resistance to discrimination.

Other findings in this study suggest that authors do not emphasize harmonious race relations. The authors referred to deliberate acts of discrimination much more often than they related incidents of racial harmony.

Table 2. Minimum and Maximum Frequencies of Theme Units.

Theme category	Minimum units in any book	Maximum units in any book
Achievements	4	80
Principal Discrimination	14	40
Deliberate Desegregation	3	28
Explained Discrimination	8	12
Non-Violent Resistance to Discrimination	3	16
Racial Harmony	10	24
Racial Violence and Conflict	5	18
Deprivation	3	12
Prejudice	0	5
Stereotypes	0	3
Expedient Desegregation	0	4

However, they mentioned racial harmony more frequently than they did racial prejudice.

The textbook writers mentioned deliberate acts of discrimination as often as they related deliberate acts of desegregation. However, they referred to deliberate acts of desegregation more frequently than they mentioned acts which lead to desegregation but were expedient gestures.

The authors depicted the achievements of black Americans in literature, music, art, science, industry, sports, entertainment, education and in other fields much more frequently than they referred to any other events which relate to the black man and race relations. For example, the physical and psychological deprivations of black Americans were rarely discussed. Thus, the achievements of individual black heroes were emphasized rather than the plight of the majority of black people in this country.

The authors of textbooks rarely used theme units which could be characterized as "stereotypes." This finding does not support the often heard contention that textbooks frequently describe Negroes in a stereotypic fashion.

A comparison of books published in 1964 and in 1968 revealed that significant changes had occurred in the frequency of several types of theme units used to discuss the Negro and race relations. Theme units which referred to achievements, violence and conflict, peaceful resistance to discrimination, and deliberate acts of discrimination occurred more frequently in books published in 1968 than in 1964. This finding indicates that textbook authors have responded, to some degree, to the demand for more comprehensive coverage of the black American in textbooks, and to the black American's increasingly active role in American life.

CONCLUSIONS AND RECOMMENDATIONS

1. This study indicates that authors rarely take a moral stand when discussing such issues as racial discrimination and racial prejudice. Those who maintain that one of the major goals of the social studies is to inculcate democratic racial attitudes will find reason here to ask for a reevaluation of the textbook author's role in intergroup education.

2. Theme units which refer to racial violence and conflict have low frequencies in elementary American history textbooks. Since racial violence and conflict are currently pervasive in our nation, a greater frequency of these units in textbooks appears necessary if that part of the curriculum is to reflect reality accurately.

3. Racial prejudice theme units appear infrequently in elementary American history textbooks. A greater number of these units might provide a context for helping children to deal with racial prejudice and conflict more intelligently.

4. This study indicates that most textbooks have "integrated" by extolling the virtues of "selected" black heroes. While both black and white youngsters need black heroes with whom they can identify, they need to know the plight of the masses of black people even more. Children cannot be expected to grasp the full significance of the black experience in America unless they are keenly aware of the social and historical factors which have kept the black man at the lower rungs of the social ladder.[14]

5. While the findings of this study support some of those of other researchers, they conflict with others. This suggests that more extensive and careful research is needed before we can derive conclusive statements regarding the treatment of the black American in teaching materials.

NOTES

1. Helen G. Trager and Marian R. Yarrow, *They Learn What They Live*, New York: Harper and Brothers, 1952.

2. David W. Johnson, "Freedom School Effectiveness: Changes in Attitudes of Negro Children," *Journal of Applied Behavioral Science*, **2** (1966), 325–330.

3. John H. Litcher and David W. Johnson, "Changes in Attitudes of White Elementary School Students After Use of Multiethnic Readers," *Journal of Educational Psychology*, **60** (1969), 148–152.

4. A partial list of these studies includes: Committee on the Study of Teaching Materials in Intergroup Education, *Intergroup Relations in Teaching Materials*, Washington, D.C.: American Council on Education, 1949; Lloyd Marcus, *The Treatment of Minorities in American History Textbooks*, New York: Anti-Defamation League, 1961; Kenneth M. Stampp, *et al.*, "The Negro in American History Textbooks," *Integrated Education*, **2** (October–November 1964), 19–24; Department of Public Instruction, *A Report on the Treatment of Minorities in American History Textbooks*, Lansing: Michigan Department of Education, 1968.

5. See Bernard Berelson, *Content Analysis in Communication Research*, Glencoe, N.Y.: Free Press, 1952; Richard W. Budd, Robert K. Thorp, and Lewis Donohew, *Content Analysis of Communications*, New York: Macmillan, 1967; Fred N. Kerlinger, *Foundations of Behavioral Research: Educational and Psychological Inquiry*. New York: Holt, Rinehart & Winston, 1966; and Walter R. Borg, *Educational Research: An Introduction*, New York: David McKay Company, 1963.

6. The six books were: Orrel T. Baldwin, *The Story of Our America*, New York: Noble & Noble, 1964; Richard C. Brown, Arlan C. Helgeson, and George H. Lobdell, *The United States of America: A History for Young*

Citizens, Atlanta: Silver Burdett Company, 1964; Mabel B. Casner and Ralph H. Gabriel, *Story of the American Nation*, New York: Harcourt, Brace and World, 1964; Stephen H. Bronz, Glenn W. Moon, and Don C. Cline, *The Challenge of America*, New York: Holt, Rinehart & Winston, 1968; Harold H. Eibling, Fred M. King, and James Harlow, *History of Our United States*, River Forest, Ill.: Laidlaw Brothers, 1968; Jerome R. Reich and Edward L. Biller, *Building the American Nation*, New York: Harcourt, Brace and World, 1968.

7. Budd, Thorp, and Donohew, *Content Analysis*, pp. 44–46.

8. *Ibid.*, p. 28.

9. *Ibid.*, p. 69.

10. The jurors were: Dr. Nancy Arnez, Professor of Education, North-eastern Illinois State College; Dr. Dewitt Dykes, Professor of American History, Michigan State University; Astrid C. Anderson, Research Associate, the Lincoln Filene Center for Citizenship and Public Affairs, Tufts University; and Irving J. Sloan, author of books on the black American and social studies teacher, Scarsdale (New York) Junior High School.

11. The five books were: Orrel T. Baldwin, *The Story of Our America*, New York: Noble & Noble, 1964; Herbert H. Gross, *et al.*, *Exploring Regions of the United States*, Chicago: Follet Publishing Company, 1966; Rembert W. Patrick, John K. Bettersworth, and Ralph W. Steen, *This Country of Ours*, Austin: Steck Company, 1965; John A. Rickard and Rolor E. Ray, *Discovering American History*, Boston: Allyn and Bacon, 1965; and, Clarence L. Ver Steeg, *The Story of Our Country*, New York: Harper and Row, 1965.

12. Department of Public Instruction, *A Report on the Treatment of Minorities*.

13. Stampp, *et al.*, "The Negro in History Textbooks," pp. 9–24.

14. James A. Banks, "The Need for Positive Racial Attitudes in Textbooks," in Robert L. Green, ed., *Racial Crisis in American Education*, Chicago: Follett Publishing Company, 1969.

THE INDIAN IN
AMERICAN HISTORY

Virgil J. Vogel

As Rome hid its debt to the Estruscans, we have obscured our inheritance from the red men. Anthropologists know that acculturation proceeds in both directions when two societies are in any kind of contact, and that even a conquered people helps to shape the destiny of their overlords. "North Americans have maintained the European level with the strictest possible puritanism," wrote psychiatrist Carl Jung, "yet they could not prevent the souls of their Indian enemies from becoming theirs."[1] For our own benefit, let us resurrect some lost truth.

Indians picked the sites now occupied by many of our great cities, and plotted the trails and canoe portages which are followed to this day by our highways, railroads, and canals.[2] We copied their dress, and not only in the fringed buckskin of Daniel Boone. From them we learned to substitute long pants for knee breeches; our women borrowed their feathers and paint, and we wear their moccasins, their parkas, and ponchos.[3] Their beads and bells are popular with our hippies. We smoke their tobacco and eat their foods: the tapioca of the Amazon, the beans, avocadoes, pineapples, chocolate, peppers, and vanilla of Mexico, the tomatoes, potatoes, and peanuts of Peru, the cranberries, squashes, and pecans of North America. The pemmican of the Plains Indian has served as food for Antarctic explorers. From the Mexican Indians we borrowed chewing gum, tamales, chili, and tortillas; from our own, hominy, succotash, corn pone and popcorn.[4]

LITERATURE, MUSIC, ARTS

They have influenced our literature far beyond Cooper's *Mohicans*, and Longfellow's *Hiawatha*, which is our truest national epic. Edna Ferber, Hamlin Garland, Helen Hunt Jackson, and Oliver La Farge are a few among many who have portrayed the Indian in novels. Thomas Wolfe and Ernest Hemingway used Indian themes in short stories, while Philip Freneau, John Neihardt, Lew Sarett, and Walt Whitman glorified them in poetry.[5] Indian mythology constitutes our most authentic American folk-lore. Appropriately, the first bible printed in the country was in an Algonquian language, John Eliot's *Indian Bible* (1663).

Virgil J. Vogel, "The Indian in American History," *Social Education*, **33** (February 1969), 200–203. Reprinted with permission of the author and the National Council for the Social Studies.

Indians have influenced composers of music; among those indebted to them are Charles Wakefield Cadman, Anton Dvorak, Anton P. Heinrich, Victor Herbert, Thurlow Lieurance, Harvey W. Loomis, Edward A. McDowell, and Charles S. Skilton.[6]

Their arts and designs have influenced our arts, jewelry, home decorations, and even our architecture.[7] Not only did early settlers imitate the Indian wigwam and palisade, but the Army modified the Plains tepee into the Sibley tent. Today, a prefabricated vacation home in the shape of a tepee, called *Wigwam* 70,[8] has been marketed by the National Design Center in Chicago. The Quonset hut, which is widely used where simplicity is demanded, has both an Indian name and an Indian design. Buckminster Fuller's "geodesic dome" is an aboriginal wigwam covered with metal or glass instead of bark. Our modern skyscrapers copy the terraced setback of the Maya. Pueblo adobe bricks became the white man's building material in the Southwest. The cube style of the Pueblos appears in the LaFonda hotel in Santa Fe, and Moshe Safdie's *Habitat* at Expo '67 in Montreal. Willard Carl Kruger's New Mexico state house is in the shape of the Zia sun symbol. Frank Lloyd Wright acknowledged his debt to the Maya and incorporated their themes in some of his buildings. Of their temples he wrote: "A grandeur arose in the scale of total building never since excelled, seldom equalled by man either in truth of plan or simple integrity of form."[9]

Not only was the Indian a sculptor, but he has inspired our sculptors as well. Leonard Crunelle, Malvina Hoffman, Ivan Mestrovic, and Lorado Taft are among those who have portrayed the Indian in stone and bronze.[10] And let us not forget that authentic American creation, the cigar store wooden Indian. Among painters who made their reputation with Indian subjects are Carl Bodmer, George Catlin, Frederick Remington, and Alfred Miller.

We borrowed Indian inventions, and even used their names for many of them: canoe, kayak, pirogue, cigar, hammock, and toboggan. We use his snowshoes, cradleboard, rubber, pipe, and cigarettes. Some of our youth play lacrosse and other games evolved from Indian sports.[11] Indian lore enlivens the program of youth organizations. Indian dance clubs and craft groups composed of white adults are flourishing in the United States and Europe.[12] Indian themes are in children's toys and juvenile literature. Indians have long been important in the movies, as they were earlier on the stage,[13] but it has only been recently that they have been portrayed on the screen with sympathy and dignity, in films like *Broken Arrow, Devil's Doorway*, and *Cheyenne Autumn*.

NAMES AND LANGUAGE

They have enriched our language. We use their names for the animals: caribou, chipmunk, cougar, coyote, jaguar, manatee, moose, opossum, raccoon, skunk, and woodchuck. The trees carry their names: catalpa, chinquapin, hickory, papaw, pecan, persimmon, sequoia, tamarack, and tupelo. Some sixty plants have Indian names, including cohosh, puccoon, pipsissewa, and poke. Because of fancy or Indian usage, other plants have names like Indian paint brush, Indian pipe, Indian turnip, moccasin flower, papoose root, and squaw vine. We use their names for topographic features such as muskegs, bayous, and savannas, and speak of hurricanes and Chinook winds. Red men taught us to say hooch, okay, punk, and pewee. From them we borrowed caucus, Tammany, pow-wow, mugwump, podunk, and tuxedo. We have come to use words and phrases like "buck," "bury the hatchet," "go on the warpath," "Indian summer," "Indian giver," "Indian file," "great white father," and "war paint."[14]

We plant Cherokee roses, Catawba grapes, Pima cotton, and Black Hawk raspberries. We drive Pontiac cars and ride in trains called *The Chief* and *Hiawatha*. We call our athletic teams Black Hawks, Braves, Illini, Redskins, and Warriors. We have Cayuse and Appaloosa ponies and Malemute dogs.

From the dispossessed we took the names of twenty-seven states, four of our great lakes, and many of our mountains and rivers, to give, as Mencken said, "a barbaric brilliancy to the American map."[15] Canada and four of its provinces and two of its territories have Indian names, as do ten nations in Latin America. We took Indian names for cities like Chattanooga, Chicago, Kalamazoo, Kenosha, Keokuk, Kokomo, Mankato, Miami, Milwaukee, Muncie, Muskegon, Omaha, Oshkosh, Paducah, Pawtucket, Peoria, Sandusky, Schenectady, Seattle, Sheboygan, Spokane, Tacoma, Tallahassee, Tucson, Tulsa, Waco, and Wichita. Some of their names we translated into colorful English and French equivalents like Bad Axe, Battle Creek, Broken Bow, Medicine Hat, Moose Jaw, Painted Post, and Red Wing; Baton Rouge, Des Plaines, and Fond du Lac.

The Indian brightens our advertising. His totem poles invite us to Alaska, his calendar stone calls us to Mexico. Indians are featured in the advertising of the Santa Fe and Great Northern railroads, and in the tourist advertising of many states. We put an Indian on a baking soda can, on a box of corn starch, on chewing tobacco, patent medicines, and other products. We use their names as trade marks: Black Hawk meats, Cherokee garments, Pequot sheets, Sioux tools, and Wyandotte chemicals. We put the Indian on coins and postage stamps. An Aztec legend is pictured on the Mexican flag, and Indian symbols decorate the state flags of New Mexico and Oklahoma.

THE INDIAN AND POLITICAL HISTORY

The Indian is an important ingredient of our political history. The colonial charters speak of trade and conversion as objects of the colonizers. The

Indian presence was a spur to efforts at colonial union, from the New England confederation to the Albany congress. The Iroquois alliance helped to defeat the French, and Indians were significant participants in all colonial wars, and later ones, both as friends and foes. Their rebellion under Pontiac in 1763 won the royal proclamation closing the West to settlement, and launched a chain of events leading to our independence. Indians are mentioned in the Declaration of Independence, the Articles of Confederation, the Northwest Ordinance, the U.S. Constitution, the constitution of the Confederacy, and in numerous presidential messages and party platforms. They figure in at least five treaties with foreign powers.[16] We have made 372 treaties with them and passed over four thousand laws affecting them. Several government agencies are involved with them.[17]

Montaigne, Rousseau, and Jefferson paid tribute to the Indian capacity to organize human affairs in a libertarian manner. The Iroquois developed a system of confederated government which, according to Benjamin Franklin, served as an example for his Albany Plan of Union,[18] and eventually for the Articles of Confederation. Felix Cohen has lashed the assumption that our democracy was born in Greece:

> . . . it is out of a rich Indian democratic tradition that the distinctive political ideals of American life emerged. Universal suffrage for women as for men, the pattern of states within a state that we call federalism, the habit of treating chiefs as servants of the people instead of their masters, the insistence that the community must respect the diversity of men and the diversity of their dreams—all these things were part of the American way of life before Columbus landed.[19]

The followers of Sam Adams masqueraded as Indians at the Boston Tea Party, and we borrowed Indian military tactics in the revolution, as the poet Robert P. Tristam Coffin has written:

> We bent down to the bob-cat's crouch
> Took color from the butternut tree,
> At Saratoga, Lexington,
> We fought like Indians and went free.

Even customs and folkways: frontier hospitality, and neighborly cooperation, such as barn-raising, were copies of Indian manners. We learned his weather and plant lore. His war whoop was the "rebel yell" in the Civil War and Tristam Coffin says:

> We even put the pow-wow on,
> We dance the night before we fight,
> Republicans, Democrats, football teams
> With red hot songs build up their might.[20]

The predominant ethnic strain in all but four of the nations of Central and South America is Indian. Indians have shaped the study of anthropology, linguistics, and archaeology, particularly in America, and have contributed to thought in psychology, sociology, law, political theory, and education. They taught us progressive, non-authoritarian ways of rearing and teaching children.[21]

CULTURAL CHALLENGE AND INDIVIDUAL RESPONSE

It is a trap to measure the worth of any people by the degree to which they have successfully participated as individuals in a rival culture. Because Indians are few in number and have lived a largely separate life, they cannot point to a large number of such persons. In athletics, however, fame came to Jim Thorpe, Louis Tewanima, Don Eagle, and Charles Albert Bender. In military service, there are Brig. Gen. Eli S. Parker (who wrote the surrender terms at Appomattox), Maj. Gen. Clarence Tinker, and Rear Admiral Joseph Clark. Indians can point with pride to artists Brummet Echohawk and Beatien Yazz, ballerinas Maria and Marjorie Tallchief, humorist Will Rogers, actor Jay Silverheels (Tonto of the Lone Ranger), William Keeler, executive vice-president of the Phillips Petroleum Corporation, present Indian commissioner Robert Bennett, and Congressman Ben Reifel.[22] Vice-president Charles Curtis boasted of his Indian inheritance.

Nowhere can we find a history book that tells more than a small fragment of these things.

NOTES

1. Carl Jung, *Contributions to Analytical Psychology*, New York: Harcourt, Brace & Co., 1928, p. 139.

2. Archer B. Hulbert, *Indian Thoroughfares*, Columbus: Arthur H. Clark, 1902.

3. "The forecast is for more and more Indian influence on fashion." Tony Minor, broadcast, WNUS, Jan. 27, 1968. The entire "Feminique" section of the *Chicago Tribune*, Oct. 2, 1967, was devoted to Indian influence on fashions, jewelry, and home decoration.

4. A. Hyatt Verrill and Otis W. Barrett, *Foods America Gave the World*, Boston: C. C. Page, 1937. Yeffe Kimball and Jean Anderson, *The Art of American Indian Cooking*, Garden City, N.Y.: Doubleday, 1965.

5. Albert Keiser, *The Indian in American Literature*, New York: Oxford University Press, 1933.

6. Gilbert Chase, *America's Music*, New York: McGraw-Hill, 1955, *passim*.

7. John Burchard and Albert Bush-Brown, *The Architecture of America*, Boston: Little, Brown, 1961, pp. 57, 236, 351–52.

8. *Tepee* and *wigwam* are the Dakota and Algonquian terms, respectively, for a dwelling. In English, the first term properly belongs to the skin or canvas tents of the Plains tribes.

9. Frank Lloyd Wright, *Writings and Buildings*, New York: Meridian Books, 1960, p. 22.

10. Marian Gridley, *America's Indian Statues*, Chicago: The Amerindian, 1966.

11. Allan A. MacFarlan, *Book of American Indian Games*, New York: Association Press, 1960.

12. Robin Richman, "Rediscovery of the Red Man," *Life* (Dec. 1, 1967), 52–71.

13. Constance Rourke, *The Roots of American Culture*, New York: Harcourt Brace, 1942, pp. 60–74.

14. Mitford Mathews, *Dictionary of Americanisms*, Vol. I, Chicago: University of Chicago Press, 1951, 866–80; A. F. Chamberlain, "Memorials of the 'Indian'," *Journal of American Folk-Lore*, **15**, 17 (April–June 1902), 107–16; *idem*, "Algonkian Words in American English," *ibid.*, **15**, 19 (October–December, 1902), 240–67.

15. H. L. Mencken, *The American Language*, New York: Alfred A. Knopf, 1947, p. 528.

16. Jay's treaty with Great Britain, 1794; Pinckney's treaty with Spain, 1795; Treaty of Ghent, 1814; Treaty of Guadalupe Hidalgo, 1848; Alaska Purchase Treaty, 1867.

17. Bureau of Indian Affairs, Indian Claims Commission, Indian Arts and Crafts Board, U.S. Public Health Service, Volunteers in Service to America. On laws and treaties, see Charles Kappler, ed., *Indian Affairs, Laws and Treaties*, 4 vols., Washington, D.C.: Government Printing Office, 1903–29.

18. "It would be a very strange thing, if *Six Nations* of ignorant savages should be capable of forming a scheme for such a union, and be able to execute it in such a manner, as that it has subsisted for ages, and appears indissoluble; and yet that a like union should be impracticable for ten or a dozen *English* colonies, to whom it is more necessary and must be more advantageous, and who cannot be supposed to want an equal understanding of their interests." Franklin to Mr. Parker, March 20, 1751, in John Bigelow, ed., *The Complete Works of Benjamin Franklin*, New York: G. P. Putnam's Sons, Vol. II, 1887, p. 219.

19. Felix Cohen, "Americanizing the White Man," *The American Scholar*, **21**, 2 (Spring 1952), 179–80.
20. Both verses from "We Put the Feathers on," in R. P. Tristam Coffin, *Primer for America*, New York: Macmillan, 1943, pp. 54–55.
21. Wayne Dennis, *The Hopi Child*, New York: John Wiley & Sons, 1965; Robert J. Havighurst and Bernice Neugarten, *American Indian and White Children*, Chicago: University of Chicago Press, 1955.
22. Marian Gridley, *Indians of Today*, 3rd Ed., Chicago: Indian Council Fire, 1960.

THE MEXICAN-AMERICAN IN CHILDREN'S LITERATURE

Gloria T. Blatt

In recent months a surprised nation has witnessed an uprising of rural Mexican-American workers and a union-organized strike by Mexican-American farm workers. For the first time, our country has been forced to face a new and unpleasant fact; Mexican-Americans are troubled with some of the same problems as Negro-Americans. Like the latter, they demand improved social conditions.

According to Helen Rowan, writing in June, 1967, *Atlantic*,[1] these problems of the Mexican-Americans have not become general knowledge for a number of reasons. Mexicans entering the United States did not come in large numbers; no war was ever fought over them (only over their land); discrimination against them is spotty. In addition, the group has wielded little political power.

DISCRIMINATION IN THE SCHOOLS

Whatever the reasons, according to Miss Rowan, many Americans share an inaccurate picture of Mexican-Americans. Often they are described as rural workers, wetbacks (people who cross the border illegally), a group without goals for advancement, particularly through education. The truth, states

Gloria T. Blatt, "The Mexican-American in Children's Literature," *Elementary English*, **45** (April 1968), 446–451. Reprinted with permission of the National Council of Teachers of English and Gloria T. Blatt.

Miss Rowan, is another matter. More than eighty percent of all Mexican-Americans live and work in cities where they perform unskilled jobs. Most are vitally interested in education for their youngsters. This, they find many times, is an unobtainable objective because of prejudice in the schools. Such an accusation is a very serious one. Bars to education cannot be tolerated. People dealing directly with Mexican-American boys and girls would do well to examine the school situation carefully. Mexican-Americans, however, are largely found in the Southwestern United States with only small numbers scattered elsewhere. Thus, many teachers do not come into direct contact with them and would plead innocent to Miss Rowan's charge. If they do not discriminate directly, is it possible that some teach their students prejudice in some subtle, indirect fashion?

Attitudes can be learned many ways, through chance remarks in class, through verbal abuse, through incorrect historical information, to mention only a few. Perhaps one of the most important is through literature, long considered most effective in learning new attitudes.[2] Could we be teaching prejudice through the children's literature on the shelves in our school libraries today?

CHILDREN'S BOOKS ABOUT MEXICAN-AMERICANS

To test this question, the writer first searched several special subject booklists for titles of children's books with Mexican-American themes. As a comparison, the same bibliographies were searched for books with Negro-American themes. Nine dealt with Mexican-American while seventy-eight treated Negro subjects. It would appear from these figures that children are learning very little about Americans of Mexican descent.

Next, thirty-two children's books dealing with Mexican and Mexican-American life were found and read for information and attitudes expressed. Both settings were used because very few books dealing with Mexican-American life could be found. In addition, from the cultural point of view the two groups are essentially the same. Finally, the writer hoped (without success) to separate negative attitudes directed toward immigrant groups from those directed toward Mexicans in general.

FACTS ABOUT MEXICANS AND MEXICAN-AMERICANS

Cultural information was gathered from *Pedro Martinez*[3] and *Children of Sanchez*,[4] both anthropological studies by Oscar Lewis. Another source that was used to gather information about this cultural group was Arthur Rubel's study of Mexican-American life, *Across the Tracks*.[5] This latter source was used to obtain facts about the group in the United States.

Oscar Lewis suggested that while there has been a marked economic improvement since the revolution, the majority of Mexicans are still poverty-stricken and over forty percent are illiterate. In the cities, because of crowded housing, people tend to be gregarious. In the country the Mexicans are often suspicious of outsiders. Particularly in urban settings there is a high incidence of alcoholism and a great deal of physical violence. There are many consensual marriages, most of which are begun and terminated freely. The resulting truncated family is mother-oriented. Men must prove their virility, *machismo*, in a number of ways, for instance, by authoritarian attitudes in the family. Women often react with a martyr complex. This situation has its effect on the children who are not given a sheltered childhood. Mexican children are frequently set to work early; less than half get an education of any kind.

On the American scene, Professor Rubel also found authoritarian parental attitudes, particularly among the men. However, while young people in Mexiquito (the area studied) spoke of their fathers as harsh, the author noted that the men were actually gentle with their families. He concluded that the old myth of authoritarianism lingered, but practices in the United States are gradually changing.

The author found some upwardly mobile families among the group studied, but he noted that the largest number are farm laborers or unskilled workers earning marginal incomes. The great majority are not well educated; a sizable number are illiterate, but increasing numbers stay in school until the sixth grade. Youngsters often meet with opposition from the schools and from their families who look on them as deserters to the Anglos, a point which suggests a story somewhat different from that of Miss Rowan.

CRITERIA FOR ANALYZING ATTITUDES

In addition to gathering facts about the Mexicans as a cultural group, the writer used some specific criteria, namely those originally suggested by Charlamae Rollins for evaluating literature about Negro Americans.

1. The characters should seem real.
2. Attitudes should be the ones we want people to have.
3. Dialects should not be overdrawn.
4. A modern story should not have nostalgia for the past.
5. Illustrations should be kindly.
6. The books should be free of derisive names.
7. The books should have literary merit.[6]

One item more was included in the list of criteria. In the opinion of the writer, too many children's books equate the customs of people with the festivals celebrated by the group. Charming as they are, these holidays do not constitute the entire cultural scene. The youngster exposed to an unrelieved diet of fiestas develops an unrealistic picture of life. *Books should therefore contain more than picturesque holidays peculiar to the group.* Those that did not were to be noted, even though the festivals were accurately depicted.

IS THE CULTURAL INFORMATION CORRECT?

In very nearly every one of the thirty-two children's books studied, Mexican and Mexican-American cultures are realistically pictured. In *My Name Is Pablo*, for instance, the life of a typical Mexican child is faithfully depicted, including the poverty of his family, the work he does to help his needy family, his stoical attitude toward a harsh world. He works every day as a shoe black while dodging the police because he has no license for his business. In the most authoritarian fashion his father had decided that Pablo's earnings would go for a donkey and not for the license. Inevitably, the boy is caught and slapped into a reformatory reminiscent of a Dickensian prison. There he remains, apparently not missed by his family, until he becomes seriously ill. In spite of all the travail, the warmth and friendliness of the Mexicans are clearly delineated. The reader readily believes Pablo when he says, "My house is yours."

Across the Tracks is another book which vividly pictures social problems. Betty Ochoa, a middle class Mexican-American, is the first of her group to run for high school office. She wins the contest even though some unknown vandal scrawls "spic" across her election posters. The entire school, ashamed of the incident, rallies around her. The prejudices of the majority, the mixed feelings of the minority are fully developed here.

Another poignantly told tale is *Citizen Pablo*, a story of life among migrant workers in the United States. Here, as in *My Name Is Pablo*, the author tells the unadorned truth, including some unpleasant facts not ordinarily found in children's books. Pablo's little sister, Rosa, falls seriously ill with a cough. The family has a choice. They can take her back to their warm, clean adobe house in Mexico where they had been starving, thanks to the drought. Or they can remain, barely sheltered, in a migrant worker's shanty, where they can earn money for food. They stay and Rosa dies. The reader is moved by the poor conditions of migrant life and by the sympathetic portrayal of Pablo and his family.

In *Magic Maize* still another cultural fact is faithfully depicted. Here the Indian's suspicion of the white man, and in fact, all outsiders, is used in the setting. Fabian's father will not permit modern farming methods or products to be used on his land, for they come from the *gringos*. Only when the magic maize saves him from starvation does he accept the white man's offering.

In general, most books that were read for this study do present an accurate picture, complete within a cultural setting. While the stories intended for the youngest sometimes lack social depth, none of them depend totally on fiestas for national flavor. *The Fabulous Firework Family*, for instance, deals with a festival and at the same time contains information on making fireworks in Mexico. In *Pedro, the Angel of Olvera Street*, the reader learns about Christmas as celebrated in Mexico, at the same time becoming acquainted with a uniquely Mexican street in Los Angeles.

Many authors do more than present accurate cultural pictures, for they also handle their characters with integrity and sensitivity. Hidalgo in *Hidalgo and the Gringo Train* is drawn with considerable understanding of human beings in general and of children in particular. Even adults have no difficulty identifying themselves with Hidalgo who wants very much to learn to read an English copy of *Robinson Crusoe* which he found near the *gringo* train. Accurate cultural background, poverty, and authoritarian family patterns are clearly delineated. At the same time the reader can share Hidalgo's feelings, his boredom as a sheepherder, his wonder at the *gringos* who flash by on the luxury train, his immense curiosity about the world beyond his father's stony land.

Even Ceci in Marie Hall Ets' *Nine Days to Christmas*, a book meant for the youngest, has the aura of reality about her. Her world is exactly the right size for a preschooler, made up largely of home, family garden, small shopping trips. Young children can wholeheartedly enter her world even though the setting is in another country.

Partly because of the warmth with which they are handled, never, in the opinion of this writer, are the characters stereotyped. David Gast, writing in the January 1967 *Elementary English*,[7] is of another opinion. He suggests that too many writers point out that Mexicans are dark, Catholic, uninterested in education, rural in their surroundings. Young readers might, according to him, learn to lump Mexicans into convenient stereotypes after reading these books.

While this writer found Mr. Gast's information correct, the characters were never found lacking in individuality and human dignity. Hidalgo in *Hidalgo and the Gringo Train*, for instance, is identified as a dark, little boy living in the country and as a Catholic. At the same time, he is pictured as an intensely curious boy, eager to learn to read a book which has captured his imagination. While Miguel in *And Now Miguel* also fits Mr. Gast's pattern, the boy reveals special qualities entirely his own, a certain wonder about himself, an eagerness to grow into responsibility. It seems, then, that Mr. Gast confuses stereotype and accurate cultural information.

ATTITUDES EXPRESSED IN THE BOOKS

These and the other books satisfy Miss Rollins' criteria in still another way. They present the information so that the reader learns desirable attitudes about Mexicans and Mexican-Americans. Pablo in *My Name Is Pablo* is made to appear the victim of circumstances rather than of thoughtless parents. Fabian in *Magic Maize* has to work because his father is ill. They worry about his welfare, but the circumstances are beyond their control. In only one book is a Mexican painted in an evil light without mitigating circumstances. Benito's uncle in *Benito* takes advantage of his ward, working him long hours with a minimal amount of care, providing him with no opportunities including the one the boy wanted most, the opportunity to paint. But even here the uncle's behavior is explained when he says that work is the only way for Mexicans to succeed in a harsh world.

Only once in all the books dealing with this group were derisive names used, in *Across the Tracks*, where Betty is called a "spic." The use of the name, however, is treated by the authors as if it were a catastrophe, making the reader understand very well the corrosive effect of such language.

Dialect is handled in an equally friendly fashion. Some authors like Marie Hall Ets in *Nine Days to Christmas* choose to use no dialect at all. Others use just enough to suggest a Spanish accent. Only once did dialect treatment appear awkwardly handled. In *Bright Summer*, the mother speaks with an accent that only the most naive could believe. In this case the trouble lies in poor writing rather than the malicious intent which often is attributed to some writers using Negro dialect.

The same is true of illustrations. A wide variety of styles are used varying all the way from realistic line drawings to highly stylized four color pictures suggestive of Mexican folk art. All are, without exception, positive in nature.

Finally, even the quality of the books seems, in this writer's opinion, high. While only a few books, like *My Name Is Pablo* and *And Now Miguel* might be considered outstanding children's literature, the great majority have literary merit. As Mr. Gast suggests,[8] Mexicans and Mexican-Americans are better treated in children's literature than they are in American text books, where they are often passed over lightly or forgotten altogether.

CONCLUSION

It appears, then, that writers of children's literature are not guilty of teaching prejudiced attitudes about Mexican-Americans. Miss Rowan may be correct in accusing the schools of prejudice; but at least the children's literature, one very important educational aid, is fair in its treatment of this cultural group. Nowhere in the twenty-nine books read were anti-Mexican-American ideas suggested. The writers commit only one "sin," the sin of omission. They seem more aware of problems south of the border than they are of similar ones in our country. They would do us all service by writing more books about Mexican-Americans in the United States.

NOTES

1. Helen Rowan, "A Minority Nobody Knows," *Atlantic,* **219** (June 1967), 47–52.

2. Louise Rosenblatt, *Literature as Exploration*, New York: Appleton-Century, 1938.

3. Oscar Lewis, *Pedro Martinez, A Mexican Peasant and His Family*, New York: Random House, 1964.

4. Oscar Lewis, *The Children of Sanchez, Autobiography of a Mexican Family*, New York: Random House, 1961.

5. Arthur Rubel, *Across the Tracks*, Austin: University of Texas Press, 1966.

6. Charlamae Rollins, *We Build Together*, Urbana, Ill.: National Council of Teachers of English, 1948.

7. David Gast, "Minority Groups in Children's Literature," *Elementary English*, **44** (January 1967), 12.

8. Gast, "Minority Groups," p. 12.

CHILDREN'S BOOKS ABOUT MEXICAN-AMERICANS

1. Bannon, Laura, *Hat for a Hero*, New York: Junior Literary Guild and Whitman, 1954.

2. ——, *Manuela's Birthday*, Chicago: Whitman, 1948.

3. Behn, Harry, *The Two Uncles of Pablo*, New York: Harcourt Brace, 1959.

4. Benelle, H. Robinson, *Citizen Pablo*, New York: John Day, 1959.

5. Buff, Mary and Conrad, *Magic Maize*, Boston: Houghton Mifflin, 1953.

6. Bulla, Clyde, *Benito*, New York: Crowell, 1961.

7. Clark, Ann Nolan, *Paco's Miracle*, New York: Farrar, Straus and Cudahy, 1956.

8. Ets, Marie Hall, and Aurora Labastida, *Nine Days to Christmas*, New York: Viking, 1959.

9. Flora, James, *The Fabulous Firework Family*, New York: Harcourt Brace, 1955.

10. Forsee, Aylesa, *Too Much Dog*, Philadelphia: Lippincott, 1957.

11. Gates, Doris, *Blue Willow*, New York: Viking, 1948.

12. Garrett, Helen, *Angelo the Naughty One*, New York: Viking, 1944.

13. Garthwaite, Marion, *Mario, A Mexican Boy's Adventure*, New York: Doubleday, 1960.

14. Griffiths, Faljean, *Hidalgo and the Gringo Train*, New York: Dutton, 1958.

15. Hader, Berta and Elmer, *The Story of Pancho and the Bull with the Crooked Tail*, New York: Macmillan, 1942.

16. Johnson, A. and E., *The Rescued Heart*, New York: Harper, 1961.

17. Kirn, Ann, *Two Pesos for Catalina*, Chicago: Rand-McNally, 1962.

18. Krumgold, Joseph, *And Now Miguel*, New York: Crowell, 1953.

19. Morrow, Elizabeth, *The Painted Pig*, New York: Alfred A. Knopf, 1930.

20. Parish, Helen Rand, *Our Lady of Guadalupe*, New York: Viking, 1955.

21. Politi, Leo, *Pedro, the Angel of Olvera Street*, New York: Scribners, 1946.

22. ——, *Juanita*, New York: Scribners, 1948.

23. ——, *Song of the Swallows*, New York: Scribners, 1949.

24. Rhoads, Dorothy M., *The Corn Grows Ripe*, New York: Viking, 1956.

25. Ritchie, Barbara, *Ramon Makes a Trade*, Berkeley: Parnassus Press, 1959.

26. Rydberg, Ernie, *Bright Summer*, New York: Longmans, 1953.

27. Sawyer, Ruth, *The Least One*, New York: Viking, 1941.

28. Simon, Charlie Mae, *Popo's Miracle*, New York: Dutton, 1938.

29. Sommerfelt, A., *My Name Is Pablo*, New York: Criterion, 1966.

30. Tarshis, Elizabeth, *The Village That Learned to Read*, Boston: Houghton Mifflin, 1941.

31. Yomans, Ben, *Roberto, the Mexican Boy*, Chicago: Whitman, 1947.

32. Young, Bob and Jan, *Across the Tracks*, New York: Messner, 1958.

REFERENCES

1. Chase, Judith Wragg, *Books to Build World Friendship*, Dobbs Ferry: Oceana Publications, 1964.

2. Crosby, Muriel Estelle, *Reading Ladders for Human Relations*, Washington, D.C., American Council on Education, 1963.

3. Eakin, Mary K., *Good Books for Children*, Chicago: University of Chicago Press, 1959.

4. Fryatt, Norma R., *A Horn Book Sampler*, Boston: Horn Book, 1959.

5. Gast, David, "Minority Groups in Children's Literature," *Elementary English*, **44** (January 1967), 12–23.

6. Lewis, Oscar, *Pedro Martinez: A Mexican Peasant and His Family*, New York: Random House, 1964.

7. ——, *The Children of Sanchez: Autobiography of a Mexican Family*, New York: Random House, 1961.

8. Rollins, Charlamae, *We Build Together*, Urbana, Ill.: National Council of Teachers of English, 1948.

9. Rosenblatt, Louise, *Literature as Exploration*, New York: Appleton-Century, 1938.

10. Rubel, Arthur, *Across the Tracks*, Austin: University of Texas Press, 1966.

11. Shor, Rachel, and Estelle A. Fidell, *Children's Catalogue*, New York: Wilson Co., 1966.

STUDY QUESTIONS

1. What kinds of errors did the textbooks studied by the Michigan Department of Education contain? How might a classroom teacher use "distorted" textbooks to teach important lessons in historiography?

2. What can a classroom teacher do to supplement textbooks that present minority groups in an unfavorable light?

3. In the final analysis, are publishers or teachers more responsible for accurate and challenging teaching materials? Why?

4. How and why do some of Banks' conclusions differ from those of the Michigan Department of Education? How are they similar?

5. What myths about American Indians does Vogel attempt to shatter? What contributions have American Indians made to our society? How might a teacher use information on these contributions to help Indian children develop more positive self-images?

6. In what ways have textbook authors treated blacks and Indians similarly? Differently? Why are there important differences in the ways that authors depict various ethnic groups?

7. Blatt maintains that Mexican-Americans are treated fairly in children's books and that authors (like Gast) who claim that minority groups are stereotyped in books confuse *stereotypes* with *accurate cultural information*. How can we distinguish between cultural information and stereotypes? Why is the distinction important?

SUGGESTED READINGS

Abramowitz, Jack, "Textbooks and Negro History," *Social Education*, **33**, 306–309, 1969

Banks, James A., "The Need For Positive Racial Attitudes in Textbooks," in

Robert L. Green (Editor), *Racial Crisis In American Education*. Chicago: Follett Educational Corporation, 1969

Bennett, Lerone, Jr., "Reading, 'Riting', and Racism," *Ebony*, March 1967

Carpenter, Marie E., *The Treatment of the Negro in American History School Textbooks*. Menasha, Wisconsin: George Banta Publishing Company, 1941

Deane, Paul C., "The Persistence of Uncle Tom: An Examination of the Image of the Negro in Children's Fiction Series," *Journal of Negro Education*, 37, 140–145, 1968

Department of Public Instruction, *A Report on the Treatment of Minorities in American History Textbooks*. Lansing, Michigan: Michigan Department of Education, 1968

Franklin, John Hope, "Rediscovering Black History: A Historical Roundup," *New York Times Book Review*, September 8, 1968

Gast, David K., "Minorities in Children's Literature," *Elementary English*, 44, 12–23, 1967

Klineberg, Otto, "Life Is Fun In A Smiling, Fair Skinned World," *Saturday Review*, February 16, 1963

Larrick, Nancy, "The All-White World of Children's Books," *Saturday Review*, 48, 63–65ff, 1965

Marcus, Lloyd, *The Treatment of Minorities in American History Textbooks*. New York: Anti-Defamation League, 1961

McPherson, James, "The 'Saga' of Slavery: Setting the Textbooks Straight," *Changing Education*, 1, 26–28, ff.33, 1967

Sahli, J. R., "Slavery Issue in Early Geography Textbooks," *History of Education Quarterly*, 3, 153–158, 1963

Sloan, Irving, *The Negro in Modern History Textbooks*. Chicago: American Federation of Teachers, AFL-CIO, 1966

PART TWO
TEACHING
STRATEGIES

The writers in Part One illuminated the negative racial attitudes and deflated self-images typical of culturally different children. They stressed the need for a curriculum that will help them clarify their racial attitudes, improve their self-concepts, and strive to better their social condition. They noted that before a teacher can structure such a curriculum, he must modify and examine his attitudes toward cultures different from his own, as well as set high expectations for low-achieving students. Part One also emphasized the need for teaching materials that adequately reflect the contributions of minority groups to American society and illuminated the problems these groups confront.

Once equipped with both appropriate attitudes and multiethnic teaching materials, the teacher must devise teaching methods that will help his students attain the objectives he has set for them. The readings in this section present promising teaching strategies—many described by creative urban classroom teachers—which will help the teacher to formulate and employ his own instructional techniques for effectively working with culturally alienated children.

CHAPTER 6
DEVELOPING INQUIRY AND
PROBLEM SOLVING SKILLS

The paucity of literature on teaching social studies to culturally different children indicates that social studies educators, like all others, have only recently shown a substantial interest in the education of lower-class and minority group children. In the past, social studies educators have been primarily concerned with devising teaching strategies to help middle-class white children learn more effectively. However, as Susan Jacoby argues in the first selection in this chapter, the current social studies curriculum is as irrelevant to the needs of middle-class white pupils of suburbia as it is to those of the poor and alienated children who live in our cities. Thus, although curriculum reform is especially needed for culturally different children, it is important that all children be exposed to a more realistic and challenging curriculum than that which is typically found in our public schools today.

As was pointed out in Part One, minority group children are typically poor, alienated, and full of self-hate and deep feelings of helplessness. Every day black Americans and members of other minority groups are confronted with blatant symbols of their impotence and inability to instigate social change—change that will enable them to more actively influence the major decisions which affect their lives and futures. The assassination of charismatic black leaders like Malcolm X and Martin Luther King, Jr. only heightened the black man's sense of helplessness and alienation. The recent verdict of an all-white jury freeing a white policeman accused of killing a black teenager at the Algiers Motel during the 1967 Detroit riots was interpreted by the black community as an indication of its powerlessness. American Indians, Mexican-Americans, and Puerto-Rican Americans, who experience many of the same indignities, have also developed intense feelings of helplessness and alienation. Unlike black Americans, however, these groups have not yet formed many strong organizations like the NAACP and SCLC, and comparatively few charismatic leaders have emerged from their ranks to articulate their discontent and aspirations.

If *basic institutional* changes are to occur in our society (as opposed to *token* changes such as those that occurred in response to the black revolt in the 1960's), we must, as David Epperson suggests in this chapter, make social critics of culturally different children. We believe with Herbert Schueler (Chapter 4) that "... education for the disadvantaged should not nurture conformity but *discontent* with the disadvantaged state, and develop the *power* and the *will* to rise beyond it" (emphases added).

In addition to making poor children both discontented with and aware of the immorality of their social condition, we must help them devise strategies to change it. We should help them formulate effective ways to attain political and economic *power*, which is absolutely necessary if they are to improve their situation. Despite the token gains that accrued from Martin Luther King's civil disobedience tactics, the farcical Poor People's Campaign illuminated the gross limitations of moral persuasion in instigating basic societal reform. Perhaps more than any other educators social studies teachers bear the major responsibility for equipping poor children with the skills they need to devise effective strategies, gain power, and help build the truly multiracial and multicultural society to which we are verbally committed.

Before culturally different children can effect societal change, they must acquire inquiry and problem-solving skills. These skills will enable them to identify and articulate significant social problems, formulate meaningful hypotheses, gather pertinent data, and reach tentative conclusions which can guide action but which are also subject to constant *reconstruction*, as Bernice Goldmark notes in this chapter.

The readings in this chapter illuminate the urgent need to help culturally different children become social critics and problem solvers. The contributors urge teachers to create a relevant social studies program by exposing children to the harsh and urgent social problems of *race*, *class*, and *power* that confront them.

SLUM AND SUBURB:
THE NEGLECTED REALITY

Susan Lynn Jacoby

Traditional American education, it is generally conceded, has failed to meet the needs of deprived children who live in the nation's teeming urban ghettos. That failure is due in no small measure to the fact that the average school curriculum has virtually no relationship to the realities of life in a city slum; indeed, it has little relationship to the ferment that characterizes American life at all social levels. Peter Schrag, associate education editor of *Saturday Review*, has written of the Boston school system a perceptive study in which he indicts traditional curricula (and curriculum planners) for dealing "in clichés, in pieties, and in the tired liturgy of obsolete Americanisms which. . . by their nature—and by their intent, minimize the negative and unpleasant in American life—they exclude the possibilities of qualification and complexity, and the richness, the dynamic energy of controversy and ambiguity."[1]

This indictment is particularly damning when applied to the broad field of social studies, which by definition is the examination of human complexity, diversity, and controversy—both past and present. The neglected areas in the homogenized history, geography, and civics courses taught in most American elementary and secondary schools are legion. The condition of the Negro, the reality of poverty, the sharp class distinctions of modern society, the increasing demands of dispossessed citizens for the kind of influence over their government that the wealthy have always held—these are only a few of the realities of American life that are daily ignored in many classrooms throughout the country.

It should be emphasized that these subjects are as neglected in the social studies curricula of white suburban schools as they are in the urban Negro ghetto schools. With the exception of a minority of courageous, perceptive teachers and an even smaller minority of innovative school systems, social studies courses seem dedicated to the proposition that to suggest the existence of anything other than the best of all possible worlds would be the equivalent of telling a dirty joke in a sex education class. This approach fails with slum children for the obvious reason that they have only to look out the classroom windows at the uncollected garbage, hopeless old men, and angry

Susan Lynn Jacoby, "Slum and Suburb: The Neglected Reality." Dale L. Brubaker, Ed., *Social Studies in a Mass Society*, Scranton, Pa.: International Textbook Company, 1969, pp. 7-17. Reprinted with permission of the author and publisher.

young men of the ghetto streets to realize that the shiny world the teacher talks about is at best a fiction, at worst a lie. Thus, the conventional social studies curriculum fails the urban child because it has no meaning in terms of his existence. The same curriculum fails the suburban child for the opposite reason: it does not acquaint him with anything outside of his own existence. The latter type of failure is graphically illustrated in *The Shortchanged Children of Suburbia*, a lengthy study conducted by a research team from Teachers College, Columbia University.

In one of the study's experiments, fifth-graders in a wealthy suburb of New York City were shown a picture of three poor white children. The youngsters in the picture were leaning against a fence, their hair stringy and dirty, their clothing ragged. Nearly all of the suburban students stoutly maintained that the children in the picture could not possibly be Americans. "You can tell by looking at them," said one fifth-grader. "No white children in our country would look like these three."[2] The teachers were astonished that their students could display such ignorance, even though they admitted that poverty was a subject rarely touched upon in the classroom. In another experiment in the same school system, children were shown a picture of a Negro boy playing with a white boy and asked which one they would choose for a friend. Nearly all picked the white boy. One second-grader explained he had chosen the white boy "because he didn't carry a knife."[3] (No knives were shown in the picture, of course.)

The Columbia study elicited an equally disturbing response from a Harlem teacher who asked his students to write a paper on their feeling about white people. Wrote one student: "White people says we Negroes need to take a bath. I saw a white man with nothing on in the window. White people want us to do all the dirty work. They don't want Negroes to have any fun." Said another: "Whites have money and jewelry and diamonds and pearl bracelets and diamond earrings."[4] The responses of the Harlem students suggest that social studies educators, despite their white, middle-class orientation, conventional social studies curricula, and teaching methods, not only are failing to grapple with the realities of slum life but are failing to convey an accurate picture of middle-class America. The Harlem children have obviously never heard of thousands of white, middle-class Americans who declare bankruptcy each year (not to mention all of the white women who have never owned a pair of diamond earrings).

The Columbia study dealt with the entire school curriculum and its effect on students; however, many of its recommendations were concerned with social studies instruction as the logical vehicle for teaching elementary school children about human differences. The responsibility for communicating a sense of what Schrag calls "the richness, the dynamic energy of controversy and ambiguity" falls even more heavily on the high school social studies teacher as a result of departmentalization at the secondary level.

Before considering what might be done to improve social studies instruction, it is necessary to understand how and why traditional social studies curricula have neglected significant areas of human experience. Ignorance and timidity have always been the major causes of such neglect. Never were they more apparent than in the sometimes uniformed, sometimes unconscionable failure of social studies educators to teach their students about the history and culture of black Americans. Social studies educators—indeed the entire educational profession—are now attempting to make amends for that failure. The history of this transition has significant implications for every neglected area in the social studies.

In a lengthy article on traditional textbooks, one Negro magazine uses the not-so-facetious title of "Reading, 'Riting and Racism."[5] However, the sins of the textbook publishers—and the classroom teachers who used their materials—were generally those of omission rather than commission. There were simply no references to Negroes in textbooks published before the civil rights revolution of the early 1960's other than an occasional paragraph on the "happy darkies" who supposedly inhabited ante-bellum society in the South. No other ethnic group was as summarily ignored in the history books for so long a period of time. The Jewish and Italian and Chinese immigrants may have been called *kikes* and *wops* and *chinks* on the street, but in their texts they could read something about the contributions of their people to world history and culture (although the publishers tended to ignore the role of all minority groups in shaping the development of the United States).

In any case, the textbook publishers are now making a major effort to correct their past omissions in the area of Negro history. It does not speak well for social studies educators that the initial change in texts was spurred by demands from civil rights groups rather than from the educational profession. A secondary social studies supervisor in a highly regarded school system once remarked that the publishers develop textbooks to please every superintendent from Augusta, Me., to Augusta, Ga. He might also have noted that educators in Maine are just as responsible for the problem as the publishers if they accept the Georgia versions without quibbling. Publishers respond with surprising speed to new demands from school systems; if the educators had asked for a thorough treatment of Negro history in textbooks, the change would undoubtedly have come earlier. During the past two years, several state legislatures have passed laws requiring the teaching of Negro history. This legislation has been supported by organizations of professional educators, including social studies teachers, but has not been initiated by them. In fairness, it must be noted that the adoption of "multi-ethnic" textbooks in large cities has been given a strong push by militant teacher unions demanding a greater voice in curriculum planning. In Detroit, a contract between the public school system and its teachers spells out the expansion of Negro history instruction as one of the terms of the agreement.

There is some evidence indicating that Negro history may be in danger of the same type of homogenization that has turned the rest of American history into a bland gruel for elementary and secondary school consumption. Every child with a textbook published after 1965 is likely to learn that Crispus Attucks, a Negro, was the first soldier to die in the Revolutionary War and that a Negro doctor named Charles Drew was the developer of blood plasma. All textbooks published after 1967 will undoubtedly record that Thurgood Marshall was the first Negro appointed to the Supreme Court. But will the same textbooks record the words of Stokely Carmichael in the steaming summer ghettos? Will the riots of Harlem and Watts receive more careful attention than uprisings of workers in the nineteenth century or earlier racial disturbances in the twentieth century? Will the agony of the Reverend Martin Luther King, Jr. over Vietnam be explored, or will the textbooks simply record that he won the Nobel Peace Prize? In viewing the past record of textbook publishers and social studies educators, it would be foolish to conclude that a new era of sophistication is in the offing simply because a few black faces have been accorded their rightful places in the history books.

In many cases, social studies educators smooth over reality with flag-waving clichés because they have too little confidence in the ability of their students to perceive complexity. Subjects such as the structure of the Negro family are often assumed to be beyond the comprehension of secondary students—not to mention elementary school children. On the basis of my experience as an observer in elementary and secondary schools, I regard this as a false assumption. I have watched a fourth grade teacher in a Washington, D.C., slum school conduct a superb discussion of the effects of slavery on the Negro family. The children—all of them classified as "slow learners"—were quite capable of understanding how and why the families of slaves were broken up in the ante-bellum South. As they advance in school, these youngsters will be just as capable of comprehending the relationship between what happened to slaves in the eighteenth and nineteenth centuries and the state of many fatherless Negro families in urban ghettos today. However, the children may not have the good fortune to encounter another teacher with enough sensitivity and courage to bring such a delicate subject into the classroom.

In general, textbook publishers, classroom teachers, and administrators share the same assumptions about the unsuitability of "unpleasant" subjects for young students. One representative of a major publishing company had this to say when I questioned him about the omission of a realistic discussion of slavery in his company's widely used fifth grade American history text: "We think the function of a student's first history text is to build patriotism, not to tell all of the nasty facts of our history. This is better for an older child." The publisher's attitude is based on two highly debatable assumptions—that the primary function of an American history course is to build patriotism and that a child is likely to be less patriotic if he learns anything about the less glorious chapters of the nation's development. Interestingly enough, the popular fifth grade history book with only a cursory treatment of slavery is used in Washington, D.C., and several other large cities for "slow readers" in eighth- and ninth-grade classes. One can only imagine the boredom with which a tough fourteen year old from a city ghetto—who is usually older in experience than a middle-class college student—greets a history book that would not challenge a bright ten year old.

The combination of ignorance and timidity that has hampered inquiring, objective social studies education is apparent in both city and suburb. The principal of Washington's all-Negro Hine Junior High School objected strongly last winter when an eighth-grader wrote a composition—later published in the city's newspapers—about how it feels to be a Negro when white people make fun of you. "You walk down the street to hear a white person call you names," wrote the student. "We will rise against our time to prove to people that we are dying to show that we are human beings, and not just some people from another world." Principal John C. Hoffman said, "I don't approve of that sort of thing. It can only cause bad feelings."[6] In neighboring Montgomery County, Md., which has the highest per capita income of any suburban community in the country, a former school board president attacked the idea of exchange programs with city schools. "I don't think there are great strengths to be recognized by mingling races or people from different economic groups in an artificial situation," he said. "For one thing, I think an exchange program between the District of Columbia and Montgomery County, Md., would make the poorer children discontented with what they have. You know—'the grass is always greener.' And I think the children in the suburbs are already aware that others are less fortunate. They get this when they give to collections for the needy at church and school, and through community services."[7] These types of attitudes are inevitably reflected in school curricula. However, a minority of bold school systems and teachers are demonstrating that this need not be so—that it is possible to devise a social studies curriculum related to the realities of life in both the urban and suburban sectors of the nation's sprawling metropolises.

Two high schools, one in Washington, D.C., and the other in Montgomery County, Md., have produced an outstanding, widely publicized example of how a carefully developed social studies curriculum can come to grips with problems such as race and poverty. Cardozo High School, with a 100 percent Negro enrollment, is located in the heart of an impoverished city ghetto and Walt Whitman High School is located in Montgomery's richest census tract. Women from the Cardozo area take the bus out of the city every day to work as maids in the sprawling $75,000 homes that surround Walt Whitman. The idea for an exchange program between the two schools originated in an American history class at Walt Whitman, where a young teacher named

Michaela Carberry was trying to tell her students something about the differences between education in an affluent suburb and in a city slum. When a student suggested that it might be useful for the class to visit an inner city school to view the differences firsthand, Miss Carberry pointed out that it would be difficult to learn very much through a "one-shot" visit. She discussed the problem with the head of her social studies department, who agreed that the social studies curriculum was a logical vehicle for piercing the economic, cultural, and racial isolation of the students at Walt Whitman. Miss Carberry's department head contacted the director of an unusual project at Cardozo which attempts to give college graduates with bachelor's degrees on-the-job training to enable them to meet the special needs of disadvantaged students. The idea was turned over to Bill Plitt, a former Peace Corps volunteer who was a teaching intern in the Cardozo project.

Both teachers wanted their classes to actually study American history together, and they held several meetings with committees of their students to plan a curriculum. The teachers suggested that the classes study a unit on civil rights as a joint venture, but the students felt they would learn more by beginning with slavery. The curriculum was ultimately worked out to include slavery, reconstruction, urbanization, and civil rights. The two classes studied the same material and met together once a week, alternating between Cardozo and Walt Whitman. Activities at the joint meetings were highly unorthodox and highly interesting to the students. At one session, a play on slavery was presented in which the white students from Walt Whitman took the parts of slaves and the Negro students from Cardozo took the parts of masters which led to a lively, open discussion about why the students had felt slightly uncomfortable in the reversed roles a hundred years after emancipation. Most of the students responded enthusiastically, although a few admitted they were not used to such frank talk and never would have thought it possible in an interracial class. The class eventually led to an exchange program in which the students lived at each other's houses and attended classes at each other's schools for a week. Parents were almost as enthusiastic about the program as their teenage sons and daughters. "My husband and I are from the South," said one Negro mother, "and we honestly aren't used to any kind of contact between white and colored. We know our children will live in a different kind of world and it seems right that the schools should prepare them." Commented a white father: "We're having all this fuss over open occupancy laws in the county. I'm convinced that half of the people who are doing all the shouting have never known a Negro as a friend. The schools should be making every effort through their curriculum to provide these kinds of experiences for kids."

The students' reactions are even more instructive. The crucial advantage of the program seems to have been that the students learned more about American history at the same time they were learning more about each other.

"I never could have learned as much about urban problems sitting in the classroom as I did through this program," said one suburban boy. "When I told the kids I was going down to Cardozo to spend a week, I got all the usual cracks about how all the Negro kids learn is street fighting in gym class. I've managed to educate a lot of my friends since I got back."

The Cardozo-Whitman program lasted for about six months of the 1966–67 school year and will be expanded next year to include more students. The program was neither expensive nor elaborate; its main ingredients were imagination and determination on the part of two teachers. In isolated instances around the country, other schools are embarking on equally noteworthy projects designed to bring the social studies curriculum to grips with the realities of urban life. At New Trier High School in Evanston, Ill., school officials felt they were not doing enough to broaden the experience of their affluent students despite New Trier's national reputation for academic excellence. Next year, they plan to use the city of Chicago as a laboratory for social studies classes. New Trier students will work in the city's schools, settlement houses, and playgrounds for credit in various high school courses. Rochester, N.Y., is involved in a far-reaching experiment that goes beyond social studies. A new school located in the central city will draw half of its enrollment from nearby suburbs and half from Rochester's ghetto schools. With small classes, outstanding teachers, and an enriched curriculum in every subject—particularly social studies, science, and English—the school already has a waiting list of applicants from the suburbs and the city. The Rochester experiment will be expensive, and a project of this kind obviously cannot be carried on by social studies educators alone. But programs such as those at Cardozo-Whitman and New Trier are within the reach of every imaginative social studies teacher and administrator; their outstanding characteristic is that they make use of the materials at hand. The development of a more meaningful social studies curriculum can only be achieved if teachers do make better use of the materials at hand to bring not only race and poverty but countless other meaningful aspects of modern civilization into the classroom. How many teachers, for example, would have the imagination to impress their students with a lesson on the Depression by having them present a play on how it feels to be evicted by a landlord? Poverty-stricken students in city ghettos live in their own personal depression; by using experiences from their lives, a social studies teacher can reach them when conventional history books fail. The same holds true for suburban schools. How many high school sociology teachers would suggest that their students study their own teenage class structure as a means of furthering their understanding of the communities in which they live? Social studies educators have too often been guilty of what the newspaper profession calls "Afghanistanism"—an overwillingness to comment on events in far corners of the globe and a noticeable reluctance to come to grips with problems at home. In an outstanding suburban school system in the East, a complete revamping of the social studies curriculum was precipitated by a caustic report outlining the irrelevence of social studies instruction at the elementary level. The report noted that one elementary school social studies unit was designed to instruct children in "Organizing an International Travel Bureau."[8] (The same curriculum did make some attempt to discuss nearby problems. One of the liveliest units: "Attracting Birds to Our School Grounds.")[9]

Incidents that may foster timidity in social studies teachers can occur in any community; some examples have been enumerated here. It is my opinion that the social studies educator—indeed, the entire educational profession—must lead public opinion rather than follow it in frightened, hangdog fashion. The specter of angry parents banging on the principal's door looms too large. Teachers and administrators are too often cowed by a vocal minority: in such cases, they fail to make the effort needed to "sell" imaginative programs to the majority of parents. Projects such as the Cardozo-Whitman exchange demonstrate that social studies courses can serve an educational function for the entire community and not merely for students enrolled in school. There is no magic formula for conquering timidity when it is deeply ingrained in teachers and administrators. Overcoming teacher ignorance, however, is a process that can be fostered by school systems through a series of logical steps.

One of the greatest hindrances to the development of meaningful social studies education is the dichotomy between secondary school teachers and college professors in the social sciences. In too many cases, outstanding high school social studies teachers are only marking time until they can earn their doctorates and move on to the college level. Having left the field to football coaches who for some mysterious reason are often pressed into service as civics and history teachers, they sneer at the poor preparation and naiveté of the students who come to them as freshman. This dichotomy is the result of an educational structure that was designed for a largely rural society. Local school boards, jealous of their prerogatives, are often totally indifferent to the idea of cooperation with nearby colleges. In the past, most colleges have been just as indifferent. However, educational planners are beginning to recognize that colleges and universities can no longer operate independently of public elementary and secondary schools as they did in the days when only a tiny minority of students continued their education beyond the twelfth grade. There are many outstanding examples of this recognition, but most of them are not in the field of social studies. In Ft. Lauderdale, Fla., the Nova Schools are developing an elementary and secondary curriculum in oceanography and the physical sciences. Students can continue in the same curriculum at a nearby public junior college and will eventually be able to do advanced work at Nova University, a private graduate school. Social studies educators have not embarked on this type of planning for a variety of reasons—most of them connected with the way elementary and secondary teachers are trained in schools of education.

Most high school social studies teachers do not know enough about their subject matter. I sat in one American history class this year in which a teacher was astonished when one of her students mentioned that the Mexican War was a topic of dissent in the nineteenth century just as the Vietnam war is today. This type of ignorance can be laid directly at the door of teacher training that places more emphasis on how to teach than on whether the teacher knows anything about his (or her) academic discipline. Social studies teachers at the high school level tend to ignore the fact that the subjects they teach *are*, in fact, academic disciplines. Consequently, the social studies teacher with a scholarly bent feels cut off from the intellectual life of his profession if he remains in a high school. All of this is not to say that a high school American history teacher should know as much about his subject as a college professor dealing with graduate students. It is to say, however, that his major field of study in college should have been history and not physical education. To improve elementary and secondary school social studies instruction, teachers must be oriented more toward the inductive approach that characterizes academic disciplines at the university level. One recent study of social studies curricula throughout the United States puts it succinctly: "Some years ago the Educational Policies Commission published a statement to the effect that the central purpose of American education is the development of rational thinking. Our task is to provide the means of accomplishing this goal.... We need and are getting more and better teacher training; we need and are getting better curriculum materials. However, we need and are *not* getting sufficient commitment on the part of teachers to inquiry-oriented teaching."[10] That commitment, backed up with knowledge and courage, is the only way to bring the social studies curriculum to grips with the realities of urban life. In essence, the social studies teacher must say to the child in a slum school: "This is your world. I understand it." To the suburban child, he must say: "Your world is not the only world."

NOTES

1. Peter Schrag, *Village School Downtown*, Boston: Beacon Press, 1967, p. 90.

2. Alice Miel with Edwin Kiester, Jr., *The Shortchanged Children of Suburbia*, Pamphlet No. 8, New York: Institute of Human Relations Press, 1967, p. 23.

3. *Ibid.*, p. 18.

4. Stanley J. Albro, "Letters to the Editor," *The New York Times Magazine* (April 1967), p. 21.

5. *Ebony*, **13**, 5 (March 1967), p. 130.

6. *The Washington Post*, March 4, 1967, p. B-1.

7. *The Washington Post*, Jan. 10, 1966, p. C-1.

8. *The Washington Post*, April 15, 1961, p. 31.

9. *Ibid*.

10. William D. Rader, "The Intermediate Grades," in C. Benjamin Cox and Byron G. Massialas, eds., *Social Studies in the United States: A Critical Appraisal* (New York: Harcourt, Brace & World, 1967), p. 49.

MAKING SOCIAL CRITICS
OF DISADVANTAGED CHILDREN

David C. Epperson

This is a proposal offered in the spirit of the Negro Revolt. It is made at a time when token concessions are being rendered to Negroes, Puerto Ricans, Mexican Americans, and other disadvantaged groups having low social and economic status. These concessions look on the surface to be significant advances, but they might well serve only to divert attention from the core issues of the moral crisis. It is my thesis that a special type of social and moral education for the disadvantaged child is called for. He not only needs to participate in an educational milieu that enriches his experiences, but he also needs to develop critical awareness of the immorality of his condition. Inspiration for this proposal comes from *A Talk to Teachers* by James Baldwin.[1]

> ... I would try to teach them—I would try to make them know—that those streets, those houses, those dangers, those agonies by which they are surrounded, are criminal. I would try to make each child know that these things are the results of a criminal conspiracy to destroy him.

Would it be fair to say that educators are participating in a conspiracy against the disadvantaged of this country? Maybe not, but many educators are unwitting contributors to the conditions which serve to perpetuate the in-

David C. Epperson, "Making Social Critics of Disadvantaged Children," *Social Studies*, **57** (February 1967), 51–54. Reprinted with permission of the author and publisher.

justice of inequitable distribution of advantages. The school board that places low priority on the needs of schools in depressed areas, the principal who denies the existence of special needs in his school, the teacher who fails to develop improved materials and techniques adapted to the needs of disadvantaged children and especially the curriculum builders, who do not sense the urgency of preparing the disadvantaged child for participation in social improvement—these are the unwitting supporters of the conspiracy. Most of these educators are good people with humanitarian dispositions, but their lack of awareness of the consequences of their actions adds them to the rolls of the conspiracy. Is Baldwin unreasonable to propose that:

> I would teach him that if he intends to get to be a man, he must at once decide that he is stronger than this conspiracy and that he must never make his peace with it.

I am sure this is frightening indeed to those agents of that conserving institution, education. But what should educators conserve—the status quo or the dignity of man?

Most experts on the subject of teaching the disadvantaged child have either an explicit or implicit conservative approach to the types of values and attitudes that disadvantaged children ought to be encouraged to develop. For example, Frank Riessman in his enthusiasm for overcoming the middle class bias of teachers has proposed that the only value that needs to be changed is that of anti-intellectualism. Others suggest that these children need to be indoctrinated into middle class values that provide them with the social graces to advance on the social ladder. These commentators seem to be saying either (1) What right do we have to change the values embraced by families of the disadvantaged? or (2) How can a child achieve adequate economic status in a middle class world without acceptable social skills? These voices are being sounded while the basic question of how the disadvantaged American can achieve a sense of dignity and personal worth in a hostile and unjust world is seldom heard.

To say that "he must never make his peace with it" is not a plea for integration into a sick world, but the appeal of a leader attempting to rally his fellow men in an effort to create a better world. It is not equality in a morally degenerate society that serves as a goal for the disadvantaged American, but membership in a reconstructed society, a society conducive to the growth of human dignity.

> I would teach him that there are currently few standards in this country which are worth a man's respect. That it is up to him to begin to change these standards for the sake of the life and health of the country.

Such an educational goal challenges a long-standing tradition in teaching, for the suggestion of taking sides on current political issues seems to be a violation of the commitment to be unbiased on one's presentation of issues. But is it wrong to take the side of justice, equality, and human dignity when they are being violated in society? To be unbiased do we need to be uncommitted to basic human rights?

We have failed in our efforts to educate the disadvantaged American unless we have inspired him to challenge the standards and values of a society which has permitted the degradation of such a large segment of its population.

I am not suggesting that the disadvantaged be encouraged to violate the conventions governing the peaceful resolution of conflict. We must help them learn appropriate and effective channels of dissent and expose them to the analysis of social issues in a manner that will encourage them to utilize the legitimate avenues of dissent to improve their lot. If there are risks involved when informed individuals have internalized the rules for peaceful resolution of conflict and concurrently are aroused to participate in social reconstruction, then we must be prepared to take these risks. But I am of the persuasion that there are in fact fewer risks with an informed and aroused group than with a group that is usually apathetic and uninformed but who come within the grip of militant dogmatic leaders.

What are the risks involved in glossing over the very real problems faced by the disadvantaged? Can pupils trust the perceptions of educators who fail to give evidence of seeing the injustice and agony the children confront each day? Recently, the case came to my attention of a Negro child who had just enrolled in a school that previously had been almost exclusively middle-class white. He would frequently cry in class and the teacher would send him out of the room. The principal came upon the child crying in the hall and asked him what was the matter. He said he did not have any friends at this school and that he had a black face. The principal replied that he had not noticed that he had dark skin! While I am sure this principal was well meaning, he had provided one more bit of evidence to indicate to the child that the perceptions of educators cannot be trusted. It is not only kindness that these youngsters need—they need a realistic appraisal of the nature of the social conditions that confront them. Many *do* have black faces and there are serious problems that grow out of this bit of reality. The more we suppress a realistic appraisal of the social injustices in their lives, the less we can count on them to trust our perceptions of the world.

I am appealing for a realistic critical attitude which will serve these children in challenging the standards and values which have perpetuated injustice. Have we encouraged the disadvantaged child to analyze critically middle class standards which are held up to him, especially through mass media, as essential for achieving status in our society? Have we challenged him to take an active part in the improvement of society or have we stayed with *Dick and Jane* for fear of generating discontent and resistance among those 30 million Americans who live a marginal existence?

Up to this point I have been appealing for another look at the goals we hold for educating the disadvantaged American. I would now like to address myself to the task of evaluating the current trends for educating the deprived child. One theme that runs through the literature is that of teaching the child a set of salable skills that will permit him to participate in the economic order. While participation in the economy may well be a prerequisite to achieving a sense of personal worth, the trend is predicated on the assumption that these children will be unequipped to participate in other than unskilled and semi-skilled trades. Isn't this assumption itself prejudical? The job of the educator becomes one of fitting the child to society. This trend in its current form is incompatible with a philosophy of reconstruction, for it is a liberal education which is called for if we are to prepare the disadvantaged child to look critically at those standards which have perpetuated the agony of his people. To make journeymen of the unskilled in no way insures justice and equality. An aggressive liberal education is called for in the time of social revolution. This is the real challenge. There is little challenge in teaching children with limited verbal skill a manual craft, but there is a challenge commensurate with the magnitude of the problem in helping him achieve skills and attitudes which permit him to analyze critically pressing social issues and then to act upon his commitments. Educational planning to achieve this type of analytical sophistication among the disadvantaged is meager if not non-existent. It would seem that there is a real need to design levels of critical analysis corresponding to the diverse abilities to deal with abstractions found within a population of disadvantaged children.

An assumption that we have been holding about the manner in which children learn to look critically at social issues needs to be re-examined, especially as it relates to the disadvantaged. We have assumed that criticism must follow the establishment of a solid foundation of information and skills. Based on this assumption, social criticism becomes a major item in the curriculum only after the child has reached the 11th or 12th grade. This assumption needs to be challenged particularly when viewed in relation to the disadvantaged. Many disadvantaged children drop out of school before they get to "criticism," and most of the remainder distrust the school and its perceptions to such a degree by the time they are late teenagers that even a well-planned curriculum of social analysis will be meaningless to them.

I am proposing that social criticism become a part of the curriculum from the very beginning. It may well be that analysis of social conditions is in fact foundational to the assimilation of information and the development of specialized skills of precise assessment. Certainly, most scholars begin with a rough analysis of a phenomenon before they accumulate the information and specialized skills to arrive at an understanding of their observations. The first grade child makes many a rough analysis of phenomena occurring in his environment. Many children wonder why they live where they do, look like they do, have fathers and mothers like they do. Are these wonderings not the foundation upon which the collection of information and specialized skills needs to be built? We need them to generate this spirit of social criticism from the very first day the child enters the school. If we are to begin along these lines we need to take a new look at the curriculum we are offering the disadvantaged child.

What of the consequences on the happiness of the child if we heighten his sensitivities to the injustice and inequality that he meets in his life? I feel that we need to risk his immediate happiness for accuracy of perception that can lead to great ultimate happiness. It is one of those many times that we must give truth priority over immediate satisfaction. Justice cannot be won without some anguish for all those participating in the task of social improvement.

It may appear that in presenting my case I have overlooked the realities of educational administration. School boards, administrators, and teachers may well be unprepared to accept and defend an aggressive posture on social issues. If this is true, then educators need to work to achieve, not a condescending missionary spirit, but the spirit of the current social protest. There are far too few generating the attitudes necessary to provide leadership for the continuing battle against injustice and inequality. Currently schools are "holding grounds" for many who feel powerless, who are estranged from meaningful participation with their fellow men, who seek meaning through violent and empty methods or who slump into apathy when they are confronted with the overwheming odds against achieving symbols of success. Is it better to be a holding operation or a training ground for meaningful participation in constructing a new order?

It may be difficult indeed to persuade the educational community of the importance of taking a fresh approach to educating disadvantaged children. Perhaps few educators would take the risk of creating unrest among their charges. If this is the case, then I feel we should be apprised of the potential consequences.

If this country does not find a way to use [the energy of the disadvantaged] it will be destroyed by that energy.

Is this a militant over-statement of the consequences of our failure to cope with the problems of injustice and inequality? It is my conclusion that while many of the actions we are taking through legislation and compromise appear to be significant improvements, many are only serving to delay a direct confrontation with the basic issues. Human dignity cannot be legislated, it must be achieved. Our job is to provide each disadvantaged child with the skills and determination to gain a sense of personal worth by actively working toward social improvement. The consequences of our failure to include this potential source of energy in efforts to change society may truly be as grave as Baldwin suggests.

If educators become persuaded that we ought to make social critics of disadvantaged children, there are immediate steps that can be taken. First, concerned professionals must insist that the schools in their communities give serious consideration to re-structuring the curriculum in a manner that will improve the chances for all students (especially the disadvantaged) to develop an intelligent awareness of social problems. Secondly, they must resist the easy solutions for educating the disadvantaged, such as blindly adopting massive vocational training programs without attending to the basic educational needs of the disadvantaged populations. Further both public and private foundations should be enlisted to stimulate improvement programs designed to test out new methods of social education for disadvantaged children. Also publishing companies should be challenged to encourage authors to prepare materials that meet the special needs of the disadvantaged. Teachers of disadvantaged children, however, are presented with the most difficult challenges. First, they must themselves be perceptive social critics. To achieve a level of sophistication as critics they must prepare themselves for this role since often their own general education fails to generate an awareness of the many facets of contemporary social problems. They also must be flexible enough to permit children to openly challenge the teacher's values and standards. If teachers are unwilling to question their own commitments, there is little hope of achieving an attitude of criticism among students.

Each of us is, in fact, in a position to encourage the development of critical skills in these potential challenges. Do we have enough confidence in the method of free inquiry to provide these disadvantaged Americans with the tools to put current social conventions to test?

NOTE

1. *Saturday Review* (Dec. 21, 1963), 42–43, 60.

INQUIRY
INTO VALUES*

Bernice Goldmark

Is there another way? Yes, there is always another way—another way just as valid, just as good, just as valuable, sometimes even more so. But, too often, in order to convince ourselves that the way we choose is the best, we will not even consider another way. What is worse, as teachers we impose *our* way as if it were not only the best, but the only way. By doing this we violate all children, for we de-value and shut off their personal meanings and values—the knowledge they gain from their *own* experiences. By doing this, culturally different children are twice violated. Not only are their personal worlds de-valued, but their out-of-school worlds—family, neighbors, community—are also de-valued.

Pre-school children are allowed some latitude in creating their own personal meanings and values in their play, their fantasies, and their art. When they come to school, however, they must abandon the creation of their own worlds; they must abandon their own symbol creations in favor of the symbols imposed upon them by adults. Gradually they learn to accept the meanings of the world around them that they are taught, and to value what they are taught to value, although these meanings and values may conflict with what they know from their own experience, and from their own feelings and wants. Gradually children cease to trust the knowledge of their own experience and become suspicious of their own desires and values. Gradually they cease to create their own meanings, for they have learned that they are not worthwhile.

Culturally different children must abandon, not only personal meanings and values, but the meanings and values of their culture also. They learn that their speech, their dress, their food, their customs, their values, are not worthwhile. They learn, therefore, that *they* are not worthwhile.

There are so many ways of living and doing that have not yet been explored. There is such a wide range of meanings and values that can be allowed in our culture without harming anyone, yet enriching all. I would like to see social studies programs developed towards the end of expanding the ways in which we do things in our worlds, creating new meanings, reconstructing values. In the sheltered environment of the classroom, and in an atmosphere of open inquiry where process rather than product is the goal, children should have opportunities to set, test, evaluate and reconstruct their ends and the means and methods of achieving these. Children

---

* Written especially for this volume.

should have opportunities to "try-on" feelings, behavior, ideas, ways of expressing themselves in the arts, non-cognitively as well as cognitively, non-verbally as well as verbally. And children should learn to ask: what do I want? how do I want to get it? should I want this and try to get this in this way? is there something else I should want? *is there another way of getting it*? This social studies program would have no pre-determined content. The children would bring the content to school with them in their gnawing concerns, their crucial problems. The teacher would expand the children's experiences so that the range of their concerns expands.

Picture an elementary school classroom comprised of a culturally homogeneous group or a combination of different cultures. The teacher is a warm, flexible human being who is not threatened by different ways of living and doing, and even values diversity of values and customs for the expansion and enrichment it brings. He enjoys diversity. The emphasis in the classroom is on *other ways* so that the children will learn to value diversity. Children in the class work on different problems in groups or individually. The problems range over a number of different areas:

a relationship with another person—how one feels and behaves

a classroom decision that needs to be made

a problem in the community, state, country or world

a personal decision that needs to be made

a practical problem of how to cook, or sew, or fix something

a problem of the curriculum and required books in the class

an aesthetic problem: making a picture, poem, dance, or song, decorating a room, designing a community

Each problem is worked out experimentally and then inquired into on several levels. First children examine what is being done and how it is being done; second, they ask why it is being done this way; third, they ask if it should be done this way, or *is there another way*. A new way can be tested, evaluated, and in turn reconstructed if necessary.

In each of these inquiries children differentiate between those ways that are distinctly individual—their own personal meanings and values—and those that are accepted by groups of people. In some instances the distinctly individual ways are preferred; in other instances the group ways are preferred. The important point is that children have *choices* and have ways of examining, evaluating, and selecting for themselves. The teacher's role is to help provide materials and resources, help children move their questions from the "what" and "how," to the "why" and "should" levels, and help children organize for "acting out" of alternatives. In their creation of personal meanings and values, children should be asked always: is there another way? Is there another way to communicate what you wish to communicate, say what you wish to say, make what you want to make, feel what you want to feel, get what you want to get, know what you want? And, finally, is there another way to find another way? It is not important for children to arrive at any particular place or point of view, nor to produce any particular product. What is important is that children learn to value diversity and the expansion that diversity brings.

It is also important that children recognize their patterns of feelings, thoughts and behavior as ways they have been *taught* to feel, think and behave. They should be aware that they are, therefore, culturally determined and restricted, no matter what their culture. Once they can recognize that their patterns of feelings, thought and behavior are only alternative possibilities that have been structured for them, then they are free to explore other alternatives, to evaluate, to choose, or to reject and recreate. The point where an individual's behavior threatens to harm others can be determined only in a specific situation, and must be evaluated and either allowed or rejected in that situation. Thus group discussion of consequences and values, group decision-making, and opportunities for minority decisions to be heard and pressed for again, are required in the classroom.

This is an exciting new frontier for human behavior and for education, and what I believe is the necessary new emphasis in social studies education. It is not possible to develop a pre-packaged program for this type of education, for it is structured by method only—a method of looking at all alternatives, evaluating them, and reconstructing them, applicable to feelings, thoughts, and behavior. Each teacher needs to tune-in to his own feelings in past experiences and draw upon the knowledge he has gained from his own feeling experiences. Only in this way can he allow others their own feelings and forms of expressions. Each teacher has to allow other ways and provide for reconstruction of ways and values.

The important aspects of this type of program are:

children select problems that are of concern to them

areas of concern are expanded

the program is structured by method, rather than by content

children are allowed to experiment with alternative means-ends-methods, not only in rational decision-making, but also in the areas of emotions and aesthetics

children learn to respect the searching, and the values, of others because they are allowed their own searching and value construction

children learn values by the ways in which they are treated

children learn that there are no right nor wrong ways, only different ways; that *they* are neither right nor wrong, only different—and that being different is all right.

While I would develop this type of social studies program for all children, it is particularly important that culturally different children participate in it so that they can test and learn how to influence the predominant values, with the blessing of the "establishment"; so that they can gain feelings of the worth of their own culture groups, and of themselves as individuals; so that they can be both "right" and "good" as people.

We can no longer be content with the forum type classroom in which judgments are debated and defended. The time has come to make the class-room a laboratory for exploring feelings, behavior and values; for evaluating these; and for reconstructing these. For, despite all of our demands in our culture for rational defenses of judgments, and all of our efforts to influence others with "reasons," we must recognize that judgment making begins with a non-rational feeling (of doubt or discomfort) and ends with a non-rational feeling (of comfort). Judgments are made on the basis of what one wants, or desires, or feels comfortable with, and these are values: non-rational directors of judgment. All reasons are rationalizations—arguments developed to defend a choice that would be made anyhow because it is the choice someone wants to make, feels comfortable with. Just as the emphasis in social studies teaching has shifted from the learning of facts, to the discovery of concepts, to the development of methods of rational decision making, so it must shift once again to the development of methods of inquiry into feelings and values that direct decision making.[1]

The key to this type of social studies education is, of course, the teacher. Unless the teacher can allow, respect, and value the different values, the different means-end-methods of the children, he cannot teach the children to do this. In her article on teaching social studies Susan Jacoby points out the lack of reality in social studies programs for slum children, and the necessity for imaginative teachers to bring the children's experiences into the classroom.[2] The culturally different child must be allowed his world, as middle-class children have been allowed their world. And all children must learn that their worlds are not the only worlds, nor necessarily the best worlds, nor the only or best possible worlds. All children must learn that there is another way, and that one can expand one's own humanity by trying another way, and, at the very least, allowing others their way.

I am not sure that the institution of public schools in our country can accomplish the task of humanizing education, of reversing our habits of imposing and coercing others because we think we know what's best for them. I am not sure that we can educate teachers towards this end so that they in turn can educate children. Perhaps it is a romantic ideal. But if we do not hold a "possible" in view so that we can try to make the "possible" happen, then we are restricting ourselves to yesterday's world. Until we can learn to do this, the education of the culturally different, and, therefore, their condition in our society, will not improve significantly. Until we can do this, the experiment in democratic living will fail miserably.

NOTES

1. Bernice Goldmark, *Social Studies: A Method of Inquiry*, Belmont, Calif.: Wadsworth Publishing Co., 1968.

2. Susan Lynn Jacoby, "Slum and Suburb: The Neglected Reality," in Dale Brubaker, ed., *Social Studies in a Mass Society*, Scranton, Pa.: International Textbook Co., 1969.

RELEVANT SOCIAL STUDIES
FOR BLACK PUPILS

James A. Banks

... the negro race is inferior to the white race, and living in their midst, they would be far outstripped or outwitted in the chase of free competition. Gradual but certain extermination would be their fate.[1]

A class of seventh grade black pupils was confronted with this argument as they analyzed a series of historical documents that their teacher had duplicated for their study. The document from which this statement was taken, like the other documents the pupils studied, was slightly edited and simplified so that they could read it more easily. Another document that the pupils read stated:

... [Negroes] were born slaves of barbarian masters, untaught in all of the useful arts and occupations, reared in heathen darkness, and sold by heathen masters.... They were transferred to shores enlightened by rays of Christianity.[2]

The pupils also read a letter written by a Virginia slave owner to his sister about a slave named Polly. It said in part:

... On last Monday week, I had to whip Polly for her impudence to

James A. Banks, "Relevant Social Studies for Black Pupils," *Social Education*, **33** (January 1969), 66–69. Reprinted with permission of the National Council for the Social Studies.

me. . . . I regret it very much but there must be one master in a family or there can be no peace. I told her that she should never be sold . . . provided she would behave herself . . . she still tells me that she is perfectly willing to be sold.[3]

Another account told about an overseer who was called Mr. Severe:

Mr. Severe was rightly named; he was a cruel man. I have seen him whip a woman, causing the blood to run half an hour at the time; and this, too, in the midst of her crying children, pleading for their mother's release. . . .[4]

In addition to reading primary sources, the pupils studied excerpts and sections from elementary American history textbooks and from Negro history books. One of the selections read:

Being indentured servants, some of the first Negroes were later freed and given land. But Negro workers proved very valuable on plantations, and more of them were needed. Gradually, settlers came to think of Negroes not as indentured servants, but as slaves who would never be set free.[5]

Another selection noted:

One famous social scientist, Nathan Glazer, has called American slavery "the most awful the world has ever known." . . . The slave in this country had no protection from society.[6]

The class read a selection from another book that included this statement:

. . . in the sale of slaves there was the persistent practice of dividing families. Husbands were separated from wives, and mothers were separated from their children. There was never any respect shown for the slave family.[7]

The pupils read *I Juan de Pareja* by Elizabeth B. De Trevino, *Up from Slavery* by Booker T. Washington, *The Book of American Negro Spirituals* by James Weldon and Rosamond Johnson, and *Amos Fortune Free Man* by Elisabeth Yates. In her poignant yet inspiring biography, Miss Yates tells the story of an African prince who was captured at the age of fifteen and enslaved in America. The author relates how Amos Fortune withstood his torture, turned hostility into humility, and dedicated his life to bringing freedom to others after forty-five years of servitude. The book vividly depicts the horrors of slavery and dehumanization of the slaves by the early American slave traders.

The pupils pondered a poem by Phillis Wheatley who tells about her own slavery in the United States. It begins:

No more America in mournful strain
Of wrongs, and grievance unredress'd complain,
No longer shall thou dread the iron chain,
Which wanton Tyranny with lawless hand
Has made, and which it meant t' enslave the land.[8]

The pupils read the primary sources, the sections from history books, and the biographical and fictional works to help them solve the problem that they had identified, "What was black slavery like in the United States?" Their teacher had helped them define their problem in clear, specific terms. The class, with the teacher's guidance, formulated specific questions related to their central problem. These are some of the questions:

How were the slaves treated?

How did people who were not slaves feel about slavery?

How did slavery in the United States compare with slavery in other parts of the world?

How hard did the slaves have to work?

How did master and slave feel toward each other?

Did slaves ever try to escape?

After the pupils had identified their problem and formulated specific questions related to it, the teacher asked them to tell what black slavery was like in the United States. They had picked up ideas about black slavery from textbooks used in previous grades, from biographical and fictional works they had read, from the mass media, and from discussions they had heard about slavery from their parents and grandparents. The pupils had many erroneous notions about slavery, as revealed below:

Many slaves were happy and contented.

While a few slaves were treated badly, most were well treated.

Most slaves worked on large plantations rather than on small farms.

Everyone except slave owners was against slavery.

Slavery in the United States was just like slavery in other parts of the world.

After they had told the teacher about their notions of black slavery, the pupils read the series of documents and selections their teacher had duplicated and searched for other sources in the school and room libraries. They viewed several films and filmstrips on black slavery, told about accounts of slavery that had been handed down in their families, and role-played a slave auction and the Vesey slave rebellion.

As the class evaluated the selections, they encountered highly divergent and conflicting accounts of slavery. In one source they read that slaves were "enlightened by rays of Christianity"; in another they read that compared with other slavery systems, "American slavery was the worst." It is difficult to accept both of these statements as historical facts. The pupils felt that if black slavery in North America was "the most awful in the world," slaves were not "enlightened by rays of Christianity." Ascertaining the validity and reliability of the sources proved most challenging for the pupils. With the teacher's guidance, the class formulated a list of questions that they used as a guide in ascertaining the value of the various sources in helping them to discover what black slavery was *really* like in America. They asked such questions as:

In what region of the country did the author live?

For what purpose was the author writing?

What audience did the author have in mind?

What were the author's probable biases?

What were the author's training and qualifications?

When was the document or selection written (approximate year)?

Does the author often use emotionally laden words?

How does his account compare with others that we have read?

Does the author cite sufficient evidence to support his conclusions?

Does the author base his arguments on fact or opinion?

What was the author's social class?

What was the author's race?

What are the author's basic assumptions about slavery?

What are the author's basic assumptions about black people?

Are the author's assumptions grounded in facts?

After answering these kinds of questions about the sources they had read, the pupils were able to generalize about the nature of history and the extent to which history has been written to support racist views. They concluded that because the historian can never discover all of the information about any single event or present all of the data that he uncovers, he must use some criterion for selection. They discovered that his selection is influenced by his personal bias, his purposes for writing, and by the society and times in which he lives and works. The discrepancies found in the accounts of black slavery that the pupils read were classical illustrations of the impact of cultural, racial, and regional influences on written history.[9]

The teacher in our example used the topic of slavery to help his black pupils develop inquiry and problem-solving skills. These skills enable black children to learn the truth about themselves, the contributions that their people have made to American life, and how history was written for years to justify, rationalize, and perpetuate racial myths that portrayed the Negro as a cruel, ruthless savage who was content in his misery. The writing of U. B. Phillips and Jefferson Davis epitomized racism in history. When black pupils gain critical insights into the nature of history as a discipline, they are able to understand why the achievements of their people are often omitted in books, and why Negroes are frequently treated in a patronizing, stereotypic fashion in textbooks. Equipped with this understanding and awareness, black pupils are better able to mitigate their feelings of worthlessness and to develop more positive self-images. Research has documented the fact that black youngsters typically have ambivalent racial attitudes, low self-images, and low occupational aspirations. Social studies teachers should implement strategies to help black pupils perceive themselves and their racial group more positively and realistically.

In addition to developing critical insights into the nature of historiography, black pupils need to make a realistic appraisal of the nature of the social conditions confronting them.[10] They should be guided to inquire into the problems of racial discrimination, the meaning and social functions of the concept of "race," and the struggle that ensues when one race dominates others in a society. Black pupils need to learn the real reasons why they are poor, full of self-hate, and possess hostility that sometimes explodes in the ghetto streets. They should understand that they are not poor because they possess certain deficient traits but because they are victims of a racist society. Without this understanding, black youth will feel that the social conditions they endure are morally justified. Clark writes:

> Children who are consistently rejected understandably begin to question and doubt whether they, their family, and their group really deserve no more respect from the larger society than they receive.[11]

James Baldwin illuminated the need for this kind of instruction when he wrote:

> . . . I would try to teach them—I would try to make them know—that those streets, those houses, those dangers, those agonies by which they are surrounded, are criminal. I would try to make each child know that these things are the results of a criminal conspiracy to destroy him. I would teach him that if he intends to get to be a man, he must at once decide that he is stronger than this conspiracy and that he must never make his peace with it.[12]

Inquiries into black power, poverty, racism, the black revolt, and historical reactions to oppression should characterize social studies for black pupils. Social studies teachers must help the black child become a social critic so that he can ". . . develop critical awareness of the immorality of his condition."[13]

Black children should not only inquire into the problems of racism in history books and into the problems of institutional racism in our society, they should be introduced to the achievements of individual black heroes who have made outstanding contributions to American life. When the Spanish explorers are studied, pupils can be introduced to the black men who accompanied the first Spanish explorers to the New World. Children will be surprised to learn about the thirty black men who were with Balboa when he discovered the Pacific Ocean. They will also be intrigued by black men such as Estavancio who was a guide for Naveza and Cabeza de Vaca. Estavancio, in search of the Seven Cities of Cibola, never reached his destination but was the first man, except for the natives, to behold what is now the state of New Mexico. When studying about Columbus's voyages, children can be introduced to Pedro Alonzo Niño, a black man who navigated one of Columbus's ships when he sailed to the New World. During a study of the Revolutionary Period famous Negroes such as Benjamin Bannaker, the mathematician and inventor, could be studied.[14]

One teacher used a creative approach with disadvantaged fourth grade black pupils. Using the book *Great Negroes Past and Present*,[15] he rewrote and duplicated the biography of one famous Negro each day along with discussion questions and study exercises. As each great Negro was studied, his picture was placed on the bulletin board. At the end of the unit the portraits of all of the Negroes under study were displayed.[16] Then each child chose one Negro whom he wanted to portray in a pageant that they wrote and presented to the school assembly. For his part each child dramatized a significant event in the life of a famous Negro whom he had studied in depth. For example, the boy who portrayed Crispus Attucks shouted, "Don't be afraid!" and fell on the stage dramatizing the killing of Attucks at the Boston Massacre, the first man to die for independence. The child who portrayed Harriet Tubman said, "You'll be free or die," dramatizing the way Harriet Tubman forced slaves to escape and join the Underground Railroad. The children also made a mural chronicling the roles that great black Americans have played in the building of this country since they landed on American shores in 1619. They called their mural "They Showed The Way."

The unit was correlated with the other learning areas so that when a famous Negro such as Gwendolyn Brooks was studied, her book of poetry *Bronzeville Boys And Girls* was read along with her biography. When Duke Ellington, Aretha Franklin, and Marian Anderson were studied, the class listened to their records. During the unit many children also read longer biographies of famous Negroes that were borrowed from the school or public libraries.

The teacher's attitudes toward the black child, his perceptions of black history and culture, and his expectations for the child are more important than the materials and methods that he uses. As Cuban insightfully notes:

> Less attention should be paid to additional books and courses ... and more to the craftsman who will use the tools. Preachers of Black History know that the person is far more important than the materials he uses.[17]

Much research indicates that teachers typically have negative attitudes toward poor and black youth. Gottlieb found that white teachers described Negro pupils as talkative, lazy, fun-loving, high-strung, and rebellious.[18] Becker interviewed teachers in an urban school system who felt that slum children were difficult to teach, uncontrollable, and morally unacceptable on all scores from physical cleanliness to the spheres of sex and ambition to get ahead.[19] It is imperative that teachers develop more *positive attitudes* toward black pupils and their culture if they are to play effective roles in helping these youngsters develop more positive racial attitudes and self-images. This is true because children can accurately perceive the teacher's attitudes, and because teachers are "significant others" for all children. In our society we acquire identity from other human beings who are "significant" to us and incorporate it within ourselves. We validate our identity through the evaluations of those who are influential in our lives. A study by David and Lang indicates that the assessment a child makes of himself is related to the assessment "significant people" make of him. The study showed that a pupil's self-appraisal is significantly related to his perceptions of his teacher's feelings.[20]

Social studies teachers must also develop *higher expectations* for black and poor youngsters. Research indicates that teachers typically expect little from the urban poor child. Teacher expectations function as a self-fulfilling prophecy. The seminal research by Rosenthal and Jacobson illuminates the cogent impact that teacher expectations have on pupil achievement. These researchers selected a random sample of elementary school children and told their teachers that these pupils were potential "spurters." At the end of the year when they were tested, they evidenced unusually high intellectual gains. Write the authors, "The results indicated strongly that children from whom teachers expected greater intellectual gains showed such gains."[21]

A "New Negro" is in the making, one who is trying to reject his old identity, shaped to a large extent by white society, and to create a new one. This "New Negro" is wearing African tikis, sandals, and costumes. He is screaming for "Black Power" and fighting to gain control of his schools, communities, and his destiny.[22] Social studies teachers must promote this identity quest by encouraging black pupils to inquire into the extent to which racism has permeated our written history and our society, to become familiar with the contributions that black people have made to American life, and by developing more positive attitudes and higher expectations for black youth. Making the social studies curriculum more relevant for the black pupil is imperative if we are to help mitigate the mounting racial crisis in our cities and help the black child gain a more positive "self."

NOTES

1. George Fitzhugh, "Negro Slavery," in Merle Curti, Willard Thorp, and Carlos Baker, ed., *American Issues: The Social Record*, New York: J. B. Lippincott, 1960, p. 522.

2. Jefferson Davis, *The Rise and Fall of the Confederate Government*, New York: Crowell-Collier & Macmillan, 1961, p. 329.

3. *See* Vincent R. Rogers, "Using Source Materials with Children," *Social Education*, **24** (1960), 307–309.

4. Frederick Douglass, "The Plight of the Slaves," in Richard C. Wade, ed., *The Negro in American Life: Selected Readings*, Boston: Houghton Mifflin, 1965, p. 27.

5. An excerpt from a fifth grade American history textbook.

6. James A. Banks, *March Toward Freedom: A History of Black Americans* (Belmont, Calif.: Fearon Publishers, 1970).

7. John Hope Franklin, *From Slavery to Freedom: A History of Negro Americans*, New York: Alfred A. Knopf, 1967, pp. 178–179.

8. From "Phillis Wheatley's Poem on Her Own Slavery," in William L. Katz, ed., *Eyewitness: The Negro in American History*, New York: Pitman, 1967, p. 39.

9. James A. Banks and Ermon O. Hogan, "Inquiry: An Important Tool in Teaching History," *Illinois Schools Journal*, **48** (Fall 1968), 176–180.

10. David C. Epperson, "Making Social Critics of Disadvantaged Children," *The Social Studies*, **35** (1966), 52.

11. Kenneth B. Clark, *Dark Ghetto*, New York: Harper and Row, 1965, pp. 63–67.

12. James Baldwin, "A Talk to Teachers," *Saturday Review* (Dec. 21, 1963), 42–43.

13. Epperson, "*Making Social Critics of Children*," p. 51.

14. James A. Banks, *Teaching The Black Experience: Methods and Materials* (Belmont, Calif.: Fearon Publishers, 1970).

15. Russell L. Adams, *Great Negroes Past and Present*, Chicago: Afro-Am Publishing Company, 1964.

16. These pictures were taken from the set *Negroes in Our History*, Afro-Am Portfolio Nos. 1 and 2, Afro-Am Publishing Company, 765 Oakwood

Blvd., Chicago, Ill. 60653. Each set contains 24 laminated portraits drawn by Eugene Winslow.

17. Larry Cuban, "Black History, Negro History, and White Folk," *Saturday Review* (Sept. 21, 1968), 65.

18. David Gottlieb, "Teaching and Students: The Views of Negro and White Teachers," *Sociology of Education*, **27** (1964), 245–253.

19. Howard S. Becker, "Career Patterns of Public School Teachers," *Journal of Sociology*, **57** (1952), 470–477.

20. Helen H. Davidson and Gerhard Lang, "Children's Perceptions of Teachers' Feelings Toward Them Related to Self-Perception, School Achievement and Behavior," *Journal of Experimental Education*, **29** (1960), 107–118.

21. Robert Rosenthal and Lenore F. Jacobsen, "Teacher Expectations for the Disadvantaged," *Scientific American*, **218** (1968), 19–23.

22. James A. Banks, "A Profile of the Black American: Implications for Teaching," *College Composition and Communication*, **19** (December 1968), 288–296.

CHILDREN LOOK AT THEIR OWN BEHAVIOR

Ronald Lippitt, Peggy Lippitt, and Robert S. Fox

Children today are avid consumers of technology. Chances are that the small boy in the third row, fourth seat knows more about the second-to-second preparations of a space shot than he does about the day-to-day work of his father at the office or plant.

Youthful enthusiasm for technology need not be limited to the race for the moon, however. It can also provide motivation for learning about matters much closer to the child's everyday world. In Michigan, for example, children

Ronald Lippitt, Peggy Lippitt, and Robert S. Fox, "Children Look at their Own Behavior," *NEA Journal*, **53** (1964), 14–15. Reprinted with permission of the authors and the National Education Association.

are learning about the ways people behave toward each other in much the same way the children might learn about the behavior of a space ship in orbit.

In the Michigan Social Science Education Project, elementary school teachers, assisted by curriculum specialists and behavioral scientists from the University of Michigan, are introducing their pupils to some of the scientifically accepted methods for studying human behavior, particularly everyday behavior experienced by the pupils in their classroom life. Begun two years ago, the Project involves several first through sixth graders in the university town of Ann Arbor and in industrial Willow Run, as well as the pupils at the University of Michigan Laboratory School.

The methods and techniques by which the children study human behavior are, of course, simplified to fit their various levels of comprehension. Nonetheless, the children are able to acquire useful information about themselves, about their own reactions to situations, about interpersonal relationships in the classroom, and about scientific method.

"Friendly and Unfriendly Feelings" is the title of one of the units introduced in the curriculums of the three participating school systems. In this unit, the children are encouraged to look objectively at their own human relations. Although the children acquire a surprising amount of knowledge about what behavioral scientists have learned about emotional behavior, the emphasis in "Friendly and Unfriendly Feelings" is on methodology—the children learn to use the scientific method as an inquiry procedure, as a way of asking and answering questions.

The learning techniques presented during this and all the units depend on the pupils' grade level and, to some extent, on the teacher's ability to work with a particular method. So far, the teachers have succeeded with learning procedures that incorporate role playing, unfinished stories, simplified interviewing and observation techniques, pupil-made graphs and charts, and group projects. The lecture-by-teacher method is rare; participation by the children is stressed.

Before the children begin the unit, they are given an orientation to what "behavior" is as an object of study and to ways of exercising their scientific curiosity.

How objectively the children are able to observe behavior is perhaps best illustrated by the experience one mother had with her little girl who was in the third grade last year. The girl was having trouble getting to sleep one night and she asked her mother's advice.

"Think about something interesting," said the mother.

"I'll think about behavior," said the child.

The mother, concerned, asked her daughter if she were having trouble at school. "Oh, no!" was the reply. "Don't you know that all actions *are* behavior?"

The purpose of the orientation is to build children's ability to differentiate between scientific observation and a value judgment. In the long run, this ability helps them to articulate and share more intelligently the many different values they have. The atmosphere of tolerance and trust in which the children learn encourages them to question and examine their own values and to develop some new and more positive attitudes toward their classmates, teachers, and families.

After the orientation period, the children undertake specific study projects. A third grade teacher, for example, may present his children with the problem of what makes people become angry. He may choose to begin with one of the laboratory exercises described in a special guide designed by some of the experienced teachers and scientists involved in developing the "Friendly and Unfriendly Feelings" unit.

Each exercise is designed to present a specimen of behavior which the children can examine and from which they can draw tentative hypotheses. For example, one exercise involves a standardized role-playing scene in which conflict develops over children taking turns.

In this case, Jim refuses to let Jack have the bat in a game of rounders. Jim says that he is not finished batting. When Jack tries to grab the bat from Jim, Jim pulls it away. Jack then hits Jim in the face.

The children observe the role-playing scene as members of observation teams. One team is given the task of collecting data on the different feelings exhibited by the actors. Afterward they tabulate the data on a chart showing how often feelings of friendliness or unfriendliness were revealed in the scene. Another team is assigned the task of observing one actor. Afterward they will be asked to make a team report on how that person reacted.

The teacher assigns the observation tasks on the basis of what the unit builders think the children should learn from the experience. The guides also include criteria for evaluating the experiences.

In the case of the children observing Jim's reaction to relinquishing his turn, they might study the accuracy of their report by comparing their independent observations. The scientists call this reliability of observation.

As the children become more adept at observing simple interaction between people, they are able to draw some conclusions from the sequences of behavior they see. For example, they may be asked to interpret "Why did Jack hit Jim?"

At this point, the children's answers involve no assigning of right and wrong in the situation, only *why* the action happened. Once they can describe and explain the action, they can seek ways of resolving conflicts with more desirable results.

In the final part of the unit, the children learn to draw parallels between the kinds of forces influencing the behavior witnessed in the laboratory exercises and the forces operating in their own minds. This ability helps them to evaluate their own behavior and to find ways for making it more rational and more effective.

Thus far, the children have shown a surprising ability to understand basic principles of human relations and to use intelligently the methods and techniques of the behavioral scientists. Boys and girls from the third grade up have learned to read and construct data charts. The children also read with understanding summaries of some experiments mentioned prominently in professional journals.

In the sixth grade last year, pupils developed skill with interview techniques. The subjects for their interviews were first graders; the purpose was to compile an inventory of attitudes toward older children. The thoroughness and objectivity represented in some of the final reports show a real grasp of the scientific approach.

Perhaps the greatest difficulty in the Project has been to orient classroom teachers to the subject matter and the teaching techniques involved. The Project staff discovered that some teachers had little college preparation in the behavioral sciences and thus had trouble in differentiating between a value judgment and a scientific analysis.

Some teachers were also unable to restrain themselves from exercising an undue amount of control over their classes. In order for the children to study human behavior, they needed the opportunity to engage in social interaction themselves. This could occur only when the teacher was willing to permit a good deal of pupil participation and interaction.

To remedy these difficulties, visiting teams composed of experienced classroom teachers, college educators, and behavioral scientists meet with the teachers early in the school year to explain the methods and assumptions underlying the Project. The visiting teams also conduct weekly, voluntarily attended seminars during the school year. In addition, tape recordings of classes conducted by teachers with backgrounds in the behavioral sciences are available to less experienced teachers.

A basic assumption underlying the Project is that having the children study human behavior rationally will make a significant difference in their attitudes toward their teachers and other adult authorities, in their concepts of such ideas as cooperation and competition, in their understanding of themselves, and in their appreciation of differences in others.

Since the Project began, several teachers have noted a marked decrease in traditional anti-teacher feelings, particularly among disadvantaged pupils. They have also noted positive changes in their pupils' concept of cooperation. Prior to the Project, many of the children regarded cooperation as nothing more than helping each other to cheat on tests—to "beat the sytem," so to speak.

The children's enthusiasm for the Project, as evidenced by the high degree of participation and skill they exhibited at all elementary school levels, has strengthened the staff's belief in its feasibility and appropriateness. Furthermore, the children are discovering that there is no subject more exciting to study than the behavior of themselves and others.

NOT UNTEACHABLE—
JUST UNTEACHED

Lawana Trout

"Wop. Nigger. Cracker. Chink!" "Like man, I'm tellin' you, there ain't no land of the free and home of the brave, and we gotta move."

I was teaching a unit on prejudice and propaganda to disadvantaged high school juniors in the Institute for Advanced Study for Teachers of Disadvantaged Youth held at Princeton University. Since that first class, I have taught the unit in several cities to classes that were all Negro, all white, and Negro-white, and to multiracial classes that included Puerto Ricans, Mexicans, Indians, and others.

President Kennedy said, "Those who make peaceful revolution impossible will make violent revolution inevitable." I wanted to evoke a peaceful revolution in my classroom—a revolution in thinking, a revolution in feeling, and a revolution in teaching. I ignored I.Q. scores and observed student performance. I forgot reading grade levels and searched for selections that spoke to the students. [I was unconcerned about haircuts and dress styles, but I did care about what students thought and how they felt.] At times I became a student, and each student became a teacher. I lost books, but I did not lose students.

During our study, I stopped periodically to discuss how different kinds of material should be covered. Should it be taught to everyone? to some? to which ones? I asked the students, "What problems do you think we will have to overcome as this class studies race problems?" The first day one boy asked, "Hey, you gonna let us talk about *Whitey* the same as us?"

Students were encouraged to disagree with anyone's ideas, including the teacher's. The one rule was, "You may say anything you like, but you must listen to everything anyone else says."

This English unit reveals how a speaker or writer achieves his goals

Lawana Trout, "Not Unteachable—Just Unteached," from "We Ain't Unteachable—Just Unteached," *NEA Journal*, **56** (April 1967), 24–26. Reprinted with permission of the author and the National Education Association.

through careful manipulation of words. It shows students the relationship between words and emotions. I selected *prejudice, propaganda*, and *protest* because they are live topics for the students and they offered illustrations of the language situations I needed. The response of many students to the unit can be stated in the reaction of one: "I wasn't board a time." Some *were* bored, but the materials were more effective than most traditional ones.

We started by finding out how words are used to evoke feelings. Since the students were familiar with advertising, I used ads to make them aware of the "feeling" of words. I asked them to choose from a collection of pictures (Hondas, cigarettes, cars, record albums) something that they would like to sell, and then to write several types of ads about it.

The ads they wrote were serious, satirical, and humorous—for radio, television, magazines, or newspapers. Students "sold" their products to the class through reading and role playing. They slanted one ad in several different ways to appeal to different groups—teen-agers, poor people, middle-aged women, young men.

The class compared different ways of expressing one idea—finest quality filet mignon: first class piece of dead cow. They played with personal slanting: "*I* daydream. *You* run away from the real world. *He* ought to see a headshrinker."

After we had written slanted descriptions of people and places, one student commented, "You can *make* people and things be anything you want them to be with the words you use."

Since the material was sometimes inflammatory and since I was a stranger to the students, tension was present until the class accepted me and my materials. Humor was my most vital ally. For example, one day I showed a cover of a popular magazine which pictured a boy carrying a small table and chair during the riot in Watts. "You are working for a magazine and you use this picture. Write one caption that will slant it positively and one that will slant it negatively."

After the class had provided several positive captions like "Innocent victim rescues furniture," I asked for some negative ones.

Student: "Boy makes off with loot."
Teacher: "Make it more negative."
Student: (all Negro class) "*Negro* boy makes off with loot."
Teacher: "More negative." (Hoping to get a word like *hoodlum, thief*) "What is the *worst* thing you could call this boy?"
Student: (With a playful glint in her eye) "WHITE boy makes off with loot."
Teacher: "I'm glad to see we've lost our prejudices in here."

From advertising we moved to the study of propaganda, which is, as one girl pointed out, another kind of selling. She noted, "Advertisers sell products, and propagandists sell ideas." We examined local newspapers for propaganda, and formulated a list of propaganda techniques.

Students examined simple editorial cartoons. Each student explained his cartoon to the class and we listed observations about what makes a cartoon. The class decided that symbolism is often used and that whether or not captions and situations have meaning often depends on the reader's familiarity with past events. Some questions were: If you were going to show hate in a cartoon, what would you use? How would you show love, peace, anger, or fear?

Our study of propaganda was not limited to newspapers; we looked at it in films like *The Twisted Cross*, which shows Hitler's rise to power, and in paintings like Picasso's "Guernica." The class was asked to give a one-word reaction to this painting. They listed *confusion, frustration, fear, struggle.* When one shy girl said, "Loneliness," the class roared with laughter. They stopped laughing when she argued, "These people are in trouble and afraid; fear makes people lonely."

We opened the study of prejudice with the book *Two Blocks Apart*, which reports the contrasting views of two New York boys from families of very different backgrounds—one, a poor Puerto Rican family; the other, a stable Irish Catholic family—on their neighborhoods, homes, schools, political views, and future plans. The book provoked many questions: Where do people get their views of others? Why do they accept them?

Students were asked to list various racial groups and to write, anonymously, positive and negative comments about each. We duplicated the combined comments and the class discussed the prejudice profile. One student observed, "People don't think about bein' prejudice. They just *be* it."

A boy reading *Black Like Me* played the role of Griffin and talked to the class about his trials in trying to understand and cope with prejudice. Hemingway's short story, "Ten Indians," and "A Question of Blood" by Ernest Haycox showed the Indian as a victim of prejudice. Several students read and liked *Letters from Mississippi*, accounts written by white students who went to Mississippi for the Student Nonviolent Coordinating Committee.

In an attempt to understand intolerance, we examined words that are weapons of prejudice. I asked for names referring to groups of people. Students supplied: Krauts, Kikes, Gooks, Frogs, Spiks, Crackers, Wops, and others. After discussing their answers, I introduced Dick Gregory's autobiography, *Nigger*. Since several copies had disappeared from the display table, I assumed that some were interested in his treatment of prejudice.

We listened to a record of Gregory's jokes about civil rights issues. I cut up his joke books, *What's Happening?* and *From the Back of the Bus*, and gave each student a joke to tell to the class. Then we talked about Gregory. Why did he entitle the book *Nigger*? Who will buy this book? Why did he say, "Dear Momma ... if ever you hear the word 'nigger' again, remember they are advertising my book"?

Students prepared roles from *Nigger* and read them for the class. One part dealt with prejudice in the classroom, and I asked how a teacher shows prejudice.

One boy responded immediately: "I once had a teacher who was always screamin' and yellin' at us. 'You dirty little colored kids are ruining our schools,'" he mimicked.

Others joined in. Some defended teachers, but others countered with comments like, "Yeah, but some teachers don't have to say anything to show they don't like you. They just give you that certain look."

Later in the lesson, I role-played several types of teachers, and the class reacted. Armed with a strong stare and a belligerent voice, I threatened, "I know all about you. I've heard about how tough you are. I want you to understand I can be just as mean as you can."

"I hate you!" exploded one boy.

After seeing the film *A Raisin in the Sun*, students discussed how the lines reveal the self-image of the characters. How did this image affect the characters' actions? What are some Negro self-images today? What are some white ones? How do these self-images affect individuals' actions regarding civil rights? What problems do they create? What is your image of the Indians? Of other races? Where did you get that image? How does one remain true to his own race and at the same time learn to live with other races?

By reading "The Odyssey of a Wop," the class got the picture of an Italian boy who denied his people until he reached manhood. Books relating to the search for identity included *When Legends Die* (Indian), *A Walker in the City* (Jew), *Autobiography of Malcolm X*, and others.

An examination of protest climaxed the unit. I searched for techniques that would help the students release their feelings. After we had looked at books of paintings and discussed expression through color and form, I had the students express some of their feelings about the civil rights struggle through finger painting.

A girl scratched her nails down the page—finger tense, face tight. "This is hate," she said.

"This is King and his sissies being smothered by black power," said a boy as he distorted the quiet routine he had traced.

With a soft rhythm, a girl's finger traced human outlines. The rhythm flared as dark patterns of terror cut over the bodies. She titled her picture "Birmingham Sunday."

When the students had finished painting, they wrote brief interpretations of what they had sought to express and put them on the paintings.

As we evaluated possible solutions to the civil rights problems, we investigated the basic principles of several groups—Ku Klux Klan, Black Muslims, believers in black power, the defenders of the nonviolence movement, and others.

They read the constitution of the Klan, and they examined copies of the Black Muslims' newspaper. They explored multiple definitions of black power, and they reacted to the newspaper put out by the National States' Rights Party, "Thunderbolt: The White Man's Viewpoint." They took notes as they listened to recorded speeches by Malcolm X, Martin Luther King, and others. From these notes, they refuted the main arguments. Students also conducted interviews, television shows, and trials. One day when I praised them for good work, a boy flicked a half grin at me with, "We ain't unteachable . . . just unteached!"

The study concluded with a debate that opened by having a representative from each group present his basic ideas. Students were allowed to join any group or to remain independent. The different factions had filled the room with propaganda, signs, slogans, pictures, and projects. As members of the class played Martin Luther King, Malcolm X, the Imperial Wizard of the Klan, Stokely Carmichael, and others, students exploded like firecrackers all over the room.

"You mean to tell me you're gonna try to move the Negroes from the South to the North? They don't want us there, either."

"Man, Malcolm and his cats just yell and scream. We cool it." (A nonviolence speaker.)

We also read from *Our Faces, Our Words; The Negro Protest; To Kill a Mockingbird; Huckleberry Finn; Crisis in Black and White*; and other books. Students read "Jewtown" from *How the Other Half Lives*, by Jacob Riis, and the article, "A Spanish Harlem Fortress" (*New York Times Magazine*, January 19, 1964). They acted scenes from *In White America* and read several poems.

This unit allows every student to be an observer, a hero, a martyr, a crusader, an avenger. He is Jew *and* Gentile as the class reads Alfred Kazin's struggle to "be a Jew" and "become an American" in *A Walker in the City*. He is Indian *and* white as a student gives Tecumseh's speech against the white man's stealing Indian land. He is black *and* white as he discovers the meaning of Kenneth Clark's words:

The great tragedy—but possibly the great salvation too—of the Negro and the white in America is that neither one can be free of the other. . . . Each one needs the other—the white to be free of his guilt, the Negro to be free of his fear.... The poetic irony of American race relations is that the rejected Negro must somehow also find the strength to free the privileged white.

In the classroom, students may bare their frustrations and fears, their loves and hates, their disillusionments in the past and their hopes for the future.

"Our English class was more instring then during the regeler time. I feel that if we had nonvolins we could all work together in one union."

"You're wasting your time. Whitey ain't chang and we are gonna get him."

"I don't think I'll ever be afraid of the word *nigger* again."

SOCIAL RESEARCH: STUDYING RACIAL BEHAVIOR*

James A. Banks

With the unprecedented accumulation and proliferation of knowledge, educators have become increasingly concerned with strengthening students' problem-solving and inquiry skills. Not only is it impossible for children to master the tremendous body of knowledge amassed, but facts become quickly outdated. The knowledge of today may be as obsolete tomorrow as the McGuffey reader. This is not to imply that facts lack utility, for problems cannot be solved in a vacuum, but to illuminate the mounting realization that we can best prepare students to function effectively and productively in the cybernetic age by equipping them with problem-solving skills and attitudes. Man's very existence assures the perennial existence of problems.

While we should not strive to make students amateur social scientists, we should provide them with practice in problem solving and data gathering utilizing the methods of the social scientist. Not only will students develop critical problem-solving and inquiry skills by participating in social research, they will learn to appreciate the difficulties involved in gathering social data and deriving conclusions. They will also become more critical and discerning readers of current social science literature. It is important that pupils become acutely aware of both the strengths and weaknesses of current social knowledge.

---

* Written especially for this volume.

One effective way to involve students in social research is to help them design and implement a small-scale descriptive study. During a unit on race relations and racial attitudes, a class could conduct a study to determine the kinds of relationships that children in two other classes have with different racial groups. In the initial stage of the study, the students will need help in *defining their problem* in clear, specific terms. A clear statement of the problem in our example might be, "What kinds of relationships do children have with other races?" When the problem is clearly delineated, the students can, with the teacher's guidance, formulate clear and *testable hypotheses*. For example, they may hypothesize that boys have more friends who belong to other racial groups than do girls. As the students are formulating hypotheses, they should be encouraged to think of ways in which they may be tested.

During the initial phase of planning, the students should secure permission to conduct their study from potential subjects and their teachers, developing in this way an appreciation for the difficulties that social scientists often confront when attempting to do research. At this point, the class might also benefit from a discussion of the ethical problems often raised by social science research. They might discuss how research may invade one's privacy, and how research results can be used in ways that are detrimental to the subjects. The class might also discuss how such negative consequences can be minimized or prevented.

In the next phase of the study, the class will need to develop *techniques and measuring instruments* which will provide objective data relevant to their hypotheses. For example, to test the hypothesis concerning the number of friends of other racial groups that boys and girls have, the students would need to include questions in their instrument soliciting specific information on the *number of friends who belong to different racial groups* and on *sex*. While the class is designing the questionnaire, the teacher can help the pupils strengthen their communication skills by emphasizing the need for language in research instruments to be precise in order to reduce the possibility of misinterpretation. Terms such as "racial groups" and "friends" must be explicitly defined so that they will mean the same or nearly the same to all of the subjects. In the questionnaire in our example, the class may define "friend" as "a person whom you are fond of and like to do things with." "A member of a different racial group" might be defined as "a person who belongs to a group that differs from yours in skin color and in certain other physical characteristics." Specific examples of different racial groups might be cited to help clarify the definition; the subjects might be told, for example, that whites, Negroes and Orientals belong to different racial groups.

The teacher should help the students to phrase questions in a way that will facilitate analysis of the data. Thus, instead of asking open-ended questions like

About how many friends do you have who belong to a racial group that is different from your own?

they might consider the merits of asking a structured question like

Indicate as accurately as you can the number of friends you have who belong to a racial group that is different from your own:

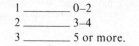

1 _____ 0–2
2 _____ 3–4
3 _____ 5 or more.

When the students have completed structuring their instrument, they should *pretest* it using a small group of subjects who will not be involved in the final study. By analyzing the pilot data, they will be able to avoid major problems in the actual study. In refining their design and instrument, the students should incorporate suggestions offered by the trial subjects as well as their own ideas for improvement.

When the instrument has been refined, *data should be collected*. The students who administer the instrument should give a detailed report to the other class members describing both the unexpected problems that arose during administration and events that took place as planned.

When the data has been collected, the pupils should attempt to *analyze* it. As a class project, analysis can be approached in several ways. The class might work in small groups, each of which computes frequencies for assigned items in the questionnaire. The students can then test their hypotheses and *draw relevant conclusions*. To test the hypothesis concerning the relative number of friends of other racial groups possessed by boys and girls, the students could construct a 2 × 2 contingency table and compute a value for *e*.* The table might resemble Table 1.

From the table, students can perceive relationships between variables. They can note, for example, that while 68% of the boys in the sample have

Table 1. Sex (independent variable)

	Friends	Girls	Boys	
Friends who belong to a different racial group (dependent variable)	0–2	20 (70%)	9 (32%)	$e = 38\%$
	3–4	6 (30%)	19 (68%)	
	Total	26 (100%)	28 (100%)	

Number = 54

*   *e* is a crude but useful measurement of the magnitude of relationships among variables. It is the percentage difference computed in the direction of the dependent variables. The perfect relationship is 100%.

three to four friends who are members of different racial groups, only 30% of the girls do. The e value gives a quantitative estimate of the magnitude of relationship; since it is 38% in our example, the hypothesis can be accepted because the predicted relationship is moderate if not high. The students would thus conclude that boys have more friends who are members of a different racial group than do girls.

In addition to testing their hypotheses, the pupils can gain valuable knowledge about sampling procedures from the data they have gathered from their population (two classes, population of 56). By assigning each subject a number and utilizing a table of random numbers (or a systematic sampling procedure, i.e., by selecting every nth number), the students can draw several random samples from their population to determine how closely the percentage distribution of several variables in each sample approximates the percentage distribution of the variables in the total population. Students are usually impressed with the close relationship between the characteristics of *each sample* and those of the *population*. Thus they come to understand and appreciate the immense value of probability sampling.

In our example, students would benefit from determining the relationship between sex and the number of friends who belong to different racial groups in a random sample of eight subjects. Determining the sex distribution in the sample and in the total population would also prove instructive.

During the implementation of a descriptive study, the teacher can introduce students to words such as *independent*, *dependent*, and *control* variables. However, the introduction of such terminology is not necessary for students to grasp the concepts that the words express or to appreciate a small venture in descriptive research.

The teacher should also ask students to think about the extent to which their findings can be *generalized*. Properly guided, they will realize that in an example such as the one described their conclusions must be limited to the two classes studied. They may wish to undertake a random sample of all the classes in the school so that they can generalize their findings to the entire school population. Other students may wish to implement a small community survey. For example, they might study the political behavior and attitudes of residents on several blocks in a black community (houses on the blocks can be randomly selected). Such an endeavor may prove especially illuminating during an election year or immediately preceding a local election.

In addition to conducting survey research, students will benefit from and enjoy small-scale observational studies. They might study the racial composition of persons who patronize black businesses, hypothesizing that more blacks than whites shop at stores owned by blacks. If they have to reject their hypothesis on the basis of their observations, they should be asked to give possible explanations of their unexpected findings. The pupils may conclude that the kinds of stores they studied and the hours of the day during which they observed patrons may have been important factors affecting their findings.

We have delineated ways in which students can gain important inquiry and problem-solving skills through small-scale descriptive studies in the area of race relations. The examples described were chosen because they can be easily executed and clearly illustrate the methods of social research. When students are selecting the type of study they will conduct, the teacher should help them choose problems that are interesting, significant, and challenging but within the scope of their research abilities.

In addition to developing and strengthening skills in problem solving and inquiry, the implementation of a descriptive study by students will give them an opportunity to improve important mathematical and communication skills. In writing the final report of their study, the students should be encouraged to strive to achieve their highest level of writing performance. By suggesting that they duplicate their report and share it with the entire school community, the teacher can effectively motivate students to strive for perfection in their writing.

The unprecedented accumulation of knowledge, the rapid outdating of "facts," and the increasing demands on our citizenry to solve urgent social problems make it imperative for social studies teachers to emphasize the acquisition of inquiry skills rather than the mastery of facts. Only in this way can we prepare the citizens of tomorrow to function effectively in our increasingly complex and confused world.

STUDY QUESTIONS

1. Jacoby indicts educators for neglecting the *realities* of urban life in the social studies curriculum. What are these realities? Why are they often evaded in the schools? What steps might be taken to make them a part of the regular social studies curriculum?

2. Jacoby challenges educators to "lead public opinion rather than follow it in frightened, hangdog fashion." Why do educators usually follow rather than lead public opinion? What are the risks involved in attempting to lead public opinion? How might the social studies curriculum be improved if educators became opinion leaders?

3. Why does Epperson think that we should make culturally different children "social critics?" How might critical-thinking skills help culturally different children to improve their lives and society? What kinds of social studies activities might help culturally different children become social critics?

4. In making culturally different children social critics, we will also make

them more discontent with their condition and therefore more hostile. How can we help them to express hostility constructively?

5. Epperson suggests that culturally different children should not only analyze and criticize society but also help *reconstruct* it. What contributions can the poor make to our society?

6. Explain what Goldmark means by helping children to move questions from the "what" and "how" to the "why" and "should" levels. Give examples of questions at these levels. Why is it important for children to develop the skill to ask questions at higher levels?

7. How did Banks use historical documents to help children develop inquiry and problem-solving skills? What are the values and limitations of this teaching strategy?

8. How might young children study human behavior in a scientifically accepted fashion? What values may accrue from such study? Why might this kind of study be especially effective with culturally different children?

9. How did the teaching strategies utilized by Trout help develop her students' inquiry and problem-solving skills? How could you adapt these techniques for use with your pupils?

10. What other kinds of problems might children study utilizing the research methods described by Banks? What difficulties might a class encounter while implementing descriptive studies? How might these difficulties be overcome?

SUGGESTED READINGS

Allen, Rodney F., John U. Fleckenstein, and Peter M. Lyon (Editors), *Inquiry in the Social Studies: Theory and Examples for Classroom Teachers*. Washington, D.C.: National Council for the Social Studies, 1968

Banks, James A., *Teaching the Black Experience: Methods And Materials*. Belmont, Calif.: Fearon Publishers, 1970

Banks, James A., and Ermon O. Hogan, "Inquiry: A History Teaching Tool," *Illinois Schools Journal*, **48**, 176–180, 1968

Clegg, Ambrose A., Jr., and James L. Hills, "A Strategy for Exploring Values and Valuing in the Social Studies," *The College of Education (University of Washington) Record*, **34**, 62–78, 1968

Clements, H. Millard, William R. Fielder, and B. Robert Tabachnick, *Social Study: Inquiry in Elementary Classrooms*. New York: Bobbs-Merrill Company, 1966

Fenton, Edwin, *Teaching the New Social Studies in Secondary Schools: An Inductive Approach.* New York: Holt, Rinehart and Winston, 1966

Goldmark, Bernice, *Social Studies: A Method of Inquiry.* Belmont, Calif.: Wadsworth Publishing Company, 1968

Goldmark, Bernice, and Morris Schmieder, "Not 'History' But Historiography," *Social Education,* **31**, 201–206, 1967

Hebert, Louis J., and William Murphy, *Structure in the Social Studies.* Washington, D.C.: National Council for the Social Studies, 1968

Massialas, Byron G., and C. Benjamin Cox, *Inquiry in Social Studies.* New York: McGraw-Hill, 1966

Raths, Louis E., Merrill Harmin, and Sidney B. Simon, *Values and Teaching: Working With Values in the Classroom.* Columbus, Ohio: Charles E. Merrill, 1966

Taba, Hilda, and Deborah Elkins, *Teaching Strategies for the Culturally Disadvantaged.* Chicago: Rand McNally, 1966

CHAPTER 7
SIMULATION, ROLE-PLAYING, AND SOCIODRAMA

A number of writers have suggested that culturally different children are anti-intellectual, action-oriented, and frequently uninterested in the traditional social studies program. In typical social studies classes such as those observed by the editors, children are asked to read passages in a basal text and to give written or oral answers to the questions posed by the author. Such an approach to the teaching of social studies probably interests the middle-class child little more than it does the lower-class child. However, middle-class children have learned how to play the school's "game." They frequently tolerate unstimulating teaching because they do not wish to endanger their chances of obtaining certain academic rewards or of getting into the colleges of their choice. Poor children often do not think in terms of such long-term rewards because they are preoccupied with the daily problems of living.

Thus creative teaching strategies are probably more necessary for lower-class children than for any others. The effective social studies teacher must select problems that are relevant to the lives of his pupils and devise techniques that stimulate their interests and involvement. Although teachers frequently complain that culturally different children have "no interests," a more valid explanation of the typically low level of involvement of these students in the social studies is that the curriculum and methods used frequently fail to capture their interests and imaginations. All human beings have interests and concerns; however, culturally different children cannot "tune in" to a social studies curriculum that is frequently very remote from their lives.

The formulation of *relevant* social problems and the utilization of *creative* teaching strategies will successfully elicit the interests of culturally different children, as the articles by Crystal and Kontos in this chapter indicate. The readings in this chapter describe teaching techniques that are especially promising for use with lower-class children. Simulation, role-playing, and sociodrama require students to become *actively* involved in the solution of relevant and timely social problems. These strategies interest *all* children, but are especially useful with culturally different children because they involve *action*. They can also be effectively used with culturally different children for another reason. We suggested in Part One that social studies should encourage culturally different children to examine and clarify their values, attitudes, and self-perceptions. Role-playing and sociodrama have been successfully used to help children do this, as well as to consider alternative ways of living and being and determine what behavior is appropriate in various social contexts.

Role-playing an interview with an employer can help the black slum child to understand how obtaining a job may be contingent on his ability to speak the standard English dialect. By simulating a racial outbreak, children may be able to perceive some of the limitations of this strategy in solving social problems, and to devise more effective problem-solving techniques. A simulation of a section of the United States governed by black militants in which all black people live will encourage children to evaluate the feasibility of separate states for black people. A few militant black leaders have suggested this arrangement as a possible solution to the black man's plight in this country; however, the idea has been rejected by the masses of black Americans. As the reader studies the selections in this chapter, he should think of ways in which he can adapt the techniques and strategies described to problems that are unique to his pupils and to minority group children in general.

THE USE OF GAMES AS A
TEACHING TECHNIQUE

John C. Attig

Inspired by the work of Professor Glenn E. Brooks, a sequence of "war games" was played in the Contemporary Thought classes at Lyons Township High School, LaGrange, Illinois. In an attempt to simulate real-life conditions of international diplomacy and to give the students an idea of the decision-making problems faced by national leaders, the two sections of the course,

John C. Attig, "The Use of Games As a Teaching Technique," *The Social Studies*, **58** (January 1967), 25–29. Reprinted with permission of the author and publisher.

meeting on alternate days, assumed the roles and functions of the two major power blocs in the world. One group assumed the roles of Soviet Union leaders; the other assumed comparable roles for the United States. In each section there were a few students representing neutral blocs and key allies, who functioned in the game as independent actors.

Each student was assigned a real-life role, i.e., President of the United States, United Nations Secretary-General, etc., and assumed the full powers and responsibilities of the role. The students were responsible for acquiring knowledge concerning 1) the powers and responsibilities of the role, and 2) the military, economic, and diplomatic characteristics and interests of the two power blocs. Each side was instructed to gain from the other actors as much as possible in the form of military, economic, territorial, and diplomatic concessions. Beginning with a crisis situation, the accidental bombing of Hanoi by an American plane, each team made a daily series of military, economic, and diplomatic moves in order to achieve the objective. Moves were made in writing and were required to be actually conceivable in real life using only real life capabilities in existence at the time of the problem. Moves were designated as public, private for designated actors in the game, or secret.

The teacher functioned in the game as observer, advisor, and umpire. In the role of umpire, the instructor reviewed each move made by the two sections in order to evaluate its realism. Less than five per cent of the moves were disallowed for this reason. In the role of advisor, the instructor gave advice if called upon to do so. All questions seeking advice concerned either a clarification of the powers and capabilities of the various roles or a desired insight as to what to do in a given situation. The former queries were answered directly and the latter were answered in the form of suggesting possible alternative moves. All moves made in the game, including the assignment of roles and tasks, were student-made decisions. The role of observer was the most enjoyable of all. It was a fascinating experience to watch the students discuss alternative moves and the problems created for them by their opposition. The teacher made no attempt to supervise the decision-making process.

The game was played with a high degree of enthusiasm and realism. It was apparent that most of the students were emotionally involved in their roles. For example, on one occasion the Soviet Union considered painting American markings on some of their North Vietnam-based planes. These planes would attack Thailand in hopes that the United States would receive the blame. The Soviet Ambassador to the United States reacted to the proposal by threatening to defect to the United States on grounds that the leader of the Soviet government was a warmonger. The ambassador's reaction resulted in the dropping of the proposal. On another occasion a Soviet note which originally demanded removal by the United States of all armed forces from Southeast Asia in the interests of preserving peace was changed from the form of a demand to that of an urgent request on grounds that the word demand was provocative and could lead to war.

An indication of student enthusiasm for the game was the number of students who desired to attend class for purposes of conferences and negotiations on days when the other section was meeting. Eleven of the thirty-nine students in the course received passes allowing them to leave study hall and attend class meetings. An additional nine students requested passes, but they were turned down because they were in other courses and not in study hall. The willingness of over half the course-members to give up their own free study time in order to involve themselves in additional game activity was unanticipated and indicated a high level of interest. At the end of the game a vote was taken on the question, "Should the game technique be used in subsequent course offerings?" The opinion of the students was unanimously affirmative.

The game technique appears to have considerable value as a teaching tool. The enthusiasm of the students for the game would indicate that it is an excellent motivation device. During the course of the game it was never necessary to prod or threaten a student into action. Because all game activities were products of the students' own creation, initiative and originality of thought were encouraged. The students were required to think realistically about the nature of the problems confronting them and were given the chance to apply theory in a simulated real-life situation. As a tool for gaining factual knowledge, the game depended on the initiative and background of the individual student. It is probably safe to say that, in general, the greater the degree of personal involvement in the role and the game, the greater the degree of knowledge gained. No definite assignments were given in conjunction with the game, but a suggested list of readings was given to all students. A student's ability to make an effective contribution to the class was influenced by the degree of factual knowledge he possessed. Because realism was a requirement of all moves and because it was necessary for most of the players to do research in order to acquire the knowledge necessary for realism, the technique probably aided the development of research skills, though not on a systematic basis. The success of the game technique is probably limited by the personalities and group dynamics of the particular class. For example, on the day that the "President of the United States" was absent, the class suffered a noticeable decline in working efficiency, which is an indication of the dependence of the class on his personal leadership.

A unique aspect of the game was the classroom-discipline situation. The law and order variety of discipline was definitely not present during most of the game. Many times the class was very noisy. If we interpret discipline to mean that the students on their own initiative set for themselves tasks which they must and do carry out of their own free will, then the game technique was outstanding. It should be pointed out that during the course of the game not once were students either prodded into action or punished for negative social behavior. The self-discipline was one of the game's most outstanding features.

Perhaps the greatest problem connected with the game technique is evaluation. A test emphasizing the subject matter involved in the game would be hard to devise. This is due to the subjective nature of the knowledge required by the various roles. The game, however, appears to offer an excellent opportunity to measure attitudes and attitude changes. Although no examination of pupil attitudes was given during this particular game experience, the remarks of the students in their own evaluations of the game indicate that certain changes of attitude did take place as a result of their participation in it. If one were to attempt to test for factual knowledge acquired during the game, one type of test would be an essay examination emphasizing the student's knowledge of his own role, its real life functions and the knowledge necessary to make the role an effective one. Another alternative would be to give separate examinations specifically tailored for each role in the game.

How did the students regard their game experience? What did they believe they learned about the subject matter of their game, international relations? At the end of the game the students were asked to evaluate their experiences. They were unanimous in their praise of the technique. In regard to international relations, most of them said that they gained a realization that the complexities of international diplomacy were much greater than they had believed prior to the game. Most students said they gained an awareness of the dangers implicit in every action of the cold war which was, in their opinion, very close to a hot war. The importance of cooperation and coordination of efforts in order to accomplish anything was another realization. Typical of student comments are the following excerpts taken from their evaluations:

I have learned from these war games that a seemingly small incident or a word in a sentence can have far reaching effects. I see now the care which must be used in diplomacy.

I was reminded that a dictatorship is resented by strong individualists.

In the cold war no one can remain truly neutral.

Being American, I used to think of all Communists as the bad guys, but now I can see the North Vietnam point of view and why they are close to both the Soviet Union and Red China.

I never realized how careful one must be when dealing with other countries. I also never realized the knowledge and planning that must go into one move.

I learned that diplomacy is a language and culture all its own. . . . I also learned that cold war is really quite hot! It can be blown into a full-fledged nuclear war proposition in a matter of hours.

I blandly assumed that the United States and France were good and true allies who felt exactly the same in respect to all sorts of things, especially the USSR. I know now that I wasn't even "hot."

I learned that the Cold War can not be won, only fought. It is a continuous series of battles, mostly, which go on and on.

I learned that the Cold War is a much more complicated matter than it would seem to be on the surface.

Cooperation is the only way to gain peace with, or advantage over, the opponent.

I realized the difficulty in coordinating the various departments of the government in diplomatic strategy.

I learned that it isn't as easy to wage a cold war as it appears—even on this level.

The significance of adequate communications was brought out by this problem.

In considering the events and actions that took place during the game, including the student suggestions as to how the game could be improved, the following recommendations should be kept in mind by anyone desiring to use the game technique. Before commencing the game itself a short period of preparation (two to five days) is advisable. The period of preparation would include reading assignments designed to give all participants a desired general background of information. During this time students would have an opportunity to familiarize themselves with their respective roles and to organize themselves into effective groups. Students should be supplied with a list of short job descriptions which would give them some idea of the duties involved in each role, thus aiding their choice of roles. It is probably a good idea to post on the bulletin board all moves of a public nature made during the game and all announcements made by the various actors. This would help to keep all players adequately informed of the actions of the game.

The game technique has a great use potential in courses of social studies. Mock United Nations Assemblies, Presidential Conventions, and United States Congresses are but some of the areas in which the technique could be outstanding. The game technique appears to be of highest value in a course in which there is a concentration of students possessing above average ability, but further experimentation with groups possessing all types of abilities is necessary before this opinion can be considered to be of considerable validity. Those who have a negative attitude toward their studies might be stirred into good motivation by the game situation, but, if not, they would create serious problems for those who are more enthusiastic about both school in general and the game in particular.

In summary, the outstanding qualities of the game included the enthusiasm of the overwhelming majority of the members of the class and their involvement in their roles. Their self-generating efforts and discipline, particularly in setting and carrying out tasks for themselves, were the keys to success. Cooperation among the members of the class was excellent. This, too, was self-generated. Positive aspects of the game would include the understandings of international relations which were gained by the participating students.

One of the negative aspects of the game was the fact that some of the roles were not clearly defined and others, important in real life, turned out to be relatively unimportant in the game situation. There is no way of determining in advance which roles will not be important and which ones will need greater clarification in order to be effective. Only actual experience in a game situation will indicate to what extent this is true. Corrective action could then be taken for future games. It should be pointed out that those students who lack a significant degree of self-motivation or who possess little initiative are going to have problems making their roles active and effective. These people probably would handicap the class as a whole.

SIMULATION, A TEACHING TOOL

Charles Christine and Dorothy Christine

Managers in industry and government responsible for training programs have been turning to an instructional technique called *simulation*. The technique involves the creation of a game-like atmosphere to demonstrate some technique or principle that an instructor desires to make real for his students. In the game, real-life conditions are simulated so that the learners become functionaries within the learning situation.

A familiar example of simulation is the U.S. Army's "war games." War games are used to instruct new soldiers in the business of combat. This instruction places the soldiers in a mock combat situation involving all the hardware, the tactics, the noises, and the hardships of a real war. Of course, in mock combat only blank ammunition is used, and almost all the casualties usually associated with war are eliminated.

Charles Christine and Dorothy Christine, "Simulation, a Teaching Tool," *Elementary School Journal*, **67** (May 1967), 396–398. Copyright © 1967 by the University of Chicago Press. Reprinted with permission of the authors and the University of Chicago Press.

Users of simulation techniques in the instruction of soldiers, real estate brokers, airplane pilots, administrators, automobile operators, and other learners have been lavish in their praise of the technique. Users have reported that simulation fosters high learner motivation, maximum learner involvement in the learning process, rapid understanding, higher instructional efficiency than more traditional methods, and high transfer of training from classroom instruction to the "real world."

The technique of simulation was used in an intermediate-grade social studies instruction period to demonstrate a concept in international trade relations. The concept was that underdeveloped nations are weak economically compared with the industrial nations in the modern world.

This technique of simulation was used in the classroom of one of the authors. The twenty-six children in the classroom were organized into six groups. Two groups had six children each, three groups had four children each, and one group had two children who acted as the teacher's helpers. The two larger groups were provided with paper, scissors, twelve-inch rulers, and crayons. The three smaller groups were provided with a supply of play money and a larger supply of paper than that given to the two groups of six children each.

COMPETITORS

The children were told that the session was to be a social studies lesson with a serious purpose. They were told that the large groups represented modern industrial nations such as Great Britain or the USSR, while the small groups represented modern non-industrial nations such as Nigeria or Malaysia. The children were further told that each group was to compete with the others in trying to provide items the teacher listed on the blackboard. Within the allotted thirty minutes, each group was to try to fill the largest number of requests the teacher listed for specific items. The items requested from the groups included a certain amount of play money, a six-inch black crayon line on white paper, a cut-out paper triangle colored blue, and a cut-out paper rectangle, five inches by two inches, colored green. The correctness of the color and the dimensions of the finished creations were compulsively checked by the teacher's two helpers while the teacher observed the activity and wrote new requests on the board as previous requests were filled.

It soon became obvious to the children that no one group had all the materials necessary to fill the teacher's requests, and they realized that trades of materials between groups were necessary.

The children in the two groups initially provided with a "manufacturing capability" (scissors, crayons, and rulers) quickly learned to maintain their advantage by not trading their manufacturing tools for "raw materials" (paper). During the initial trial of the game, one of the small groups was able to trade paper and play money for a crayon and a twelve-inch rule, but this did not happen during later repetitions of the game. Instead, the larger groups traded finished products needed by the smaller groups for ever increasing supplies of play money and paper.

RULES OF THE GAME

Certain ground rules were established to insure that the game progressed in an orderly manner. The children were told that:

1. Trade negotiations could be carried on only at a special negotiations table located near the teacher.
2. Only one child could absent himself from each assigned table at any one time.
3. All trades would be final and lease agreements would not be allowed.
4. Measurements and colors of completed "manufactured goods" must be exact.
5. The object of the game was to fill the largest number of the teacher's requests for finished products in the allotted thirty minutes.

Predictably, the larger groups that had initially been supplied with crayons, rulers, and scissors far outpointed the smaller groups by filling the most teacher requests within the time allotment.

After the game, the children discussed the activity. They readily drew analogies between the game experience and the dilemma of underdeveloped nations in the industrialized twentieth century. During the discussion, a flood of questions was loosed. The children asked: "Why don't nations without machines go broke as we did?" "Why don't we give them some machines?" "What did the paper represent?" "Who writes the stuff on the board so the nations know what to make?"

CLASH

During the game, a "war" (a near fist fight) developed over a difficult trade negotiation between one large group and two small groups. The incident gave the teacher a convenient vehicle for pointing out one source of conflict between nations.

The technique of simulation had much appeal for the children. The technique was used later to demonstrate other concepts: the greater efficiency of the production line in comparison with earlier methods of manufacture, the inflation of a monetary system, the ascendancy of the factory system of manufacture over the independent craftsman, and the peculiar difficulties that landlocked nations meet in trying to engage in world trade.

The use of simulation in the social studies program offers great possibilities. All the simulations inspired lively class discussions, enthusiastic research, a beginning understanding of the concepts demonstrated, and a heightened enjoyment of the elementary-school social studies program.

The illustrations of simulation experiences presented here are limited to topics usually treated in fifth- or sixth-grade social studies programs. The technique can be used in other areas of study, in American history, for example. Simulation is a widely useful tool for developing many understandings throughout the entire social studies program for the intermediate grades.

ROLE-PLAYING IN A
TROUBLED CLASS

Josie Crystal

In the spring semester of 1967 I transferred from an upper-middle-class public school in west Los Angeles to teach Negro children in a school in central Los Angeles. This community has changed much in the past four to five years. Most of the stable families have moved farther west into "better" sections and have been replaced by more transient families.

Many of the recent newcomers are families without fathers. More than half of the children in my class had no father living at home. The unemployment rate seemed to be well over 50 per cent. The responses of this class on the Federal Impact Survey for May, 1967, indicated that nearly 70 per cent of the parents were unemployed. The per cent may be inaccurate, since the form is unclear, and it is possible that some parents did not fill out the place of employment because of misunderstanding.

Most of the homes in the community are individual dwellings, small, modest, frame houses moderately well kept. This description gives an impression of better conditions than really exist. Several families may live in a single dwelling. Relatives who have just come from the South often spend weeks and months with cousins, aunts, or grandmothers.

There are pockets of poverty on the fringes bordered by Western Avenue, the main street. This is an area of ramshackle apartments, shacks behind other

Josie Crystal, "Role-Playing in a Troubled Class," *Elementary School Journal,* **69** (January 1969), 169–179. Copyright © 1969 by the University of Chicago Press. Reprinted with permission of the author and the University of Chicago Press.

houses, and the kind of slum conditions associated with back-alley life.

My first impression of my class was its explosiveness. Typically, between the time the children came into the class at nine and recess at ten-thirty as many as three fights broke out in the classroom. On the playground the children rarely played with one another. They usually fought for the balls and then ran away with them. Unruly behavior is a way of life among highly disturbed children. During the semester there was not a child in this class who was not involved in a physical fight. Usually boys fought boys and girls fought girls, but sometimes fights broke out between boys and girls.

The outbreaks were usually over name-calling: "He called my mother a dirty name. He was messin' with me." These, of course, were only external causes. Repeated failure, constant frustration, unsuitable home conditions, inadequate diet, lack of sleep, and inability to talk out problems took their toll. The children's self-concept and sense of worth were weak and negative.

SCHOOL—A DRAG

School re-enforced some of their worst inadequacies. These sixth-graders saw school as a prison, a place to avoid if possible, a trap of all their weaknesses. On the street, some of the children, especially the boys, had already earned status, but at school it was taken away. Among eleven- and twelve-year-olds, it was very "uncool" to be positive about anything having to do with school, even if one did find something attractive about it. The better the show of antagonism toward school, teacher, and lessons, the tougher one appeared and the higher one's status in the peer group.

The children's interest was extremely difficult to capture. As a group they were never able to remain calm for more than five minutes at a time. Any kind of instruction had to be given in as short a time as possible.

Ideally, teaching should have been done individually or in small groups. There was a negligible amount of group cohesiveness. On a sociogram made during the second week of the semester, no child received more than three choices. Some leadership developed, but it was effective only occasionally.

Group discussions and evaluations were almost impossible, since the children reacted with barrages of accusations and counteraccusations; tempers flared immediately and a brand new fight broke out. Riot-like conditions were not uncommon. One fight led to others in and out of the classroom.

During individual talks with children involved in some difficulty, there was rarely any sign of objectivity or of understanding the dynamics of the incident. Reasoning it out with a child did not seem to work. The confronted child always seemed to feel unjustly accused, persecuted, resentful, and blameless. It seemed impossible to help a child see the other guy's side, regardless of guilt. It seemed that the child always felt that he had been the sole recipient of injury so that no understanding could be reached and there were often recurrences the next day.

At this point it seemed reasonable to try role-playing.

Role-playing provides experience in seeing the relationship between cause and effect. Since wise choices depend on foreseeing probable consequences, role-playing would hopefully lead to the habit of using forethought and break the existing behavior pattern of impulsive physical outbursts.

A PREFERENCE FOR ACTION

Muriel Crosby,[1] Hilda Taba,[2] and Frank Riessman,[3] all specialists in the study of disadvantaged children, have reported that children from low income families respond more fully and directly to action than to talk. Role-playing offers many opportunities. The informality, the humor, and the empathy-arousing drama catch young people's interest, involve them, and hold their attention. Slum children, whose crowded homes and play settings condition them to working together, find the group aspects of role-playing natural. In contrast to their lack of attentiveness in ordinary discussion and their hesitancy to answer questions, they respond to role-playing more spontaneously and enthusiastically.

PANTOMIME

Since my pupils were reluctant to approach any activity that appeared unfamiliar or different, I thought it best to start the role-playing sequence with short, quick, warm-up exercises in which simple situations could be enacted in pantomime. I tried suggestions that Mark Chesler and Robert Fox made in their book[4] *Role-Playing Methods in the Classroom*:

> walking on pebbles barefooted
> looking for a lost puppy
> arguing with a silent umpire
> eating potato chips, a lemon, pickles, cotton candy
> throwing an ice cube, a feather, a hot potato, a ball
> having a cinder in one's eye
> carrying a heavy water bucket
> lifting a heavy load
> putting on a pull-over sweater
> stand facing another student pretending to be his reflection in a mirror
> walking a tightrope

The authors list pantomimes that require some show of emotion, though no words.

How do you feel when:

it rains on the day of a picnic.
a large dog is running toward you.
you find a dead bird.
your baseball bat is broken.
you see people teasing a dog.
you are watching a funny film.
you get an *A* or an *F* on a test.
you see a friend who has been telling lies about you.

The authors also list problem situations for one main character:

two good friends ask you to go to two different places at the same time.
your best friend tries to talk to you while you're listening to an explanation of a lesson in math.
a friend tries to get you to sneak off the playground at noon.
you see two kids who are about to get into a fight.
you're walking by a fruit stand and your friend tries to get you to steal.
you're in the middle of a good game and some outsider runs away with the ball.
you're sitting doing your spelling work and the person sitting across from you starts shooting paper clips.
a neighbor tries to look at your answers during a test.

I began the pantomimes about the fourth week of school. The whole class was enthusiastic. It was the first time the class responded unanimously to anything I suggested. There were many volunteers, and I had my first opportunity to see the children in a fairly natural situation. They had been extremely guarded about any spontaneous expression outside of anger or hostility. We had not laughed together once before this first pantomime session.

Unrecognized talent emerged. Children who posed the worst behavior problems were the most enthusiastic participants and among the most gifted actors. Through the dramatizations, it became evident that many of the children were very observant of their physical environment, very much aware of weight, distance, pain, balance, temperature, and taste. They were not at all lacking in the involvement that seemed characteristic of their ordinary classroom behavior. For the first time I saw them laugh at themselves. For the first time I saw them show delight, amusement, and the kind of child-like joy that is easily found among middle-class children in ordinary situations.

For the first half-hour session, the children actually enjoyed one another in an unhostile, friendly, and accepting way. It seemed as if they were discovering things about one another they had never recognized. They would clap spontaneously at someone's good performance and look to where I was sitting as if to say, "Wasn't that great?"

ENCORE

The children who showed the most remarkable response were the two most hostile and most belligerent boys in the room. It seemed as if all the attention they had been lacking was suddenly available to them, and they clamored for more "pantomime" long after it was over.

The sessions gave me the first genuine opportunity to praise the two boys for something they felt great about doing. Previously, I had given praise honestly, but I sensed their rejection of it almost every time, since praise from Teacher was usually considered "uncool."

AFTER RECESS—NO CHANGE

I must add that my big disappointment came when after the first few panto-mimes several children lost interest because they were not personally involved. I had asked some of them to take the roles, but they refused. After the first ten or fifteen minutes they showed signs of restlessness, but did not disturb those who were still acting. During that first session none of the children who presented serious behavior problems lost interest. It was also disappointing that after recess the children showed no change in general behavior even though they had left the classroom with high *esprit de corps*.

I realize now that any change would have been miraculous. We had many long sessions before any sign of improvement appeared. What misled me in my expectations was that in every other teaching situation, any such activity—whether dramatic play, construction, or art—yielded almost immediate results in building group cohesiveness. But not here in central Los Angeles.

After this initial pantomime session, I used every opportunity that lent itself to dramatization. In our social studies we were studying Nigeria. Any information that we read that could be acted out was dramatized on the spot. I found that this made the children eager to read more in order to be able to "pantomine." We pantomined every aspect of our study, from tapping rubber trees to boiling palm oil. Perhaps the greatest value of role-playing was that it gave the children a legitimate opportunity to get out of their seats.

At the time I was reading them African folk tales from various sources written especially for children. The stories are excellent for dramatization, since they stress action rather than conversation. Furthermore, they are often about inanimate objects that come to life or animals that have anthropomor-phic qualities. The stories can be used almost exactly as they are without any modification. They are short and follow a simple line of action in much the same way that *Aesop's Fables* do. The tales are ideal to build groundwork for more complicated role-playing. Many children who refused to take the role of a person accepted the role of an animal.

A PLEA FOR PLAYS

After several weeks, role-playing or dramatization became a part of the curriculum. Certain children often said to me: "What we were doing can be acted out. Could we please?"

We played one folk tale for the principal and any visitor that happened to come to the class. This was an activity the children definitely "felt" in the experiential sense.

Still, the intense behavior problems continued. The fighting did not lessen. Peer hostility did not taper off. Perhaps the most positive outcome so far was that the children seemed to enjoy school more than before. During this period several of my worst offenders in the schoolyard and in the classroom were threatened with transfer to other classes. They met the threat with begging and pleading for another chance. I decided to perceive this as a positive outcome, though I was not ready to establish any connection between dramatization and the desire to remain in class.

A PROBLEM STORY

During the tenth week of school I introduced the first problem story. "But Names Will Never Hurt Me," from the book *Role-Playing for Social Values*[5] by Fannie R. Schaftel. Though I had warned the children that there would be no ending, they were quite agitated that it was so.

Many wanted to act out the story, but refused when they were called on. I suspect that they refused because of the ambiguity and the fear of making a mistake or of being unable to make the proper ending.

We discussed possible solutions, which I listed on the board under two headings, "positive" and "negative." We laboriously acted out each solution, and I was gratified and encouraged to hear the children say:

"Well, couldn't you talk it over before you started to fight?"

"Hey, come on don't fight; it ain't gonna help."

"Let's go call the teacher."

"Callin' names ain't nothin' so bad."

There was also the usual, "I'm gonna get my brother, punk, don't mess with me." There was one mock fight, which the actors ended themselves.

When we took a final vote, the children decided on one of the negative solutions, much to my disappointment. I was perplexed at the time by the public sanctioning the vote seemed to give to fighting, but decided to keep trying.

I realized that it was easy for me to contaminate any kind of genuine expression if I too openly showed approval or disapproval at the time of the evaluation. It was entirely possible that they might be voting just to thwart the teacher's expectations, since they were so hostile toward any authority figures.

PUPILS BECOME PLAYWRIGHTS

After recess I had a pleasant surprise. They asked me whether they might act out a play they had made up on the playground just before. Reluctantly I allowed it—but after arithmetic. I was determined to do some teaching that day, and they were quite stimulated from the excitement of the morning.

One difficulty of allowing "acting out" is that children tend to become perhaps even "higher" immediately after it is over. The teacher must decide whether she can stand the stress that accompanies such behavior. I tried to have a recess period immediately after the sessions. It was always difficult to judge when to stop and when to continue. One has to sense whether the class is becoming so "high" that the rest of the morning will be impossible. Whenever I could, I chose not to threaten the children with total elimination of the activity, since it would have defeated my ultimate purposes.

The play that the children worked out by themselves was quite simple and unrefined in presentation, as I had expected. Loosely put together, though full of spontaneity and enthusiasm, it was about two children who had been in a fight and were now being represented by older brothers and sisters. There was a great deal of fast and loud arguing. A mock fight broke out, but it was quickly ended by some of the more peaceful adversaries and a firm matriarchal figure, who finally said, "Well, if you ain't gonna apologize, then just go home." This ended the play. The negative tone of the earlier play that morning was now replaced by a much more positive manner. I was encouraged.

The rest of the day classroom behavior seemed more acceptable, probably because of my own optimism over the second play. The two natural leaders in the class had enjoyed the venture. They were much more co-operative than usual in helping to get the class in order for dismissal. These same two leaders were the loudest, most stubborn, and often most unruly members of the class. They could swing in either direction. Dramatization brought out their better qualities more consistently than any other classroom activity.

PROBLEMS IN THE AUDIENCE

About half of the pupils in the class were still non-participants, however. When the plays dragged, these children showed a great deal of boredom and became so disturbing that they interfered with the play acting. The biggest problem was still how to involve everyone.

At the following session, the children again acted out a play written by the children themselves. Several girls were spending their free time writing plays with long elaborate lists of characters, little dialogue, and sketchy descriptions of the action. Since few of the children would be able to "read" scripts even if they were more adequately prepared, I decided at this point not to interfere with the playwriting.

ON SOCIAL LIFE

A large group of children formed to enact one of these plays and begged for time to practice. The play they wanted to do was about a camp situation in which the boys and the girls came together and were expected to socialize. Since this was a pre-adolescent group, it seemed a natural theme. Meetings and introductions were elaborately enacted. An amazing degree of personality was revealed. Each boy or girl introduced himself and then interacted in a "social teen-age" atmosphere. I found the play useful for understanding some of the children's self-concepts. Some revealed a brand new side I had never suspected.

Again, leadership was clearly shown. I was beginning to recognize increasingly why certain children held power over their peers. I saw that the children who were decisive and fast-talking were the most popular. Quick action, regardless of its appropriateness in a given situation, was the quality that was most admired and respected.

Georgene and Stewart, the two emergent leaders, had a great deal of "style" and were unquestionably considered "hip". Both were extremely aggressive and often brutal in their treatment of their peers. I am fairly sure that neither child was well liked, but both were feared and given the kind of respect that accompanies fear. It is not surprising that the children attached themselves to such authoritarian types. This is the kind of personality that has probably had the most influence in their own personal lives.

STANDARD ENDING

The play ended in the usual "fight" between the boys, much to the girl's disdain. The playwright protested vociferously that she had not written the script that way, but no one was paying attention to the script anymore.

I was not overly distressed by the "violent" end, for a great deal of co-operation and accommodation had gone into the rehearsals. I had steered clear of giving any direction. I accepted the invitation to watch the final rehearsal on the playground, but made no recommendations. I wanted to see how the children acted toward one another when they had a common goal about which there was a fair amount of commitment. It was gratifying to see that they seemed to interact with more cohesiveness, self-direction, and harmony than I had ever seen in them before.

The next play the children presented was "Johnny Kotowski," from the book by Schaftel.[5] Somehow the story did not reach them. No one wanted to accept a part immediately. Reluctance and lack of interest were obvious. The performance was artificial and muddled.

SHIFT TO THE CASUAL

I decided to go back to simpler story plots in which the action was confined to a single scene. It was hard for the children to change scenes without a great deal of direction from me; my interruptions tended to stifle spontaneity.

Also, I tried a more casual approach to the sessions. Often in the middle of the day when I sensed that the children were so restless that little constructive activity would be possible, I would say, "I need two people at the front of the room to do a play. You're going to act out a situation in which your best friend tries to talk you into leaving the playground at lunch time. Who wants to try it?"

The response to such spontaneous skits was enthusiastic. The results were becoming more natural and more delightful. The whole class became far more involved when the plays were short and quick than when they were long. Often we would end with a good laugh at something funny that had happened and then resume curriculum activities. I sensed that the children—actors and audience—tended to forget themselves and become deeply immersed in the action.

I asked Georgene and Stewart to do the disciplining during these short skits. Since both were keen on acting, they ruled with an iron hand and order was easily maintained. I felt that this was useful, for peer-group control was developing. It allowed me to become part of the audience, free to observe and show approval without having to act as part-time referee.

The skits that dealt with stealing and other illegal behavior showed a lack of concern with morality; the only concern was fear of being caught. The ramifications were obvious. I had discussed the rightness or wrongness of an aggressive act with the children, but I now realized that this approach was inappropriate. At this point all that should be emphasized was the realistic danger inherent in an aggressive act, not the morality of it. This was no small discovery.

A WELCOME GUEST

At this time the principal asked to observe some sessions. The children and I welcomed the opportunity to have her as a guest. The children were pleased because her visit gave them an important personage in the audience. I was glad because I knew that her presence would make some deeper evaluation possible. Fewer children would openly attack each other as in previous evaluations. The attempts at evaluation had all too frequently turned into vicious accusations that created brand new conflicts. It must be said that this principal is an exceptionally sensitive, perceptive, and sympathetic person, who encourages any innovation that may have even the remotest chance of reaching children.

THE SPELLING TEST

For the occasion two children enacted a skit about cheating during a spelling test. The skit was extremely well acted by the two culprits as well as the girl who played the role of teacher. When she discovered the cheating, she silently pulled one child away from his friend and went right on with the spelling test without uttering a single syllable of reproach.

We were able to have a discussion on cheating—how it feels to have someone copy answers from your paper, how the teacher feels about it. The class said that it was not really that bad to miss many words. All that happens is that you have to take the test again after you have had a chance to study the words once more. The children were unanimous in their approval of the "teacher's" method of handling the cheater. They were glad that she did not embarrass him. Having to cheat was embarrassment enough.

This was certainly the most successful session so far. Watching the children at their most "mature" level gave the teacher and the children renewed hope. Because this class set a high premium on negative behavior, this experience with maturity was a revelation.

In the afternoon of that same day, we had class elections, which were held about every two weeks to give many pupils a chance to hold office. The children voted out the incumbent officers, Georgene and Stewart, and chose a quiet but powerful boy who said little, but could fight anyone on the schoolyard. The former leaders were miffed and threatened to be disruptive under any new officer. Subsequently, they refused co-operation on every occasion, but the class and I did our best to ignore them. Unfortunately, the next day, the new president got into a heated battle with a girl during arithmetic and had to be suspended from school. The suspension gave the former leaders fuel for their fires. I was uncertain whether to reinstate him or to rule him out, as several pupils suggested. The problem promised to be a good topic for the next role-playing session.

The following day the children were hostile. Fearing an excess of punitive reaction, I did not bring up the question of keeping the new president, Brian, in office.

TOWARD GIVE-AND-TAKE

We played a scene in which two smaller children were being bullied by the classroom tormentor and another child tried to intervene. Three sets of children played the scene. After the plays were over, I asked the class to vote on which was the best solution. Then I asked them to vote on the best solutions as they thought their own mother might vote, as they thought the principal might vote, and as they thought their best friend might vote. To my surprise, they agreed unanimously on the most positive solution. It was—in each election—the solution that offered a compromise.

A BREAK FROM OLD PATTERNS?

Each of the three scenes showed a definite increase in verbal rather than physical efforts to solve problems. At the risk of excess optimism, I hoped that the children were beginning to realize that there is a way besides physical reaction. I doubted that any of the role-playing would influence their daily interactions, for when emotions run high, reason runs low. Still, the fact that the children were beginning to even think of other solutions in their calmer moments might be a sign that the role-playing was having an effect. I chose to hope it was a beginning.

The Schaftel story "Trick or Treat" created eager participation.[5] In the story a mild prank results in a serious injury for which two innocent children are blamed. The children enacted the scene in which one boy attempts to persuade the other culprit to own up. Interesting arguments were offered:

"You ain't gonna be able to sleep if you don't."

"Your conscience is really gonna hurt your head."

"You gonna go straight to the devil."

"Man, if you don't tell, you got no soul."

As usual, the children who are in trouble almost daily are the ones who talk most freely along these lines. Yet on the day this play was presented I was distressed to see a knock-down, drag-out battle between the two boys who had made the most contributions in the discussion after the play. Evidently, any kind of transference would require far more play acting.

The trick-or-treat tale ended with the consultation of a juvenile officer, who took the pair of boys down to be fingerprinted. This turn of events led to a heated argument over what happens at juvenile hall. I explained briefly the appearance before a judge and punishment depending on the seriousness of the offense. One boy then asked whether the culprits in our story would receive a milder sentence if they agreed to pay for the damages. The whole class was excited by this suggestion, but some realists reminded their classmates that money cannot really compensate for physical injury.

GROWTH

I believe that I saw growth in the application of reasoning to problems when they were isolated in this way, but the lack of visible carry-over is discouraging and makes me wonder whether role-playing is worth the time and energy. Dare I take heart from the belief that though the children may not always come up with proper behavior, they continue to give the problems thought when they are alone or perhaps in a more comfortable atmosphere? That hope, it would seem, justified continuing this daily exercise.

"Keeping the faith" is not easy!

In "Shutter-Bug," from the Schaftel book, an individual has to make a decision as to whether to consider his desires or the needs of the group.[5]

The outcome was not especially meaningful. As I watched the presentation, I was wondering whether the story was appropriate when I overheard a small buzz group discussing the problem privately. "This," they were telling one another, "was just like the time when. . . ."

GUIDELINES FOR TOMORROW

At that moment I had a flash of insight that these experiences in the classroom may have far more value sometime in the future when the children will recall them, perhaps even as guidelines for their own plan of action. Right now because of emotional immaturity, the children may not yet be able to apply some of the solutions offered. Later they may well recall a similar situation and how their peers reacted. Maybe it is this process of laying bare the reactions of their peers that will ultimately be most meaningful. The recognition that everyone has similar experiences and has to meet conflicts that are more alike than different may give the children a measure of security they might not otherwise have.

The experience of watching and participating in these make-believe situations that are real and life-like gives the viewer a storehouse of experiences in human relationships he would not otherwise have. When children are removed from the emotionally charged context in which conflicts usually occur, they are likely to come to an intellectual understanding of what is going on. Whether their immediate subsequent behavior is affected is perhaps not so important—however desirable from my point of view—as the opportunity to observe and evaluate in an unthreatening environment. The fact that the children verbalize their conclusions poorly does not mean that they lack understanding.

I am making no final judgments on the basis of this semester's activities. I am far more certain of the potential value this process holds for "typical" classes than for the one I taught. I am also aware of my limited knowledge and experience in guiding these sessions. In the hands of a trained guidance counselor or psychologist, role-playing is probably far more likely to be effective. I cannot even be sure that the ordinary classroom teacher ought to tamper with this sensitive area. Few principles would have permitted it, I am sure. I am grateful for the opportunity to try it and will continue my efforts.

The time to reach disadvantaged children is now. Role-playing offers some hope.

NOTES

1. Crosby, Muriel, *An Adventure in Human Relations*, Chicago: Follett, 1965.

2. Taba, Hilda, *Teaching Strategies for the Culturally Disadvantaged*, Chicago: Rand McNally, 1966.

3. Riessman, Frank, *Helping the Disadvantaged Pupils To Learn More Easily*, Englewood Cliffs, N.J.: Prentice-Hall, 1966.

4. Chesler, Mark, and Robert Fox, *Role-Playing Methods in the Classroom*, Chicago: Science Research Associates, 1965.

5. Schaftel, Fannie R., *Role-Playing for Social Values*, Englewood Cliffs, N.J.: Prentice-Hall, 1967.

REVOLUTION AND JUSTICE: ROLE-PLAYING IN SOCIAL STUDIES

Peter G. Kontos

One of the Trenton teachers was concerned, after he had observed my 1965 class, with the fact that I had refused to define the word revolution when asked to do so by the students. I had instead asked them what they thought it meant. I asked him, an art teacher, if there were many of his brush strokes on the canvases of his students. He answered that he didn't put his brush to their work, and that if he did, the canvases would not truly be the pupils' works of art but, rather, extensions of his own ideas. I told him that I tried to avoid the same pitfall in teaching history.

This conversation typifies much of what we were about—explaining and demonstrating the inductive method. The pupils were "discovering" the answer to a problem by using their experience and reasoning abilities. Each was painting his own canvas. It is the method that Dr. Charles Keller of the John Hay Fellows Program calls "drawing it out instead of pouring it on." It is the method that was used in the social studies classes in the Princeton-Trenton Institute.

Basically, the curriculum and techniques used were chosen to serve as a showcase for the inductive method of teaching. The curriculum in social studies revolved around two themes which lent themselves well to two in-depth studies using the discovery method—the idea of revolution and the concept of justice. Three techniques—role-playing, discussion, and composi-

Peter G. Kontos, "Revolution and Justice: Role-Playing in Social Studies," from P. G. Kontos and James J. Murphy, ed., *Teaching Urban Youth*, New York: John Wiley & Sons, 1967, pp. 92–98. Reprinted with permission of the publisher.

tion—complemented the inductive inquiry and allowed some concentration on the development of basic skills necessary for the study of history.

Role-playing was used as a motivational device in order to stimulate interest and to involve the pupil in class participation. This device sparks pupils' interest almost immediately because it creates an attitude of controversy and conflict. The student becomes involved in class discussion because he is comfortable in a situation in which he is not penalized for making mistakes. If the student is wrong, it is the character of the role being played that is wrong, not the student who is playing the role.

A class discussion in which the pupil is urged to participate, rather than a teacher's lecture, provides an arena for testing a pupil's conceptions against other pupils' arguments and for the testing by the teacher of the credibility of pupil responses.

Composition called for a final restatement of the students' historical position in a logical and organized argument and, at the same time, it encouraged the correct use of basic communication skills.

Each of the techniques used in a sequence would complement and reinforce the others. It was not essential, however, to begin with role-playing and to follow in sequence with discussion and composition. The three techniques could be used interchangeably.

The classroom investigation of revolution was scheduled for a four-day period. The fifth day was usually reserved for a trip or other miscellaneous activity which, as it turned out, might or might not be related to the social studies curriculum. The pupils began the first day by taking a quiz which was not graded or collected. The quiz was based on five misconceptions of revolution discussed by Carl G. Gustavson in the chapter on revolution from his book *A Preface to History*. The students were asked to identify as true or false the following statements:

1. A revolution is caused by the misery of the people.

2. One of the principal reasons for a revolution is the tyranny and brutality of the government.

3. The transfer of power occurs when people storm the citadels of the government in the course of a civil war.

4. In a revolution, the people rise spontaneously and take power.

5. The result of a revolution is to gain greater freedom for the people.

After taking the quiz, the students were asked to defend or attack the validity of the statements. Most of the pupils felt that these statements were fairly accurate generalities regarding revolution. The teacher then made the statement that he thought that all of the statements might be false. The reason for this conclusion was not given by the teacher at this time, even though the pupils pressed him for his reasons. Instead, the teacher said that the statements would be re-examined at the end of the four days to see if the pupils had changed their minds.

It was important to emphasize at this point that the pupils' arguments were just as valid as were the teacher's, and that perhaps the teacher did not have the correct answers. The teacher suggested that perhaps they could get closer to a better analysis of the statements if they studied the idea of revolution in depth. The pupils were then asked how they would plan a revolution if the teenagers of Trenton decided to take over the city. Through the inductive method the pupils realized that one of the elements necessary to the planning of a revolution was a knowledge of how other revolutions had occurred, and that by examining past revolutions they might be aided in planning their "revolution." They also discussed methods of gathering data and types of historical testimony by distinguishing between primary and secondary evidence.

The class decided on the American Revolution and the civil-rights movement as their case studies. These were selected because they were both relevant to the pupils' own experiences, and because the class felt that there would be ample resource material available for their analysis. The class assignment was to find and read as much as possible on the cause of the American Revolution for class discussion the next day. Possible sources for this investigation were discussed.

On the second day a role-playing situation was structured. A summit meeting was to be held between American colonists and the British government, supposedly just before the outbreak of hostilities in 1775. The students were asked to try to resolve the differences between these two factions. The class was divided into two groups. One of the groups was designated American colonists, the other, representatives of the British government. Both groups were given copies of the Declaration of Independence (although it was pointed out that it had not yet been written), Patrick Henry's "Liberty or Death" speech, and a selection from Thomas Paine's pamphlet *The Crisis*. The students were also encouraged to use and share another resource material they had found as part of their homework assignment.

Each group met separately during the first half of the class period and planned its presentation, trying to interpret the historical positions of the group it represented. During the second half of the class period, the students held their "summit meeting" and argued from the point of view either of the colonists or the British. Their homework assignment was to write a composition presenting the view of the opposition and a restatement of their own position.

On the third day the compositions were discussed and a decision was usually reached as to whether there was any relationship between the principles and causes of the American Revolution and the present civil-rights movement. The entire class listened to a recording of Dr. Martin Luther King's speech "I

Have a Dream." Another role-playing situation was then structured. The group that had played the American colonists were asked to play a host of roles representing various attitudes of segregationists. The group that had represented the British point of view were cast in the roles of civil-rights workers. The time was established as the present and the place as Mississippi. The two groups were to meet and discuss their differences in another mock "summit meeting."

The civil-rights group was given a *Springboards* reading selection entitled "Civil Rights" and selected testimony drawn from *Mississippi Black Paper*, which was compiled by the Misseduc Foundation, Inc. The segregationists were also given a copy of the same *Springboard* lesson and selected articles from *Life* magazine which quoted attitudes of Ku Klux Klan members and other segregationists. The pupils were encouraged to find additional sources. The groups met individually for the remainder of the period to organize their arguments and to explore possible sources of additional information.

On the fourth day the role-playing situation was allotted the first 20 minutes of the period. The class discussion after the role-playing compared the American Revolution with the civil-rights movement. The students were then asked to re-examine the original statement regarding revolution and to write a composition defending or attacking the original statements by Gustavson.

The investigation of the concept of justice was also planned to cover a four-day period. Selections from Edwin Fenton's *32 Problems in World History*, the essay "We Are Not Superstitious" by Stephen Vincent Benet, and the entire film, "The Ox-Bow Incident" were the curriculum materials for the study of justice.

The Fenton materials were introduced on the first day. They consisted of selections from Hammurabi's Code of Law and from the Old Testament. These readings expressed the "revenge theory" of justice. The teacher played the role of Hammurabi during the course of the first period and defended Hammurabi's point of view to the students, who played the roles of senate investigators. The class in the discussion which followed decided that punishment alone was not an acceptable form of justice. During the entire course of the four-day period, the pupils were encouraged to keep a written journal defining their conception of justice.

On the second day the students read the Benet essay which described the Salem witch trials. The pupils again assumed roles and passed judgment on the teenagers in history who had instigated the witch hunts. They found, however, that they used punishment and revenge as justice. A situation was created in which the teenagers had revolted against the adults in society and were now faced with the task of establishing a new society. In their discussions they arrived at the conclusion that, in order to have justice, they must first establish, like Plato, a "just state." The state that the teenagers felt would work best closely resembled the American democratic society.

The pupils viewed "The Ox-Bow Incident" on the following day and, on the fourth day, discussed safeguards against the breakdown of justice in a democratic society.

The pupils studying the concept of justice were exposed to the historical skills of using and evaluating primary and secondary evidence. They also learned to withhold historical judgment until they had weighed the factors which had contributed to the actions and decisions of past societies and individuals. They were, however, neither encouraged nor discouraged in interpreting history according to contemporary moral standards. Making moral judgments became an individual concern to each pupil, as it is and should be with the trained professional historian.

This was generally the plan and activity of the classroom demonstrations. There were, of course, slight variations in some of the classes. Larry Cuban, of the Washington, D.C., Cardoza project, for example, taught two of the classes for one day and discussed the causes of the American Civil War. There were also differences in the individual makeup of each of the classes, and the various interests of the pupils caused some of the ideas to be more fully developed than others. One class, for example, might express more interest in the ideas of freedom and its application to revolution than would the other classes.

It was interesting to note that a few of the teachers had never known that the role-playing method existed, and they completely rejected its use in a classroom situation. By the end of the session, though, many teachers and some of the few skeptics were discussing ways by which to improve and implement the role-playing technique in their own classes in Trenton.

A few other incidents merit recording. Early in the Institute a teacher volunteered to teach part of the class period. His topic was to be a comparison of the French and American Revolutions. This portion of the class turned out to be a lecture, in which the teacher spoke for 18 of the 20 minutes allotted. The teacher asked questions, but the pupils simply did not respond. Halfway through the questioning period, the teacher said, "I just don't know how to get you kids to answer." His admission and recognition of this problem was a beginning. He began to question some of his methods. He returned at the end of the Institute and asked for and received world history materials which were problem-centered and which required more pupil participation than did the traditional textbook.

During the final week of the Institute, two of the teachers assumed roles which would have made a traditional teacher uncomfortable and perhaps vulnerable. A situation was structured in which the teenagers had taken over America and had called on the two teachers to defend the ideas and attitudes of the adult world. The teachers in this session allowed the teenagers to question openly the values and traditions of adult society. I think they would not have felt as secure in a similar situation at the beginning of the Institute. Another teacher was overheard early in the Institute to say, "Nothing can be done with these students." But later he said, "Before anything can be done, it is the teacher's responsibility to know all that he can about his students." This remark represents a striking shift in attitude.

The pupils were a joy. It was remarkable and thoroughly enjoyable to witness a transformation in their thinking. They became more inquisitive; they were no longer satisfied with a pat or glib answers from their peers and, possibly most important, they relied more upon and were more confident in their own abilities than had been the case during the first week of classes. Two incidents are illustrative of this change. The first occurred when, during the third week of classes, the pupils began to define the words *patrician* and *plebeian* by the way they were used in the readings rather than by asking me for the definitions or simply skipping over the words as they had done during the early weeks of classes.

The second incident occurred when one of the students was challenged by another to define the word *freedom*. Her definitions proved weak and unconvincing. Challenged again to provide a definition, she replied, "Well, maybe I don't know now, but I've got all week-end to find out." On the following Monday she produced a well-written, well-documented essay on the meaning of freedom. I had neither assigned nor prompted her to write this essay. Instead, the stimulation had been provided by another pupil.

I think that I shall never forget these students. It would be difficult to forget a group of students represented by a girl who said to me after the first week, "Thank you. You are the first teacher that ever told me I did something good."

Much of what was done this summer can never be described fully, even if the most minute records were kept; for teaching, I feel, is an art form. Any description of a work of art, whether the work be good or bad, can never really do that piece of art justice. Nor has anyone yet written *the* manual for effective teaching. I suspect that no one ever will. Teaching must be demonstrated, it must be viewed, and a teacher should do both, during a relatively short period of time, to appreciate and work toward an understanding of the art of teaching. Herein lies the strength and justification of the Institute. It became a living laboratory for teaching practices. It became a place where the feel and the indefinables of teaching were shared and expressed as a common creative experience.

SOCIODRAMA AS A
TEACHING TECHNIQUE

Grace Graham

Not long ago a young man whom we shall call John Jones, a West Coast college student, applied for a teaching position in a small Eastern city. After submitting his recommendations and exchanging several letters with the superintendent of schools, he was given a contract which he signed. John and Mary, his wife, bought a trailer in which they made a leisurely trip across the United States, arriving at their destination a week before the opening of school.

The next morning John visited Mr. Brown, the superintendent.

Mr. Brown was very upset when he saw John Jones. "You did not tell me you are a Negro," he said. "We have never had a Negro on our faculty and the community would not stand for it. I don't know what we can do about you. I'll call a meeting of the School Board to discuss the matter. But I can assure you, Mr. Jones, you will not be allowed to teach here."

John Jones went home to tell his wife the bad news and to discuss with her what they should do.

A story such as this is ideal for the implementation of sociodrama as a teaching method. After telling the story, the teacher would tell her class:

"Now we shall act out possible solutions that John and Mary might find to their problem. Tim, you play the role of John, and Jane, you play the role of Mary. Remember, you decide what you are going to do and also how you think the person whose part you are playing will *feel* and talk."

The teacher then chooses one or two other casts and sends the couples out of the classroom to discuss the problem briefly. While they are outside, the rest of the class quickly list various possible solutions, such as these:

1. sue in court for a year's salary;

2. plead with the Board for a chance, agreeing that John will leave after a trial period if he does not make good;

3. appeal to the National Association for the Advancement of Colored People for help;

4. get another job in the vicinity;

5. settle for compensation for time and expenses of trip;

6. get a job in a Negro school.

Grace Graham, "Sociodrama as a Teaching Technique," The *Social Studies*, **51** (December 1960), 257–259. Reprinted with permission of the author and publisher.

The casts return and *extemporaneously* discuss the problem and decide what they will do. Often the couples hit upon the same or a combination of the same solutions that the class suggested, but sometimes they act out an entirely different ending. The feeling that each pair puts into the dramatization usually varies from belligerency to dejection on the part of one or the other of the characters.

Following the role-playing, the class analyzes the solutions and the feelings portrayed in terms of reasoning, psychological authenticity, and possible consequences of alternate courses.

This sociodrama is an example taken from a college course in Social Foundations of Teaching where problems of minority groups are studied. The setting is present-day America, but any problem situation involving human relationships—current or historical—can be studied through sociodrama.

Classes in social studies that have learned the issues in a labor-management controversy might use a situation involving a meeting of leaders from both groups. A class might enact a scene in which the local town council discusses a problem. The mock United Nations meetings attended by high school representatives in many states are actually large-scale sociodramas. Family living courses offer innumerable problems of parent-child, brother-sister, child-peer group relationships that are natural plots for sociodramas. In sociodramas such as these, the primary purpose might be to present opposing views rather than arriving at a solution to the problem.

While stories for role-playing may come from today's headlines, they may be as old as recorded history. For example, the dilemma of Hans Van Loon, a wealthy patroon in New York who must choose sides in the American Revolution, or of Tom Smithson, a Northern States-Righter at the time of the Civil War, might be emphasized through sociodrama. In historical settings, probably imaginary characters in hypothetical situations are better material for role-playing than well known personages because the choices actually made by the latter tend to restrict creativeness.

Perhaps you are thinking, what is the advantage of this method over the usual informal class discussion beyond the fact that it adds a little variety? The chief advantage is that frequently the players and perhaps the class, too, *identify* with the roles being portrayed. In studying current affairs, their social sensitivities are developed because they learn how it feels to be in someone else's shoes. Identification with the aspirations, disappointments, troubles, and fears of others is especially important today when so much of our society is living in tight little subcultures of suburbia.

Sociodrama may help also to make everyday people who lived long ago come alive, problems seem real, and social history become more significant. They may, furthermore, add another dimension to good teaching of history: the concept of social change. Although problems of human relationships are as old as man, the solutions chosen by persons long dead might have been different had they known what we know today. Consequently, pupils must orient their thinking to that of the period being studied. Part of the evaluation of the sociodrama would entail the historical accuracy of the data cited in support of a decision. At the same time, children would be reminded that in like manner, some of the choices we make today might be unwise from the vantage point of 2500 A.D.

HOW TO TEACH USING A SOCIODRAMA

Planning Select a problem of human relationships that fits the maturity level of your pupils. If you are lucky you may find a short story that serves the purpose which you will read to the class. You may, however, write your own story or simply describe the characters and the situation in which they are involved to your class. In any event, the number of characters should be limited, how the story ends will not be suggested, and several different endings are possible.

Procedures

1.   Prepare the pupils to identify with the characters by explaining that you will choose some of them to act out the ending of the story you are about to tell or read.

2.   Read or tell the story. This should not take more than fifteen or twenty minutes.

3.   Choose the cast or casts. (At first, you may find it helpful to choose the actors before you tell the story.) Since you want your first sociodramas to be successful, you might choose boys and girls who would cooperate willingly and be able to talk readily. After you have used the technique a number of times, you should then choose pupils who would gain most from playing the role. For example, when you know a boy has no sympathy for unions, you would cast him in the role of a labor leader. The assumption is that he would learn something of labor's point of view from taking the role.

4.   Send the actors out of the room for a three to five minutes' planning session.

5.   Let the class suggest solutions. Some teachers may prefer to omit this step, but others find it useful in getting involvement from the whole class.

Perhaps with first attempts, you might prefer to spend the time in helping the class think through how they will evaluate the role-playing. At this time, you would also suggest that the class should be sympathetic with the performers and refrain from laughing.

6.   Students act out the conclusion of the story. While the play is in progress, you should sit with the class and not interrupt the players unless they are

obviously changing the facts of the situation as described. You should, however, recognize when a decision is reached, end the scene, and thank the performers. Sometimes the pupils themselves do not seem to realize when this point is reached.

7. Evaluate in terms of (a) emotional reactions portrayed; (b) facts cited; and (c) consequences of various courses of action. Sometimes teachers assume that they can evaluate their pupils' emotional reactions, too, on the basis of how they play roles. Thus they confuse sociodrama as a teaching method with psychodrama, a projective technique used by psychiatrists and psychologists. Since analyses derived from projective techniques are sometimes questionable even when made by expert psychologists, teachers should beware of amateur diagnosis. After all, you asked the pupil to play a role. Let's assume that he is doing just that.

A final word Plan carefully so that you will establish a clearcut problem situation that is interesting. Nevertheless, don't be discouraged if your first effort fails. Sociodrama will work on any age group from kindergarteners to adults, but older persons are more likely to laugh and be self-conscious and less likely to identify on first tries than younger children. After a little experience, the chief limitation of the technique is the lack of ingenuity of the teacher.

BLACK-WHITE CONFRONTATION:
HOW DOES IT FEEL?

Dale L. Brubaker

"Our nation is moving toward two societies, one black, one white—separate and unequal." Who is to blame for this separatism? Who is responsible for the ghetto? "White institutions created it, white institutions maintain it, and white society condones it."[1] In short, the National Advisory Commission on Civil Disorders concluded that the United States is a racist society and had better move quickly and visibly to correct its racial ills. One year later, in March of 1969, we were told that America failed to respond to the race warning issued by the National Advisory Commission. This warning was issued by Urban America, Inc., and the Urban Coalition, both nonprofit Washington organizations concerned with city problems.[2]

Dale L. Brubaker, "Black-White Confrontation: How Does It Feel?" Unpublished manuscript, printed with permission of the author.

It becomes clear, after recognizing the gravity of the present black-white confrontation, that changes in the attitudes and behavior of those who support the racist society are a necessity. The part our social studies programs have played, can play, and should play in this reconstruction of belief systems is the subject of the remainder of this essay.

Given the state of the present crisis in black-white relations, one cannot validly argue that social studies programs have been effective in preventing the United States from becoming a racist society. In fact, traditional approaches in social studies education, primarily cognitive in nature, have seemingly done little in effecting changes in students' attitudes and behavior with respect to the matter of racism. Some critics will reply by saying that classroom instruction can never change students' attitudes and behavior with respect to racial conflict.[3] It is asking too much to expect the school to make a difference in these matters. The writer would respond by saying that the schools in general and social studies teachers in particular cannot afford to fail to make the effort given our present crisis in black-white relations. That is, it is the writer's thesis that we must question traditional philosophical assumptions and approaches to social studies instruction and explore new ways of trying to change students' attitudes and behavior in confronting our present racial conflict.

COGNITIVE AND AFFECTIVE APPROACHES

Social studies objectives and methods have primarily been cognitive. That is, they " ... emphasize remembering or reproducing something which has presumably been learned, as well as ... the solving of some intellective task for which the individual has to determine the essential problem and then reorder given material or combine it with ideas, methods, or procedures previously learned."[4] The lecture or lecture-discussion method is very popular in social studies classes and the textbook serves as the major source of influence on social studies instruction.[5] Both support the cognitive approach. Obviously, those approaches which are primarily cognitive have failed to change student attitudes and behavior enough to prevent our society from becoming racist.

Those approaches which as yet have been given too little opportunity to make a difference in students' attitudes and actions may be labelled "affective". That is, they " ... emphasize a feeling tone, an emotion, or a degree of acceptance or rejection."[6] It is necessary, at this point, to disgress for a moment. A distinction between *objectives* and *teaching methods* is important; traditionally, the primary objective for the social studies has been "good citizenship".[7] The word "good" is affective; likewise, those involved in social studies education have said that they are teaching values. Yet those who have held the affective objective "good citizenship" as their primary goal in the social studies have primarily employed cognitive methods in attempting to reach their objectives. The paradox is obvious.

The remainder of this essay is devoted to a discussion of some affective methods which have largely been untapped in social studies instruction.

GETTING IN TOUCH WITH YOUR FEELINGS

It is the thesis of this essay that social studies teachers and students need to identify and understand their feelings about the black-white confrontation before their belief systems can be altered in order to precipitate action or behavior conducive to healthy black-white relationships. That is, the teacher and his students should get in touch with their own feelings and the feelings that others in the black-white confrontation have.

The following are some examples of affective techniques designed to achieve the objectives cited in the previous paragraph.[8]

The social studies teacher in an all white suburban school sits in a circle with twenty of his students. The following occurs:

Teacher: Close your eyes for a few minutes and imagine yourself in front of a large mirror. (Students have three minutes of silence to get themselves in the proper mood.)

Look very carefully in the mirror at your face. Notice your eyes, nose, and lips. Concentrate on your face.

Now imagine that your face is black. (Students think about this for a few minutes with their eyes closed.)

Please open your eyes and tell us what you experienced.

Some of the following student reactions have been recorded. "I kept withdrawing. I couldn't stand to be close to the mirror." "I felt terribly lonely." "I felt conspicuous. Everyone was staring at me." I was frightened. It was scary. I didn't know what my friends would think."

The teacher, having accomplished his goal of getting the students in touch with their feelings about blackness, moved on to a class discussion concerning why the students reacted as they did. The class discussed contemporary social forces and historical bases for present conditions with respect to black-white relations.

On another occasion the teacher and his students were discussing relations between blacks in the ghetto and the police, primarily white policemen.[9] The teacher wanted his students to experience the distrust and suspicion which exists between the two groups. One reason for this conflict is the use of informants in order to get information about those who are suspected of breaking the law.

The teacher asked each student to write his name on a slip of paper. The teacher then mixed these names in a hat and had each student draw a name not his own. Each student was asked to keep this name a secret. Then the participants related their own names orally so that the holder of the card knew his "target". The teacher told the students that they were to be police "spies" whose function it was to observe the person whose card they held. They were asked to observe any behavior that would be of use to the police. Next, the teacher told the students to informally mill around while at the same time observing the "target".

After ten minutes of this activity the students returned to the circle. Each student was then asked to inform orally on the person whose card he held. The level of suspicion and distrust was very high. Having experienced this conflict, the students discussed the black ghetto reaction to the use of these tactics by the police and how tension might be lessened between police and those living in the ghetto.

The teacher also wanted the students to understand some of the feelings a white policeman has in working in the ghetto. In order to achieve this goal, the teacher distributed cards, all but one of which had the name of a single student on them. The single student received a card with another student's name on it. The same "spy" game was then played with all attention on one person. In this way the single student experienced the suspicion and distrust a white policeman often feels in the ghetto.

Another feeling, consistent with the findings of the Kerner report, is the conflict between the "haves" and the "have nots", the rich and the poor, America and the "other America".[10] The teacher divided his students into two groups with ten in each group. Five of the ten students in each group were told that they have it, and the other five told that they want it. The five who had it immediately bunched together and joined hands to protect themselves. Those who didn't have it initially tried to talk the other group into giving it to them. When this didn't work they tried to physically break into the group that had it in order to get it. Intense anger developed between the two groups.

One student who didn't have it related the following: "At first I couldn't believe that I didn't have it. Then I tried to get it in any way I could. I got angry. When I realized that I couldn't get it, I felt frustrated. There wasn't any hope."

The same technique was used on another occasion with students paired— one having it and one not having it. Similar results occurred.

During one class discussion, a girl expressed her anger at black militants in general and Eldridge Cleaver in particular. The teacher placed an empty chair in the circle and said to the girl, "Eldridge Cleaver is sitting in that chair. Tell him how you feel!" The girl began slowly, finally conducting an angry tirade against Cleaver. The teacher then asked the girl to sit in Cleaver's chair, play the role of Cleaver, and respond to her previously made remarks. She tried to play Cleaver's role but finally admitted that she couldn't because his position made her too angry. At least she had gotten in touch with her own feelings on this matter even though she couldn't play Cleaver's part.

On another occasion the teacher divided the class into groups with five students per group. The students were asked to present a play dealing with the theme "The White Point of View." One group simulated an ice cream store. A white student walked in and asked for a dip of chocolate and a dip of vanilla. The dip of vanilla was on top. Two other students asked for the same thing and also got the dip of vanilla on top. A second group presented a skit based on a cafeteria scene. Four white students sat at a table. When a black student walked by the whites were overly friendly in asking him to sit down. When the black student didn't sit with them but instead moved on to another table the following comments were made by the white students: "What's wrong with him? Why wouldn't he sit with us?" "That's the way *they* are! They always stay together."

PROBLEMS AND PROSPECTS

The writer has argued that the gravity of the black-white confrontation calls for bold new approaches to the teaching of the social studies.[11] It is not being argued that the cognitive should be eliminated from social studies instruction. It is being argued that we need to initiate approaches that are primarily affective in order to influence the attitudes and behavior of students. What then are the problems and prospects if such approaches are initiated in social studies programs?

The major problem with affective approaches, in the view of the writer, is that they can lend support to an intellectual game that inquiry disciples sometimes foster in their students. This game works as follows: The student analyzes a controversial issue and mentally plays out the action that he feels is appropriate. (The same game may be played with affective approaches.) At the point where the students reaches the threshold of action in the larger society, he stops! The game is a relatively safe one to play for the school as a social system isn't upset too much. The game has been confined to the classroom. The simulation is an end in itself. The writer would therefore argue that we must develop continuity between affective approaches in the classroom and action in the larger society. We must explore avenues for student action in the larger society rather than confining ourselves to affective experiences in the classroom.

A second problem is that teachers who are expected to initiate affective approaches have themselves been exposed to a great deal of cognitive teaching and very little affective teaching. This is one reason why many teachers are cautious about trying out affective approaches even though they think they may be a good idea. The only advice that can be given is to try these approaches and see how they work. Of course, there are many teaching styles, some of which lend themselves more to affective innovation than others. Yet in the writer's view all teachers can profit from giving attention to such innovation. The teacher who will have the most difficult time with affective approaches is the one who is obsessed with structure and control at the expense of flexibility. At the same time he is the teacher who would profit the most from affective approaches. Highly structured schools and a "don't rock the boat" attitude also work against affective innovation in social studies classrooms. Those who use affective techniques can expect instant exposure and the attention of if not the wrath of *some* colleagues and administrators.

In short, the use of affective techniques in social studies instruction is not for the faint of heart. Yet, difficult times call for new approaches and affective approaches provide one exciting new alternative to traditional social studies instructions.

NOTES

1. *Report of the National Advisory Commission on Civil Disorders*, New York: Bantam Books, 1968, p. 1–2. The fact that white racism rather than black agitation was cited as the root cause of city riots immediately made the report a controversial document.

2. Vincent J. Burke, "White America Didn't Respond to Race Warning, Study Finds," *Los Angeles Times*, March 2, 1969, Part 1, pp. 1, 6.

3. For a review of the literature concerning attempts to change values in social studies instruction, see Dale L. Brubaker, "A Comparative Cultures Approach to the Teaching of Vocational and Citizenship Education in Secondary Schools," unpublished Doctor's dissertation, Michigan State University, 1965, pp. 12–21. See also Milton Rokeach, *Beliefs, Attitudes, and Values*, San Francisco: Josey-Bass, 1968, pp. 152,155.

4. David Krathwohl, Benjamin Bloom, and Bertram Masia, *Taxonomy of Educational Objectives*, New York: David McKay Co., 1956, p. 6.

5. C. Benjamin Cox and Byron G. Massialas, ed., *Social Studies in the United States*, New York: Harcourt, Brace & World, 1968.

6. Krathwohl, *et al.*, *Taxonomy of Educational Objectives*, pp. 6–7.

7. See Dale L. Brubaker, *Alternative Directions for the Social Studies*, Scranton, Pa.: International Textbook Co., 1967, Chapter One, for a consideration of the "good citizenship" argument.

8. The writer is indebted to Professor George I. Brown and his doctoral students, Aaron Hillman and Robin Montz, for the affective techniques discussed in this essay. For a more conprehensive treatment of humanistic

education, see George I. Brown, *Now: The Human Dimension*, Big Sur, Calif.: Esalen Institute, 1968.

9. Affective methods involving police-community confrontation were developed in teacher education workshop meetings held in Santa Barbara, Calif. These workshops were sponsored by the Civic Education Project under the leadership of Dale Flowers, University of California, Santa Cruz.

10. For an excellent discussion of this conflict, see Susan Lynn Jacoby, "Slum and Suburb: the Neglected Reality," reprinted in Chapter 6 of this volume.

11. It is clear that students will continue to accelerate their drive for more voice in school matters. By a vote of seven to two, the United States Supreme Court ruled that school officials cannot legally prevent students from staging peaceful demonstrations in support of causes that may be unpopular with authorities. (*Los Angeles Times*, March 2, 1969, Sec. G, p. 5.)

STUDY QUESTIONS

1. Would the game described by Attig interest most culturally different children? Can you think of other problems to which this technique could be applied that are closer to the lives of lower-class children?

2. Attig suggests that the game technique *might* be best used with students of "above-average ability." How would you evaluate this statement if you accept most of the assumptions about *ability* delineated in Chapter 3?

3. How can simulation and gaming be used to teach children important social science concepts and generalizations? Why might this technique appeal to culturally different children?

4. What are some of the special problems involved in the use of simulation? How might they best be solved?

5. How can simulation enable students to learn from unwise decisions without suffering their consequences in real life?

6. How can role-playing be used to help culturally different children solve some of the social problems which permeate their lives and environment?

7. Explain how role-playing and sociodrama can help children to devise alternative solutions to social problems and to consider and evaluate the possible consequences of different courses of action. Give specific examples of lessons and topics.

8. Brubaker argues that we need to "initiate approaches that are primarily affective in order to influence the attitudes and behavior of students?" Do

you agree with his argument? Why or why not? What problems might a teacher encounter in implementing the activities described by Brubaker? Can these problems be solved? How?

SUGGESTED READINGS

Boocock, Sarane S., and E. D. Schild (Editors), *Simulation Games in Learning.* Beverly Hills: Sage Publications, 1968

Carlson, Elliot, "Games in the Classroom," *Saturday Review*, April 15, 1967

Carlson, Elliot, *Learning Through Games.* Washington, D.C.: Public Affairs Press, 1968

Cherryholmes, Cleo, "Developments in Simulation of International Relations in High School Teaching," *Phi Delta Kappa*, **46** 227–231, 1965

Chesler, Mark, and Robert Fox, *Role-Playing Methods in the Classroom.* Chicago: Science Research Associates, 1966

Christine, Charles, and Dorothy Christine, "Four Simulation Games That Teach," *Grade Teacher*, **85** 109–120, 1967

Farran, Dale C., "Games Work With Underachievers," *Scholastic Teacher*, **62** 10–11, 1967

Grambs, Jean D., *Intergroup Education: Methods and Materials.* Englewood Cliffs, N.J.: Prentice-Hall, 1968

Grambs, Jean D., "Dynamics of Psychodrama in the Teaching Situation," *Sociatry*, **1** 383–399, 1948

Hogan, Arthur J., "Simulation: An Annotated Bibliography," *Social Education*, **32** 242–244, 1968

Klein, A. F., *How To Use Role-Playing Effectively.* New York: Association Press, 1959

Morasky, Robert L., "The Case Method Approach to Teaching History," *The Social Studies*, **57** 257–259, 1966

Nesbitt, William, *Simulation Games for the Social Studies.* New York: The Foreign Policy Association, 1970

Roselle, Daniel, (Editor), "Simulation: The Game Explosion," *Social Education*, **32** 176–199, 1969

Shaftel, Fannie R., and George Shaftel, *Role-Playing for Social Values: Decision-Making in the Social Studies.* Englewood Cliffs, N.J.: Prentice-Hall, 1967

Zinsmaster, Wanna M., "Contributions of Creative Dramatics to Teaching Social Studies," *The Speech Teacher*, **14** 305–313, 1965

CHAPTER 8
TEACHING DIFFERENT
CULTURES AND GROUPS

Chapters 6 and 7 describe teaching strategies which can be used effectively with children who emanate from diverse cultures. This chapter explores some unique problems involved in teaching specific groups, such as children of American-Indian, Afro-American, Mexican-American, and Puerto Rican-American descent. Some of the articles describe promising approaches to use in teaching children from these groups; others describe ways to teach their cultures to any group of children.

Many of the approaches and techniques recommended for use with specific groups can also be used effectively with other poor children. Smith describes strategies he used to augment the self-concepts and occupational aspirations of black children. However, a similar method could be used to help American-Indian, Puerto Rican-American, and Mexican-American children feel better about themselves and their cultures. As is pointed out in Part One of this volume, youngsters from these groups also experience a *cultural conflict* in school; they have deflated self-concepts, little confidence in their ability to succeed, and hostile attitudes toward the educational establishment. This is not to suggest that children from different cultures do not have unique problems. However, we should be cognizant of the problems that children of poverty share. As teachers we should also realize that while culturally different children need to know about their cultures, such knowledge is also *imperative* for children from affluent groups.

Research on children's racial attitudes discussed in Chapter 1 indicates that both black and white children prefer white to black as early as age 3. Studies by the Clarks, Morland, Goodman, and Trager and Yarrow support this postulate. In all-black inner-city classrooms, the senior editor has often observed children calling each other "black" when trying to hurt or intimidate their classmates. "Black" is often used in such classrooms as a curse word.

Even though black militant leaders and intellectuals have begun a "black is beautiful" campaign, numerous all-black classrooms have apparently as yet been unaffected by their efforts. Since many children are still ashamed of being black, as Jean Lloyd points out in her beautifully and sensitively written article, the school must design a systematic program to help children deal with "blackness."

THE SELF-IMAGE
OF A SMALL
BLACK CHILD

Jean Lloyd

It's June, and I'm tired and cross. But I've had at least three superbly satisfying moments this month.

The first came when a Montessori teacher in a well-known middle-class community told me that he could not see any difference between his kindergarten class and mine. When you consider that my pupils are all Negro and live in Harlem and that his pupils are all white and came to school with excellent vocabularies, his remark is high praise indeed. I shall not take all the credit, because my pupils are an experimental group and have had the benefit of much frenzied attention. Still, they are a rip-roaring group.

The second moment of bliss came when Kim's mother told me how her little girl responded to a taunt. Another five-year-old called Kim "a black . . . !" Kim answered, "I'm black. So are you, and you should be proud of it." Pure gold!

The third moment came at the end of a story that weakened me with guilt. Helen, a pretty, dark-skinned child, confided that every time she told her mother the lesson that I had taught her ("I know I'm black. So are you, and you should be proud of it"), she got a whipping. I was shaken when I realized that I was exposing my pupils to physical punishment. I did not dare tell the child that her mother was wrong and that I was right. But Helen gave me a touching kind of reassurance. I asked her flatly, as I always ask my pupils when I get stuck, "Helen, what are we going to do?" This five-year-old

Jean Lloyd, "The Self-Image of a Small Black Child," *Elementary School Journal*, **67** (May 1967), 407–411. Copyright © 1967 by the University of Chicago Press. Reprinted with permission of the author and the University of Chicago Press.

kindergartener answered, "We have to make her understand. We have to keep telling her till she understands." I had a conference with her mother the next day, and I gave Mrs. Bannister "the lesson on race" just as I gave it to the children. No one can tell me that that dark-skinned woman was not grateful for a mode of handling the kind of slur that sooner or later every Negro gets hurled at him. This little story has a happy ending. Mrs. Bannister recently came in to tell me that she and her husband are so happy with Helen's school experience that, although they have eight other children, they have decided to take out an insurance policy that will mature when Helen is ready for college. They want her to have that chance.

The "lesson on race" that Mrs. Bannister received is the keystone of a method that helps my children develop positive images of themselves. It is my answer to the problem of classroom fights where the word *black* is a verbal club.

My pupils were responding to this hurting word like most Negro children, in or out of ghettos. They had already developed negative feelings about their status as minority-group members. Because I was their teacher and, more importantly, because I am a Negro, I felt that I should try to replace their devaluation of self with definite feelings of race pride. This kind of learning is just as important as academic skills and abilities that foster self-confidence and self-esteem.

When I sought help on the matter, a supervisor suggested that when the word *black* was used to hurt, the children be told that they were "chocolate brown." Thus they would identify with something pleasant, something they liked to drink. I preferred to confront the question of *blackness* squarely. If I told a child that he was brown and his playmate called him black, the taunt would still rankle as an insult. But if he could reply with equanimity, "I know I'm black. So are you, and we should be proud of it," he could no longer be attacked on this level.

I was excited by the chance to grapple with this question of *blackness* because I was well aware of its national, international, and cultural implications. For some time now the Negro intellectuals of the U.S.A. have been expressing a steadily growing pride in the idea of *blackness*. The close bond that they feel with their African brothers has certainly been tightened by exposure to the African concept of *negritude*, an expression and affirmation of the African's potential and humanity. A strengthening pride in his ancestry, together with a determined surge toward civil rights, has given the American Negro a new and satisfying opinion of himself. Influential publications like *Ebony*, the *Negro Digest*, and the *Amsterdam News* consciously reflect this new image. Action groups like the Congress of Racial Equality and the Student Non-Violent Co-ordinating Committee, moderate groups like the National Association for the Advancement of Colored People, and extremist groups like the Muslims agree at least on this one thing: they accept the once insulting designation *black* without hesitation. If this new attitude had not yet filtered down through the levels of society in the ghetto so that Harlem's school children could benefit from a changing racial-image, perhaps I could help.

When a child reported to me, "Tommy called me black," I answered slowly, "I'm black, he's black, and you're black, too." The fact that I so labelled myself made a tremendous impression. I would sometimes amplify, "Be angry if he calls you stupid. Because you're not stupid. But don't be angry if he calls you black. I'm black. You are black. He is black." Or I'd just say, "I know I'm black. So are you, and you should be proud of it." I was not interested in having the children discover these ideas for themselves. In good Montessori fashion, I was systematically presenting the material I wanted them to learn.

They discovered other important information in group discussion. One day I placed a picture of a Negro child and a white child (equally attractive) side by side. I asked the class: "What's the difference between them?" The children answered easily that one was "black" and one was "white." My new curriculum was paying off. I told the children the different names that black people used for themselves—*colored*, *Negro*, *Afro-American*. They learned that there were three groups of people in the world: white, black, and yellow (so far no one has asked me about the Indians, so we will let sleeping dogs lie).

During this discussion Kim was at a corner table cutting out material for our service project. She showed me that she had been listening by bringing me a full-sized picture of an oriental child. Someone in the group remarked that the child was Japanese. I followed this discussion up by putting a box of colored Japanese post cards out on the work-play shelves. The children handled them regularly and compared the pictures of Japanese with the pictures of Negroes and whites on display in the classroom.

On another occasion when I remarked that in our class everybody belonged to the black group, those who had reservations spoke up. "Gail and Yvonne are not black. They're white," someone said. Gail and Yvonne both have fair complexions. "I'm not," said Gail. "I'm black." I emphasized many times that our skin colors might be different (we all compared) but we still belonged to the black group.

As time went by, I found many ways to boost the children's egos. I enjoyed passing these ideas along to white teachers who were also interested in developing self-concepts and self-images. I bought hand mirrors to be used in the doll's corner so that the children could study their faces or admire themselves when they used the "dress up" box and made themselves into mommies and daddies. I went broke taking pictures of them with my camera. The children took some of the pictures home; others were posted in the class-room. I took one set of pictures and printed small name cards to match. One of the children's favorite games was to match their names to the pictures. (They also learned to read one another's names.) I took all the familiar group games and play-party songs and inserted the children's names. "Did you ever see a lassie?" became "Did you ever see Debby?" Anybody who visited my classroom was recruited to write down the children's original stories, poems, or jokes; and these were made into booklets to take home.

I was thrilled with the children's passion for African drum music. Our sessions on creative rhythms became cultural high points. Many of the children had seen African dance troupes at the World's Fair, on television, and at local dances. They taught their classmates little dances with steps and movements that I recognized as authentic Nigerian or Ghanaian.

I shall never forget little Cynthia, her hair unbraided and *au naturel*, announcing proudly, "I'm wearing my hair African-style today." We found Africa on the map, and we admired carved ebony Masai statues from Kenya.

When I felt particularly industrious, I used the light from the slide projector to throw the children's silhouettes on black paper. I traced, and they cut and mounted; and for the first time we made really interesting Mother's Day presents.

Later that year I found another effective way of teaching a lesson on race. I had been delighted to see more frequent use being made of black people in television ads, in movies, in theatre. I knew that if, as Kenneth Clark proved in his famous study,[1] a Negro child already has negative feelings of self by the time he is three or four years old, one reason may be that long before he enters school he has been bombarded by all manner of communications media with which he cannot identify. Cinderella is always a blonde, and so are the girls in the shampoo commercials.

To help the children develop a more positive self-awareness, and at the same time encourage a love of books and reading (my other pet project), we began a class campaign to buy books about Negro children. The class was encouraged to bring in pennies, nickels, or dimes. As I seldom send home written messages, because I want my pupils to develop their memory skills, I only spoke to parents who wanted more information. I asked the children to explain our project to their parents. The innocent tots who skipped in each morning with a nickel for a lollipop at noon were quickly separated from at least two cents. Everybody else "upped the ante" without too much trouble. (My pupils have unbelievable amounts of spending money.) Soon each of my twenty-five pupils was able to buy a book that cost a dollar. This project was a continuing one, and the nickels and dimes kept pouring in (voluntarily or with a little persuasion).

Life continued, productively and pragmatically, when my crisis-of-the-month overtook me. My superiors decided to test my class to discover the positive effects of a conscious development of the self-image in a school setting. They were particularly intrigued with my attempts to develop positive attitudes about "blackness." A control class, innocent of any such classroom influence, was chosen, and the two groups were tested.

To explain why my class "failed," I would probably have to reveal more about the educational experiment from which I have recently become unglued. Let it suffice to say that a test which asks the question "Which color do you like—red or black?" cannot be much good. Still, I was distraught. I began a period of soul-searching in the wake of the criticisms I received. The psychologist who made up the test has suggested that I might even be damaging my pupils, since the tests showed a negative response to "blackness." He suggested that I was creating conflict in my pupils about this subject.

I pondered the observable results of my teaching. First of all, racial classification had become a normal unit of study in my kindergarten classroom. My pupils responded informationally to the idea of *blackness* or *whiteness*. When they were confronted with the idea, there was little emotionalism. Value judgements were not generally forthcoming. Except for one child, they no longer used the designation *black* as an insult. Now when attacked verbally, they gave learned responses. It is true that these were rote responses, but because they were rote responses they were effective in emotion-charged situations. My desire to help my pupils grow in self-esteem stems from an awareness of the negative influences that operate around them. They are growing up in homes where their parents often use *black* as a slur, probably because they struggle or drift in a society where their minority-group status and lack of progress have combined to give them a negative self-image.

But I panic easily, and I am completely intimidated by a psychologist who has a Ph.D. I felt like Snow White (Ha, another example of "white being right!") biting the poisoned apple when I learned that the experimenters had decided to have a conference to examine some of their projects, discuss some of their findings, and generally bat the experimental ball around a bit. I was asked to discuss my little effort in studies of the self-image, and I agreed (suspiciously). Sure enough, the conference agenda allowed me thirty minutes to speak before a presentation by the psychologist who had tested my group and had terrified me. I was hysterical now. I felt like a lamb being sacrificed on the "publish-or-perish" scrap heap. He would surely present a clear, well-organized-research paper that was all science and logic and statistical facts and that would make my folksy little observations seem dangerous and probably ungrammatical.

I spent nearly a week crying in my beer before I thought of a source of rebuttal. I called a Negro psychiatrist who practices here in New York. I told him of my classroom experiments and of the possible damage that I might be inflicting on my pupils. His response was breath-taking: "It is better that the Negro child experience conflict about his worth than be convinced that he is worthless." He explained to me that conflict, like fear, could be a useful tool.

I realized that my young pupils might be confused by the differences between my new curriculum and the attitudes they heard expressed elsewhere, but at least I was giving them a choice. And if I had taught them well enough, the painful tension that I might generate and the clash of contradictions would resolve into a positive, forward-looking attitude.

Last week at discussion time I was thumbing through the newspapers. "I can't find what I want," I muttered. Finally I said, "I've found it," and held up a picture of an integrated group of men on strike.

"What was I looking for?" I asked my class. "Negroes!" someone said. "Black people!" someone else said. "Black people and white people!" a third child said. Not bad, I thought to myself. Not bad at all.

NOTES

1. Kenneth Clark and Mamie P. Clark, "Emotional Factors in Racial Identification and Preference in Negro Children," *Journal of Negro Education*, **19** (Summer 1950), 341–350.

A SPEAKER MODELS
PROJECT TO ENHANCE
PUPILS' SELF-ESTEEM

Donald H. Smith

A Negro child raised in an urban slum does not have nearly the same chance for the promise of America that other children, Negro or white, have who are born into more fortunate circumstances. The Negro slum child is both a product and a victim of a culture of poverty.

Inhabitants of America's slums are dreadfully poor. Most of them have little education and few skills that are marketable in an automated society which is rapidly phasing out jobs that call for simple manual skills. To be Negro and poor—and most Negroes are poor—is to have the added burden of being denied the opportunity to hold a decent job and to earn a decent living. Racist customs and gentlemen's agreements which deprive the Negro of job opportunities also enforce invisible housing codes which force the Negro to live within narrowly confined ghettos.

The child who grows up in the ghetto has his view of life filtered by rat

Donald H. Smith, "A Speaker Models Project to Enhance Pupils' Self-Esteem," *Journal of Negro Education*, Spring 1967, 177–180. Reprinted with permission of the author and publisher.

infested tenements; by crime and vice, co-evil effects of deprivation; by fathers and older brothers who daily stand on street corners instead of having jobs to go to; and by the picture of himself that the ghetto reflects. The child who sees only poverty and squalor all about him, and who also sees that everyone around him is Negro begins to conclude that poverty and squalor and being Negro go hand in hand. Very early in life Negro children become aware that their race is different, and frequently they believe that being Negro is something to be ashamed of. The social-psychological research of Clark and Clark[1] was the pioneer study of racial identity in Negro children. The Clarks found that as early as three years of age Negro children have a negative awareness of race. When the Clarks offered young Negroes their choices of Negro or white dolls, the children invariably selected the white dolls, even in instances where the white dolls were dressed unattractively and the Negro dolls were beautifully adorned. The more recent research of Goodman,[2] of Morland,[3] of Stevenson and Stewart,[4] and of Trager and Yarrow[5] confirm the Clarks' findings of self-deprecation and self-rejection of Negro children.

Society communicates in many ways to the Negro child that he is allegedly inferior. A father who cannot get a job, racial epithets, brutality from police, and history books which omit the deeds of Negro Americans all help to inculcate and reinforce a self-image of worthlessness. An experience I had when I taught elementary school will help to amplify the point. I was a substitute teacher, fresh out of college, temporarily assigned to teach first grade in a disadvantaged area. Like all newly assigned teachers I decided to give my children a sociogram. Therefore I asked these Negro, Spanish, and white first-graders the following question: "Suppose I were to change your seat tomorrow. Write the names of the two students you would most like to sit next to." The results are illuminating. Without exception the Spanish children chose other Spanish children. White children were about even in their choices of the Spanish children and of other white children, but no Negroes. The Negro children most often chose Spanish children and occasionally white ones, but almost never themselves, and this in a class where Negroes were in the majority. Within this little first grade classroom I found a phenomenon which has been well documented in social science research on American life: not only are Negroes rejected by others but frequently they reject themselves and others like themselves. It is probably a normal reaction that in a social order which constantly tells a people they are inferior, those people seeing little evidence to the contrary will begin to believe in their own unworthiness, and they will develop hatred for themselves and other unfortunates like themselves. Convinced that their low station in life is just in the nature of things, their concept of self and their aspirations of progress will be accordingly low.

In June, 1961, I was informed by the principal of the disadvantaged high school where I taught that the following September I would be privileged to teach a freshman honors English class, all but one of whom were Negroes. The other child was a Japanese boy who had been raised by Negro foster parents. During the summer as I pondered what I would teach those freshmen I was aware that what I tried to communicate in the way of literature, grammar, and composition was only a part of the teaching job I had to do. Unless I could also convince those youngsters that they were important, worthy human beings and that life had more to offer them than it had offered their parents, they might never realize the potential their test scores indicated. The ghetto has a way of reaching out its tentacles and reclaiming those who try to escape. Many able youngsters who enter high school desperate to find a path to a better life soon become discouraged by a society that expects them to fail and by a school system that is insensitive to their needs. I have known many cases of bright students who should have gone to college, who should have been able to make a large contribution to society but who instead dropped out of school to haunt the streets and become part of the social dynamite to which Mr. Conant refers. What could I do to help my freshmen beat the incredible odds against escape? Perhaps the most important thing I could do would be first to give them hope that with diligent study and achievement in school they might have their chance and second, to give them the courage to set their aspirations high. Hope and aspiration are the springs to vault the ghetto wall. Michael Harrington has expressed this idea poignantly in his sensitive social document, *The Other America*. Harrington states passionately: "If a group has internal vitality, a will—if it has aspiration—it may live in dilapidated housing, it may eat an inadequate diet, and it may suffer poverty, but it is not impoverished."[6] And so it was my clear duty to help these children cling to whatever aspirations they had, while at the same time raising their sights to levels they never imagined possible. One of the measures I took is the title of this paper: a Speaker Models Project to Enhance Pupils' Self-Esteem.

Once a month, for an entire year, I brought to our class outstanding Negroes, most of whom were themselves former slum dwellers but who had managed to achieve outstandingly in spite of adversity. The purpose of the project was twofold: first, to bring live models of Negro achievement before the children. Success in the flesh is far more inspiring than an attempt by the teacher to communicate some abstract possibilities of the future. And second, to use the diverse careers these models represented as examples of professions that Negroes have been able to pursue.

The speakers who participated were either personal friends of mine or were recommended by friends. In selecting the speakers I tried to choose models who were credible. A Willie Mays would not do, for Willie Mays is superhuman and not even a white boy, except perhaps a healthy Mickey Mantle, could hope to be the Giants centerfielder. Included among the speakers were a teacher in the school who was also a civil rights activist, an engineer, an anthropologist, a journalist, an attorney, a poetess, the secretary of a U.S. Congressman, a doctoral divinity student, and a psychologist. Each speaker talked for about twenty minutes, giving biographical details and telling something about his work. Following this the pupils asked questions for about twenty minutes. There was never any lack of response on the part of the students. Sometimes their questions were so penetrating I was thankful that the guest, not I, had to answer.

Perhaps the high point of the program was the presentation of Pulitzer Prize winner Gwendolyn Brooks. In addition to relating events of her life Miss Brooks read some of her poetry, and the children were enthralled. During the course of the year the pupils were to do some writing of their own. Six had their essays published in the High School Essay Anthology and one young poet published in the High School Poetry Anthology.

These twenty-four children and I were together for a year, and it was my great pleasure to see them grow intellectually, and to perceive what I hope was a strengthening of their self-concepts. It would be both unscientific and unrealistic for me to contend that this project alone was responsible for any behavioral change among these students. I have no scientific data to support my assertion that among other influences the speaker models project helped to convince these youngsters that it is all right to be a Negro and to have lived in a slum, that in spite of their physical destitution America promised them prospects of a good life. I have only inference to support my conclusion that they began to think more of themselves because of the speaker models. I believe they also reasoned that if their teacher thought enough of them to have such a project, and if those important people thought enough of them to come at 8:00 A.M. then they must be pretty good little people. One indication of the program's value is that when, at the end of the year, I asked the students to write a course evaluation, not a single child failed to mention the program and most of them expressed praise.

I was unable to be with these children after the one year, but I have followed their progress. In a school whose dropout rate is greater than 50 per cent, twenty-one of the twenty-four are known to have graduated, though three completed their work at another high school. The whereabouts of three others who transferred are not known. The class produced two valedictorians, one who graduated a semester early. In a school where less than 25 per cent go on to college, fifteen of the twenty-one graduates are known to have entered college. One brilliant girl who scored at the 99th percentile on the freshman Differential Aptitude Test won a National Achievement Scholarship. She was accepted by Smith College, but lacked adequate financial support so she enrolled at Carleton College. An exceptional boy, who later transferred on scholarship to a private school, is now a scholarship student at Dartmouth and a member of the freshman football team. Other students are enrolled at Knox College, the University of Illinois, Southern

Illinois University, Bethel College, and various junior colleges in the Chicago area.

I will not guarantee that anyone who attempts a program such as I have described will be successful. I cannot even be sure that I was successful with my own project. As in the case of the classic Hawthorne Effect we can never be sure whether the real influence is the elaborate projects we set up or is simply that the children are responding to the fact that someone thinks they are worth doing something special for. Perhaps it really doesn't make any difference. Sometimes faith in a fact can help to create the fact.

In spite of the personal joy I derived and in spite of the apparent good the project accomplished, as I reflect upon it I cannot help but think of its tragic aspect. For I submit that it is a deep national tragedy that any American children should be so badly scarred and humiliated by racial prejudice that part of their school curriculum must be devoted to the rehabilitation of crushed egos. If their fathers had jobs and received a decent wage and if unfair housing practices were abolished so that these children could live beyond the walls, in time the scars would heal. But without the chance to belong to a family that is self-sustaining, the children's wounds will grow deeper. As Daniel Moynihan, former assistant to President Johnson, put it: "Employment . . . is the primary source of individual or group identity. In America what you do is what you are: to do nothing is to be nothing; to do little is to be little. The equations are implacable and blunt, and ruthlessly public."[7] And I might add to Mr. Moynihan's statement they are also "ruthlessly private."

Until the practitioners of government and the titans of industry and the American people at large decide to remove the psychological and physical barriers that maim and distort the self-images of children, we who teach must be as concerned about their emotional development as their intellectual development; we must paste and patch and do whatever else we can to give these children the same chance for happiness that is promised to all Americans.

NOTES

1. Kenneth B. Clark and Mamie P. Clark, "Racial Identification and Preference in Negro children," in T. M. Newcomb and E. L. Hartley, eds., *Readings in Social Psychology*, New York: Holt, Rinehart & Co., 1947, pp. 169–178.

2. Mary E. Goodman, *Race Awareness in Young Children*, New York: Macmillan, 1952.

3. J. Kenneth Morland, "Racial Recognition by Nursery School Children in Lynchburg, Virginia," *Social Forces*, **38** (1958), 132–137.

4. H. W. Stevenson and E. C. Stewart, "A Developmental Study of Racial

Awareness in Young Children," *Child Development*, **29** (1958), 399–409.

5. Helen G. Trager and Marian R. Yarrow, *They Learn What They Live*, New York: Harper & Row, 1952.

6. Michael Harrington, *The Other America*, New York: Macmillan, 1962, p. 10.

7. Daniel P. Moynihan, "Employment, Income, and the Ordeal of the Negro Family," *Daedalus*, **94** (1965), 746.

THE AMERICAN BLACK GHETTO: A GEOGRAPHIC APPRAISAL

Don C. Bennett

Possibly one of the most relevant, timely, and challenging subjects that the social studies teacher could offer his students today is that of the black ghetto in the United States. Many of the most acute social, political and economic problems are currently concentrated in the ghettos, and since the ghettos are concentrated in cities they become urban problems. The subfield or urban geography is presently the largest and most rapidly expanding within the discipline. This subject, then, is eminently suitable as a logical study in a geographic context.

In this article we will discuss specifically the Negro or black ghetto although the word "ghetto" can be applied to any urban areas to which a specific group is largely confined in housing. Ghettos can be areas where the restricted group is clearly in the majority as in the core areas of the large ghettos or places where the restricted group is residentially concentrated but is not numerically dominant as in the border zones around large ghettos or in small ghettos.

The purposes of this article are (1) to suggest a few geographic approaches that social studies teachers might employ in studying a ghetto and (2) with this framework in mind, to cite some information already known about black ghettos. The geographic aspects which we will consider are: distribution, location, nature of the boundaries, size, shape, the association of phenomena in ghettos, and the interaction of ghettos with other parts of the city or metropolitan area. In considering these aspects of black ghettos, we will

Don C. Bennett, "The American Black Ghetto: A Geographic Appraisal," *News and Notes on the Social Sciences*, (October 1968), 2–12.

employ three geographic scales of analysis: small, intermediate and large. At the small (micro) scale we will consider distribution: at the intermediate (meso) scale, the focus will be on location, size, the association of phenomena in the ghettos, and the interaction of ghettos with other areas of the city; at the large (macro) scale we will examine shape and the arrangement of phenomena within the ghetto.

Specific study suggestions, or projects, are given at various points throughout the paper to facilitate teacher utilization of the ideas being discussed.

AT THE SMALL SCALE OF ANALYSIS

Distribution   The basic information for this topic is a map of the U.S. which depicts the distribution of urban Negroes. ("Negro Population as a percent of the Total Population," Bureau of the Census, GE-50, # 16, $0.50.) The Bureau of the Census data are the main source.

A primary concern in studying a distribution, in this case the black ghettos of the U.S., is to determine what other phenomena the distribution is closely related to. What has caused the distribution to be as it is? A standard method for gaining insights is to make maps of other phenomena which one thinks may be closely related and then compare these, visually or by overlaying them, to the map of the ghettos.

Some of the known information is:

1)   The *size of ghettos* is related to city size, i.e., the largest ghettos, in general, are found in the largest cities or metropolitan areas. Apparently Negro migrants consider that there are greater opportunities in large cities than in the small ones.

2)   The *ratio of whites to blacks* in a city varies considerably both regionally and locally. The cities of the Great Plains and mountain states have much lower percentages of blacks than those in other parts of the nation.

3)   The *rate of growth of ghettos* is related to city size and ghetto size. Growth is faster in the larger cities and where there are existing large ghettos.

4)   The *degree of segregation of blacks and whites* in a city is *not* related to region, city size, or the ratio of whites and blacks and it is increasing. The black populations in U.S. cities are highly segregated residentially in all parts of the nation, in cities of all sizes and irrespective of the number or ratio of blacks in the city.

Projects

1. Make and compare maps of the cities of your state or region. Consider: (a) city size, (b) rate of city growth, 1950–1960, (c) size of black population

in cities, (d) percent of city population which is black, (e) rate of growth of black population.

2. Determine the degree of segregation which exists in the cities of your state or region. Use the following Index of Segregation:

$$\text{Segregation Index} \; + \frac{b}{B} - \frac{w}{W} \times 100,$$

where b and w are the black and white populations of the census tracts (or other areas for which there is information) in which blacks exceed the city average. B and W are the total black and white populations of the city.

Steps in working the formula:

a) Determine the percentage of blacks in a city.
b) Identify all census tracts in which blacks exceed the city average. Label them "Black tracts." It is usually very easy to identify these tracts. Record the black and white populations of only the Black tracts.
c) Determine the number of blacks and whites who live in the combined Black tracts.
d) Divide Black tract blacks by all blacks.
e) Divide Black tract whites by all whites.
f) Subtract (e) from (d).
g) Multiply (f) by 100. This is the Segregation Index.

This index has a range from 0–100, with 0 representing perfect integration and 100, total segregation. An index of 70 means that 70% of the blacks would have to move in order to achieve perfect integration. With this index one can compare the degree of segregation in cities by region, by size, by proportion of blacks to whites, over time, by city growth rates, etc.

AT THE INTERMEDIATE SCALE OF ANALYSIS

At this scale of analysis we focus on just one city. As used in this article, the term "functional city" refers to a single urban concentration with a central business district (CBD), industrial and residential areas including the suburbs. From a plane at night the functional city is clearly delimited by the dense concentration of lights. Characteristically, functional cities are considerably larger than a political or administrative city, e.g., the areas over which a mayor has jurisdiction. Large functional cities will include dozens or scores of politically separate areas, most of which are only suburbs or local shopping areas of the functional city.

In this section we will discuss ghetto location, the association of phenomena in ghettos, and the interaction of ghettos to the other areas of the city.

Location

1. Black ghettos are characteristically located in the heart, or core area, of the functional city, adjacent to the central business and industrial districts. This central location is the traditional area that foreign and other poor immigrants have initially settled. With all other immigrants there has been a migration out of this undesirable location as soon as possible—usually in two or three generations.

2. There may be several distinct and separate ghettos in a large functional city. Ghettos almost never completely surround the central business area but rather develop in a number of separate places near to the business district. Some of these may coalesce with time. With rising affluence and numbers, new smaller ghettos may develop away from the city center, even in the suburbs.

Spatially associated phenomena Viewed within the areal context of a functional city, many characteristics have been determined to be spatially identifiable with the ghetto areas. The following are examples.

a) among the highest population densities
b) among the highest birth rates
c) among the highest death rates, especially infant mortality rates
d) among the highest communicable and deficiency disease rates: influenza, tuberculosis and rickets
e) among the lowest levels of educational attainment
f) among the highest rates of unemployment
g) among the lowest income
h) among the highest incidence of substandard housing
i) among the highest rates of persons on welfare
j) among the highest crime rates

These examples make the point that there are a large number of undesirable conditions spatially indentified with ghettos. These conditions may arouse fear and criticism in the white population of the city but to many blacks who live there they represent a daily struggle against overpowering odds. It should be noted that for each of the above 10 characteristics, the word "among" was used. In none of these 10 conditions are the ghetto residents or the ghetto areas unique; all functional cities contain non-ghetto white areas and populations that share these dismal conditions. In a very real sense the problems of the black ghetto are the problems of the poor.

Projects

1. Examine your home town or a nearby city in terms of the distribution of the ten characteristics above or others for which data are available

from the Census Bureau or students could also conduct sample neighborhood surveys.

2. Trace the history of your town to determine: (a) which factors appear to have influenced the selection of certain areas for ghetto development, and (b) the locational stability of the ghettos through time.

Area interaction Area interaction refers to the various ways one area is linked to other areas. A city is like an industry; it is a highly integrated system of specialized labor and specialized areas. The ghetto, as a distinct area of American cities, is linked in a variety of ways to the other areas of the cities. Linkage can be one-directional or reciprocal. The things exchanged can be goods, services, money, labor or information. Important aspects of the exchange pattern would include its kind, volume, regularity, continuity, route, source and destination areas and distance.

Some areal linkages already established include:

a) Those due to personal and public insecurity in the ghettos, especially border zones, and in the nearby business area. Public expenditures on security measures are usually disproportionately high in these areas. Residential restrictions imply dislike and create alienation and hostility which may result in crime and violence in any part of the city but more so in the areas designated.

b) Many central city public facilities and private businesses are underused or losing their market because of the perceived or real insecurity of the area at night. Examples are libraries, galleries, theatres and shopping areas.

c) The insecurity in the vicinity of the central business district is a factor in the migration of certain business and industries to the suburbs.

d) Jobs are becoming further removed from the central city (ghetto) residents as the downtown loses its trades and as new businesses locate in the city periphery. Unemployment rates in the ghetto tend to increase: welfare, crime and disease increase.

e) Commuter traffic within the city rises as black residents are increasingly separated from their jobs.

f) The problem of equalizing educational opportunities, i.e., the unequal allocation of the educational budget to certain areas, increases as black residents are physically separated in ghettos. Bussing or other kinds of pupil and teacher transfers could be reduced and potentially eliminated if there were no residential concentrations of blacks.

Projects

1. Examine the interaction in your city by having your students plot their family's use of the various parts of the city for work, shopping, recreation.

2. Determine how the public budget is allocated within the city regarding recreation, police, education, and streets for the past year.

AT THE LARGE SCALE OF ANALYSIS

At the large scale of analysis a variety of detailed aspects of ghettos may be examined. The nature of ghetto boundaries, the size and shape of ghettos, and the kinds and arrangement of land uses and activities within a ghetto are appropriate topics.

Ghetto shape and size   The shape and size of many regions vary according to the criteria used. A criterion of 50% black families in a given block or census tract will define a ghetto of one size and shape—that of 35% will produce another. There is frequently no *best* definition; it changes according to the purpose of the investigation. However defined, size and shape are important considerations when examining internal and external relationships. The ratio of boundary to internal area can be important. For example, a circular shape provides the least amount of boundary contact with the remainder of the city.

Ghetto shapes have not been thoroughly studied. From evidence available it appears that ghettos tend to be compact with little development or interdigitation of white and black blocks.

The total area occupied by all black ghettos in a functional city is usually quite limited. Certainly they are smaller than the size of the black population would suggest because ghetto population densities are generally much higher than the city averages. The public has become aware that the black population of several major political cities such as Chicago, Philadelphia, Detroit, and Cleveland is or will probably be in a majority within 15 years. It is a misconception to think that the functional city is becoming black; the great majority of the functional city population is white and will no doubt remain white.

Ghetto boundary   While boundaries are often established by a single criterion, and so drawn with a line, e.g., the percent of black families in a block, the boundary of the phenomenon may be very transitional in nature. It is always important to consider the extent to which the mapped border corresponds to the nature of the real world border. In some instances the concept of border zones should be used rather than border lines. Other important aspects of boundaries are their stability through time, i.e., their rate and direction of change.

Black ghetto boundaries appear to have these characteristics:

1. The transition from all-black to all-white blocks may be either very abrupt or very gradual. Most of the ghetto boundary is rather broad, frequent-

ly several blocks in depth. This does not necessarily mean that the percentage of blacks in the border zone blocks changes constantly from the ghetto core to the all-white blocks. That change may be quite abrupt.

2.   The ghetto boundaries are unstable in some sectors and are expanding outward. The major territorial adjustment to the continuous increase of the black population in U.S. cities is an expansion of existing ghettos rather than (a) dispersing the population or (b) creating new ghettos. The ghetto area seldom, if ever, contracts.

3.   The ghetto boundaries are stable or have slow rates of change where the adjacent land use contrasts sharply with the ghetto conditions and/or where there is some type of physical separation such as a major highway, river, or commercialized zone. Boundary changes tend to be more rapid where the adjacent land use is residential and of a value that is similar to that of the nearby ghetto. Much appears to depend on the attitude of the whites who occupy the adjacent areas and on their patterns of restrictions.

4.   The process a neighborhood or block goes through in changing from white to black occupants has traditionally been called an "invasion by the blacks." This terminology appears to show a white ethnocentric bias; it is more accurate to think of the change as "a retreat by the whites." Most ghetto housing is quite old by the time it is first occupied by blacks and the ghetto seldom grows by the construction of new housing on its edge. The growing edge is almost always into a well established white neighborhood. Blacks occupy new blocks only *after* whites have moved. The temporal and spatial pattern of white retreat on the growing margin of a black ghetto still needs a great deal of study to determine the regularities and irregularities but it appears that changeover occurs gradually up to a critical range of white-black mixture and that beyond that point, white retreat accelerates. The "tipping point" appears to lie between 5 and 30% blacks.

Intra Ghetto Spatial Arrangements   One frequently unstated but assumed misconception among whites is that the ghetto area and its population are homogeneous. Nothing could be further from the truth. Compared to a similarly sized white residential area in a large city, the ghetto population will exhibit a greater range of education, income and ability than the whites. The reason is that essentially all blacks, irrespective of personal achievement, are similarly restricted in their housing choices and forced to live in proximity to each other in well defined areas whereas the white pattern operates to separate the resident population by income, education and occupation. Ghetto residents have a greater variety of backgrounds and attitudes than their white counterparts. Large ghettos include everyone from the unemployable to top professionals; from no earned income to six-figure incomes, and from second grade dropouts to Ph.D's.

Just how ghetto residents spatially sort themselves out within their restricted area has had little study. Based on other experience, it seems likely that they would attempt to follow the typical American patterns of separate neighborhoods with residents of relatively similar background. Larger ghettos would probably have more homogeneous sub-neighborhoods than smaller ghettos just as neighborhoods in large cities have more homogeneity than in small cities.

Virtually all ghettos contain some nonresidential activities in contrast to many white neighborhoods which are solely residential. This land use mixture results from the segregation of blacks from most white private social activities such as churches and clubs and until recently, from many of the low order commercial possibilities such as movies, bowling and pool halls, barber and beauty shops, ice cream parlors, etc.

Where the ghetto is large enough to support a number of them, the nonresidential functions are frequently concentrated along one or a few business streets. A comparison of ghetto business streets with their counterparts in white areas reveals much that is similar. The kind, size, quality and frequency of stores and other functions are primarily related to the generally low income and educational levels of the ghetto population rather than to the Negroness of it. Thus the middle class white's image of the shoddy condition and higher frequency of pawn shops, taverns and liquor stores, small private grocery shops rather than chain stores, small restaurants, used clothing stores, store front churches, pool halls, etc. are all characteristics of populations of low income and education rather than black ghettos as such. These conditions may just as easily be seen in some white neighborhoods. The generally low income nature of the areas population is also reflected in the visible aspects of old age, quality and state of repair of buildings; in the small size of the individual store; in the amount of vacancy and turnover of proprietorships; and in the number of establishments that require little capital, e.g., barber and beauty salons, dry cleaning, etc.

The eye, ear, and nose appeal of the business streets, however, may vary considerably from white to black areas. Ghetto menus feature more fish, fowl and pork and deep fry methods of preparation; ghetto taverns are more likely to be eye-catching with bright paint and fancy names as well as clearly audible jazz music than their white neighborhood counterparts; ghetto barber and beauty shops may not feature aseptic conditions; to suggest just a few of the superficial differences that may create a unique atmosphere but which can be very misleading to the observer if he considers them as substantial differences.

Projects

1. In racially mixed schools the social studies class could prepare and compare land use maps and lists of ghetto and non-ghetto business

activities. Care should be taken to insure that the two neighborhood populations are similar in income and educational background.

2. Travel diaries of students, comparing ghetto and non-ghetto residents could be kept and mapped to illustrate how and to what extent people use an area and the entire city.

To summarize, we have considered the black ghetto as a particular area within American cities. The basis of their existence has been to separate blacks from whites residentially. Residential separation has tended to produce many other types of spatial separation as well so that the ghetto has become much more than a special type of neighborhood. We have examined aspects of their existence and condition from the vantage point of three geographic scales of observation and analysis. Within each scale of observation, certain questions or problems were focused on as illustrative of what could be done at that scale but they are in no way exhaustive of the possibilities that social studies teachers and students might profitably pursue.

SUGGESTED READINGS

Lieberson, Hanley, *Ethnic Patterns in American Cities*. New York: Free Press of Glencoe, 1963.

Taeuber, Karl E., and Alma F. Taeuber, *Negroes in Cities: Residential Segregation and Neighborhood Change*, Chicago: Aldine Publishing Co., 1965.

FOR YOUR LIBRARY

Shaver, James P., and Harold Berlak, eds., *Democracy, Pluralism, and the Social Studies: Readings and Commentary*, Boston: Houghton Mifflin, 1968, 438 pp. This paperback very nicely sets forth the various positions currently contesting for the intellectual loyalty of social studies teachers. Unlike many books of social studies readings, this volume includes articles by scholars in the social sciences and other areas such as psychology. No attempt has been made to paper over the basic differences currently a part of the social studies scene. Introductions to each section are provocative, and alone will provide the interested teacher with an overview of the controversy now raging in the profession. The book is organized into six sections: objectives, conceptions of the society and their relationship to the social studies curriculum, history and the social studies, the social sciences and their relationship to the curriculum, thinking about thinking, and research and social studies instruction. Two years ago Frederick Smith made a plea in a Guest Commentary for social studies departmental meetings that were intellectually stimulating. In this issue James Cierzniak argues for monthly seminars run by and for departmental members. Various sections of this book would provide an excellent springboard for such discussions. . . .

Faucett, Verna F., *et al.*, *Social Science Concepts and the Classroom*, Syracuse: Social Studies Curriculum Center, 1968, 64 pp. This booklet serves as a companion volume for the Center's earlier *Major Concepts for the Social Studies* and is intended as an introduction to the growing body of literature devoted to the conceptual approach. . . .

WHY INDIANS?

Frederick O. Gearing

I like American Indians, it happens, and that creates a certain handicap in pursuit of the current purpose. Liking something is a nice but rather trivial reason for suggesting that students study it, at least during the already crowded school day. The purpose here is to suggest that non-trivial, fully serious educational profit can be realized in the schools through the study of Indian communities, past and present. The case could perhaps be made more compellingly by an anthropologist who knows Indian life and finds that life personally unattractive. (Of which anthropologists there are, contrary to public myth, many; furthermore, to be such an anthropologist is quite respectable.)

Why Indians? I shall put the question in this form: What serious educational profits would accrue to a student who, after study, does not find Indian life especially attractive or fascinating or even interesting in and of itself?

North American Indians form, of course, a highly varied array of communities. Southwestern groups are best known to most and include farmers settled in tightly knit villages, as the Zuni, and include other groups, nomadic and seminomadic, who once lived by hunting and gathering and by raiding. Along the northwest coast, from southern Alaska to northern California, is another array of Indian communities which, as the Kwakiutl, were blessed by bountiful nature (in the form of salmon, mainly) to the degree that they spent a good deal of their time gathering quite useless surplus wealth and giving it away in a stylized, often arrogant way. Southward from that area

---

Frederick O. Gearing, "Why Indians?", *Social Education*, **32** (February 1968), 128–131, ff. 146. Reprinted with permission of the author and the National Council for the Social Studies.

and into the desert interior lived the economic opposites of the northwestern groups, the very poor, as the Paiutes, whose lives often were an unceasing struggle for survival, so much so that their various cultures seemed to include virtually any practice that would help keep body and soul together. Through the entire eastern half of the continent, from Florida into the far northern interior of Canada, lived a very large array of groups—those south of the Great Lakes were gardeners and hunters, and those north of there solely hunters. The Eskimos covered the entire northern fringe of the continent. Finally, after the coming of Europeans and the horse, there occurred a cultural explosion of sorts which resulted in the creation, overnight as it were, of the horse-and-buffalo cultures of the High Plains, as among the famous Dakotas (Sioux) and Cheyenne. All these peoples spoke over 150 mutually unintelligible languages which fall into five large language families. Among these peoples are found all the basic forms of human kinship organization, a welter of forms of political organization, a wide variety of religious belief and ritual.

It of course follows: one does not in the schools "study Indians," but one may study some selected group of Indians. For serious educational purposes, it does not matter which, provided only that decent materials are available.

Such materials are becoming more readily available. For example, a recently published annotated bibliography gives as a sampler an outstanding group of books on North American Indians[1]—a survey book, a volume of illustrations and descriptions of two cultures within the area (respectively, *Red Man's America* by Ruth M. Underhill; *The American Indian* by Oliver LaFarge; *The Great Tree and the Longhouse* by Hazel W. Hertzberg; *The Ten Grandmothers* and *Kiowa Years*, both by Alice Marriott).

The serious educational profits to be gained from such study are, I judge, two. First, a proper study of an Indian community will permit a student to recognize that *any culturally patterned behavior, however bizarre it may at first appear, at bottom makes plausible sense, is believable and fully human* (not personally attractive, necessarily, nor "good," necessarily, but humanly believable).

Educated men, perhaps misled by what they take anthropologists to have said, have become too much preoccupied as to whether one is sufficiently accepting or respectful of an alien culture he might encounter. There is some question as to what one can do about those things; good intent and will power go only so far. A better objective for the schools would seem to be firmly to implant in student minds the working assumption that culturally patterned behavior makes sense, and that any such behavior becomes believable to any man if he knows enough about it. Then, in some future real encounter across cultural boundaries, when an item of behavior is paraded which appears bizarre, or inscrutable (and this is inevitable), a bell should ring in the observer's head which means, quite simply: What don't I know? The first answers will be questions and these may be highly various; and no adequate final answer may be forthcoming, then or ever. But the mind-saving result follows in any case. The observer says, "The behavior appears to me bizarre, because there is something I don't know." He is at least, answer or not, set to looking. He will say to himself, "I wonder why those people are doing that," rather than saying, "Look at those crazy people." This shrunken world would perhaps be a bit less riskful were the concrete visceral recognition more widely spread that culturally patterned behavior at bottom makes human sense.

It is the overwhelming anthropological experience that culturally patterned bizarre behavior does in the end make sense. It is also the anthropological experience that, when men keep looking and look well, respect and the like tend to follow; in any event, it is then and not before that thinking men are able meaningfully to ask whether that behavior is "good."

The proper classroom study of any Indian community can provide serious educational profit. Given materials that are adequate, bizarre Indian behavior will inevitably be paraded and, as the study moves forward and additional facts come under scrutiny, some of that bizarre behavior will come to make sense, will be revealed to the student as humanly believable.

An example: Among many Eskimo groups (and among Paiutes as well) very old people are simply abandoned by their sons, or those old people voluntarily walk off into the cold and soon freeze, or they ask their sons to strangle them. All these things are not rare but very common. At best such behavior seems to us so bizarre as to be beyond the pale of normal human behavior. It perhaps helps one somewhat to take note of the extreme harshness of the Eskimo environment, of the very large demands made by that environment on sheer physical stamina, and thereby to note that Eskimos have, after all, little choice. It perhaps helps somewhat more to note that the question is not simply whether the old will live for a while longer. Rather, the question would concretely appear to a young adult, who is son to his aged parent but simultaneously father to his own young child, in this form: whether the old parent and the young child will live some short while, or whether the old parent will die now and the young child have a chance, at least, to live to maturity. Now, of course, the problem is recognizable as not merely a matter of necessity or utility, but also as a moral dilemma which demands a difficult and highly moral choice. Even so, the behavior—the killing or abandonment or suicide of the old people—seems at best, to an alien observer, hardly humanly tolerable, one cannot quite say, "Yes, knowing all these things I can imagine myself an Eskimo and can imagine myself, faced with that real choice, doing what I see Eskimos doing." However, the mind of the observer is additionally helped over this very difficult intellectual hurdle by still further information, by some brief glimpse into the mind of the old man himself. Humans, unlike other animals, remember and anticipate; a human career is in some large measure memories and anticipations. Out of this can emerge a quietude, surprising perhaps but humanly compelling, in the face of the inevitable end. The Eskimo writer of the following poem knows he will quite soon walk off into the cold.

1
Often I return
To my little song.
And patiently I hum it
Above the fishing hole
In the ice.
This simple little song
I can keep on humming.
I, who else too quickly
Tire when fishing—
Up the stream.

2
Cold blows the wind
Where I stand on the ice,
I am not long in giving up!
When I get home
With a catch that does not suffice,
I usually say
It was the fish
That failed—
Up the stream.

3
And yet, glorious is it
To roam
The river's snow-soft ice
As long as my legs care.
Alas! My life has now glided
Far from the wide views of the peaks
Deep down into the vale of age—
Up the stream.

4
If I go hunting the land beasts,
Or if I try to fish,
Quickly I fall to my knees,
Stricken with faintness.
Never again shall I feel

The wildness of strength,
When on an errand I go over the land
From my house and those I provide for—
Up the stream.

5
A worn-out man, that's all,
A fisher, who ever without luck
Makes holes in river or lake ice
Where no trout will bite.

6
But life itself is still
So full of goading excitement!
I alone,
I have only my song,
Though it too is slipping from me.

7
For I am merely
Quite an ordinary hunter,
Who never inherited song
From the twittering birds of the sky.[2]

I have cheaply tricked the reader, it is evident. I set out to show that serious educational profit accrues, as I said, "to a student who, after study, does not find Indian life especially attractive or fascinating or even interesting in and of itself." And to that purpose I have cited a bit of human drama which cannot but grip one.

I now move to more bland, even "academic," facets of Indian life. Two examples are drawn from earlier Cherokee life: A Cherokee addresses a dozen or so specified male kinsmen, including his father, by a single term roughly translatable as "father" and some of these "fathers" may be a generation younger than he, others his own age, others much older; he addresses another dozen kinsmen, including some as old as his grandfather or others as young as his grandson, as "brother"; there are other such bizarre uses of kinship terms. These are, it should be noted, in no sense figurative extensions of kinship terms, but are the sole proper modes of address of these specified kinsmen. These facts do not come to make sense simply by learning that such are Cherokee customs; rather they make sense by putting those facts of customary usage together with other similar facts and by recognizing the systematic logic of the whole. The kinship usages at hand are transformed for the observer from the apparently bizarre to the eminently logical when it is recognized that Cherokee life is organized around an array of matrilineal kin groups. Every Cherokee automatically joins, at birth, the kin group of his or her mother; a man must marry outside his own (his mother's) kin group, and he usually resides, after marriage, with his wife's kin group; nevertheless he remains a member of his own kin group throughout his life. Most critically, all *these matrilineal kin groups act like corporations*: for example, land is owned by these corporate groups, and the rights to use land are passed from female to female within the kin group, thus a married man helps work gardens on his wife's land and lives off that produce; similarly, these kin groups act like corporate individuals in political life, thus when political decisions are to be made a married man leaves his wife's group for the moment and joins fellow males in his own kin group, and that group tries to arrive at a corporate opinion about the matter at hand. In general, in everyday life each Cherokee "sees" his community as a set of such "lines," matrilineal groups which in many critical realms act like corporate individuals; of course his welfare is variously affected by the actions of these groups, his own, his wife's, and others. The logic of those "fathers" is by these comments but dimly suggested.

Similarly, a second example: Cherokees once encouraged young men to go on the warpath and gave them formal honors for their noteworthy deeds at war; at the same time, they held the more successful warriors at arm's length and actively disliked many of them. This evident inconsistency similarly makes human sense, not merely because it was Cherokee custom. Rather, Cherokees placed very high moral value on extremely unaggressive behavior inside the group (for example, most kinds of political decisions were made unanimously or not at all), and, generally, the men who precipitated out as the best warriors were temperamentally a bit "pushy" at home and so—by these severe Cherokee moral standards—were immoral men.

These Eskimo and Cherokee facts are of little or no importance in and of themselves, and it matters little whether the student finds them fascinating or whether he, for whatever reason, feels drawn to such a pattern of life. What matters is that the student repeatedly experience the transformation of the bizarre into the humanly believable. This is done by encountering bizarre behavior, then seeking additional information, and finally recognizing the ultimate sense of the no-longer-bizarre behavior first encountered. And what matters even more is the resulting visceral belief that, a priori, bizarre, culturally patterned behavior is, whether comprehended or not in any particular instance, humanly believable if and when knowledge is complete. Perhaps, with such a mental set, one can live in a profoundly heterogeneous nation and world in some measure of comfort and with some measure of effectiveness.

The proper study of an Indian community can yield a second serious profit. Such a study can powerfully *help a student to see well—accurately and in some measure of completeness—the social world immediately around him,* his own social world which is often too familiar to quite see. To study Indians is, through comparison, to see ourselves.

Other social science disciplines work in the classroom under a handicap; these other disciplines are in the position of trying, as the saying goes, to teach a fish about water. The anthropological impulse is to toss the fish onto the bank and there to instruct it some brief while about sand and dirt and dry leaves, and ultimately about oxygen. The anthropological faith is that a thinking fish, returned to the stream, would thereafter perceive water differently and better and would, indeed, be then better prepared for serious instruction, by anyone so inclined, about water, oxygen, gills.

The overriding purpose of the social sciences in the schools is to help students to see well. To this task, we are saying, anthropology brings especially the crucial heuristic device of comparison. It seems to be an unyielding and probably neurologically based fact that men perceive best through comparison and that the broader and more varied the comparison, the more nearly adequate the perception becomes. Comparison assists powerfully in unclouding the senses. Thus, anthropologists do most literally insist that a student cannot adequately "see" pricing mechanisms in a market economy until he has looked also at pricing mechanisms in a non-market setting where the exchange price appears, superficially, to be firmly established by traditional usage; that a student cannot adequately see the flow of political influence through impersonal mass media and legislatures until he has also watched influence flow through a community-wide network established by some configuration of kinship relations; that a student cannot see status mobility until he also looked closely at communities where the sole "mobility" is to move from the status of infant to that of ancestor; that, generally, a student cannot see his own very big society until he has also viewed some array of very little societies.

Broad and varied comparison has hardly found its way into social sciences curricula in the schools. Curricula strategy could, to much profit, be exactly reversed and take the position that all junctures in curricula where broad comparison is not explicitly exploited would have to be specially justified.

The study of any Indian community provides just such dramatic comparison in the realm of economics, politics, social organization, subject only to the availability of adequate and appropriate materials. In several Plains groups a man gains stature by giving things to the point of rendering himself (and his family) virtually destitute; this could bring to a student a fresh perception of America's wealth-and-status system which might otherwise be too familiar and "natural" to see clearly. Many Indian communities, as we saw with Cherokees, make certain kinds of political decisions unanimously or not at all; perceiving this comparison acts to reduce, to some profit, the sense of contrast between modern liberal democracies and other more centralized systems, since both, in comparison, seem a bit "hard" on the dissenting few. And so on.

Two special applications of such comparison can be briefly named. First, where classrooms are markedly heterogeneous in respect to race and economic class and where there is, in the minds of the students, some anxiety about that heterogeneity: Indian studies, especially drawn so as to focus the student's attention on realms of experience which particularly "matter" to him (variously, according to his age, as the host of new "rules" in the classroom and on the playground must mystify and deeply bother a kindergartener or first-grade child), can be made to serve as a useful stimulus to cause the members of the class to look newly into their own diverse parallel experience (as to "rules" at home and in the neighborhood and now at school, for example) at first severally then perhaps collectively. Members of the class can frequently in such a context "triangulate," each with the alien culture and with his fellow's and with his own. This is especially useful in that, not only does the comparison cause students to see familiar things newly, in fresh perspective, but also the student is left to ponder privately or to discuss publicly, at his discretion, whatever he thinks he has seen in his own experience or in that of his fellows. In heterogeneous classes where heterogeneity itself seems to the students especially touchy, this "third culture" strategy is perhaps the only way to get the students to think afresh about themselves and each other.

A second application can be made in respect to realms of self-realization which are particularly bothersome to students. Materials which depict an array of diverse cultural handlings of such realms provide a measure of detachment which may in turn help the student resolve such a matter adequately for himself. Study of a variety of Indian patterns of restraint on sexuality would be an example; these range from great liberality to restraints of unusual severity. Adolescent students go into "sex education" classes with one over-riding question, and that question is the only one *not* answered. The question or course is, "Shall I? or shall I not?" A cross-cultural study doesn't answer the question, but it may help the student better to see in nontrivial terms the nature of the question and why he is asking it. Which is, at bottom, what a liberal education is about.

It should, finally, be noted: a class would not, as a rule, elect to pursue the first objective *or* the second, but both simultaneously. Time in the classroom is always at a premium. The study in some breadth and depth of one or two specific Indian communities gives the student much more than would some broad survey of equal duration of some single facet of the life of many Indian communities. The bizarre emerges frequently in in-depth studies and only in such studies is there chance that the bizarre will be transformed into the humanly believable. At the same time, in such in-depth studies, comparison will have a chance, in planned and unforeseen ways, to work its magic.

The thoughtful reader will have by now asked: Would not the Pago Pago serve as well? The answer is: Yes.

NOTES

1. Kurt W. Johnson, "Two Dozen Anthropology Books." Available from Anthropology Curriculum Study Project, 5632 Kimbark Avenue, Chicago, Ill. 60637.

2. Paul Radin, "The Literature of Primitive Peoples," *Diogenes*, **12** (Winter 1955).

TEACHING ABOUT
THE AMERICAN INDIAN

William Crowder

You cannot stop the locomotive any more than you can stop the sun or moon, and you must submit to do the best you can.

Lt. Gen. William T. Sherman

These words, spoken to the Sioux Indian chiefs in North Platte, Nebraska, at the 1867 signing of one of the last great Indian treaties, were unwittingly prophetic of the white man's future policy. He would force the Indians farther westward. Then, when pushed westward, he would neglect them and leave them to their own resources.

Now, a hundred years later, a great deal of attention is turned in the direction of Indians, and the conscience of Americans who neglected them and failed to discharge their responsibility has been jarred awake.

Patently, it is of the utmost importance that social studies teachers bring into the classroom specific instruction concerning the educational, vocational, social, and economic development of these native Americans. They are small in number (approximately 600,000); their tribes are relatively isolated, both from one another and from large cities; they are a quiet, retiring people who have, for the most part, articulated their grievances and aired their problems only to a small audience.

William Crowder, "Teaching About the American Indian," *Civic Leader*, **46** (April 22, 1968), 4–5. Reprinted with permission of the author and publisher.

BASIC CONSIDERATIONS

It cannot be emphasized too strongly that the material used in a unit on Indians should be authentic. It should be realistic as well as accurate, and the sources drawn upon—whether the lecture, films, books, pamphlets, newspapers, or other materials—should conform to similar standards.

Not many years ago a unit on Indians, prepared especially for the elementary school, featured a wigwam constructed of burlap or paper, stories and songs, and a war dance. Such instruction probably did more harm than good because it gave a highly romantic, misconceived notion and was so general that a child would come away thinking all Indians lived in teepees, walked in soft-soled shoes on beautiful green meadows, beat their drums, etc. In reality, tribes differed greatly in their activities, methods of making a livelihood, home construction, and customs.

BUILDING A BACKGROUND

A unit can be started in any one of a number of ways, a few of which are offered here.

One of the teacher's first tasks is to become informed about Indians and their problems. This information may be gained from inexpensive, up-to-date, readable, and easily obtainable materials which later may be used by the students as they get into the work. In addition to books available in most public libraries, the pamphlets listed below can be easily filed for future use. The series of booklets *Indians of New Mexico*, etc., is one of the best sources. Each booklet is available for 15¢ from the Government Printing Office, Washington, D.C. 20402. Some of them give a historical description of the tribes, tell of their present ways of making a living, and discuss the relations of tribes to the Federal government. For example, the booklet, *Indians of New Mexico*, begins with a history of Pueblo Indians and how they were discovered in the 16th century by white explorers seeking the fabled, seven gold-filled cities. It gives data about present tribes, and tells of the Apaches and Navahos. A map on the back page shows the location of present reservations.

Teachers may decide to have the class study the Indians who occupied the area in which their school is located. The *Visual-History Wall Map* produced by CES, as well as other maps from encyclopedias, indicate the approximate places where various Indian tribes lived.

The development of a list of main ideas or generalizations for the class to learn will have to be done by individual teachers who best know their classes. For some groups a study of the Red Man from an anthropological point of view may be feasible; others may be interested in the economic aspect of his plight. Still other classes may decide to focus on cultural deprivation and to work out ways of helping minorities whose unstimulating experiential home background, inadequate educational facilities, lack of incentive, and general discouragement have contributed to their present situation. A high school class beginning the unit on Indians may afterwards go into a study of modern developing nations, their problems and potentialities.

ATTITUDES

One of the most important aspects of this unit should be a study of the present-day conditions of these neglected people and an attempt to develop appreciative perception of their predicament.

1. What problems do minorities face in efforts to gain social acceptance in a white-dominated country?
2. How does the isolation of a reservation contribute to the plight of the Indian?
3. Why is it harder to get a job and to be promoted if one is a member of a minority group?
4. Why do some Indians appear to be antisocial?
5. Specifically, what steps should be taken to assist Indians?
6. What problems facing a minority must be solved by the group? Which ones can individuals and the Federal government help them solve?
7. What contributions has the Indian cultural heritage made to our own?

Implicit in this unit would be development of skills such as locating information, reading to verify facts, making reports, taking notes, and engaging in problem solving.

ACTIVITIES FOR THIS STUDY

There are a large number of activities which may be carried out to enrich the unit. The class may construct transparencies showing cultural areas and the general locations of Indian tribes today. A series of transparencies with overlays might depict the location of the following: Woodmen of the Eastern Shores, Hunters of the Plains, Pueblo Farmers, Navaho Sheepherders, Desert Indians, Seed Gatherers, and Northern Fishermen.

Another project related to both history and geography would be that of making a map or another transparency showing the distribution of tribes about the time Columbus discovered America.

Using the pamphlets listed below, the class may be divided into groups to present reports on home building, dress, customs, etc., of specific tribes. A tape recording of this presentation would be useful for later review.

A study of the lives of great American Indians may be pursued. Some of them are: Tecumseh, Sacagawea, Sitting Bull, Jim Thorpe, Charles Curtis, Robert Bennett, Benjamin Reifel, Will Rogers, and Maria Tallchief, to name only a few.

After studying Indians of the United States, some students may become interested in the Aztecs of Central America, the Mayas of Southern Mexico and Guatemala, and the Incas of Peru. A comparison of their civilization with Europe's past may be carried out by the more advanced students. What kinds of transportation system, communication system, code of laws, etc., did the early explorers find in those countries? What kinds of cultures did these "uncivilized natives" have to offer the Spanish soldiers? What happened to these people as a result of the white man's coming?

Some classes may plan to make an indepth study of current efforts to assist Indians. A $500-million program, recently requested by the President, is a milestone in the efforts of the Federal government to help the Indians help themselves.

A culminating activity for the unit might include a review of problems facing minority groups and a consideration of what each person can do to help in this struggle.

The teacher must be careful not to attempt to "promote" Indians, nor should he adopt a paternalistic attitude or attempt to glamorize them. Indians need quality education, equality of opportunity, vocational training, and guidance to help them become citizens in the fullest sense of the word.

SOURCES OF MATERIALS

The Bureau of Indian Affairs, Department of the Interior, publishes pamphlets and booklets useful to both teacher and student. Titles may be obtained by requesting a price list from the Superintendent of Documents, United States Government Printing Office, Washington, D.C. 20402. Offerings include:

1. *A Suggested Reading List* concerning Indians' relationship with the Federal Government contains 49 titles, which are usually available from most large public libraries or may be borrowed through an inter-library loan. Examples of the listed books include: *The American Heritage Book of Indians*, and *Early Man in the New World*.

2. A leaflet, *Reference for Young Readers*, lists 113 books, many of which are for use in the elementary and junior high schools, plus 18 books describing handicrafts.

3. *Indian Record*, a monthly publication of the Bureau of Indian Affairs, provides a wealth of information.

4. A brochure, "New Indian Series," announces a 13-booklet series on Indians of different geographical parts of the United States. For example, *Indians of New Mexico, Indians, Eskimos, and Aleuts of Alaska, Indians of Arizona*, etc.

5. "Three Maps of Indian Country," a pamphlet.

6. *Federal Indian Policies*, a summary of major developments from the pre-Revolutionary period to the 1960's.

7. *American Indians and the Federal Government*.

Civic Education Service publishes an excellent *Visual-History Wall Map* on American Indians when the white men came.

Editor's Note: The CES Map mentioned by Dr. Crowder not only provides a pictorial presentation of the main cultural divisions of Indians at the time the white men came, but also portrays the kinds of homes in which each group of Indians lived, their means of a livelihood, tools they used, and much more. Also shown are major Indian tribes and their locations, present reservations, major Indian battles, and some leading Indians—past and present.

The map is available for $1.50 each. It is part of a set of *10 Visual-History Wall Maps* which also includes *Exploration and Discovery; Colonization; American Revolution; Western Frontier; Immigration; House Divided; Civil War; Literary America*; and *20th Century America*. The entire set of 10 maps, including Teacher's Guide and file folder, is available for $9.95.

NEW TRANSPARENCIES

New from CES is a series of transparencies which includes a unit on *Indians Before White Man*. This series includes the following:

1. *Came from Siberia.* Large groups of Indians crossing frozen waters into North America to seek new hunting grounds. Includes inset map of the crossing.

2. *Colorful Map.* Clearly shows how anthropologists and historians have divided American Indians into various groups. Interesting teachers' guide explains these groupings, and raises challenging questions.

3. *Pueblo Indians.* America's first apartment dwellers are examined as to their culture and history; also colorful pottery and handicraft.

4. *Hunting Buffaloes.* Indians dressed up in wolfskins to hunt near-sighted buffalo. Products and uses made of skin and meat.

5. *Indian Fishing.* Using plants to drug fish and make them come up for air was just one of many ingenious Indian devices.

6. *Variety of Crops.* You name it—they grew it—from squash to tomatoes to corn to beans to pumpkins.

7. *Women's Duties.* Tidying up the wigwam was only one of many duties for Indian women. They were often farmers, weavers, and developed such products as maple sugar.

8. *Sign Language.* Varieties of signs vividly illustrate how the stoical Indians often communicated without a sound.

9. *Word Symbols.* Even without a written language, most Indians carved pictures to represent words. Fascinating study.

10. *Chief & Council.* Who governed the Indian villages? Where did clan members fit in? These and other interesting questions are explored in the picture and teachers' guide.

11. *War Rituals.* Each tribe had strict codes of ethics in conducting wars. An insight into Indian heroics and character.

12. *Skilled Craftsmen.* The intricate process of canoe-building is examined.

13. *Buffalo Dance.* What Indian dances achieved, and what the movements meant.

14. *Religion.* Sun worshippers and medicine men are strikingly portrayed. Indian religion tried to explain the violent, often cruel, ways of nature.

Write for illustrated brochure and price list for first semester: Civic Education Service, 1733 K Street, N.W., Washington, D.C. 20006.

TEACHING ABOUT
THE PUERTO RICAN

Board of Education of the City of New York

PROBLEM SITUATIONS

In newly integrated schools, situations which are new are bound to arise and old situations with a new twist will continue to be with us. It is impossible to anticipate all of the possibilities.

This section will present some situations which have arisen or are likely to arise. In addition to the situations, we will present certain clues for ways of dealing with them. These fall into two groups, immediate response and follow up. In some cases no follow up may be indicated.

It should be noted there is no pat answer to any educational problem. The clues given should only be seen as suggestions. Differences in school population, class population, teacher and pupil personalities, and teacher-pupil rapport make it necessary that the individual teacher adapt the suggestions to meet the demands of his particular situation. . . .

1. A boy states, "My grandfather had to learn English before he could vote. Why should Puerto Ricans vote if they can't even speak English?"

Immediate Response: "Puerto Ricans are citizens whether or not they speak English. They have the same responsibilities as others and should enjoy the same rights."

2. A child states, "My mother says that you can't pass laws to make people like one another."

Immediate Response: "Your mother is right. Laws do not change people's feelings. Laws enable the government to enforce civil rights."

POSSIBLE LEARNING ACTIVITIES

Topic Puerto Rico and the Puerto Ricans in New York City

Aims

1. To learn a few facts about Puerto Rico and the Puerto Ricans who migrate to New York City.

New York Board of Education, "Teaching About the Puerto Rican." Adapted from *Teaching About Minorities in Classroom Situations*, Curriculum 1967–68, Series No. 23, pp. 6–10, 58–64. Reprinted with permission of the Board of Education, City of New York.

2. To find out what Puerto Ricans are doing and what we ourselves can do to minimize causes of conflict, and to promote better relations.

3. To foster among pupils a feeling for the difficulties faced by people coming into a culture different from theirs, where the language may also be unfamiliar.

4. To discuss some of the myths that are being circulated about the Puerto Ricans and by the use of facts and figures, dispel some of these myths.

Possible approaches

1. Show a film, such as "This is Puerto Rico," which emphasizes the progress made in Puerto Rico in the social, economic, and political life of the people.

2. Where there are Puerto Rican youngsters in the class, ask volunteers to recount an outstanding experience of their life in the city.

   a) A composition may be assigned beforehand where youngsters are asked to write about the most important experience of their lives; youngsters who are fairly recent arrivals and who have some command of the language may be encouraged to write about their first few days, or weeks or months in New York City; those who are not sufficiently competent in the use of English may tell their story to a classmate who will translate it and/or write it for him.

   b) Teacher and/or pupils will bring in clippings from newspapers and magazines which they will discuss for accuracy and expression of attitudes.

   c) Make a survey of the class to find out how many youngsters have been to Puerto Rico or have relatives who have been to Puerto Rico, how many have Puerto Rican friends, and how many have parents who know Puerto Ricans or work with Puerto Ricans.

Development

1. Elicit from class topics that should merit the consideration of the class for intensive study, for example:

   a) *Background*
   What is life like in Puerto Rico?
   How do people make a living there?
   Why do they come to the Mainland?

   b) *The Puerto Ricans in New York City*
   What is life like in New York City for the Puerto Rican?
   Who is the Puerto Rican who comes to New York City?
   Why do some Puerto Ricans have difficulties in adjusting?

2. Pupil volunteers for topic of particular interest. Some may prefer to work individually, but where a group of youngsters appears to be interested in a particular topic, they should be encouraged to form a committee, choosing a leader or chairman from the group. The topic they choose may be further subdivided for more detailed study, for example, under *"What is life like in Puerto Rico?"*, they can study:
   a) The geography and climate
   b) Social advances
   c) Economic growth
   d) Political development
   e) Educational advancements

   The topic *"Why do they come to New York City?"* can be further subdivided in the following manner:
   a) Reasons for migration
   b) Periods of greatest migration
   c) Migration today as compared to migration in the 40's and 50's
   d) Out-migration to other cities on the Mainland.

3. Pupils report to class the results of their findings, with every effort being made to encourage pupils to use varying methods of presentation, such as:
   a) Presentation and discussion of a film or a film-strip
   b) Panel presentation with chairman to present speakers and summarize, as well as lead the discussion
   c) Recording of interviews conducted
   d) Use of speakers from among parents or interested community members, or from organizations such as the Commonwealth of Puerto Rico Office, Aspira, etc.

Application Return to question of myths, and with the use of material presented by the committees, elicit from students evidence for their rebuttal of the stereotypes.

Follow-up

1. Urge youngsters to clip articles from newspapers and magazines written specifically about Puerto Ricans, bring to class for group reading and interpretation (use opaque projector).

2. Encourage volunteers to write letters to newspaper editors with an evaluation of the article in question.

3. Keep a permanent bulletin board of current literature about Puerto Ricans.

4. Have a debate on the advantages and disadvantages of the present "Commonwealth status" for Puerto Rico.

Materials

1. Teacher and pupils check on availability of materials in school and/or neighborhood library.
2. Committee of students write to agencies such as the Commonwealth of Puerto Rico for information on Puerto Ricans.

THE PUERTO RICAN PEOPLE

Puerto Rico is a roughly rectangular island, 1600 miles southeast of New York. Its territory includes three smaller islands, Vieques, Culebra and Mona. The climate is sub-tropical. Puerto Rico became a U.S. possession as a result of the Spanish American War.

I. Internal migration in the United States has generally been a rural to urban movement. The lures of more lucrative employment and greater cultural and educational opportunities which were to be found in the cities were compelling attractions.

   A. Overpopulation has been a great spur to Puerto Rican migration. The population density of Puerto Rico is 687 persons per square mile. The population density on the U.S. mainland is 51 persons per square mile.

   B. The primarily agrarian economy cannot provide sufficient employment for the labor force. In 1960–1961 more than 11.1% of the labor force was unemployed. Many of these unemployed people came to the United States seeking work.

   C. Many Puerto Rican soldiers who served in the armed forces during World War II decided to take advantage of the greater opportunities offered by the mainland.

   D. The cheap rapid air travel also encouraged immigration.

II. Puerto Rican migration to the mainland correlates closely with economic activity. During periods of recession, such as in 1957 and 1961, there is a sharp drop in migration.

Year	Net Migration to United States	New York City
1909–30	1,986	
1931–40	904	
1945	13,573	
1946	39,911	
1947	24,551	
1948	32,775	
1949	25,698	
1950	34,703	29,500

	Net Migration to	
Year	*United States*	*New York City*
1951	52,899	42,300
1952	59,103	45,500
1953	69,124	51,800
1954	21,531	16,100
1955	45,464	31,800
1956	52,315	34,000
1957	37,704	22,600
1958	27,690	17,000
1959	29,989	18,000
1960	16,293	9,600
1961	1,754 Net outflow	—
1962	10,800	6,500
1963	5,479 Net outflow	—
1964	1,370	822
1965	16,678	

III. The unskilled agricultural laborer entering an industrial center is faced with many problems of adjustment even in a racially homogeneous situation. The Puerto Rican migrant faced, and faces, these and other problems.

A. Most Puerto Rican immigrants cannot speak English.

B. Most Puerto Rican migrants are unskilled laborers. The lack of salable skills plus the inability to speak English limit the migrant to menial, low-paying jobs.

C. Because of the housing shortages and discrimination unscrupulous landlords demand exorbitant rentals for substandard housing.

D. Securing an adequate education was a problem for some Puerto Rican children in the late forties and fifties. The enrollment of Puerto Rican children in the city's schools rose from 24,350 in 1947 to 146,430 in 1959. The schools were not equipped to handle this influx of largely non-English speaking children.

E. Racial prejudice is particularly galling to the Puerto Rican immigrant. Restrictions based on racial considerations are not as common in Puerto Rico. The Puerto Rican identifies himself culturally or ethnically rather than racially.

F. The Puerto Rican immigrant is the victim of many stereotypes and misconceptions. Some of them follow.

   1. "They created slums". Slum dwellers are estimated at 20% of the population, and Puerto Ricans make up about 5% of the population. There were three times as many non-Puerto Ricans as Puerto Ricans living in slums.

   2. "Puerto Ricans come to New York City to go on welfare." Data

from the N.Y. Dept. of Welfare reports that 85–95% of the Puerto Rican population of the city is self-supporting. During the recession preceding Korea 14% were reported to be on Welfare; after April 1957 11%; during periods of prosperity 5 to 6%.

3. "Puerto Ricans contribute more than their share of delinquents." They contribute just about their quota, according to official estimates. An article appearing in *Time* June 23, 1958, claims that Puerto Ricans who form about 8% of the population contribute slightly more than 8% to the crime rate.

4. "All Puerto Ricans are colored". Some are, some are not. The United States Census classifies the people of Puerto Rico as 79.7% white and 20.13% non-white. The 1950 census showed that 7.7% of the persons of Puerto Rican birth living in the United States to be non-white. Census figures also show that fewer non-whites come to the United States from Puerto Rico than whites.

G. The cultural differences at times create conflicts with mainland groups. An activity, such as playing dominoes on the street is perfectly acceptable in Puerto Rico; in many mainland communities it is considered objectionable.

IV. The recent waves of Puerto Rican immigration have had significant impact on our mainland society.

A. There has been an increased public interest in Latin American culture such as food, music and dance.

B. There has been increased enrollment in Spanish classes in our public schools.

C. In time of war Puerto Rican soldiers have made notable contributions. In World War II over 65,000 Puerto Rican men served in the armed forces; in the Korean War 91% of the 43,434 Puerto Rican men who served were volunteers.

D. In the area of race relations Puerto Ricans living on the mainland may well influence the thinking of their neighbors in terms of the development of better interracial relationships.

E. Puerto Ricans in our labor force, especially in New York City, profoundly affect the production of goods and services. They also form a large segment of the consumer market.

F. Puerto Ricans have begun to take an effective part in our political life. Carlos Rios is a Manhattan Councilman, Herman Badillio is Borough President of the Bronx, Manuel Gomez and Felipe Torres are judges.

G. Many Puerto Ricans have made contributions in the arts, industry, sports, business, the professions, and politics. Jose Ferrer and Juano Hernandez are actors of international reputation. Graciela

Rivera is a singer of note. In the major leagues Ruben Gomez, Juan Pizzaro and Jim Rivera are only a few of the outstanding players from Puerto Rico.

V. Impact of America on the Group

A. The strongly patriarchal family system is weakening. Economic necessity has forced many Puerto Rican women to work; in some cases she becomes the chief breadwinner. This tends to undermine the authority of the father.

B. Women because of their earning power and the example of their North American neighbors are gaining new respect and status and playing a more important role in community social life.

C. An unfortunate result of acculturation is the increase of color prejudice among Puerto Rican people.

D. The development of anti-social gangs took place among urban Puerto Rican youngsters. Such gangs were unknown in Puerto Rico.

VI. Highlights of its Historical Development

1. Puerto Rico was discovered by Christopher Columbus on his second voyage to the New World, on November 19, 1493. The Indians called the island Borinquen, but he named it San Juan Bautista (which today is the name of its capital). Quanica, the name of the town on the west coast of the island where this landing supposedly took place, is the only part of the United States where Columbus actually landed.

2. It was not until 1508 that conquest and settlement took place under the leadership of Juan Ponce de Leon, some 100 years before the English settled in Jamestown in 1607. The first settlement was near the site of San Juan today, the oldest city flying the American flag. History reports that this was a peaceful occupation because of the unaggressive nature of the Arawaks. As early as 1544 it was reported that these Indians as a distinct ethnic group were fast disappearing. Unaccustomed to working in mines, great numbers died. Others fled to the mountains or neighboring islands. However, we can still find traces of this Indian past in the physical features of some Puerto Ricans of today.

3. From the earliest times Puerto Rico was valued by its mother country Spain for its strategic position. It was used by Spain as a supply depot for its expeditions to and from the other possessions and as a defense outpost to protect its shipping and insure the stability of its empire.

a) This strategic importance was likewise recognized by the English, the French and the Dutch, all of whom engaged in a series of attempts to take the island away from Spain, from 1528 to as late as 1797. England succeeded in occupying San Juan for five months in 1598, but finally had to withdraw because disease was decimating her men.

b) It was in order to protect San Juan and its excellent port from attack that Spain decided to build a wall and series of forts around it. Names were given to these fortifications—La Fortaleza, El Morro, San Cristobal—all major tourist attractions today.

4. Because of the decimation of the Arawaks alluded to above, early in the 16th century Negroes were brought in as slaves. Manumission of slaves appears to have been common from the outset, a fact which motivated slaves from neighboring islands to flee from their masters and seek sanctuary in Puerto Rico.

a) From about 1850 the sentiment in favor of abolition grew and in 1868 children born of slaves were freed.

b) Slavery was abolished in 1873, without reported incidents. Vagrancy laws at that time were rigidly enforced to prevent a drastic reduction in the labor supply.

c) To the law freeing slaves was added the stipulation that slaves were to remain with their former owners for three additional years.

5. During its first three centuries under the rule of Spain, Puerto Rico's economic development was practically nil. By the 18th century it was trading more with Spain and the Spanish West Indies. Coffee was then its most important export crop. It wasn't until 1815, when the trading policy was liberalized and the island was allowed to trade with the United States, Europe and South America, that it started becoming aware of its great agricultural potential. The amount of land under cultivation increased, with a greater proportion of the land being devoted to export crops.

6. Population expanded rapidly during the 19th century:

a) The Cedula de Gracias of 1815, in addition to opening foreign ports to the Puerto Rican trade, also permitted foreigners of the Catholic faith to settle in the island.

b) Many royalist refugees from the Latin American revolutions sought haven there.

7. The economic activity of the 19th century contributed to the rise of an important and powerful class of merchants, professionals and wealthy local planters. This group assumed an important role in the struggle for greater political freedom. This national consciousness opposed to Spanish rule was evidenced by:

a) The rebellion by slaves in certain sections of the island (Vega Baja and Ponce).

b) The Insurrection at Lares in 1868 (Grito de Lares) an example of rebellion against autocratic rule.

c) Participation in Cuban revolts.

d) Activities of leaders, such as Hostos, Betances, Baldorioty de Castro, Luis Munoz Rivera today hold prominent places in the historical development of Puerto Rico towards freedom.

8. A Charter of Autonomy was obtained by Luis Munoz Rivera (father of the Governor of Puerto Rico, Luis Munoz Marin) from Spain in 1897. This charter granted the island "dominion status" and allowed it a much more powerful elected legislative body.

9. Very soon after the Charter was proclaimed, General Miles and his United States Contingent landed near Guanica, on July 25, 1898, to plant the American flag on Spanish soil. Under the provisions of the Treaty of Paris, following the cessation of hostilities on August 13, Puerto Rico was ceded to the United States. The Commander of the American forces and subsequent governors ruled as autocratically as Spain had.

10. In 1900 under the first Organic Act (known as the Forakar Act) a civil government was instituted (less democratic in form than provided in charter secured from Spain in 1897). With the exception of the members of the lower house of the legislature, which was elected, Washington took over all political activity, from the appointing of the governor and the key official of the executive branch to the naming of the members of the upper house of the legislature and the justices of the Supreme Court.

11. As a result of persistent requests for more autonomy in government, this act was amended in 1917. The name of this new Organic Act was The Jones Act. Its most important provision was the granting of citizenship to the Puerto Ricans. It liberalized the political structure to the extent that they could now elect members to both houses of the legislature.

12. Puerto Rico started toward self-government in 1947 when Congress passed a resolution allowing Puerto Ricans to elect their own Governor. On January 2, 1949, Luis Munoz Marin, the first elected governor, took his Oath of Office.

13. According to the Constitution of 1952, Puerto Rico is now neither a state nor an independent country. It is a Commonwealth, an associated free state to use the literal translation of "Estado Libre Asociado", a "new concept in government" as it has been described by political scientists. Insofar as local affairs are concerned, it governs itself like a state, except that it has no representation in Congress, and its citizens may not vote for President. (There is a Resident Commissioner in Washington representing the interests of

the Puerto Rican Government, but he has no vote). It does not pay federal taxes, an obvious advantage. Washington exercises some of the authority it does over a state. However, its revenue and customs money goes into the insular rather than the Federal Treasury.

14. There have been repeated protests from certain segments of the population for greater political autonomy, if not outright independence. On the other hand, a larger group seeks to have Puerto Rico become the fifty-first state. But the great majority of the Puerto Ricans have supported the party of former Governor Luis Munoz Marin and its concept of the Commonwealth.

15. The United States has contributed much to help Puerto Rico on the road to a higher standard of living. Although the per capita income is about one half that of the poorest state in the United States, it is the second highest in Latin America.

    The migration to the mainland has helped with the problems of over-population and lack of employment in Puerto Rico. But the migration has had undesirable as well as desirable effects in Puerto Rico.

STUDY QUESTIONS

1. How did Smith and Lloyd help their children to confront "blackness?" Do you think these approaches were effective? Why or why not? What other teaching techniques might be used to augment the self-images of black children?

2. What are the disadvantages of using information about black heroes to help black children improve their self-concepts? What are the advantages?

3. What techniques could you use to help Mexican-American, American-Indian, and Puerto Rican-American children to improve their self-images?

4. Minority group children are seldom exposed to lessons dealing with the ghettos in which they live. Why?

5. Why might a study of the ghettos in which they live be especially important for minority group children? What approaches to studying the black ghetto does Bennett recommend? Do these approaches seem helpful and practical? Why or why not? How might the approaches recommended by Bennett be used to study the Puerto Rican ghetto?

6. According to Gearing, how might children benefit from studying Indian cultures? In what ways is a study of Indian cultures especially valuable for Indian children?

7. Why are Indian peoples frequently stereotyped in teaching materials?

How might a teacher use distorted materials to teach important lessons about the derivation of social knowledge?

8. What are the strengths and weaknesses of the teaching strategies described by the New York Board of Education for use in classrooms with Puerto Rican children? How might these strategies be improved?

SUGGESTED READINGS

Banks, James A., *Teaching The Black Experience: Methods and Materials.* Belmont, Calif.: Fearon Publishers, 1970

Banks, James A., and Jean D. Grambs, *Black Self-Concept.* New York: McGraw-Hill, in press

Clark, Kenneth B., *Dark Ghetto.* New York: Harper and Row, 1965

Cleaver, Eldridge, *Soul on Ice.* New York: Dell Publishing Company, 1968

Collier, John, *The Indians of the Americas.* New York: Mentor Books, 1947

Detroit Public Schools, Department of Social Studies, "Bibliography on Afro-American History and Culture," *Social Education*, **33** 447–461, 1969

Forbes, Jack D. (Editor), *The Indian in America's Past.* Englewood Cliffs, N.J.: Prentice-Hall, Inc., 1964

Glazer, Nathan, "The Puerto Ricans," in Vincent R. Rogers (Editor), *A Sourcebook for the Social Studies*, pp. 220–230. New York: Macmillan, 1969

Grier, William H., and Price M. Cobbs, *Black Rage.* New York: Bantam Books, 1968

Gruber, Ruth, *Puerto Rico, Island of Promise.* New York: Hill and Wang, 1960

Hagan, William T., *American Indians.* Chicago: University of Chicago Press, 1961

Handlin, Oscar, *The Newcomers.* Cambridge, Mass.: Harvard University Press, 1959

Jarolimek, John (Editor), "Social Studies Education—The Elementary School: Focus on Minority Groups," *Social Education*, **33** 429–446, 1969

Lewis, Oscar, *La Vida.* New York: Random House, 1966

Morine, Harold, and Greta Morine, *A Primer for the Inner-city School.* New York: McGraw-Hill, 1970

New Voices of the Southwest. Washington, D.C.: National Education Association, 1967

Padilla, Elena, *Up From Puerto Rico.* New York: Oxford University Press, 1958

Pettigrew, Thomas F., *A Profile of the Negro American*. Princeton, N.J.: D. Van Nostrand, 1964

Rand, Christopher, *The Puerto Ricans*. Oxford University Press, 1958

Roselle, Daniel (Editor), "Black Americans and Social Studies," *Social Education*, **33** 385–428, 1969

Rubel, Arthur J., *Across the Tracks: Mexican-Americans in a Texas City*. Austin: University of Texas Press, 1966

Silberman, Charles E., *Crisis in Black and White*. New York: Vintage Books, 1964

Verrill, Hyatt A., *The Real Americans*. New York: G. P. Putnam, 1954

Vogt, Evon Z., "The Acculturation of American Indians," in Vincent R. Rogers (Editor), *A Sourcebook for the Social Studies*, pp. 237–244. New York: Macmillan, 1969

CHAPTER 9
TEACHING
BLACK HISTORY

With the emergence of the black revolt in the 1960's, black people began to shape and perpetuate a new identity. They rejected many of the cultural components of the dominant white middle-class culture and searched for elements from which they could form a new identity. Such elements include intensified racial pride and cohesiveness, a search for power, and an attempt to identify cultural roots in Africa.[1] African dashikis, tikis, "natural" hair styles, and Swahilian phrases emerged as new cultural components. Written history is an essential and important part of a people's heritage. As the black revolt gained momentum, black people demanded that textbooks be rewritten so that their role in the making of American history would be more favorably and realistically depicted. Civil rights groups pressured school districts to ban lily-white history textbooks from the schools, and school districts in turn pressured publishers to include blacks and other minority groups in textbooks and other teaching materials.

School districts throughout the nation are urgently concerned about implementing relevant and successful programs in black studies. Many districts have produced curriculum guides on black studies, hired consultants in black history, and conducted workshops in black studies. The market is flooded with black history and "integrated" textbooks, many whose quality is being seriously questioned. All-white textbooks have been revised and sprinkled with success stories of selected black heroes. Despite these efforts, there is still debate among teachers and administrators about the appropriate content of and approaches to use in teaching black history. This chapter discusses some critical issues related to the teaching of black history, as well as some perennial issues regarding historical bias and objectivity and the purposes of history. Although many of these problems have been debated by historians for centuries, they are receiving renewed attention today because of the attempt to reconstruct American history so that it presents a different perspective on the black man's role.

NOTE

1. James A. Banks, "A Profile of the Black American: Implications For Teaching," *College Composition and Communication*, **19** (December 1968), 288–296.

TEACHING
BLACK HISTORY

Nathan Hare

To paraphrase Stokely Carmichael, who appeared to take the words out of my mouth, the essential character of a course in black history or/and culture revolves around its perspective and its methodology, from which its content is more or less naturally derived.[1] All three elements are, of course, dependent in turn on the goals of the teacher and the course. However, any course, or system of education, has the function, in one way or another, of transmitting skills, loyalty, and deportment appropriate to some institutional or normative order. This is no less true—nor should it be—in the case of black courses.[2]

To illustrate, let us discuss in detail each of three elements—perspective, methodology, and content—which distinguish a course in black history or/and culture from a general course in history and culture.

PERSPECTIVE

The cry for courses in black history and culture has arisen in a new black push for an invigorated collective ego-identity or group self-respect and self-direction. This quest for black consciousness and nationhood, in the absence of a territorial and political autonomy, must inevitably rest, as would any idea of nation or peoplehood, on a common sense of history

Nathan Hare, "Teaching Black History," from "The Teaching of Black History and Culture in the Secondary School," *Social Education*, 33 (April 1969), 385–388. Reprinted with permission of the author and the National Council for the Social Studies.

and/or culture. This sense of pastness, or collective density, in turn is viewed as a springboard to a new collective future.

Therapeutic value Having acquired a new self-image as a result of pride in his race and its pastness, the black student will, other things being equal, seek to convey this image to others.[3] This may be a major key to the current problems of "motivating" black youth which typically is approached from an individual standpoint alone.

In this regard, a course in black history or culture which does not derive from the black perspective loses much of its therapeutic value not to mention intellectual integrity. This is true whether the teacher is a black individual or not. While, other things being equal, it is expected that, within the present racial context of this country, the black student—socialized in a "racist" (white-dominated) society—will relate better to the black teacher, this is not always the case. The cry for black teachers for black history is merely a reflection of the credibility gap inflicted on the black race by the history of white conduct vis-à-vis black history and development. Indirectly, of course, the cry for black teachers has the function of increasing the admission of black teachers in a society with traditionally white-biased criteria of teacher selection.[4] However, this is not to suggest that a black (or Negro) teacher can feign to teach black history merely because he treats the subject of "the Negro" from a conventional, white perspective while hiding behind the badge of a black skin.[5]

At the same time, there are the ultra "objective" who, though they think nothing of teaching a "regular" history course without ever mentioning "the Negro" except as a slave and a spark for the Civil War, are quick to wail self-righteously that to teach from a black perspective is political rather than academic. This is no more accurate than the fact that to teach from a white perspective (in a society self-defined as racist) or neglect black contributions entirely is political. It is just as political to campaign or work for an existing regime as to work for its removal. In any case, all education seeks to better its community, as so perceived by the guardians of its institutions, and to prepare persons to play better roles in that regard. Thus, the teacher of black history and culture must also have a vision or picture of the kind of black history and culture black people want to build in America and the kind of society they wish to help America become in relation to themselves. Inasmuch as America will house the black American's culture, the teaching of black history and culture must be geared to both a new black community and a new America.

Transformation versus transmission The danger from political dogma or abstract absolutist ideologies is dampened, while a number of positive factors are achieved—more about them later—through a wedding of the teaching process and the black experience toward what is currently called "relevant education." This encourages creativity instead of passive assimilation of dogmatic perspectives.

For, in addition to transmitting knowledge about black history and culture as it has already emerged, the teacher of black history and culture—as in the case of any history or culture—must be an agent for transforming that history and culture, making the student as well a part of that transmission and ultimate transformation. To quote Maulana Ron Karenga, founder and chairman of the U.S. organization, "we must tell Blacks they are great and then make them so."[6]

Thus, the teaching of black history and culture not only should seek to save black history and culture and all that is good therein, it should involve or integrate the student into his community, augmenting his functioning in the community and, indirectly, in society and the world at large.

The fostering of identity with the black community, the development of community consciousness, black consciousness (including black America, Africa, and the black spectrum around the world) would, other things being equal, commit the black student more to the task of helping to build the black community, when once his studies are done, in contrast to the currently induced frenzy (within the educational institution and elsewhere) to escape the black community.

METHODOLOGY AND CONTENT

Inasmuch as the content of a black history and culture course is derived from the black experience, the black struggle and its needs, it is largely empirical or/and experimental in nature. Hence, textbooks, for example, direly lacking anyway, will typically be disdained in preference for creative syllabi (produced often with student collaboration) and guidelines culled from the laboratory of life.

This includes directed activities to get the student into the community and allow him to live, instead of memorizing, what he is learning. Experiments, discussions, audio-visual aids and the like likewise would tend to replace perfunctory lectures and textbook perusals, and should be supplemented in turn by field work and apprenticeships in the community where the student can experience the phenomena treated in the classroom.

A class in black history and culture might require, as an individual or a collective assignment, the establishment of a Black History Club or a Black Culture Club. This has the effect of organizing the community around its own identity as a by-product of the learning process. Panels of students could be obliged to hold discussions on black history and culture before elementary school groups, if only informally in church basements or wherever.

Additionally, the mere presence of the students would provide models of purposeful endeavor for younger black children in slum districts currently characterized by high dropout rates. This would be compounded in the case of college students, and those high school students of black history and culture who took part in the organization and production of cultural affairs would develop relationships which in turn might cement their commitment to the black community and its ideals in post-college life.

Other things equal, the black student would be impelled to read more in order to succeed better in his field work activities connected with his courses. Thus, a course ordinarily regarded as of little practical value or, at the least, non-utilitarian, is placed in a framework of pragmatism which goes far beyond the expressive component of merely salvaging a damaged collective ego and ego-sustenance.

BLACK HOLIDAYS AND HEROES

The teaching of black history and culture might also be tied in with black holidays and/or heroes current and future. Most holidays are generally regarded as having arisen by some kind of divine decree or, at the least, are taken for granted. This is in spite of the fact that Mother's Day, for example, was proclaimed initially by Woodrow Wilson some fifty-four years ago. Even Christmas as an annual celebration in this country is said by the *Encyclopaedia Britannica* to be slightly more than 100 years old. There are many precedents, then, as well as a need, for the establishment of major black holidays just as there is St. Patrick's Day for the Irish, though celebrated by others. Yom Kippur, for example, a Jewish holiday, might be duplicated by a Black Winter Break, beginning with February 21, the day of Malcolm X's assassination (whose life and death could be studied by the class), passing over February 22, the birthday of George Washington (a slavemaster and president of a slave-holding nation), and ending with February 23, the birthday of W. E. B. DuBois, early black leader and one of the world's greatest scholars.[7]

This combines black holidays and black heroes (currently typically white), whose birthdays and other significant dates could be celebrated in some way if only by a field trip or pageant. Thus, the student experiences some fabric of the history and culture as he learns it. This also helps eliminate the risk, too often victimizing would-be black change-makers, of getting bogged down in history, glorifying and magnifying the folk contributions and, frequently, makeshift heroes of the past to the point of neglecting to make a new future. While they are thus preoccupied with a static study of the past, others largely make their current history and shape their future culture for them.

At the same time, the students are led to study, from firsthand and raw sources, the contributions of the black race to American history and culture with special reference to the given community. There are, for example, many black persons living in black communities whose parents, let alone their grandparents, were either slaves or freedmen or soldiers in the Union Army or members of the ranks of black cowboys (currently estimated by respectable historians to have numbered as much as one-third of all cowboys) who helped clear the American frontier westward. These individuals comprise an untapped fund of data on black history and culture handed down to them at fireside by their parents but now already fading away and destined largely to die with their generation. Many other types of community experts in some form of culture (such as jazz and blues music) could be utilized for classroom presentation of various kinds designed to enhance the student's knowledge as well as appreciation of the intricacies of black culture.

Black history and culture as taught in the schools must be, above all, the story of the struggle and aspirations of the black race; not merely a catalog of the white race's undernourished if not infected conception of the black race and its goals—a view endorsed in one way or another by black assimilationists[8] as well as the white majority. Black reconstructionists, who wish to reconstruct a repressed black culture on the assumption that the black race as a distinct category and much of its past contributions are worth saving as well as developing, by contrast are committed to a new black perspective as a cornerstone for building a viable consciousness of a black community. In such an enterprise, the key partner is the teacher.

> Teacher Irving Sloan, in an AFT booklet reviewing U.S. history texts' treatment of Negroes, had this to say: Only when we have teachers—as distinguished from texts—who are well-versed in integrated history will our secondary school students gain both facts and perspectives about the Negro in the history of our national past. This will come only as a result of specialized courses for teachers on the college level and a heightened sense of commitment by teachers about the importance of the subject.[9]

And a heightened sense of commitment by teachers about the importance of the teacher with appropriate new perspectives, methodology, and materials as well as the importance of the teacher and the student—the educational process—as agents of cultural transmission, development and transformation.

NOTES

1. Lecture delivered before an all-nonwhite audience, Main Auditorium, San Francisco State College, Nov. 5, 1968.

2. "Black" courses are distinguished from "dark" or "Negro" courses in that the former are taught from a "black" (nationalistic or pluralistic or reconstructionist) perspective—more about that later—as distinct from a "white" (dominant group or assimilationist) perspective. Old or

traditional courses in "Negro history" and "race relations" and the like are all too frequently dusted off and rushed forth under the "black" label.

3. Already in our program at San Francisco State College, there is evidence that students subjected to even an embroyonic black studies program tend to do better not only in their black courses but in their "white" courses as well. The white student also gains a healthier self-image set against a more realistic image of the black race. "If it is wrong to deny the Negro a record of his past, it is equally wrong to cheat the white student, who . . . is resentful when he realizes that he's only half educated in American history and only half prepared for the American future." From Charles H. Harrison, "Black History and the Schools," *Education News* (Oct. 21, 1968), reprinted in *Ebony* (December 1968).

4. Recently a school teacher of twelve years experience in five school systems from Chicago to Washington, D.C. applied for a job in California. She held a master's degree plus thirty hours and had received the Junior Chamber of Commerce's "Outstanding Young Educator" award for all of Washington, D.C. The personnel counselor still assumed that she was not qualified on the assumption that she had not passed the rather irrelevant National Teachers Exam. When she stated that she had passed that exam in her field plus one other, she was told that she would have to take five additional courses (including the state's political history) in order to qualify. More recently, on the other hand, a California state educational governing body voted to certify persons with two years of college who had received majors in black studies in order to fill the budding shortage of black history teachers in high schools.

5. "Black nationalists" are beginning to distinguish the words "black" and "Negro." A Negro is assimilationist-oriented or "white-minded" in that view.

6. Clyde Halisi and James Mtume, eds., *The Quotable Karenga*, U.S. organization, 1967, quoted in Floyd B. Barbour, ed., *The Black Power Revolt*, Boston: Porter Sargent Publishers, 1968, p. 170.

7. The "Black Christmas" movement sponsored by Chicago's Operation Breadbasket program (1968) suggests another possibility of integrating blackness into existing holidays. Black history and culture also should, of course, be integrated into regular courses, but for quite some time yet—and to some degree indefinitely—there is a need for black courses per se.

8. See Nathan Hare, *The Black Anglo-Saxons*, New York: Marzani and Munsell, 1965.

9. Harrison, *"Black History and the Schools,"* p. 114.

BLACK HISTORY,
NEGRO HISTORY,
AND WHITE FOLK

Larry Cuban

Booker T. Washington is an Uncle Tom; Nat Turner is a Freedom Fighter; Abraham Lincoln is a white supremacist, and the first President of the United States is just another honkie. Mali, Songhay, and Timbuktu are enshrined, and hog maws, chittlings, and black-eyed peas are ennobled. This is the stuff of Black History. Heroes are all black and struggle for freedom. Villains are all white and oppress for profit. Black History, a tool in the hands of race-conscious activists who wish to create a sense of people-ness among black people, bursts with righteousness, pride, and outrage.

Negro History, on the other hand, corrects distortions and fills in the enormous gaps of information about people of color in this nation. Restraint and balance mark this approach: injustice is soberly catalogued. Colored inventors, soldiers, and artists enter their proper chronological niches and tell Americans that this country is indebted to the invisible man. A history unit on the westward movement, for instance, includes adequate treatment in text and pictures of Jim Beckworth (fur trapper), Nat Love (Deadwood Dick of the 1880s), and the Indian pacification efforts of the Ninth and Tenth Cavalry units.

Negro History, in short, speaks to the mind of the white man and to the middle- and upper-income Negro over thirty-five. Black History speaks to the soul of black men, especially the young.

The distinction, of course, is not absolute. But the differences in style, content, and audience between the two histories have crystallized sufficiently in recent years to become clear. Indeed, the split over aims and audiences mirrors the larger conflicts over the whys and wherefores of race consciousness.

Consider the recent flood of books and materials on the Negro. Much criticism has been directed at books that glorify such individuals as Crispus Attucks, who is, at best, a shadowy historical figure. What critics fail to realize is that such materials are part of a determined effort to counter the white propaganda that has blanketed public schools since their inception. In the process, such materials create a pantheon of black heroes that

Larry Cuban, "Black History, Negro History, and White Folk," *Saturday Review* (Sept. 21, 1968), 64–65. Copyright © 1968 by Saturday Review, Inc. Reprinted with permission of the author and publisher.

children can point to with pride. Movements need heroes—martyrs, preferably—and Attucks, Nat Turner, and Malcolm X can be used to convince black people that they counted years ago and they count now.

To evaluate a book on Attucks solely by the canons of scholarly objectivity and historical accuracy is missing the point—it ignores the necessity of creating black counterparts to the Nathan Hales and Molly Pitchers of the white past. That equally shadowy white heroes have been manufactured in the name of patriotism should give pause to those critics who attack such books without considering their purpose or audience.

The basic issue is whether black mythology will compete with white mythology—commonly called "social studies"—or whether mythology, black or white, belongs in the public schools at all.

To the proponents of Negro History there seem to be three main purposes which competent, well trained teachers can hope to achieve: 1) offer Negro and white students a more balanced picture of the American past, 2) improve racial relations, and 3) improve the self-concept of Negro children. Black History advocates accept the first, care little if at all for the second, and emphasize the third most strongly. Pride, dignity, and self-respect are the vocabulary of Black History.

This poses the question of whether studying Negro or Black History actually will improve the self-concept and instill pride. The only answer has to be: No one knows. No evidence has been produced to demonstrate whether children will see themselves and their race in a more positive light as a result of instructional materials or a course in high school. That no evidence exists, of course, does not mean that increased self-esteem and pride are not produced. But it is clear that creating a course or writing a book for the express purpose of instilling racial pride requires a selection of content that stresses only the positive, only the success story, only the hero, only the victory. And this is propaganda. I don't know whether it works, but I do know that its place is in the storefront, not the classroom. Its teacher must be a true believer, not an inquirer; and it can only be taught by a race-conscious black man, not a white man.

Within the framework of a public school, the only legitimate goals for ethnic content that can be achieved are to offer a balanced view of the American past and present, including racism and democratic ideals, and to equip students with the skills to analyze the meaning of the black American's experience in this country. Whether this combination of knowledge and analytical skills will raise self-esteem or invest youngsters with dignity is debatable, but both could help students to know and think about the many dimensions of the American experience, free of propaganda.

But the activists are dissatisfied with "integrated" history—and with some reason. Most efforts to incorporate the role of the Negro into the course of study simply haven't worked because of the fear, unwillingness, and ignorance of teachers and administrators, both black and white. Consider Washington, D.C., where 80 per cent of the schoolteachers are Negro. In 1964, the Board of Education published a curriculum guide on Negro history for teachers that corrected the distortions and omissions. Yet in visiting classrooms in the District, one finds a tiny fraction of the teachers using the guide, and a majority seldom even incorporate ethnic materials into the conventional content. School people must learn what black activists already know—it is not the materials but the teacher that makes the difference.

When we turn to the contrasting opinions over who should teach history to black children, the answers seem deceptively clear. To most Negroes and whites the answer hinges upon the academic training and competency of the teacher, regardless of race. To Black History advocates, concerned less with the facts than with redefining blackness in a positive manner, only a black man can teach the subject. But the first point of view fails to accept the reality of experience, and the second advocates a kind of educational apartheid that inflates skin color to the single most important variable in teaching—which it isn't.

On his pilgrimage to Mecca in 1964, Malcolm X discovered that he could break bread with a blond, blue-eyed Moslem and be treated as a brother; the trip convinced him that skin color is less important than point of view. Awareness, not pigment, is crucial. Black students learn the same thing when they discover that many of their Negro teachers care little for the issues that confront youth today. And it is doubly galling when they see a young white teacher who is not afraid to raise issues of racial conflict, protest movements, and poverty. Bitterly, they wonder who exactly is "white" and who is "black."

Less attention should be paid to additional books and courses, then, and more to the craftsman who will use the tools. Preachers of Black History know that the person is far more important than the materials he uses. Advocates of Negro History have yet to learn this. There is much to be learned about teaching and learning from the unorthodox, intuitional growth of the Black History movement. But only so much.

Black History aims at revitalizing the African heritage, specifying white racism and the race's liberation from it, and defining a positive black culture—all of which is geared to producing a proud people capable of initiating basic changes in society. It is necessary. It should be supported. But it belongs to a parochial, not a public, education. Its place is outside the public schools. It belongs in the after-school classes established by CORE and the NAACP in Cleveland, the private schools created by Black Muslims in Chicago and other cities, and in the many storefront classes developed by Afro-American societies across the country.

The movement is a growing, vital force capturing the imagination and soul of black youth. If Black History can recruit youngsters and instill in them a passionate race consciousness, the public schools will benefit from youth who know themselves and are committed to use education to shape their future in this country. Not fear but support is essential for after-school centers, cultural exhibitions, and private schools. Fear becomes an issue, however, when Black History becomes the pretext for the thrust toward black control of schools where the goals of public education become unraveled by the search for a political power base.

And Negro History? Its place is in the public schools. It is essential to the growth of both black and white students. Borrowing some of the content, approach, and emphasis of Black History, effective teachers of Negro History, of either race, can begin the enormous task of eliminating the white mythology that has dominated the public schools for too long. The two histories, Black and Negro, need not strain against one another. Rather they can mesh gears and begin moving Americans toward an examination of themselves and their past. Something this country needs badly.

CRISPUS ATTUCKS

Jean D. Grambs

It is not usual to accord a lengthy review to a book written for 4th or 5th grade students in American schools. This is unfortunate. Public and school libraries have shelves of such books; the market is good and is growing with each new injection of Federal money.

One portion of this market, growing faster than any other, are books which have anything to do with Negroes, today or yesterday. The volume reviewed here* is a "natural" for enjoying a wide and profitable market; for young children, it is a book about a Negro whose name occurs in American revolutionary history, but is not controversial. Thus, we are teaching Negro history and can tell Black Power leaders to hush.

Jean D. Grambs, "Crispus Attucks," from "*Crispus Attucks, Boy of Valor*, by Dharathula H. Millender," (book review), *Harvard Educational Review*, **38** (Summer 1968), 605–611. Copyright © 1968 by President and Fellows of Harvard College. Reprinted with permission of the author and publisher.

*Dharathula H. Millender, *Crispus Attucks*, *Boy of Valor*, Indianapolis: Bobbs-Merrill, 1965.

Many educators, white and Negro, are justly critical of American history for its continuing distortions of the history and influence of Negroes, both individually and as a major ethnic group. We are naturally eager that these distortions be corrected, the blank places filled in, and the appropriate data reported accurately. In an effort to overcome the ignorance of Negro and white teachers and historians, new books and articles devoted to Negro history, African history, or biographies of Negroes are appearing at a great rate. It is to be hoped that librarians and educators will see to it that these volumes take their place with other works on American history, and that the data reported become a standard part of students' historical study of America from the very earliest grades. Hopefully, too, textbooks will reflect balanced versions of the African, British, and Spanish Caribbean backgrounds of American Negroes, a more realistic view of the demeaning aspects of slave life prior to the Civil War, a reasonable as well as accurate discussion of the Reconstruction period, and a balanced report of the struggle by Negroes and other ethnic minority groups to gain full access to the privileges and responsibilities of American citizenship.

The contribution of the book reviewed here, however, is a major disservice to these commendable goals. Works of this kind assign to history a dubious name in education and to the Negro an equally dubious role in American life. To change our sentimental view of the past it is one thing to present authentic, historic material, but it is quite another matter to twist or invent material. That the Negro has been ignored or lied about in American history does not justify our telling other historical lies to repair the damage. Unfortunately, that is exactly what Millender does in her "biography" of Crispus Attucks.

Despite the absence of historical data regarding Attucks' life, Millender reconstructs a complicated family, complete with conversations purporting to show how happy the slaves were with their New England masters.

Historical reviews of Attucks' life indicate no authentic data, other than an advertisement to pay a reward for his capture as an escaped slave, his appearance and sudden death in front of the Boston Customs House on March 5, 1770, and disputed, contradictory evidence at the trial of the British soldiers involved.

Questions may be asked, too, about the kind of "history" which has Attucks' father, in the book by Millender, recounting to his son his own life in Africa.

. . . Tell me about your father.

Well, my father was known best for his efforts to make the people of his kingdom prosperous. He encouraged them to be farmers and to trade with other people. . . .

My father told his people that they needed to go to school in order to learn how to be prosperous or successful. Our schools were different from the schools in this country, but they were suited to the needs of our people. They taught our people how to read and write our own language. We had doctors and scientists, too, and many other kinds of workers. . . . Then one day my father was killed and I was sold as a slave.

How awful, Father!

No, not awful, son. Anyone captured during a war was thought of as a slave. That's the way things were in those days. Slaves were the property of the chief of a tribe or the head of a family, and could be kept or sold as the owner wished. Most of them became trusted members of the tribe or family and were free to carry on many activities. But others were sold and taken to other countries. I was one of these.

What happened to you?

I was sold to some traders from the West Indies, who brought me here.

The father explains that now they are the property of Colonel Buckminster. Crispus does not seem to like the idea, but his father remonstrates

Not many slaves have their own cottages, Prince [Attucks' father] explained. I have my own plot of ground just as I might have had in Africa, though not as large. You have always been happy here and you can keep on being happy. The important thing is that you are my son and I'm proud of you . . . (pp. 33–35).

Where are the horrors of the Middle Passage? What about the less than gentle slave trading resorted to by African tribal chiefs? What a delightful picture of the life of a slave in colonial Massachusetts! One wonders just what kind of history Millender was writing, and for whom? Such a benign picture would warm the hearts of book selection committee members from Texas to Mississippi.

Millender provides no footnotes or lists of references to indicate the sources from which she has reconstructed the home and family of Crispus Attucks as he grew up. It would appear that the author has done some study of the lives of Indians, colonial customs, and the incidents leading up to the Boston Massacre. But what is "true" and what has been fabricated by the author cannot be untangled. To pretend that this book provides an authentic story of the life of Crispus Attucks is to mislead in the grossest possible fashion.

In writing the "biography" of Crispus Attucks, Millender closes her volume by saying

Much has been written about the beginnings of the American Revolution. Strangely enough, few United States history books have ever given sufficient attention or credit to Crispus Attucks, the first to fall for American Independence (p. 187).

What Millender fails to point out, as we will document below, is that Crispus Attucks became a martyr for the evolving American Revolution by an accident of history.

But Miss Millender is not alone in desiring a larger-than-life role for her "hero." Unfortunately, other historians have similarly distorted the role of Attucks. For instance, according to C. Eric Lincoln

> Crispus Attucks, a Negro sailor who sought to rally the confused Americans in the face of the British fire, was the first to give his life for America.[1]

Another eminent Negro Historian, John Hope Franklin, also falls into the chauvinistic trap:

> Attucks could hardly be described as a saucy boy. [By whom?] Nor was he deserving of the other harsh things John Adams had to say about those who fell in the Boston Massacre. He was more than forty-seven years old and had made his living during the twenty years after he ran away from his Framingham master by working on ships plying out of Boston harbor. As a seaman he probably [sic] felt keenly the restrictions which England's new navigation acts imposed. He now undertook [*sic*] to make the protest in a form that England would understand. Attucks's martyrdom is significant not as to the first life to be offered in the struggle against England. . . . The significance of Attucks's death seems to lie in the dramatic connection which is pointed out between the struggle against England and the status of the Negroes in America. Here was a fugitive slave who, with his bare hands, was willing to resist England to the point of giving his life. It was a remarkable thing, the colonists reasoned, to have their fight for freedom waged by one who was not as free as they.[2]

On what basis Franklin dismisses John Adams' comments and produces his own probabilities one cannot discern.

Quarles, unlike some of his colleagues, does not let being Negro distort his historical appraisal:

> John Adams later [after the event] observed that the men who lost their lives that night were "the most obscure and inconsiderable that could be found upon the continent." His remark had some justification. Crispus Attucks, "the first to defy, and the first to die," was a Negro of obscure origin, with some admixture of Indian blood. Presumably he had been a slave . . . Attucks's obscurity prior to the Boston Massacre was in dramatic contrast to his role on that occasion . . .

Whatever Attucks actually did that night, his prominent role in the Boston Massacre owed much to John Adams, who, as counsel defending the British soldiers, chose to make him the target.... It was Attucks "to whose mad behavior, in all probability, the dreadful carnage of that night is chiefly to be ascribed."[3]

Quarles argues that there is little historical evidence that Attucks was motivated by patriotic principles, and that in all likelihood—as John Adams in the defense of the British soldiers states—Attucks was merely part of an unruly and drunken mob enjoying the prospect of goading the nervous British. Yet, he continues, it is historically *possible* that he was influenced, as were other Bostonians, by anti-British sentiment. But *all of this is inference*, as Quarles admits.[4]

In his collection of first-hand accounts of events in Negro history, Katz summarizes the events of the mob action which resulted in the Boston Massacre by reporting:

A group of Boston patriots met a company of British soldiers, but this time the usual name-calling, scuffling, and throwing of snowballs ended in bloodshed.

The leader of the crowd of Boston men and boys was Crispus Attucks, a tall runaway slave who had become a seaman. When Attucks waved his cordwood club and urged the crowds forward, someone gave the order to fire and the British muskets cut down Attucks and four other Bostonians.[5]

The actual "eyewitness" account, however, does not quite jibe with the above summary. Katz quotes an observer, also a Negro, who stated in court:

... a stout (heavy set) man with a long cordwood stick, threw himself in, and made a blow at the officer; I saw the officer try to ward off the stroke, whether he struck him or not I do not know; the stout man then turned around, and struck the grenedier's gun at the captain's right hand, and immediately fell in with his club, and knocked his gun away, and struck him over the head, the blow came either on the soldier's cheek or hat. This stout man held the bayonet with his left hand, and twitched it and cried kill the dogs, knock them over; this was the general cry; the people then crowded in, and upon that the grenedier gave a twitch back and relieved his gun, and he up with it and began to pay away on the people.[6]

From the eyewitness account, it sounds as though Attucks was foolhardy in the extreme; had the soldier not retrieved his bayonet and fired, it is likely that he would have been the one lying dead. Katz, the author of page

44, should read his own page 56. There is absolutely no supporting evidence that Attucks was a "patriot," except in the sense that he was the first man to fall, mortally wounded, in a brawl with the British soldiers in Boston in 1770. This fact, however, does not qualify him *as an individual*, Negro or white, for elevation to the Hall of Fame.

By contrast, the classic history of the United States of Charles and Mary Beard provides this comment, and only this comment, on the Boston Massacre

> ... school children (of Boston) now emulated their elders by jeering at soldiers and officers; indeed, one of the first Americans killed in the conflict was a school boy shot by an informer who resented childish ridicule.
>
> This affair was shortly followed by the "Boston Massacre" of March, 1770, starting in comedy as some youths threw snowballs and stones at a small body of British regulars and ending in tragedy with the killing and wounding of several citizens.[7]

In writing her fantasy biography of Crispus Attucks for children, Millender has him attending the trial of Richardson, who shot the taunting schoolboy. Nothing in the historical record would indicate that Attucks would do such a thing, particularly since his official status as a runaway slave would make such public appearance rather dangerous. Courthouses, in those times, were not large and impersonal places; a person of Attucks' appearance would have certainly drawn comment, whereupon his former master could have had him seized; Millender ignores the other "probabilities" of history in order to invent those more suited to her purpose of inflating an individual tragedy to the level of heroic martyrdom.

A more recent "popular" history of the United States summarizes the Boston Massacre in these terms:

> The Townshend Acts bore most heavily on Massachusetts, and for its protests against them that colony's General Court was dissolved in 1768. Violence broke out soon after when a mob attacked customs agents trying to collect Townshend duties from John Hancock's sloop, *Liberty*. This prompted the governor to ask for troops. On March 5, 1770, a snowball attack on some of the soldiers brought the unfortunate order to fire, and after the melee four [*sic*] Bostonians were lying dead.
>
> New England seethed over the "Boston Massacre"; but when the new Lord North Ministry repealed all duties but that on tea, quiet seemed to have been restored ...[8]

The charge that the Beards and William Miller, being white, are thus insensitive to the role of the Negro might be worthy of further examination. One might pick up any current American history and find similar quotations. Few general histories today do an adequate job of placing the Negro in perspective *throughout* our history, and indeed, one could cite the absence of Crispus Attucks in "white" history books, and school textbooks. Suffice it to say that, historically, those who died provided a rallying cry for the American patriots. Yearly, the anniversary was

> duly observed ... in a public ceremony, which took on a ritualistic pattern. Bells would toll during the day, and at night lighted transparencies depicted the soldiers and their victims, giving a substance of sorts to the "discontented ghosts, with hollow groans" summoned to solemnize the occasion. The highlight of the evening was a stirring address by a leading citizen which, as the contemporary historian David Ramsay observed, "administered fuel to the fire of liberty, and kept it burning with an incessant flame." The propaganda value of the Boston Massacre cannot be minimized. . . .[9]

Is it not a bit ironic for another Negro historian proudly to quote George Washington: "Remember it is the 5th of March and avenge the death of your brethren,"[10] when that same Washington was most reluctant to allow Negroes, free or slave, to be recruited and treated as regular soldiers?

The necessary question remains: must we make a hero out of Crispus Attucks? At a critical point in American colonial history, a traumatic event occurred whose propaganda value, as Quarles indicates, played a useful role in rallying wavering colonial sentiments and stiffening the resistance to British rule.

One small nagging question might occur to the careful reader: what about those other Bostonians killed along with Attucks? John Adams, in supporting the defense witness who stated that it was to Attucks' "mad behavior, in all probability, the dreadful carnage of that night is chiefly to be ascribed," added " . . . a Carr from Ireland and an Attucks from Framingham, happening to be there, at the head of such a rabble of negroes, etc. etc. etc., as they can collect together, and then there are not wanting persons to ascribe all their doings to the good people of the town."[11] No one, however, in writing the history of the Irish in America makes much claim for Patrick Carr for having lost his life in the same fracas. The backgrounds and forebears of the others who died have faded into the fogs of history. Why such efforts to resurrect Crispus Attucks?

Perhaps the important point is that when Negroes have appeared in these small but critical points in American history they have somehow become "white-washed." The impression conveyed to the innocent and the ignorant is that Negroes appear in American history as slaves, over whom the states quarreled and therefore had a bloody and unnecessary war, and who then, after living in animal conditions for decades, once more (circa 1954) have become visible and voluble on the American scene.

A reasonable request might be, then, to "color them black" when, indeed, black faces appear as they do throughout our history. But is it necessary to go further and create heroes out of non-heroes, black, white, or in-between? The life of Crispus Attucks by Millender is only one in a series of over 100 titles published by the same firm. One can justly ask what kind of historical authenticity guides the production of these volumes, and what kind of publishing responsibility is demonstrated?

At a time when authentic history is more essential than ever, we must refrain from creating non-history. We, who tittered over the revisions of Russian history to discredit Stalin and then Khrushchev, have perhaps a little house-cleaning to do at home. Indeed, the usually-impeccable *Encyclopedia Americana*, might do well to review its reference to Crispus Attucks as "American patriot and leader of the demonstration that lead to the Boston Massacre...."[12] An impressive list of textbook studies over the years shows that educators have been well aware of the errors of omission and commission existing in books of all kinds, and particularly in history books.[13]

Future historians can, however, at least settle the problem of Crispus Attucks by turning to the definitive discussion of the incident in a recent essay by Fleming. As Fleming persuasively argues, the true import of the event was not who did or did not provoke the bloodshed, but that a bloody confrontation had indeed taken place, and furthermore, that men who were to play leading roles in the ensuing evolution of the American Revolution took opposing sides in the trial of the British soldiers: Samuel Adams and the Liberty Men against his cousin John Adams and the rule of law and reason. John Adams, reviled by other Bostonians for taking on the defense of the British, won the case through his skill with courts and procedures, and thus gained time for the coming revolution to mature. He and Sam Adams became friends though they never agreed on tactics. In the end, Fleming observes:

That John [Adams] won the larger place in history should not be surprising to anyone who penetrates beyond the patriotic myth to the interior drama of this great but little-understood trial.[14]

Are these subtleties of history too difficult for little children? Must we, then, give them fantasy? I for one would opt for genuine make-believe, the great myths and fairy tales, the sagas and ballads, Paul Bunyan and Ulysses. Let youth, in all good time, ponder some of these obscure and dramatic by-ways of authentic history, from which lasting ethical and moral insights may, in all truth, also be gained.

NOTES

1. C. Eric Lincoln, *The Negro Pilgrimage in America*, New York: Bantam Books, 1967, p. 18.

2. John Hope Franklin, *From Slavery to Freedom*, 2nd ed., New York: Alfred A. Knopf, 1965, p. 127.

3. Benjamin Quarles, *The Negro in the American Revolution*, Durham: University of North Carolina Press, 1961, pp. 5–6.

4. *Ibid.*, p. 8.

5. William L. Katz, *Eyewitness: The Negro in American History*, New York: Pitman, 1967, p. 44.

6. *Ibid.*, p. 56.

7. Charles and Mary Beard, *The Rise of American Civilization*, rev. ed., New York: Macmillan, 1934, p. 221.

8. William Miller, *A New History of the United States*, New York: George Braziller, 1958, p. 102.

9. Quarles, *Negro in the American Revolution*, p. 7.

10. Charles H. Wesley, "Editorial," *Negro History Bulletin*, **30**, 3 (March 1967), p. 4.

11. Thomas J. Fleming, "The Boston Massacre," *American Heritage*, **18**, 1 (December 1966), pp. 6–11ff.

12. *Encyclopedia Americana*, vol. 2, New York: The Americana Corporation, 1967, p. 662.

13. Barbara Finkelstein, Loretta Golden, and Jean D. Grambs, "Textbooks in Social Context: A Bibliography of Studies of Textbook Contents," College of Education, University of Maryland, 1968. [Mimeographed.]

14. Fleming, "The Boston Massacre," p. 111.

VARIETIES OF HISTORY:
NEGRO, BLACK, WHITE

James A. Banks

In a provocative review of Katz, *Eyewitness: the Negro in American History* (*Harvard Educational Review*, Summer 1968), Larry Cuban makes a distinction between "Black History" and "Negro History." In Black history, "Heroes are all black and struggle for freedom. Villains are all white and oppress for profit. . . . Ignored facts are dusted off and celebrated, while previously scorned items are converted into virtues and extolled" (p. 612). Booker T. Washington is portrayed as an Uncle Tom; Abraham Lincoln as a white supremacist. Black History ". . . bursts with righteousness, pride and outrage" (p. 612). While Black History distorts, Negro History ". . . corrects distortions and fills in the enormous gaps of information about people of color . . . Restraint and *balance* mark this approach . . ." (p. 612). Ethnic content, Cuban argues, should offer a *balanced* view that ". . . correct errors of *fact* . . . and accurately describe the Negro's role in the American past . . ." (p. 616). (All italics in this letter are mine.)

In the same issue Jean D. Grambs reviews a recent biography of Crispus Attucks and raises issues similar to those discussed by Cuban. Like a growing number of white "liberal" educators, these authors are alarmed by what they perceive as attempts by black militants to "distort" history by glorifying the black man's past in order to imbue pride in black students. Grambs accuses Millender, the black author of Attucks' biography, of telling "historical lies to repair the damage" done by previous distortions of black history (p. 606). Grambs maintains that "appropriate data" should be reported "accurately" and that textbooks should reflect "*balanced* versions" of black history. She writes, ". . . it is one thing to present *authentic*, historic material, but it is quite another matter to twist or invent material" (p. 605). The author posits her own canons of historical objectivity and uses her standards to ascertain the "accuracy" of the treatments of Attucks given by two black historians. She argues that Benjamin Quarles *accurately* portrays Attucks because he depicts him as a shadowy historical figure. "Quarles," writes Grambs, "unlike some of his colleagues, does not let being Negro distort his historical appraisal" (p. 607). The author vehemently attacks

---

James A. Banks, "Varieties of History: Negro, Black, White," from "To the Editors: Varieties of History: Negro, Black, White," [letter], *Harvard Educational Review*, **39** (Winter 1969), 155–158. Copyright © 1969 by President and Fellows of Harvard College. Reprinted with permission of the publisher.

John Hope Franklin, an eminent historian, for falling into the "chauvinistic trap" and portraying Attucks as a significant historical personality.

Cuban and Grambs err when they assume that there is such a phenomenon as unbiased, objective, and balanced written history. Both believe that the historian, by carefully gathering data, can derive historical statements which are balanced, factual and without distortions. This assumption emanates from a confusion of *historical facts* with *past events*. These two authors imply that historical facts are hard and stable, waiting to be uncovered by the studious, objective historian. Grambs argues that Quarles portrays Attucks as he really was, while Franklin distorts the *real* Attucks. The Boston Massacre is a *past event*. It has taken place and will never occur again; neither Quarles nor Franklin will ever be able to observe Attucks' participation in that historic battle; neither can go back in time. Even if they could they would probably perceive Attucks' role in that battle differently. Thus, the historian can never deal with actual past events, but must deal with *statements about events* written by biased individuals with divergent points of view. Moreover, the historian necessarily and inevitably reflects his own biases in his attempts to reconstruct the past. Using various sources to find out about past events, the historian *must* select from the statements which he uncovers those which he wishes to report and to regard as factual. The historian can never discover all of the "facts" about a past event; his selection and interpretation are greatly influenced by his personal bias, cultural environment and his reasons for writing. His statements are actually symbols for past events, and it is difficult to argue that symbols are true or false. As Becker notes, "The safest thing to say about a symbol is that it is more or less appropriate."[1]

We cannot, like Cuban and Grambs, contend that any versions of history are "balanced" and without distortions, because historical facts are products of the human mind and are not identical with past events. The most we can say about any version of history is that its statements are regarded as factual by a greater number of historians than other statements which comprise other varieties of history. The versions of history accepted as most factual by historians vary greatly with the times, the culture, and the discovery of artifacts and documents. The present heavily influences how historians view the past. Becker, the noted historian, writes: "The past is a kind of screen upon which we project our vision of the future; and it is . . . a moving picture, borrowing much of its form and color from our fears and aspirations."[2] Commager, like Becker, argues that we look at the past through our own eyes, ". . . judging it by our own standards, recreating it in our own words or reading back into the language of the past our own meanings. . ."[3]

Implicit in Cuban's argument is the belief that statements which constitute Negro History are more widely regarded as factual by white, liberal historians than the statements which constitute Black History. He assumes that because these statements are more widely accepted by "established" white historians they more accurately describe past events than statements which constitute Black History. Similarly Grambs believes that Attucks is a shadowy historical figure because he is described as such by most established, white historians. We cannot accept consensus within the community of white, established historians as adequate evidence for historical accuracy. This is true not only because there is rarely agreement among historians on controversial issues, but because historians in different countries and in different times regard highly conflicting statements as factual.

Grambs reveals her cultural and personal biases when she accepts Quarles' interpretation of Attucks and rejects Franklin's. Which historian's portrayal of Attucks is more congruent with the actual past is a moot question. Provided that she diligently searched all available data, carefully considered all points of view, and reached her conclusion through critical reflection, Grambs is justified in regarding Attucks as an insignificant figure; but she is not justified in contending that her conclusion is the "right" conclusion and that Quarles' view of Attucks is more accurate than Franklin's. She can only argue that she *believes* that Quarles' portrayal is more accurate. We must grant Cuban the right to prefer Negro History to Black History, but he cannot claim that the statements which make up Negro History more accurately reflect past events than statements which comprise Black History. Both histories are products of the human mind; both reflect the historians' personal biases, cultural backgrounds and purposes for writing.

The writers of Negro History attempt to construct history which reflects the opinions of established historians (most of whom are white); writers of Black History write history primarily to imbue pride in black students; writers of white schoolbook history write to glorify the United States and to develop patriotism in white children. Because of the tenuous nature of history, we are more justified in questioning the *aims* of these different varieties of history than we are in challenging the accuracy of the statements which they promulgate. Since black people are vehemently complaining about the treatment of the Negro in schoolbooks, which were written by white established historians and educators, we cannot assume that the professional white historian has fewer biases than the black militant historian.

Cuban and Grambs, and other educators who are alarmed over recent attempts to create a black version of history, grossly misinterpret the proper role of history in the public school. These educators assume that there is *an* "accurate" version of history, and that it is the role of the teacher to help youngsters become effective consumers of this authentic and balanced history. Actually, the role of the school, as Bolster says, is to help students ". . . create their own accounts of the past and to pit their conclusions against those of other writers of history."[4] As I have argued elsewhere, by approaching the study of history in this way, students will realize that there are alternative ways of looking at identical events and situations; consequently, their reasoning and critical powers will be strengthened.[5]

In writing their own accounts of history, students should determine for themselves which versions of history are more accurate and balanced. *To do this, they must be exposed to all types and varieties of history, including Negro History, Black History and White Schoolbook History.* Students should also be exposed to different versions of history because thinking occurs when students are forced to consider conflicting interpretations and points of view. To ban any version of history from the public school is to deny the student academic freedom. Students should not have to go to the storefront school to encounter versions of history which conflict with *the* version endorsed by established institutions.

By reading historical documents, examining historical artifacts, reading accounts of history written by others, and writing their own versions of history, students will discover that written history is at best accounts of events from particular points of view. The conclusions which students derive about the accuracy of historical statements, and the versions of history which they construct will be greatly influenced by their own personal biases and cultural environment. We cannot confiscate the student's right to reach his own conclusions regarding the accuracy of historical statements and to construct his own accounts of history. Rather, we should encourage students to carefully consider all points of view and to responsibly defend their own judgments. If a student concludes that Crispus Attucks is a significant historical figure, we cannot accuse him of falling into a "chauvinistic trap." If we disagree with his conclusions the most we can do is to encourage him to begin inquiry anew, for the ultimate goal of social education is to help students develop a commitment to inquiry and not to make them unthinking consumers of any version of history.

NOTES

1. Phil L. Synder (editor), *Detachment and the writing of History: Essays and Letters of Carl L. Becker*, Ithaca, N.Y.: Cornell University Press, 1958, p. 47.

2. *Ibid*, p. 59.

3. Henry S. Commager, *The Nature and The study of History*, Columbus: Charles E. Merrill, 1965, p. 46.

4. Arthur S. Bolster, Jr., Review of *History and the Social Sciences: New Approaches to the Teaching of Social Studies* by Mark M. Krug, *Harvard Educational Review*, **38** (Summer 1968), p. 599.

5. See James A. Banks and Ermon O. Hogan, "Inquiry: A History Teaching Tool," *Illinois Schools Journal*, **48** (Fall 1968).

AN END
TO INNOCENCE

Julie Paynter

It should be obvious today that few American youth, black or white, will settle for illusions over reality where the past is concerned. By continuing to put forth a mythology in our history books which has little basis in fact, we shall be teaching contempt for history and for the white world which is its purveyor, as well as contributing to the already considerable degree of cynicism among many American young people today.

"It is a complex fate to be an American," Henry James is said to have observed. If that is a perception which has not been widely shared by fellow citizens, it is undoubtedly because Americans have been told again and again how marvelously simple and self-evident is their destiny.

In some respects, of course, Americans *have* been heirs to an unusually innocent past. The United States had a visible beginning and since that time a relatively short history. The ideals of the Founding Fathers—incorporated in the phrase, "the American Creed,"—were uncomplicated enough to become a part of the value system of virtually every American. Until very recently, the fact of physical isolation kept the majority of our citizens out of touch both with others of the world's people and with the tensions which would inevitably have accompanied a great proximity. Perhaps most important is the fact that, throughout her history, America has been the beneficiary of a set of favorable conditions probably unmatched in the history of the world: isolation, constant population growth, and abundant natural resources, not the least of which was a vast quantity of land. Certainly Americans have "rarely if ever known defeat and humiliation as a national experience."

The understanding which Americans have of themselves has tended to exaggerate these aspects of simplicity to the point of distortion. Biography has often seemed a substitute for history, and American citizens have been too easily seduced into assuming an identity based on the individual success story and the *American* experience—that "log cabin to the White House" theme. Only in America are men *self-made*. Our endless celebration of the unusual individual reveals, as James Baldwin has pointed out, an awful disrespect for human life and human achievement. The past has typically been seen as an unbroken upward line of continuity and progress, attributed to "the genius of the American people," while conditions favoring that success have been allowed to fade into the background. Furthermore,

Julie Paynter, "An End to Innocence," *Journal*, **7** (January 1969), 3–7. Reprinted with permission of the publisher.

Americans have been too easily satisfied with the *forms* of change, seldom pushing behind the facade to see if the day-to-day experience of the nation's people has been affected *in fact*. Not the least of all the problems is the fact that the generalizations about our national character have been formed in white America and have been possible only, in effect, by reading black people out of the past. Such a national self-image is the history not of a people but of a dream—a dream which has yet to be realized for the majority of Americans.

Exchanging this national naïveté for a more honest and just conception of ourselves is not going to be easy. Myths are not mere fairy tales arbitrarily arrived at; they are socially functional. In the American experience, they have served as a source of national identity. Ever since Crèvecoeur first asked the question, "What then is the American, this new man?", Americans have debated the issue, defining and redefining who they are. A phenomenon peculiar to the United States, this ceaseless quest of identity is in part a consequence of life in a relatively open society. Erik Erikson makes the historical point that America's short past has been filled with extreme contrasts and abrupt changes which have had the cumulative effect of endangering individual autonomy and making a firm sense of identity a hard commodity to hold onto. In surveying the contemporary scene, James Baldwin has correctly observed that the problem is bigger than race alone: "It is not really a 'Negro revolution' that is upsetting this country. What is upsetting the country is a sense of its own identity."

The second function served by the American mythology has to do with the status insecurity suffered by many Americans. While it is rooted in the society's mobility and constant flux, it also involves the focus on potentiality and the future rather than on present reality. The point relentlessly driven home to numberless Americans that they haven't quite "made it," seems to inspire endless striving which cannot for a moment be given up. As it is difficult not to interpret the national preoccupation with American identity as a compensation for individual identity confusion, so too the constant building up of the national ego indulged in by Americans appears to be one way of achieving at least vicarious status or prestige. Many outstanding citizens throughout our history have suggested that the United States should serve as an example to the rest of mankind. Relinquishing this sense of mission, as well as the paternalism and proprietary interest which has characterized our view of other peoples, will necessarily involve something of a national loss of face. On the individual level, too, many whites— however inarticulately—will see themselves as having nothing to gain and a great deal to lose by adopting a more comprehensive view of the past. This is particularly true today, when whites have been stunned by the overnight disappearance of the hat-in-hand Negro and antagonized by the sudden emergence of the militant black. Regardless of the goals pursued by Afro-Americans, where the status of whites is concerned the tactics of coercion are not at all the same as those of cajolery and gratitude. Even leaving black militance out of the equation, as Adam Walinsky strongly stated four years ago, middle-class Americans perceive real threats to their status in the attention lavished on youth by the mass media and in the inauguration of programs which no longer have as their aim "keeping the poor in their place."

Finally, the problem of distortion in our national self-image affects far more than today's middle class: it is rooted in a great deal of American historiography, making it that much more difficult to eliminate. Daniel J. Boorstin, a leading commentator on the American past, has noted a quality of provincialism in the collective memory of American historians which has led them to overemphasize the importance of individual events at the expense of institutional realities in American society. Many chroniclers of the American past have become caught up in the panorama of the national political process; others have been champions of the "melting pot" romance. Yet surveys of the national character have been written in recent years by eminent historians in which the words "Negro" and "race" can scarcely be found in the index. What is missing from these colorless, conflictless, essentially static versions of the American past are the hard facts of life on *class, power* and *race*.

The point has been made that we cannot, as individuals or collectively as a nation, approach social maturity as long as we continue to prop ourselves up with false images which prevent us from seeing the past as it was. Rather, we must develop the ability to see culturally different individuals for who they are (or were), ourselves for who we are, and human beings as they are. On the individual level, this will involve new self-concepts for all Americans. The unearned sense of inferiority which has been a large part of the national legacy to black people must be traded for a new sense of pride in themselves and their past. In this there is potentially a very large gain. Oscar Lewis, pointing out that the "culture of poverty" would be far more difficult to eradicate than mere material poverty, said: "Any movement . . . which organizes and gives hope to the poor and effectively promotes solidarity and identification with larger groups, destroys the psychological and social core of the culture of poverty." Whites, too, must divest themselves of the falsely inflated notions of self and of the unspoken but apparently impregnable sense of superiority which has been their unearned historical increment. Significantly, the second of the two changes is the one more often omitted by spokesmen for a new national history, though it may well necessitate a more difficult and painful transition. *The two changes are equally important*: both races must learn, in Thomas Pettigrew's phraseology, a new "equal citizen's role." Nothing less than our character as a nation—and perhaps even national survival—is at stake.

These remarks presume what is almost universally accepted as the primary goal of the social studies: education for citizenship. If this assumption holds up, it becomes necessary to look at the world in which American citizens will be called upon to function. At home, at the present time, we are a conflict- and hate-ridden people, torn apart over the issue of race. Overseas, we shall increasingly be called upon to relate to "the other two-thirds of the world"—for the most part, non-Christian, non-Western, non-affluent, and non-white—a world bearing little resemblance to the American experience. These two tasks are not unrelated, for the United States has in the Afro-American background a major link to the experience of the majority of the world's people.

Awareness of the aim of citizen education points to a fundamental dilemma in goals pursued: namely, telling the truth about history *vs.* promoting the welfare of the polity. This tension between *accuracy* and the *social good* inheres in all historical study, but is particularly acute in teaching about the Afro-American experience: first, because of the nature of the audience, which includes young people whose values, habits, etc., are presumably being formed; and second, because the subject is at once the one aspect of American history that is least reconcilable with the American Creed and the single most pressing domestic issue of our times. It is not certain that a student entering such a study would come away from it with his commitment to the American polity intact. For example, in studying various atrocities, some students would have trouble avoiding the conclusion that inhumanness was a necessary consequence of whiteness. But these students should be helped to see that simply to condemn the past has no more merit than mindless celebration of it.

American students especially find it hard to realize that every human being is born into an institutional framework which limits his actions somewhat (which is neither to excuse an individual from historical responsibility nor to endow him with unlimited freedom). Students must be challenged to grapple with such hard historical questions as what changes were possible; when and for whom; what underlying conditions would have been necessary in order for change to have occurred; and what would have been the consequences of certain lines of action in other spheres of American life. Obviously none of these approaches constitute a panacea since even the location of problems in their full historical context does not guarantee that understanding will be achieved.

Occasionally—when trying to make a case for the black American experience as a *cultural whole*—non-integration is justifiable. As Frederick Gearing states, "to study (another culture) is, through comparison, to see ourselves." Does the Afro-American experience constitute another culture? Those close to the black experience who have emphasized the radical disjunction between white (middle-class, especially) and Negro (especially lower-class) life-styles argue convincingly that it does. Thus, insofar as the Negro American experience *is* a culture whole, it ought to be transmitted as such, as well as integrated into the national story where appropriate.

The task of dealing with the black experience as a subculture requires the imposition of an essentially social-science conceptual scheme on American history. However, rather than attempting to see the social system at any point in time as a whole, and setting out to analyze only one carefully delineated element of that structure, historians of the American experience have tended, on the one hand, to lift out the sagas of individual Americans and put these forward as the American experience in microcosm, and on the other hand, to attempt comprehensive surveys of relatively vast periods of time. Both approaches typically operate to perpetuate the national mythology. The latter alternative would not be so damaging if it were not for the tendency of some writers of history to delude themselves—and worse, their readers—into concluding that "their" period has then been "covered," rather than qualifying the significance of their work by identifying it as dealing with a single small aspect of that period as seen through only one angle of vision. The historical discipline is perhaps the most unconsciously and unmethodically selective of all of the social sciences, thus leaving itself peculiarly vulnerable to cultural bias; the survey approach in particular, by getting more and bigger conclusions from less research, is deceptively efficient.

This somewhat haphazard selection process is pregnant with consequences for any minority group. In the area of Afro-American history, the tendency has been—when blacks are included at all—to select out those Negroes whose lives best reflected what was purportedly "American": those included generally have resembled the middle-class white American "on-the-make." Putting forth this overly assimilated version of our history as the American story is particularly unfortunate in a country whose richness and variety of population are almost unparalleled in history.

Where the black American experience as a whole is concerned, what is called for is the transmission of that culture *with its differences intact*— not the presentation of a group Americanized beyond recognition, featuring Negroes as no more than "white men colored brown." Ironically, if this is done, cries of opposition will be heard from some liberal quarters, where any attempt at differentiation is seen as discrimination. Equality is not sameness, however. If a reasonably accurate conception of American history is to be developed, this course (among others where appropriate) must be followed.

More frequently, the grouping of Negro Americans together in *blocs* is not done in order to consider the Afro-American experience as a unified whole, but as an artificial construct. When this is the case, black Americans tend to be treated essentially as Negro rather than as American figures.

For example, William Katz has pointed out that Frederick Douglass is usually studied as an escaped slave and black Abolitionist rather than on the same stage with other Americans as a major leader in nineteenth-century reform movements. To isolate minority Americans in special categories of their own without justification is not only to distort the truth but to imply that their history is not worthy of consideration as a part of the national experience. Unfortunately, this has been the approach taken recently by some publishers adept at producing texts segregated in their "integration." One common practice is to concentrate all of the book's Afro-American history in a short supplemental section sandwiched between chapters or at the end of the book. These "new," 1960's-variety, separate-and-unequal versions of the nation's racial past have dubious educational value.

In trying to deal with the racial complexity of the nation's past, one quickly becomes aware of the fact that there are a number of different ways—more accurately, degrees—of integrating American history. None of these modes of integration is adequate by itself; some, however, are more pernicious than others when used in isolation.

The easiest—and the least effective—way to arrive at an interracial history is, as Spelman College's Vincent Harding has derisively paraphrased it, simply by dropping an occasional individual "chocolate drop" into the national melting pot. Thus in some books we read that Jan E. Matzeliger invented the shoe lasting machine, Matthew Henson accompanied Admiral Perry to the North Pole, and Garrett Morgan, a Cleveland Negro, invented the traffic light. This approach is insufficient. First, the black individuals chosen for inclusion are often those who are least offensive to the white American's image of himself and who, in their times, least threatened to upset the racial status quo. Even in cases where blacks and whites are chosen on the basis of comparable historical criteria, the picture is still not a complete one. This is because—much of American historiography and most of her conventional wisdom notwithstanding—there is no very good reason for assuming the typicalness of the American Illustrious Individual, whatever his color. Thus a great many American history books provide us with a picture of a certain kind of upwardly mobile elite, but little in the way of a chronicle of the experience undergone by the majority of Americans or of a description of the structural factors shaping American life. Since this individualist approach (whether singly or in blocs) is the one most often followed today in "correcting" American racial history, we are in danger of manufacturing a whole new set of darker-hued Horatio Alger heroes—and leaving the rest of American history unaltered.

There is another way to perpetuate the injustice done to black American citizens in the history books even while including them. Benjamin Quarles identified it when he criticized American historians for making the Afro-American into an "unperson" by portraying him solely as part of a monolithic *mass*, which in turn was seen as the cause or the effect of something. For instance, under the institution of slavery blacks have typically been seen exclusively as a labor force; later, during the Civil War, they were often analyzed as a mass in terms of their potential as resource or liability to the war effort. Many accounts give no hint that Afro-Americans were anything other than docile and obedient slaves before the Civil War, or that not all Negroes were then slaves, or that individual blacks distinguished themselves in any way. Ironically, sometimes this treatment of Negroes only as part of a mass comes at the hands of liberal historians who, in their eagerness to establish the persistent fact of white racism in America and to absolve blacks from any of the onus of the past, reconstruct social reality in such a way that Negroes are left with only one role to play: objects of oppression. Quarles is right in contending that to write American history treating Negroes solely as part of an undifferentiated mass is to denigrate that race—regardless of the intention.

In spite of the impression conveyed to us by textbooks, the history of a nation is neither merely the sum total of the stories of the individuals within it, nor the mute tale of masses of men. Drawing on the vast gains made in the social sciences in this century enables the historian to organize the experience of a society over time in another way. Contemporary social-science concepts applied to history make it possible to analyze American society at any point in time as a *social system*: to identify the Afro-American's role within that structure, and to study the evolution of social change in an incredibly dynamic society. Thus, not only are individuals actors, but *organized groups* and social movements also can influence and be influenced by history. Key social institutions such as the family and the church have a great part to play in black American history reconstructed; groups such as the N.A.A.C.P. and A. Philip Randolph's Brotherhood of Sleeping Car Porters become important especially in the study of social change. Greater attention should be devoted to Marcus Garvey's "Back to Africa" movement of the 1920's and the civil rights and black power movements of our times.

The experience of blacks as a minority group can be compared to that of other minorities (racial, ethnic, and religious) in the American past; "the minority group experience": (if one can be identified) should also be examined *vis à vis* that of the majority. In any case, America should be viewed as a coherent but constantly changing social structure, the component parts of which can be broken down and analyzed separately as well as in relation to one another and the whole.

Once a social structural approach is taken to the study of American history, *white racism* will be seen for what it is: an *institutional phenomenon* with deep roots in all facets of our society. We will no longer be able to explain away the injustices inflicted on blacks by white Americans through verbal euphemisms which obscure more than they explain. We cannot read that injustice out of the national past by seeing it as a fundamentally un-American happening entirely alien to the "real" American history. Nor can we take the overly sanguine view that white racism did exist, but only as a momentary lapse which was cleared away by the Civil War and its aftermath. It should be obvious to every American in the 1960's that if there ever was a time when we could indulge ourselves in such illusions, that time is not now. Almost twenty-five years ago, Gunnar Myrdal identified the "problem of the Negro" as "predominantly a white man's problem"— and one which cannot be treated in isolation. Any careful student of the Afro-American past will be hard put not to conclude that white racism *and* black degradation have been constant and pervasive factors interwoven throughout American history. Until that painful past is affirmed we shall remain ill-equipped to confront the problems of the insistent present.

FREEDOM SCHOOL EFFECTIVENESS: CHANGES IN ATTITUDES OF NEGRO CHILDREN

David W. Johnson

> ... [my father] had a terrible life; he was defeated long before he died because, at the bottom of his heart, he really believed what white people said about him.
>
> JAMES BALDWIN, *The Fire Next Time*

David W. Johnson, "Freedom School Effectiveness: Changes in Attitudes of Negro Children," *The Journal of Applied Behavioral Science*, **2** (1966), 325–330. Reprinted with permission of the author and publisher. The investigator wishes to express his appreciation to Isaiah Robinson, chairman of the Harlem Parents Committee, and to Robert Washington, director of the Freedom School, for their cooperation in conducting this study. The investigator also wishes to express his appreciation to the children in the Freedom School, to the Freedom School staff, and to the members of the Harlem Parents Committee for making this study possible.

The investigator is deeply indebted to Dr. Robert Dentler, director of the Institute for Urban Studies, Teachers College, Columbia University, for his unfailing encouragement and indispensable help and for his financial support of the study.

Grateful acknowledgment is also extended to Dr. Morton Deutsch and Dr. Matthew Miles for their valuable assistance in carrying out this study.

PROBLEM

There is a large volume of research which states that Negroes have the same prejudices and attitudes toward Negroes that the white majority have. Much of the literature on Negro children states that they have negative self- and racial attitudes. More specific research has shown that the Negro's negative self-attitudes affect his (1) attitudes toward society, (2) maturation processes, (3) motivations and aspirations, and (4) academic and vocational performances.

It can be concluded that in order "to bring the Negro into the mainstream of American society" it is necessary to change such attitudes. One of the few direct attempts at changing the self-attitudes of Negro children is the programs which teach Negro history. These programs are based on the hypothesis that through a positive presentation of Negro history and culture the distorted and disparaging views which many Negroes have of themselves will be ameliorated. *If proved effective, Negro history courses could easily be instituted in public schools as a means for rapid and widespread change in the self- and racial attitudes of Negro children.*

One of the first permanent, long-term programs teaching Negro history was initiated during the academic year of 1963–64 by a civil rights organization primarily concerned with the education of Negro children living in the ghettos of New York City. This was a "Freedom School," organized and administered by the Harlem Parents Committee. The Freedom School was founded for two basic purposes (taken from an HPC publication):

1. To teach our children to reclaim and proudly identify with their history and culture;
2. To teach all people that the heritage and culture of the American Negro is not a barren one.

The Freedom School met every Saturday morning for two hours during the school year of 1963–64. In organization it consisted of three groups: (1) an adult workshop, (2) teenagers, and (3) children from eight to 12. The curriculum covered both African history and the history of the American Negro. Staff members were members of the Harlem Parents Committee and public school teachers who volunteered their time without pay.

METHODOLOGY

The design used in the study was a panel design, where two interviews, four months apart, were given to a random sample of half the children participating in the Freedom School. Only children between the ages of eight and 13 were used in the study.

To control for the effect of the first interview on the second, a control group of 12 children who received the second interview but did not receive the first interview was used. To control for the effect of the racial membership of the interviewer on the subjects, Negro interviewers were used. Finally, the set of statistical norms given for Cattell's Child Personality Questionnaire was used as a control. This compared the children in the Freedom School with the "average" American child.

The ten children studied were primarily middle-class children from intact homes with parents who were involved in the civil rights movement. Four were boys, six were girls. Most of the children had civil rights experience. The majority of the children's parents were members of the Harlem Parents Committee.

Two instruments were used in the study. They were: (1) selected factors of Cattell's Child Personality Questionnaire and (2) an attitude questionnaire.

RESULTS

From Table 1 it is seen that on Factor G (Super-Ego Strength) the panel decreased significantly ($p < .05$). However, the boys did not change signif-

Table 1.   Child Personality Questionnaire

	Change Between Two Interviews Given Four Months Apart to Ten Freedom School Children				
Factor	$\overline{X}_1$	$s.d._1$	$\overline{X}_2$	$s.d._2$	Probability of No Differences*
C (Ego-Strength)	2.90	0.88	3.10	1.08	
Male	3.00	0.82	3.25	1.26	
Female	2.83	0.98	3.00	1.41	
G (Super-Ego)	3.40	1.08	3.00	0.82	.05
Male	3.25	1.71	2.75	0.96	
Female	3.50	0.55	3.17	0.75	.10
O (Insecure)	1.70	0.95	1.20	1.03	
Male	2.25	0.50	0.25	0.50	.01
Female	1.33	1.03	1.83	0.75	.05
Q_3 (Self-Sentiment)	3.80	0.79	3.80	1.13	
Male	3.50	1.00	3.25	0.96	
Female	4.00	0.63	4.17	1.17	
Q_4 (Tension)	1.50	1.08	1.10	0.99	
Male	2.25	0.50	1.75	1.26	
Female	1.00	1.10	0.67	0.52	

*   t-test of Mean of a Population of Differences Between Two Measures for Each Individual.
Males: $n = 4$
Females: $n = 6$

icantly, while the change for the girls was of only marginal significance (p < .10). On Factor O (Insecurity) the boys became much more confident in themselves (p < .01), and the girls also became more confident (p < .05). No other differences on the CPQ were found to be significant.

From Table 2 it is seen that the panel changed significantly (Scale 1) toward the attitude that Negroes and whites are equal (p < .025). This was true for the boys (p < .05) and marginally true for the girls (p < .10). The boys also increased significantly in their attitudes toward Negroes (p < .05) and civil rights (p < .05). It should also be noticed that the boys felt more solidarity with Negroes at the termination of the Freedom School than did the girls, at a marginal level of significance (p < .10).

The Freedom School, therefore, seemed to have some effect on the boys in the areas of self-attitudes, equality of Negroes and whites, attitudes toward Negroes, and attitudes toward civil rights. That is, they became more confident in themselves, more convinced that Negroes and whites are equal, more positive toward Negroes, and more militant toward civil rights.

In the Negro community it has often been noted that compared with girls,

Table 2. Attitude Questionnaire

Scale	$\overline{X}_1$	$s.d._1$	$\overline{X}_2$	$s.d._2$	Probability of No Differences*
Change Between Two Interviews Given Four Months Apart to Ten Freedom School Children					
1. Equality	11.80	1.99	12.80	2.04	.025
Male	11.50	2.65	12.25	2.22	.05
Female	12.00	1.67	13.17	2.04	.10
2. Negroes	20.10	1.98	20.40	1.84	
Male	19.25	2.50	20.35	1.71	.05
Female	20.67	1.51	20.50	2.07	
3. Solidarity†	12.10	1.98	11.70	1.70	
Male	11.75	2.36	12.50	1.29	
Female	12.33	1.86	11.17	1.84	
4. Whites	18.40	2.37	18.20	3.19	
Male	17.50	0.58	17.75	2.06	
Female	19.00	2.97	18.50	3.94	
5. Civil Rights	24.50	1.84	25.40	1.43	
Male	24.50	1.30	26.00	0.82	.05
Female	24.50	2.26	25.00	1.67	

* t-test of Mean of a Population of Differences Between Two Measures for Each Individual.
† Difference between Male $\overline{X}_1$ and Female $\overline{X}_2$ is significant (p < .10).

boys show inferior academic, personal, and social adjustment. The reasons given for this are the matriarchal nature of the family, the greater accessibility of good jobs to females, and other similar reasons. It would thus seem that it is the Negro male who most needs programs such as the Freedom School and, at the same time, that programs such as the Freedom School are most effective with the Negro male.

The most striking effect of participation in the Freedom School is the increased conviction that all people are equal. This is illustrated by the following remarks made by the children studied: "When I was younger I thought whites were better than Negroes, but since I've been attending Freedom School I've learned that there is no superior race"; "The white man isn't any better than the Negro"; "I found out that whites are not better than Negroes, and that all men are the same." Such attitudes, if they continue, should help in effective academic and vocational competition with whites.

When the scores of the children studied were compared with the norms for the CPQ it was found that they did not show the negative self-attitudes ordinarily found in studies of Negro children. This warrants further study, as it is possible that subgroups in the Negro community do not hold negative self-attitudes. The control group data also show that the first interview did not affect the responses given on the second interview. Due to space limitations these data are not presented here, and the interested reader is referred to the larger research report.

It should be noted that there are a number of shortcomings connected with this study, primarily because of the difficulty of studying a program developed and run by a voluntary civic organization, the lack of wide representation in the sample, the small number of subjects, and the investigator's limited access to the program.

The findings of the study, however, can be taken as tentative evidence that programs such as the Freedom School, which teach Negro history and culture, can be effective in raising Negro boys' attitudes toward self and toward Negroes.

STUDY QUESTIONS

1. Is it possible for a knowledge of black history to help black children shape and perpetuate a new identity? Why or why not?

2. According to Hare, what are the proper aims of black history? Do you agree or disagree? Explain.

3. What are the two varieties of history discussed by Cuban? Do you feel that one can justifiably delineate different varieties of history? Is Cuban's distinction valid? Why or why not?

4. Do you believe that it is possible to write *balanced* and *accurate* history? Explain.

5. According to Grambs, how might new versions of black history become as distorted as older versions? Are the concerns voiced by Grambs warranted? Why or why not?

6. Grambs believes that history should be rewritten so that it includes the role and contributions of minority groups, but that it must be accurate and not "a major distortion" of history. Does the author clearly delineate how historical accuracy and the canons of historical objectivity are derived? Explain.

7. Banks attacks Cuban and Grambs for assuming that we can write un-biased, objective, and balanced versions of history. What arguments does he advance to support his views? Refute or defend his position.

8. What instructional implications can we derive from the arguments promulgated by Cuban and Grambs and by Banks? How would a black history course structured by Cuban and Grambs differ from one taught by Banks? Which course would you prefer for your students? Why?

9. In her cogent and perceptive article, Paynter bemoans the national myths that we have created and perpetuated in the public schools. How can we distinguish historical facts from mythology? Explain how the debate between Cuban and Grambs and Banks relates to this distinction.

10. In the final selection in this chapter, Johnson concludes that courses in black history and culture "can be effective in raising the attitudes of Negroes toward Negroes." What methodological flaws do you recognize in this research? What are its instructional implications?"

SUGGESTED READINGS

Banks, James A., *March Toward Freedom: A History of Black Americans*. Belmont, Calif.: Fearon Publishers, 1970

Banks, James A., *Teaching The Black Experience: Methods and Materials*. Belmont, Calif.: Fearon Publishers, 1970

Franklin, John Hope, *From Slavery to Freedom: A History of Negro Americans*. New York: Vintage Books, 1969

Grant, Joanne, *Black Protest: History, Documents and Analysis*. Greenwich, Conn.: Fawcett Publications, 1968

"How To Integrate Your School District's Curriculum," *School Management*, pp. 20–25, August 1968

Hughes, Langston, and Milton Meltzer, *A Pictorial History of the Negro in*

America. New York: Crown Publishers, 1968; [C. Eric Lincoln co-authored the latest edition.]

Hurt, Franklin, "Integrating American History," *Today's Education*, January 1969

International Library of Negro Life and History—Ten Volumes. New York: Publishers Company, 1967, 1968. [Sponsored by the Association for the Study of Negro Life and History.]

Jackson, Miles M., *A Bibliography of Negro History and Culture For Young People*. Pittsburgh: The University of Pittsburgh Press, 1969

The Journal of Negro History. [Published quarterly by the Association for the Study of Negro Life and History, 1538 Ninth Street, N.W., Washington, D.C.]

Katz, William Loren (General Editor), *The American Negro: His History and Literature*. New York: Arno Press, 1968. [45 volumes which have been favorably reviewed.]

Katz, William Loren, *Teacher's Guide To American Negro History*. Chicago: Quadrangle Books, 1968

Krug, Mark M., "On Teaching Negro History," *The School Review*, **77** 1–17, 1969

Miller, Elizabeth W., *The Negro in America: A Bibliography*. Cambridge: Harvard University Press, 1968

The Negro Heritage Library. Yonkers, N.Y.: Educational Heritage, 1966

Ploski, Harry, and Roscoe C. Brown, *The Negro Almanac: The Negro His Part In America*. New York: Bellweather Publishing Company, 1967

Salk, Erwin A., *A Layman's Guide to Negro History*. New York: McGraw-Hill, 1967

Welsch, Edwin K., *The Negro in the United States: A Research Guide*. Bloomington: Indiana University Press, 1966

Woodward, C. Vann, "The Hidden Sources of Negro History," *Saturday Review*, pp. 18–22, January 18, 1969

Young, Beatrice, and Benjamin Solomon, "Joy and Conscience in Teaching American History," *Changing Education*, pp. 3–7, Fall 1966

PART THREE
PROLOGUE
TO CHANGE

This volume has explored some of the critical and salient issues involved in creating a relevant and challenging social studies curriculum for children from diverse cultural groups. The need to make social studies meaningful for Afro-Americans, Mexican-Americans, American-Indians, Puerto Rican-Americans, and other oppressed minority groups has been emphasized. The contributors have also urged that the teacher critically examine his own perceptions and predispositions, and clarify his attitudes so that he can work successfully with children who come from subcultures different from his own. The teacher must *appreciate* and *accept* cultural differences, and promote an acceptance of all groups in the classroom setting.

Culturally different children must not be required to abandon the unique attributes of their indigenous cultures; rather they should be taught to value them. However, they *should be encouraged to explore alternative ways of living and being, and helped to evaluate the possible consequences of various courses of action in different social contexts*. We should also make culturally different children social critics so that they can accurately perceive their predicament in this society. They must become effective problem solvers in order to successfully identify problems and devise strategies to solve them. These skills will enable them to attain the *power* needed to change their lives and society.

These basic issues are restated in this part, and strategies for effective change are illuminated.

CHAPTER 10
PROPOSALS
FOR CHANGE

In a real sense, the theme of this book is the need to change the social studies curriculum so that it is more relevant, interesting, and challenging to poor children from diverse cultural groups. Part One of the book devotes considerable discussion to the delineation of the problems involved in properly educating poor children. However, even in this section the need for *change* is discussed. The articles in this chapter summarize the ideas presented in this volume, re-emphasize the urgent need for reform in the urban school, and make constructive proposals for change. The improvement of the social studies curriculum cannot be accomplished in a vacuum. Unless *basic* changes are made in the attitudes and expectations of teachers, the control of the public schools, and the general curriculum, efforts to improve the social studies will prove futile. These selections delineate the need for basic changes in the educational establishment; several also discuss the need for reform in the social studies and posit promising proposals for achieving it.

MINORITY GROUPS
IN AMERICAN SOCIETY:
IMPERATIVES FOR EDUCATORS

William W. Joyce

> *Little Indian, Sioux or Crow,*
> *Little frosty Eskimo,*
> *Little Turk or Japanee,*
> *Oh don't you wish that you were me.*

Admittedly the world has shrunk dramatically since Robert Louis Stevenson penned this stanza. But the spirit if not the intent of this blatantly chauvinistic attitude toward other cultures has endured, deriving its sustenance from an "accepted" view of the social studies that in theory advocated such values as the dignity and worth of the individual, the inviolability of the human personality, and the belief in justice and equality of opportunity, but in practice negated even the best-intentioned efforts of teachers to inculcate these values in their pupils. An examination of instructional materials and curricular documents used extensively in elementary schools throughout our nation strongly suggests that over the years teachers have given their children a distorted view of American minority groups, one that has extolled the virtues and accomplishments of the white, Anglo-Saxon, Protestant sector of society, while denigrating the role of the Negro, the American Indian, the Spanish-American, and the Oriental—four groups that in varying degrees have been barred from assimilation into American society.

Indeed, our nation's experiences in minority group relations demonstrate that the proverbial American melting pot has been a colossal fraud perpetrated by a dominant white Anglo-American majority for the purpose of convincing society at large that all cultural groups, irrespective of race or ethnic origin, were in fact eligible for full and unrestricted participation in the social, economic, political, and religious life of this nation. To be sure the American melting pot did achieve reality in some instances—initially for the white Western European immigrant and later for his Eastern European counterpart, but for the non-European, non-white immigrant, the melting pot had little meaning.

It is no mere accident that the process of amalgamation had little effect on other minorities—particularly American citizens of American Indian,

William W. Joyce, "Minority Groups in American Society: Imperatives for Educators," *Social Education*, **33** (April 1969), 429–433. Reprinted with permission of the National Council for the Social Studies.

Chinese, Japanese, African, and Spanish descent. These people differed significantly from the dominant American image—in racial, religious, and other ethnic characteristics. Various theories have been offered as explanations of why the dominant white majority has denied minority groups access to the mainstream of American society. Couched in anthropological, economic, sociological, and psychological terms, these theories range from simplistic rationalizations to highly sophisticated hypotheses. The essential elements of these theories as recounted by Arnold Rose, the eminent sociologist, are summarized below:

1.   *The race-difference theory* postulated that man has an instinctive aversion to people who are different from himself, and that these feelings of repulsion are confirmed and strengthened through incidental social contacts with the offending group.

2.   *The theory of economic competition* maintains that prejudice is absent when minority and dominant majority groups earn their livelihoods in separate sectors of the economy, but when thrown together in direct competition for limited jobs and resources, the majority group will oppress the minority.

3.   *The traumatic experiences* explanation states that racial prejudice is a consequence of painful or unpleasant emotional experiences suffered at the hands of the minority group.

4.   *The frustration-aggression theory* states that a person thwarted in his attempt to attain a given goal often experiences an internal tension that can be relieved by lashing out against the source of his frustration or toward an innocent third party. Typically this theory of prejudice is known as "scapegoating."

5.   *Trait-factor theories of personality* attempt to describe the interrelationships between authoritarian personality types, familial and other socialization experiences, and prejudiced attitudes.

6.   *The social control or caste structure theory* hypothesizes that the dominant and often ascendant sub-culture or caste within a society will strive to maintain its hegemony over other sub-cultures by rigorously imposing various physical, social, psychological punishments and rewards.[1]

In recent decades a growing body of sociological, psychological, and anthropological research has documented the devastating effects of white racism on minority-group children. The vast majority of these studies focus on the Negro and variously underscore his negative racial attitudes, his poor self-image, and his low educational and occupational aspirations and achievement. Granted, the dearth of authoritative research prevents us from ascertaining the extent to which these generalizations apply to American children of American Indian, Spanish, and Oriental ancestry, but there is sufficient evidence to indicate that these children have suffered at the hands of a society that has knowingly perpetrated social injustices against them.

RACIAL ATTITUDES HELD BY WHITE CHILDREN

But what about the white child? What are his attitudes toward American minorities? There are many serious gaps in the literature, but several studies reveal an emerging, if not fragmented, picture of racial attitudes held by white children. Moreland's study of social perception in Southern children reveals that racial self-recognition was significantly higher in white than in Negro children, and more significantly, white children accepted the socially communicated distinctions of racial inclusion and exclusion at an earlier age than Negro children.[2] Trager and Yarrow found that over two-thirds of their white subjects in the primary grades verbalized hostility toward Negroes.[3] That negative racial attitudes intensify as children grow older was revealed in a study reported by Radke, Trager, and Davis.[4]

How have these attitudes affected the mental health of children? Here too the evidence is scanty, but increasingly psychologists express growing concern over the long-range effects of racial and ethnic prejudice on white children. As early as 1955 the psychologist Kenneth B. Clark hypothesized:

> In observing normal forms and expressions of prejudice among average Americans, one observes certain types of reactions, which if demonstrated in relations with other members of an individual's own race, would be considered symptoms of emotional disturbance.[5]

Since that time other psychologists have confirmed Clark's suspicions.

Why have our children acquired negative attitudes toward minorities? If we accept the proposition that American schools reflect the society they serve, then our total educational enterprise must share the guilt for propagating a white, Protestant, Anglo-Saxon view of society that is totally inconsistent with the past and present realities of American life. In some educational circles it has become fashionable to label the publishing industry as the prime offender. If we acknowledge that universally the textbook has been and still is the most widely used teaching device, it becomes axiomatic that the text largely determines the social studies content that is taught in American schools.

THE "SLANTED TEXT"

In recent years a growing number of critics have documented the failure of social studies textbooks to present our children with an intellectually honest view of American society. Witness the following statement by Vincent R. Rogers and Raymond H. Muessig:

> Too many texts are filled with slanted "facts," stereotypes, provincial and ethnocentric attitudes, and superficial, utopian discussions which skim over conditions as they actually exist in life today. Texts which have sections devoted to "life in our United States," for example, too often portray "Americans" as white, Anglo-Saxon, Protestant, white collar, and middle class. Perusing a number of books, one gets the impression that all Americans live on wide, shady streets in clean suburban areas, occupy white Cape Cod style houses, drive new automobiles, have two children (a boy and a girl, of course), and own a dog. Characters in texts have first names like Bill, Tom, and John, rather than Sid, Tony, and Juan and last names like Adams, Hill, and Cook rather than Schmidt, Podosky, and Chen. . . . [6]

A recent study on the treatment of minorities in American history textbooks used in elementary and secondary schools in Michigan reinforces these allegations. Although the primary focus of the study was on the Negro, the conclusions and recommendations apply to other minority groups as well:

> Through errors of both omission and commission, through their avoidance of nearly everything of a controversial nature, through their reliance on outdated and even antediluvian historical research, and through their inadequate treatment of the current Civil Rights scene and the backgrounds to it, these books. . . . are historically inaccurate, misleading, and distorted. . . . These reviews do indeed constitute a severe indictment of the American history textbooks that are in widespread use in the state of Michigan, and undoubtedly in other states as well.[7]

The publishing industry maintains that because of their heavy investment in textbooks (often a publishing house will have invested $250,000 or more in a single social studies text before realizing one dollar of income), they need to insure that their products will sell on a nationwide market. And as Hillel Black points out, "This means he will censor his own books if he thinks the offending passages may hurt sales, [or] submit to censorship from outside sources if the potential market is big enough. . . ."[8]

The effects of such censorship are legion throughout the publishing industry. One executive, addressing a seminar sponsored by the American Educational Publishers Institute and the National Council for the Advancement of Educational Writing, remarked,

> . . . educational materials will be as good as the market-place wants

them to be ... those of us in the publishing business [know] that when we have tried to do innovative things we very often have taken a blood bath.[9]

One firm that found this to be an expensive lesson was the Follett Publishing Company of Chicago, one of the first houses to produce an integrated social studies series. When Follett released these books in 1959, there were few purchasers, presumably because school systems found them too advanced for the times. Robert Follett, the firm's president, ruefully recalls:

Even New York was not asking for the integrated text then. ... Nor was there an overwhelming demand in the suburban areas except for those communities heavily populated with liberal Jewish people. You know, I have the feeling we'll be selling our integrated books in Atlanta and Dade County before we sell them in some of our lily-white suburbs.[10]

This is but one of many instances over the years where publishers have taken the initiative in advocating social change—and paid dearly in the process. Viewed from this perspective, their reluctance to become innovative becomes a bit more understandable.

TRADEBOOKS PROJECT DISTORTED IMAGES

Social studies textbooks have not been the only proponents of white racism. Children's tradebooks have been equally guilty of projecting distorted images of minority groups. After surveying more than 5,000 tradebooks published during the period 1962–64, Nancy Larrick concluded that only 6.7 per cent included one or more Negroes. Indeed, among the four major publishers of children's books, the percentage of books including a Negro in text or illustration is one-third lower than this figure. But even these figures may be misleading, since more than half of the books dealing with Negroes placed them outside the continental United States or prior to World War II, an event that Larrick contends is "... as remote to a child as the Boston Tea Party."[11] Further, the author noted that only four-fifths of one per cent of the entire list of books surveyed dealt with the American Negro in today's world.

A study conducted by David K. Gast focused on the treatment of contemporary American minority groups in children's literature. Gast's findings not only underscore the biased, distorted portrayals of American Negroes but also reveal the tendency of tradebooks to ascribe distorted characterizations, concepts, and stereotypes to American Indians, Chinese, Japanese, and Spanish-Americans.[12] A few basic conclusions reported by Gast are summarized below:

American Indians, Chinese, Japanese, and Spanish-Americans are portrayed as having adopted such dominant middle-class American values as cleanliness, kindness, intelligence, ambition, and hard work. The stereotypes associated with these groups are complementary, but with one exception: "Negroes are musical."

Children's tradebooks depict American Indians, Chinese, and Spanish-Americans as possessing lower-class status. Negroes are shown to be of lower- and middle-class and Japanese are treated as middle-class.

Occupational stereotypes are associated with all minority groups except the Negro, who appears in many occupations, including white-collar and professional positions. The Indian craftsman, the Chinese cook, the Mexican shopkeeper, the Japanese gardener, and the Spanish shepherd persist in these books.

Tradebooks foster the impression that Japanese and Negro minorities have been assimilated into the dominant culture and have more social contact with Anglo-Americans than American Indians, Chinese, and Spanish-Americans. In contrast, they relegate Indians to reservations, Chinese to Chinatown, and Spanish-Americans to rural areas.

American Indians and Spanish-Americans are depicted as living simple, serene, and virile lives, close to nature. The male-superiority tradition permeates books dealing with these minorities, while males and females appear to enjoy equal status in books dealing with Negroes, Japanese, and Chinese.

Few instances are cited when American Indians, Chinese, and Spanish-Americans have lost or abandoned their ethnic cultures; rather, the reader is led to believe that these minorities are fiercely proud of their traditional life styles and have accepted few economic motivations from the dominant culture.

Primary-grade books in particular stereotype American Indians and Mexican-Americans as wearing their ethnic garb, presumably as evidence of their resistance to assimilation and their desire to be treated as friendly foreigners of the American Southwest.

Stereotypes associated with physical characteristics are changing. Today's tradebooks portray Negroes as brown-skinned people with straight hair and Caucasoid facial features—a marked departure from traditional portrayals which caricatured Negroes by exaggerating facial features, kinky hair, and coal black skin.

Social acceptance is a persuasive theme in books about the Negroes but receives incidental treatment in books about American Indians, Chinese, and Spanish-Americans. These books create the impression that the Japanese-American has encountered no prejudice and has gained total acceptance by the Anglo-American majority.

HOW REALISTIC SHOULD BOOKS BE?

Pervading these criticisms is the constant, recurring theme that the contents of social studies textbooks and tradebooks are not only inconsistent with social reality but that they consciously or unconsciously promote, reinforce, or perpetuate racial and ethnic prejudice. But how realistic should these books be? Should they expose children to the social injustices endured by American minorities? Should they explain why and how these injustices were perpetrated? Should they tell the story of American "like it is"? Bruce R. Joyce maintains that "A textbook *can* be constructed to teach children about human interaction, and a sophisticated social studies textbook *can* be used to teach them how to use the strategies of social science to analyze human relations." Nonetheless, he questions whether society is actually ready for realistic textbooks at the primary level.[13]

Admittedly the situation is beginning to improve, as evidenced by recent efforts of publishers to produce materials that present accurate portrayals of American minority groups. *William, Andy, and Ramon*; *Five Friends at School*; and *Living as Neighbors* are noteworthy efforts on the part of Holt, Rinehart, and Winston to publish primary-grade textbooks that tell about the lives of minority-group children. McGraw-Hill's *Skyline Series* utilizes printed materials, films, and filmstrips in depicting problematic situations confronting children in the inner-city. One of the stories in this series, "A Place of My Own," is a poignant account of how a little Puerto Rican girl copes with a perennial problem confronting many people of the inner-city—overcrowded living conditions and the resultant loss of privacy.

Increasingly publishers are developing non-verbal materials, some of which deal with minorities. The John Day Company's *Urban Education Series* is a brilliantly executed collection of photographs on American cities, while Fannie and George Shaftel's *Words and Action Series* is a role-playing kit employing photographs depicting everyday problems of Negro and white children. Both series should be especially useful with pupils encumbered by reading problems and by those encountering difficulty in analyzing social situations.

These are but a few of the new teaching resources on minority groups that have appeared on the market. On display at the annual meeting of the National Council for the Social Studies in Washington, D.C. last November were other promising materials, particularly an amazing array of tradebooks for children. Despite recent cutbacks in Federal aid to education, school systems will purchase many of these materials to partially alleviate the shortage of intellectually honest, accurate resources for teaching about American minorities.

THE ROLE OF THE TEACHER

But what about the teachers? Over the years we have subscribed to the time-honored principle that teaching materials are only as good as the teachers using them. This principle, coupled with the inescapable fact that educators, like most other Americans, are likely to harbor negative attitudes toward racial and ethnic minorities, suggests that before the classroom teacher can present his pupils with the accurate, realistic image of minority group relations that is so desperately needed, he will need to re-examine, clarify, and modify his own attitudes and predispositions toward minorities. In these times he can ill afford to do less.

NOTES

1. Arnold M. Rose, "The Causes of Prejudice," in Milton L. Barron, ed., *A Textbook of Readings in Intergroup Relations*, New York: Alfred A. Knopf, 1957, pp. 82–92.

2. J. Kenneth Moreland, "Racial Recognition by Nursery School Children in Lynchburg, Virginia" *Social Forces*, **37** (1958), 132–137.

3. Helen C. Trager and Marian R. Yarrow, *They Learn What They Live*, New York: Harper and Brothers, 1952, pp. 140–155.

4. Marian Radke, Helen C. Trager, and Hadassah Davis, "Social Perceptions and Attitudes of Children," *Genetic Psychology Monographs*, **40** (November 1949), 440.

5. Kenneth B. Clark, *Prejudice and Your Child*, Boston: American Book Company, 1963, p. 77.

6. Vincent R. Rogers and Raymond H. Muessig, "Needed: A Revolution in the Textbook Industry," *The Social Studies*, **54** (October 1963), 169.

7. *A Report on the Treatment of Minorities in American History Textbooks*, Lansing, Michigan Department of Education, 1968, p. 15.

8. "Textbook Publishers Discuss Their Product," *Phi Delta Kappan*, **50** (November 1968), 190–191.

9. *Ibid.*, p. 191.

10. Hillel Black, *The American Schoolbook*, New York: William Morrow, 1961, p. 117.

11. *Ibid.*, p. 64.

12. David K. Gast, "Minority Americans in Children's Literature," *Elementary English*, **44** (January 1967), 12–23.

13. "The Primary Grades: A Review of Textbook Materials," in C. Benjamin Cox and Byron G. Massialas, ed., *Social Studies in the United States: A Critical Appraisal*, New York: Harcourt, Brace and World, 1967, p. 22.

TEACH THEM
THE ARTS
OF FREEDOM

Lawrence C. Howard

Too little of the education of the disadvantaged has either the content or the spirit of the humanities. Since the disadvantaged are those who are limited, and the humanities are concerned with liberating man—this void is hard to understand. Part of the problem may be that "disadvantage" has been viewed too narrowly as a deficiency of the child, and education not enough as the enlargement of freedom. This brief review of its nature, history, and current focus suggests the humanities should have a central role in the education of the disadvantaged. And since the humanities are the arts of freedom, such a shift may well permit the disadvantaged to help in the re-education of America.

Much is now being written about the concept of "disadvantage" to describe problems confronting the child, or rather certain children. Yeshiva University in New York has a center, using semi-automatic data processing techniques, called IRCD (Information Retrieval Center on the Disadvantaged). The center's director, Professor Edmund W. Gordon, wrote in a recent *IRCD Bulletin* about "disadvantage" when approached as the child's problem.

"Disadvantage," he indicated, is rooted in the condition of poverty and discrimination in which the child grows up. He is in an American sub-culture, that of poverty or low status, which has inadequately prepared him to function in the middle-class world of employment and suburban living or, in our frame of reference, for functioning effectively in the educational system. Youngsters are "disadvantaged" in the sense that the preparation they receive is inadequate for successful competition in the larger society.

This kind of "child disadvantage" has been described in great detail by Bloom, Davis, and Hess in their new volume, *Compensatory Education for the Culturally Deprived*. They trace what it means to have poverty and discrimination nagging at you; what a limited diet, inadequate clothing, and shelter can mean in terms of a poor start in life; how these can affect the child during the prenatal period. They note the deficits of early childhood in this setting in inadequate perceptual and linguistic stimulation and in a poverty of experience. When such children reach the first grade, school for them is an unfamiliar and frustrating experience. There is inadequate counseling and an absence of appropriate models. They fall behind in grade, especially in reading skills. By adolescence they are the dropouts; they display a decline in IQ rating over time. The education experience simply does not take, and ahead are social problems. This picture of the disadvantaged child has prompted the conclusion that he needs compensatory education, started early and continued relentlessly, and more enlightened programs to focus upon cognitive development, that is, helping him learn how to learn.

The child is said to have a cumulative deficit that he must overcome: he's non-verbal, has a limited attention span, poor time perspective, limited response to all stimuli; he is the product of a broken home, reared under a matriarchy, is inadequately guided by adults; few things belong to him, he's under-motivated, and has a negative self-image. This is the conception of the disadvantaged child.

There is a divergent view. It states that disadvantage is a societal problem, a critical flaw in democratic America. The existence of poverty, rather than a problem of the poor, is seen as a weakness in our economic system—much the same as depressions used to be viewed. Persisting discrimination, especially against the Negro, reveals America's underdeveloped morality. Gunnar Myrdal has called this the American dilemma: mouthing words of high ideals and Christian precepts, but acting in relentless patterns of prejudice toward Negroes. "Disadvantage" then becomes the problem of the "advantaged." It reflects the middle-class preoccupation with the material, and insensitivity to the human, the strong taking advantage of the weak, the power structure corrupted by its own power. Archibald MacLeish, commenting about disadvantaged America more recently, said, "There is vulgarity everywhere. There are pockets of ignorance and hatred—not only in the Deep South. Our relations with each other lack richness and tenderness." The very existence of ostracized subcultures reinforces this view, points up our historic insensitivity to certain groups—not just the Negro and the poor—the Indian, Mexican, and Filipino as well.

Those who stress disadvantaged America reject the economic deprivation thesis. While they agree limited income is important, they tend to emphasize the powerlessness of the poor, how they are socially invisible in the eyes of those more affluent. Compared with himself, the Negro economically is better off today than he was ten years ago. Yet Thomas Pettigrew has shown that disadvantage has grown steadily more acute. Relative, not absolute, poverty and isolation are the rub. Similar in relative positions are the continuing conditions of the disadvantaged when compared to the ever-increasing promises of amelioration: antipoverty programs, civil rights reforms, urban renewal projects. Only by comparisons can one know his own inferior position.

With so little known about the poor, and even less about their intellectual development, the cumulative deficit thesis is also questioned. The void is exposed by terms like "cultural deprivation" and descriptions of disadvantage couched in absent middle-class values. Ralph Ellison has also denied the relevance of the Americanization of immigrants or Jewish experience with discrimination as models for understanding the "disadvantaged." In a debate with Irving Howe, he remarked, "Things don't look like that from the black skin looking out."

To be disadvantaged, concludes this view, is to feel the pain of being labeled disadvantaged. It is defenselessness against compensatory programs hastily assembled by those whose true objective is to preserve white neighborhood schools. It is being ministered *at* by social workers who stigmatize "the clients" and, in fact, increase dependency. When ignoring the moral failures in our history, we demand that the disadvantaged overcome their background by rejecting home and family, the disadvantaged protest, "I cannot so easily put aside my identity."

Discrimination is common ground to both views of "disadvantage." Those who emphasize America's flaw point less to overt bars and more to subtle acts that come from "doing things as usual." The words "de facto segregation" have grown up to describe societal discrimination in housing, jobs, and schools. While not supported by laws, their effect is equally deadly. In this connection the compensatory approach in schools can provide no real solution. Schools remain white-controlled and segregation continues to expand. It thus comes as no surprise that civil rights demonstrations are active where compensatory programs are in greatest prominence. The drive for integration is not a drive to enter white schools, but one to broaden the cultural base of all schools for educational objectives. It is also to make them truly public. Quality education, if our goal is a free society, is not achievable for anyone—Negro or white—without the integration of our schools.

When some are barred and others intolerant, mankind as a whole is the loser. It is this understanding that should turn our attention to the humanities rather than to the more prevalent psychological emphasis which seeks to get the child "undeprived" before he gets any "learning." The humanities embrace all learning and skills which accelerate man in his becoming what he can be. It is because the humanities are fundamentally concerned with the human condition and its betterment that they have such high relevance both to a group stigmatized as "culturally deprived" and to a society with pervasive patterns of inhumane behavior.

The humanities, in a sense, have always been concerned with man's disadvantages. Originally they included the *trivium* on words (grammar, logic, and rhetoric), and the *quadrivium* of things (geometry, arithmetic, astronomy, and music). The content has changed since classical times, with secularism, science, and the study of society—but all along a basic unity remains: concern with what men can do, and knowledge to reach those goals. It is understandable that the disadvantaged themselves dwell too much on limitations to be overcome, on the legal-social barriers, and too little on the fruits that will accrue to all when man's wholeness is achieved. It is harder to account for the American Council of Learned Societies' failure to mention the "disadvantaged" in the *Report of the Commission on the Humanities* (1964).

The quest to free man, the historical concern of the humanities, is no less the focus today. The forms this takes, according to Richard P. McKeeon, are those of increasing man's discovery power, refining his ability to use the past, and bringing men to act when knowledge and power are at hand. Thus, in a sense, the concern with the humanities today remains as with the Greeks: the proper human uses of relevant words and things.

The first item, as in Shaw's *Pygmalion*, is better use of words. The art of utterance, the ability to communicate thought with power and fluency, is one of the fundamental needs of the disadvantaged. Behind the words must be experience, the basis of communication. Appreciation of structure and design, comprehensiveness of view, of insight, and of system, come hard without experience. Nor can one be assured these several arts will develop simply by exposure blessed by middle class or social power. It is being read to as a preschooler, having books in the house, the trip to the museum, that are required. Cultural enrichment is that which prompts the child to expand his view of reality; it promotes his spirit of wonder. Thomas Merton writes inside a monastery, Schweitzer in a jungle. It is not things or places so much as systematic discouragement that dries up one's experience.

Words grounded in experience illuminate values. And here, too, is relevance, for the disadvantaged are often told to change their values or else to go and get some. The humanities' approach would require that these demands, these moral judgments, rest in understanding. The first step is to weigh the various perspectives on reality including those of the poor and ostracized. No war on poverty, mindful of the humanities, would have delayed so long before including the poor. Judgments of others, in short, should follow, not precede, inquiry. The task of the humanities, and, one would think, of all good education, is to strive to understand what understanding is. Socrates, for one, believed that knowledge of the good would leave man pursuing nothing else.

Values formulated in words and expressed in action are not enough. There must be style, if one would remain true to the humanities. The esthetic dimension is communication so efficient and action so purposeful that elegance is radiated. The discordances have been removed. Is not the unlovely way the disadvantaged are seen much of the problem? To be known as disadvantaged blocks out much of anything else. The label "problem" increases social separation and may itself justify the mistreatment the disadvantaged receive.

This cursory look at the humanities prompts one to ask what has greater relevance for the education of the disadvantaged. How has it happened that schools of education and social work, rather than those of the liberal arts, have dominated this field?

Even for those still emphasizing the child's needs, there is a large place for the humanities in our schools. It is to literature that teachers should turn to overcome the poverty of experience. Are not Grimm, Carroll, Graham, Aesop the basic readers, and the lifeless *Dick and Jane* at best for suggested-reading lists? Would not the deportment task of teachers diminish if students had ample opportunities for acting out? Drama, a transliterated Greek word, means a thing done. To live up to this meaning is more than talking literary forms or discussing characters. The fine and performing arts are personalized expressions of conflicts, aspirations, and fears. The tense of drama is current—the present working itself towards destiny. *Hamlet* is a poet's construct; his reality is in the reader's mind. It is we who are Hamlet. "More than any other art," wrote Arthur Miller, "theater calls for relevance. The play must convince that this is the way it is now in human intercourse." Drama is a tool for understanding. It permits telling others who the actors are, as well as letting actors know a world beyond themselves. Much great drama, too, is familial. For those who see family relationships as crucial there is limitless material in *Antigone*, *Agamemnon*, and virtually all of O'Neill.

Much that is familiar can also be found in poetry, because it is concentrated expression of the human mind in rhythmical language. This should be particularly appropriate for the disadvantaged whose attention spans are said to be short, for those for whom nothing but the existential is of interest. There is even more when poetry is set to music, especially in folk songs, spirituals, the blues, and now the songs of the Civil Rights movement—for they rise out of the disadvantaged themselves.

But more than content, the humanities suggest to teachers attitudes necessary for teaching disadvantaged students. At heart this is belief that freedom is man's proper condition. Carl Rogers's *On Becoming a Person* and Philip Morrison's *Experimenters in the Classroom* draw heavily on this spirit by presenting teaching as the art of liberating the student. De-emphasizing content, they seek not good listeners or good memorizers, but real experimenters, not the empty "why?" but the internalized insight that often comes from manipulation of objects. They see the formulation of questions by students as more important than teacher-supplied answers. Both have high tolerance for the novel. They urge teachers to enter the students' world of feeling and meaning. To see things as the student does requires withholding judgment—the teacher must cultivate openness in himself to see reality in a new way. The attitude of the teacher then becomes one of warmth, interest, respect, and expectation, because the teacher now is learning with the student. The belief that the disadvantaged child has something of value to offer is precisely that attitude of which he is most deprived!

The teacher who would liberate must see student potential at least in equal measure to statistics suggestive of his limitations. Greater use of the humanities would help produce this balance. It would shift the focus— a little—from the failings of the child versus the middle class to the America that could be. In that new emphasis the teacher would see that the disadvantaged have much to teach America, especially about the nature of freedom. It is true that those who have not had freedom are most preoccupied with it. In America the Negro has been concerned with little else. Those with negative thoughts about the disadvantaged should read Frederick Douglass, Henry McNeal Turner, or W. E. B. DuBois; see Martin Duberman's *In White America*; or sing aloud "We Shall Overcome!" The idea that the disadvantaged bring what America long has needed is not new. Alexis deTocqueville in 1831 visited our prisons and wrote the first reasoned account of democratic government in America. In *De la Democratie en Amerique* he pointed out America's problem as being born free and therefore perhaps not knowing the real value of freedom.

To continue to deprecate the disadvantaged child, his home and culture is to prevent the disadvantaged from giving to America what America most needs. The price of this imposed separation, this social ostracism, even— or especially—when accompanied by impersonal compensatory educational and welfare programs, can only bring the social breakdown that Baldwin predicted and Los Angeles now presents in sample form. The approach of the humanities could perhaps turn us away from discordances of guilt and hatred, and toward the harmony of an integrated society.

To be in the learning enterprise with the disadvantaged is in our time an exciting opportunity. The enlargement of freedom is what education is about. So, educators, drink deep from the humanities, the arts of all— even of disadvantaged—mankind.

BLACK LIBERATION
AND THE SOCIAL
STUDIES CURRICULUM

Gerald A. McIntosh

Traditional approaches to social studies instruction have, by and large, provided the student with information about the great achievements of European societies, and little if any information about the contributions and achievements of non-white civilizations. This approach has been particularly detrimental to the liberation struggle of Black people, whose attention should be directed toward the various forces controlling and affecting their lives. Out of such understandings should develop a unified commitment to bring about needed social change and changes in power relationships.

C. Wright Mills argues that educational institutions are established to train persons to fit into slots in society, and to produce a few select persons who can move into power positions.[1] He further states:

> If the centralized state could not rely upon the inculcation of nationalist loyalties in public and private schools, its leaders would promptly seek to modify the decentralized educational structure.[2]

Herein lies the major purpose of educational institutions as we know them. Throughout the history of this country, education has been idolized as the "avenue to the good life." The common school concept developed in the early stages of public education purported to provide equal education for all people. The implication was that everyone needed the same or similar skills and knowledge to attain success. Few persons have strongly questioned the basic tenets and goals of American public education, and still fewer have attempted to analyze its effects on Black people, its role in their subjugation, and its potential in their struggle for liberation.

Black people have long believed that education was the key to equal opportunity and freedom. Even during the early days of slavery, when it was illegal to educate Blacks, many of them strove to become educated under the threat of mutilation and even death. The reasons for this tremendous faith in education are many. However, one of the main reasons was that persons they saw succeeding in life (those that had power and wealth) were highly educated. They, therefore, hypothesized that if so educated, they could also gain the

---

Gerald A. McIntosh, "Black Liberation and the Social Studies Curriculum." Unpublished manuscript, printed with permission of the author.

same degree of success. This belief was clearly demonstrated in W. E. B. Dubois's professed reliance on the "Talented Tenth" as the solution to the problems of exploited Blacks. He also stated that:

> Black folk connected knowledge with power, who believed that education was a stepping stone to wealth and respect, and that wealth without education was crippled.[3]

That belief has proven true for most Americans. However, because of the capitalistic, exploitative, racist nature of American society this dream has not been fulfilled for Black people. As Malcolm X stated, a Black person with a Ph.D. in the eyes of whites is still a nigger.[4]

The problem, then becomes that of deciding the role education truly has in the struggle of Blacks, and how they can most effectively restructure educational institutions so that they more successfully meet the needs of the Black community.

Harold Cruse, in his book, *The Crisis Of The Negro Intellectual*, strongly criticizes Black intellectuals for their inability to develop viable programs and organizations that truly reflect the cultural, political, and economic needs of the Black masses. One of the main reasons for this inability may lie in the whole indoctrination process that Black intellectuals are subjected to in our public schools, which renders them incapable of effectively developing alternative strategies to the traditional, acceptable, legitimate (in the eyes of the power structure) methods of redress. Robert Hess describes the role of schools in this manner:

> In addition to the task of conveying information about the political systems and its processes, the school also acts to promote and teach political values and traditions. In this sense, political socialization in the school is a form of political indoctrination, designed to perpetuate the dominant values of the present system.[5]

The results of this political indoctrination are complacency and total uncritical acceptance of governmental action which results in an extremely uninformed and apathetic citizenry. This form of political awareness (or lack of) is extremely detrimental and dysfunctional to the liberation struggle of Black people. Therefore, an attempt must be made to restructure the educational curriculum (the total school experience) so that it disseminates a more realistic picture of America and provides students with opportunities to analyze federal, state and local political structures and determine their effects on them as individuals and as members of an ethnic group.

Students should become intimately involved in local politics, and have experience in efforts to influence or change political thought and action. The major thrust must be an attempt to increase participation in the ideas, emotions, and actions of politics so that the end product of the school experience is a *political activist* rather than an uninterested observer.

The struggle as it relates to education is one of institutionalizing radical thought and action. Radical in that the school becomes an instrument of the Black community to instill, develop, and mold the minds and bodies of young people so that they:

1. Have pride in themselves and, collectively their racial group.
2. Have a dedication and commitment to the liberation of their people.
3. Have a dedication, commitment, and desire to develop their own intellectual skills so they are better prepared to analyze and create new and different social structures that will benefit their people.
4. Above all, they should recognize and believe in group solidarity as the major and most effective weapon at their disposal, rather than the traditional individualistic manner of thinking and acting.

Robert Maynard maintains that in order to effectively develop a program of action that attempts to liberate Black people (both physically and mentally) those institutions that disseminate knowledge, ideas, and concepts must be controlled by Blacks. He states:

> Black nationalism has other goals at the community level, principally commerce and the police, but the schools are being focused upon as all-important to the fostering of the ethic of Black pride and Black self-determination.[6]

Education which purports to be relevant to the needs of Black people (kindergarten—higher education) must be developed and derived from the Black experience. That is, it must reflect the cultural, economic (other than capitalism), and political needs (based upon new radical approaches) of the Black community. It must train youth to control the territory in which they predominate, for example: "if the glories of European culture and the Renaissance are being taught to White children, then the glories of African culture, of the Dahomneys and Ashantis, must be taught to Black children. Beyond that, the role of education in the nationalist scheme of things is to interrupt the cycle of self-abnegation, the forces that cause young Black children to see themselves as less than human."[7]

The obvious components that are absolutely necessary for such an approach to education are:

1. *That the process be largely problem solving and experience oriented.* At all levels, dependent upon age and maturation level, students should be exposed to real life situations that are operative in their indigenous situation. That is not to say that they should not be concerned with the larger com-

munity and/or world, but the educational experiences should be sequential, so that they have had total exposure and have dealt thoroughly with their own situation before attempting to generalize beyond it.

2. If the process is to gain its direction from the Black experience, then it must necessarily be planned and implemented by Black people (more specifically, Blacks who have a commitment, dedication, and knowledge of the Black experience i.e. history, culture, and needs of the community seeking liberation). Therefore, if whites have a role to play in those attempts, they are of a supportive and facilitative nature. They cannot determine curriculum because they are not of the "Black experience" and cannot effectively translate it into curriculum goals and objectives.

Since the present curriculum serves the purposes of the present order, it is at best naive to consider its control and/or restructuring being allowed through the use of moral persuasion tactics. Those concerned with the liberation of Black people must develop strategies to force the system to make changes in its approaches and relinquish control. It has become increasingly evident that those in power are committed to protecting their vested interests, and will only respond in meaningful ways when tactics are employed that will render the system inoperable until justified and needed changes are made.

However, teachers and curriculum planners do have a major responsibility to play in developing more meaningful programs. They must re-evaluate their personal attitudes as they relate to subject matter as well as people and institutions. In addition they must begin the process of curriculum change by analyzing the present approaches, and in cooperation with laymen begin developing and implementing programs that more truly reflect the realities of being Black "In White America."

NOTES

1. C. Wright Mills, *The Power Elite*, New York: Oxford University Press, pp. 62–63.

2. *Ibid.*, p. 6.

3. W. E. B. Dubois, *Black Reconstruction in America: 1860–1880*, New York: World Publishing Co., p. 64.

4. *Autography of Malcolm X*, New York: Grove Press, p. 284.

5. Robert D. Hess, "Political Socialization in the schools," *Harvard Educational Review*, **38**, 3 (Summer 1968), p. 529.

6. Robert Maynard, "Nationalism and Community Schools," Washington D.C., December 1968, p. 3. Unpublished paper prepared for the Brookings Institute Conference on The Community School.

7. *Ibid.*, p. 5.

RACE AND EDUCATION:
A SEARCH FOR LEGITIMACY

Charles V. Hamilton

An article on public policy, race, and education in the United States in the late 1960's cannot overlook the clear existence of tremendous ferment taking place in the various black communities in this country. The nature of that ferment is such that, if we would devise relevant policy for educating vast numbers of black people today, we cannot focus merely, or even primarily, on achievement in verbal and mathematical skills as criteria for educational improvement. At one time, possibly to the mid-1960's, it was possible to talk about educational policy largely in terms of "integration" (or at least, desegregation) and assume that plans to implement integration would be dealing with the core of the problem of educational deficiency. This is no longer the case.

Today, one hears wholly different demands being raised in the black community. These demands are better represented by the kinds of resolutions coming out of the workshops of the newly formed (June, 1968) National Association of Afro-American Educators than by the conclusions reached by the report on *Equality of Educational Opportunity* (Coleman Report). These demands are reflected more clearly in the demonstrations of black high school students in many cities for more emphasis on Afro-American history and culture and for better science lab facilities than by the findings of the United States Commission on Civil Rights (*Racial Isolation in the Public Schools*). These demands are more clearly illustrated in the positions taken by the Harlem chapter of the Congress of Racial Equality (CORE), calling for an independent school system for Harlem, and by many of the Concerned Black Parents groups than in policy recommendations found in the statement issued by the Board of Education of Chicago, Illinois in August, 1967 (Redmond Report).

First, I would like to indicate why it is more important at this time, from a socio-political point of view, to put more credence in the wishes of the black community than in the statements and findings of the experts. Second, I would like to give examples of the kinds of things on the minds of some of those black people taking an active interest in new directions for education in the black community. Third, I want to present a sketch of a proposal for

Charles V. Hamilton, "Race and Education: A Search for Legitimacy," *Harvard Educational Review*, **38** (Fall 1968), 669–684. Copyright © 1968 by President and Fellows of Harvard College. Reprinted with permission of the author and publisher.

dealing with some of the problems in some of the large, urban areas. I am not sanguine that the proposal will be applicable in all places (I assume it will not be), but neither do I believe it possible or necessary to develop one model to fit all occasions. My proposal attempts to combine some of the fervent wishes of a growing number of black people with the clear need to think in wholly new institutional terms. I am fully aware that public policy in this area has been influenced by such dichotomies as "integration vs. segregation" (*de jure* and *de facto*) and "integrated education vs. quality (compensatory) education." My presentation will not use these terms as primary focal points, but it is clear that the main thrust of my proposal will support the involvement of more parents in the school system and the improvement of educational opportunities within the black community. Some critics will view this as an "enrichment" proposal, or as an effort at "compensatory" education, or even as a black power move to maintain and further divisiveness in the society. I simply acknowledge these criticisms at the outset and intend to let my proposal stand on its own merits.

A CRISIS OF EDUCATIONAL LEGITIMACY

It is absolutely crucial to understand that the society cannot continue to write reports accurately describing the failure of the educational institutions *vis-à-vis* black people without ultimately taking into account the impact those truths will have on black Americans. There comes a point when it is no longer possible to recognize institutional failure and then merely propose more stepped-up measures to overcome those failures—especially when the proposals come from the same kinds of people who administered for so long the present unacceptable and dysfunctional policies and systems. Professor Seymour Martin Lipset once wrote:

> Legitimacy involves the capacity of the system to engender and maintain the belief that the existing political institutions are the most appropriate ones for the society. The extent to which contemporary democratic political systems are legitimate depends in large measure upon the ways in which the key issues which have historically divided the society have been resolved.

> While effectiveness is primarily instrumental, legitimacy is evaluative. Groups regard a political system as legitimate or illegitimate according to the way in which its values fit with theirs.[1]

And in another place, he has wrtten:

> All claims to a legitimate title to rule in new states must ultimately win acceptance through demonstrating effectiveness. The loyalty of the different groups to the system must be won through developing *in them*

the conviction that this system is the best—or at least an excellent—
way to accomplish their objectives. And even claims to legitimacy of a
supernatural sort, such as "the gift of grace," are subjected on the
part of the populace to a highly pragmatic test—that is, what is the
payoff?[2] [Emphasis added.]

The United States gradually acquired legitimacy as a result of being
effective.[3] [Emphasis in original.]

The important point here is that loyalty, allegiance, is predicated on
performance. What decision-makers *say* is not of primary importance, but
it is important what black people *believe*. Do they *believe* that the school
systems are operating in their behalf? Do they *believe* that the schools are
legitimate in terms of educating their children and inculcating in them a
proper sense of values? With the end product (i.e., their children graduating
from high school as functional illiterates) clearly before their eyes at home
and with volumes of reports documenting lack of payoff, it is not difficult to
conclude that black people have good reason to question the legitimacy of
the educational systems.

They begin to question the entire process, because they are aware that
the schools, while not educating their children, are at the same time supporting a particularly unacceptable situation. They know that the schools are one
of the major institutions for socializing their children into the dominant value
structure of the society. Professor V. O. Key, Jr. concluded in his book,
Politics, Parties and Pressure Groups:

> In modern societies the school system, in particular, functions as a
> formidable instrument of political power in its role as a transmitter
> of the goals, values, and attitudes of the polity. In the selection of values
> and attitudes to be inculcated, it chooses those cherished by the dominant
> elements in the political order. By and large the impact of widely accepted
> goals, mores, and social values fixes the programs of American schools.
> When schools diverge from this vaguely defined directive and collide with
> potent groups in the political system, they feel a pressure to conform.[4]

The relevance of all this is that makers of policy and their advisers
must recognize that there is a point beyond which vast numbers of black
people *will* become alienated and will no longer view efforts on their behalf,
however well-intentioned, as legitimate. When this happens, it behooves
decision-makers, if they would search for ways of restoring faith, trust,
and confidence, to listen to the demands of the alienated. The "experts"
might see integration as socially and educationally sound and desirable,
but *their* vision and empirical data might well be, at this juncture, irrelevant.
Unless this is understood, I am suggesting that public policy might well find
itself in the position of attempting to force its programs on a reluctant

black community. And this is hardly a formula for the development of a viable body politic.

A clear example of a paternalistic, objectionable policy is contained in the report of the Chicago Board of Education, *Increasing Desegregation of Faculties, Students, and Vocational Education Programs*, issued August 23, 1967. The Report called for bussing black children into all- or predominantly white schools. It contains the very revealing paragraph:

> The assignment of students outside their neighborhood may be objected to by Negro parents who prefer that their children attend the segregated neighborhood school. This viewpoint cannot be ignored. Prior to implementation of such a transfer policy the administration must take steps to reassure apprehensive sending area parents that transfer will be beneficial not only in terms of integration but of improved education for their children. The generation of a favorable consensus in the designated sending area is important. *If such a consensus is unobtainable, the transfer program would have to proceed without a popular base.* In the light of the dismal alternatives such a program perhaps should proceed even without consensus, but every effort should be made to attain it.[5] [Emphasis added.]

This is a perpetuation of the pattern of telling the black community what is best for it. My point is that this position will only increase alienation, not alleviate it. At the present time, when the educational systems are perceived as illegitimate, it is highly unlikely that such a policy could lead to success. In order for the program to work, support *must* be obtained from the black community. This means that educational achievement must be conceived more broadly than as the mere acquisition of verbal and mathematical skills. Very many black parents are (for good reason) quite concerned about what happens to the self-image of their black children in predominantly white schools— schools which reflect dominant white values and mores. Are these schools prepared to deal with their own white racism? Probably not, and a few summer institutes for white, middle-class teachers cannot prepare them. Are these schools prepared to come to terms with a young black child's search for identity? Will the black child indeed acquire certain skills which show up favorably on standardized tests, but at the same time avoid coming to grips with the fact that he or she should not attempt to be a carbon copy of the culture and ethos of another racial and ethnic group? Virtually all the social scientists, education experts, and public policy-makers who emphasize integration overlook this crucial, intangible, psychological factor. Many concerned black parents and teachers do not overlook it, however. And their viewpoint has nothing to do with black people wanting to perpetuate "separate but unequal" facilities, or with attitudes of "hate whitey." This concern is simply a necessary reaction to the fact that many white (and black) liberal, integration-oriented spokesmen are tuned in to a particular result and overlook other phenomena.

They fail to understand that their criteria for "educational achievement" simply might not be relevant anymore.

What I am stating (in as kind a way as possible) is that setting criteria for measuring equal educational opportunity can no longer be the province of the established "experts." The policy-makers must now listen to those for whom they say they are operating; which means of course that they must be willing to share the powers of policy-making. The experts must understand that what is high on the liberal social scientist's agenda does not coincide with the agenda of many black people. The experts are still focusing on the effectiveness of existing educational institutions. Many black people have moved to the evaluation of the legitimacy of these institutions.

American social scientists generally are unable to grasp the meaning of alienation when applied to certain groups in this country. (Most of the recent perceptive literature on alienation and modernization deals with new nations of Africa and Asia.)[6]

Consequently, Grant McConnell, in an important book, *Private Power and American Democracy*, could write:

> In general the use of government has depended on a particular group's capacity to isolate the relevant governmental agency from influences other than its own and to establish itself as the agency's constituency— at once giving an air of validity to its own ends and endowing it with the added disciplinary power of public authority over its own members.[7]

And later:

> ... farm migrant workers, Negroes, and the urban poor have not been included in the system of "pluralist" representation so celebrated in recent years.[8]

Then finally:

> It can be readily agreed that if explosive mass movements are a genuine threat to America, a politics of narrow constituencies might be desirable to counter the danger. Small associations probably do provide order and stability for any society. In the United States some associations may serve in this manner to a greater degree than others. The American Civil Liberties Union and the League of Woman Voters have given notable service to American democracy. Trade unions and farm organizations have undoubtedly also been similarly useful at various times. Nevertheless, it should be clear that a substantial price is paid for any guarantee against mass movements provided by a pattern of small constituencies. That price is paid in freedom and equality. Although the price would be worth paying if the danger were grave, it can hardly be argued that such an extremity is present.[9]

There are voices in the black community (accompanied, as we well know, by acts of expressive violence) saying precisely that the danger *is* grave and that the extremity *is* present. The educational systems are particularly vulnerable, because of their very conspicuous inability to "pay-off."

AN ALTERNATIVE AGENDA

It is instructive, then, to examine some of the major items presented by certain voices in the black community. Clearly, one source of constructive ideas would be black teachers, those persons who not only teach in ghetto schools, but whose children attend those schools (in most instances), who, themselves, grew up in the black community, and who, for the most part, still live in black communities.[10] Approximately 800 such teachers met in Chicago, June 6–9, 1968, in a national conference and formed the National Association of Afro-American Educators. They did not spend the four days discussing the Coleman Report or the report of the U.S. Civil Rights Commission. One could identify four particular areas of concern at that conference, and these areas coincide to a great extent with the issues raised by associations of Concerned Black Parents as well as various Afro-American History clubs in the high schools around the country.

1. Control It was generally concluded that the existing educational systems were not responsive to the wishes of the black community. Therefore, those structural arrangements now operating should be changed substantially. The decision-making process in most ghetto school systems was challenged. The workshop on the black school and the black community issued the following statement:

> Whereas, the educational systems of this nation have criminally failed the Black youth of this country,
>
> Whereas, Black parents have not had a voice in determining the educational destiny of their youth,
>
> Whereas, the Black youth and Black parents are demanding relevant education to meet their needs,
>
> Therefore, be it resolved that we encourage, support and work to organize local communities to control their own schools through local or neighborhood school boards and further that this organization go on record to immediately implement such plans.
>
> The goal of the National Association of Afro-American Educators should be Black control of the Black Community schools.[11]

One hears these kinds of statements increasingly among newly politicized people in the black communities. The focus has shifted; emphasis is now on viable ways to gain enough leverage to drastically revise a system. Black people, having moved to the stage of questioning the system's very legitimacy, are seeking ways to create a new system. This is difficult for most Americans to understand precisely because they have assumed the continuing legitimacy of the present educational system.

2. Parent involvement and alliance with black teachers   It is becoming clearer and clearer that the major agents of control should be black parents in the community working closely with the teachers in the school. For this reason, if no other, many black spokesmen do not favor various compulsory plans for bussing black children out of their communities into white schools, in some instances, miles away from home. Are we to assume that black parents, likewise, will travel miles across town in the evenings to attend PTA meetings—frequently to be surrounded by a sea of white faces, more articulate and with more organized voting strength? The principle of bussing overlooks the very important factor of facilitating black parent participation in the child's schooling. If in fact the home has a critical role to play in the educational process, then we would be well advised not to pursue policies which would make that role more difficult.

The participation of black parents in the child's schooling is one of the points high on the agenda of some black people. And it is clearly at odds with one of the stated objectives of the Redmond Report: to bus black children into white schools, but to maintain a quota (no white elementary school would be over 15 percent black; no high school over 25 percent black), in order to guard against the possibility of a white exodus. James Redmond, Superintendent of Schools in Chicago, said: "Chicago will become a predominantly Negro city unless dramatic action is taken soon ... School authorities (must) quickly achieve and maintain stable racial proportions in changing fringe areas."[12] Trying to placate whites simply is not a matter of top (or high) priority to many black people, especially if it must be done by manipulating black children.

Discussion of parental involvement and control has serious implications for the standards of professionalism we adopt. Black parents might well have different notions about what is methodologically sound, what is substantively valuable. They might well be impatient with some of the theories about teaching reading and writing. And at this stage who is to say that their doubts are not valid? The present approaches have hardly proved efficacious. Therefore, when we get sizeable black parental participation, we are opening up the profession to question and challenge about what constitutes educational legitimacy. No profession welcomes such intrusion from laymen. This is quite understandable; professionals have a vested self-interest. All those years of college courses and practice teaching certifying exams, all those credentials of legitimacy may be going by the board. But that is precisely what happens in societies which are modernizing, in societies where new group-ings—alienated from traditional norms—rise to make new normative demands. It is disturbing, disruptive, painful. It is change. And this is the phenomenon American social science has been unable to come to terms with in the latter half of the twentieth century—especially with reference to the issue of race relations.

3. Psychological impact   A third matter of concern to these new black voices is the psychological impact of educational institutions on the black children. Many black people are demanding more black principals in predominantly black schools, if only because they serve as positive role models for the children. Children should be able to see black people in positions of day-to-day power and authority. There is a demand to have the schools recognize *black* heroes with national holidays. There is concern for emphasizing group solidarity and pride, which is crucial for the development of black Americans. And there is very serious question whether a predominantly white, middle-class ethos can perform this function. Again, the Coleman data measure verbal skills and mathematical abilities, but there are other areas of equal importance. One should not assume that symbols of cultural pride are unim-portant. Professor Lipset was correct when he described the impact of these symbols, but he was incomplete when he applied them to the United States—when the growing awareness of black Americans is taken into account. He wrote:

> A major test of legitimacy is the extent to which given nations have developed a common "secular political culture," mainly national rituals and holidays. The United States has developed a common homogeneous culture in the veneration accorded the Founding Fathers, Abraham Lincoln, Theodore Roosevelt, and their principles.[13]

The schools serve as a major instrument to transmit such a common homogeneous culture. And yet, we are beginning to see black Americans call for the recognition of other heroes: Frederick Douglass, Martin Luther King, Jr., Malcolm X, and so forth. Students are demanding that the traditional Awards Day programs at their schools include such awards as a Malcolm X Manliness Award, a Marcus Garvey Citizenship Award, and Frederick Douglass and Martin Luther King, Jr. Human Rights Awards. We see black writers challenging the idea of a common secular political culture. John Oliver Killens and Lerone Bennett, Jr. are two prominent examples. Killens captured the mood when he wrote:

> We (black Americans) even have a different historical perspective. Most white Americans, even today, look upon the Reconstruction period as a horrible time of "carpet-bagging," and "black politicians," and "black corruption," the absolutely lowest ebb in the Great American Story . . .

We black folk, however, look upon Reconstruction as the most democratic period in the history of this nation; a time when the dream the
founders dreamed was almost within reach and right there for the taking;
a time of democratic fervor the like of which was never seen before and
never since . . .

For us, Reconstruction was the time when two black men were Senators in
the Congress of the United States from the State of Mississippi; when
black men served in the legislatures of all the states in Dixie; and when
those "corrupt" legislatures gave to the South its first public-school
education . . .[14]

Even our white hero symbols are different from yours. You give us moody
Abe Lincoln, but many of us prefer John Brown, whom most of you hold
in contempt as a fanatic; meaning, of course, that the firm dedication of
any white man to the freedom of the black man is *prima-facie* evidence of
perversion or insanity.[15]

And Lerone Bennett, Jr. challenged much of American historical scholarship
when he challenged the role and image of Abraham Lincoln:

Abraham Lincoln was *not* the Great Emancipator. As we shall see, there is
abundant evidence to indicate that the Emancipation Proclamation was
not what people think it is and that Lincoln issued it with extreme mis-
givings and reservations.[16]

A growing number of black Americans are insisting that the schools begin
to reflect this new concern, this new tension. We simply cannot assume a
common secular political culture. If we continue to operate on such false
assumptions, we will continue to misunderstand the very deep feeling of
alienation in the black community. And misunderstanding cannot be a viable
basis for enlightened public policy. Likewise, it is not only important that
Afro-American history be taught in the black schools, but that it also be
incorporated into the curriculum of white schools throughout this country. It
is not sufficient that only black children be given an accurate historical
picture of the race; all Americans must have this exposure—in the inner city,
the suburbs, the rural schools.

Who can predict what the "tests" will show when we begin to expose
black children to these kinds of innovations? What sort of impact will this
have on the motivation of those "slow learners," those "high risks," those
(and here is the misnomer of them all) "culturally deprived?" The legitimacy
of the "standardized tests" must be questioned as long as they overlook these
very essential components.

4. Curricula and instructional materials Closely related to the third point
is a concern with the kinds and content of materials used, especially in black

schools. How are black people portrayed? Do the textbooks reflect the real experience of black Americans in history and in contemporary society? The workshop on instructional materials at the Afro-American Educators Conference concluded:

> In each local community black educators must develop a criteria for selection of materials which will be presented to the Board of Education, to local textbook committees, and to the major publishing houses which provide text and supplemental materials to that community. It is incumbent upon us, if we are to serve this society, that instructional material which we select be both educationally sound and incorporate a strong black orientation.
>
> Black classroom teachers must help black students to speak the language of the market place and assist them as they move back and forth between "their own thing and a white American thing." Since all groups usually speak two languages, one at home and within their group and another in the economic world; by nurturing and respecting our own language and effectively manipulating the other we will become a truly bilingual people. This is necessary to achieve a viable economic base . . .
>
> Black teachers must become connected with major textbook publishing firms as authors, editors and consultants to create the materials available on the market. We must pressure major publishers to reflect the needs of black children in schools. We will work for a factual inclusion of the scientific contribution of black scientists to medical and scientific advancement. For example, Dr. Daniel Hale Williams (open heart surgery) and Dr. Charles Drew (developer of blood plasma) must receive their rightful place in elementary and secondary science texts.[17]

These are some of the things on the agenda of many black people as they consider possible solutions of our vast educational problems. It is far too soon to evaluate the results of most of these proposals—in some instances they have not even been implemented. And in most cases they are in the embryonic stage. We are without precedent in these matters, and it would be presumptuous of American social scientists to attempt to prejudge results, or even to suppose that they could. Black people are searching for new forms of educational legitimacy, and in that kind of modernizing atmosphere the traditional criteria for measuring effectiveness might well be irrelevant and anachronistic.

AN ALTERNATIVE MODEL

The rhetoric of race and education, as stated earlier, is prolific with dichotomies of segregation vs. integration, quality education vs. integrated education, compensatory programs vs. bussing, and so forth. Too much is assumed by these simplistic terms, and a superficial use of these labels frequently restricts and predetermines discussion at the outset. While this is unfortunate, it is probably unavoidable, given the historical context and the highly emotional atmosphere. Those persons favoring "neighborhood" schools and opposing bussing have traditionally been, in the North, white parents and taxpayer groups, usually identified as anti-Negro in their basic racial views. These groups would normally be found opposing open housing laws as well. Therefore their motivations are questioned when they argue that they are essentially concerned about "educational standards" and property values. When it is pointed out to them that white students do not suffer academically and (if panic selling is avoided) property values do not go down, they do not listen. And their intransigence leads their opponents to label them as racial bigots and segregationists.

Proponents of bussing and integration see a positive academic and social value in racially heterogeneous classrooms. Integration to these people is virtually synonymous with quality. And black people who once worked for desegregated schools but who no longer do so are viewed as having given up the fight, as having joined the white racists, and, indeed, as having become black racists and advocates of "Black Power separatism."[18]

I state this simply to acknowledge an awareness of some of the positions taken before I proceed to suggest an alternative educational plan. The fact that my ideas would appear more closely akin to the views of some white segregationists whose ultimate goal is to deny educational opportunity to black people is an *appearance* I cannot avoid. It is important however to point out that a close examination of the ultimate goals of my suggestions will indicate a clear divergence from views held by the segregationists. In other words I am motivated by an attempt to find an educational approach which is relevant to black people, not one that perpetuates racism. The plan I am suggesting is not a universal panacea; it is not applicable in all black ghettos. Where it is feasible—particularly in the large urban communities—I strongly propose it for consideration.

This is a model which views the ghetto school as the focal point of community life. The educational system should be concerned with the entire family, not simply with the children. We should think in terms of a Comprehensive Family-Community-School Plan with black parents attending classes, taking an active, day-to-day part in the operation of the school. Parents could be students, teachers, and legitimate members of the local school governing board. A similar plan is already in operation in Chicago: the Family Education Center. There are two centers, the Westinghouse and Doolittle Centers, which provide basic adult education, prevocational and vocational training, and work experience programs.

Mr. William H. Robinson, Director of the Cook County Department of

Public Aid, has stated:

> The Center's most unique feature is the Child Development Program for the students' (parents') pre-school children, who come to school with their mothers and spend the day in a well-equipped, professionally staffed nursery school. Mothers can attend classes with the assurance that their children are receiving proper care and mental stimulation. Thus, the program makes participation in an educational program possible for many recipients who were prevented previously because they could not obtain adequate child care services.[19]

Since the inception of the program two years ago, 1,300 adults and 500 children have been involved in the centers.

This concept should be expanded to include fathers as well, those unemployed and willing to obtain skills. Many of these parents could serve as teachers, along with a professional staff. They could teach courses in a number of areas (child care, auto mechanics, art, music, home economics, sewing, etc.) for which they are obviously now trained. The Comprehensive Plan would extend the school program to grades through high school—for adults and children—and it would eliminate the traditional calendar year of September to June. (There is no reason why the educational system could not be revised to take vacations for one month, say in December of post-Christmas, and another month in August. The community educational program would be a year-round function, day and evening.)

The school would belong to the community. It would be a union of children, parents, teachers (specially trained to teach in such communities), social workers, psychologists, doctors, lawyers, and community planners. Parent and community participation and control would be crucial in the hiring and firing of personnel, the selection of instructional materials, and the determination of curriculum content. Absolutely everything must be done to make the system a functioning, relevant part of the lives of the local people. Given the present situation of existing and growing alienation, such involvement is essential.

If it can be demonstrated that such a comprehensive educational institution can gain the basic trust and participation of the black community, it should become the center of additional vital community functions. Welfare, credit unions, health services, law enforcement, and recreational programs— all working under the control of the community—could be built around it. Enlightened private industry would find it a place from which to recruit trained, qualified people and could donate equipment and technical assistance. The several advantages of such a plan are obvious. It deals with the important agencies which are in daily, intimate contact with black people; it reduces a vast, fragmented service bureaucracy which now descends on the black community from many different directions, with cumbersome rules and regulations, uncontrolled by and unaccountable to the community. It provides the black people with a meaningful chance for participation in the very important day-to-day processes affecting their lives; it gives them educational and vocational tools for the future. All these things reflect the yearnings and aspirations of masses of black people today.

The Comprehensive Plan envisions the local school as a central meeting place to discuss and organize around community issues, political and economic. All of the establishments functioning under the plan would provide relevant intermediary groups to which the people could relate. The size of the community involved would vary, with several factors to be considered: geography, number of participating agencies, available funds (from federal, state, and local governmental sources), and manageability. At all times, the primary concern would be about the active involvement of people and about their possession of real power to make decisions affecting the Comprehensive Plan. They would hire consultants and experts whose legitimacy would be determined by their relevance to the community, not by a predetermined set of criteria superimposed from outside.

The proposed Comprehensive Plan attempts to come to grips with the understandable alienation discussed in the first section and with the appropriateness of the agenda items described in the second section of the paper. This plan is better understood when one keeps in mind the premise presented earlier: black people are questioning, evaluating the *legitimacy* of existing educational institutions, not simply searching for ways to make those institutions more *effective*. I am suggesting that we are at a point in the process of modernization and social transformation when we must begin to think and act in wholly new normative and structural terms.

NOTES

1. Seymour Martin Lipset, *Political Man: The Social Bases of Politics*, New York: Doubleday, 1963, p. 64.

2. Seymour Martin Lipset, *The First New Nation: The United States in Historical and Comparative Perspective*, New York: Basic Books, 1963, pp. 45–46.

3. *Ibid.*, p. 59.

4. V. O. Key, Jr., *Politics, Parties and Pressure Groups*, New York: Thomas Y. Crowell, 1964, pp. 12–13.

5. *Increasing Desegregation of Faculties, Students, and Vocational Education Programs,* Chicago: Board of Education, 1967, p. B-20.

6. See: Myron Weiner, ed., *Modernization, The Dynamics of Growth*, New York: Basic Books, 1966; David Apter, *The Politics of Modernization*,

Chicago: University of Chicago Press, 1965; S. N. Eisenstadt, *Modernization: Protest and Change*, Englewood Cliffs, N.J.: Prentice-Hall, 1966; Edward Shils, *Political Development in the New States*, New York: Humanities Press, 1964; Thomas Hodgkin, *Nationalism in Colonial Africa*, New York: New York University Press, 1957; K. H. Silvert, *Expectant Peoples: Nationalism and Development*, New York: Random House, 1964; Lucian W. Pye, *Politics, Personality and Nation Building: Burma's Search for Identity*, New Haven: Yale University Press, 1962.

7. Grant McConnell, *Private Power and American Democracy*, New York: Random House, 1965, pp. 346–347.

8. *Ibid.*, p. 349.

9. *Ibid.*, pp. 355–356.

10. In a column entitled "Quality Teaching in Decentralized Slum Schools," Fred M. Hechinger, education editor of *The New York Times*, wrote: "It seems more realistic and, for the long pull, more constructive to face the fact that part of the answer to the crisis must come through the efforts of Negro teachers. If young Negro college graduates can be channeled into these schools and if their greater identification with the children's and the parents' own background can more easily gain the pupils' confidence and attention, then to sacrifice some of the present licensing requirements may be a small price to pay." (*The New York Times*, April 29, 1968.)

11. Excerpt from notes of discussion and reports of workshops of National Association of Afro-American Educators, Chicago, 1968. [Mimeographed.]

12. Quoted in an editorial in *Chicago Sun-Times*, Jan. 12, 1968, p. 27. The editorial, which favored the Redmond Plan, further stated: "That part of the Redmond Plan that has excited opposition calls for fixing immediately a balanced racial enrollment in those all-white schools that are in the way of the Negro expansion. It would be roughly 90 per cent white, 10 per cent Negro. The Negro pupils (who are from middle-class families) would be acceptable to white families and keep them anchored in the neighborhood, whereas they would flee to the suburbs if the Negro proportion became greater than 25 per cent. The plan may not work. If it does it is at best only a holding action until the entire metropolitan area faces up to the demographic realities of our time. But it should be tried."

13. Lipset, *Political Man*, p. 68.

14. John Oliver Killens, *Black Man's Burden*, New York: Trident Press, 1965, pp. 14–15.

15. *Ibid.*, p. 17.

16. Lerone Bennett, Jr., "Was Abe Lincoln a White Supremacist?", *Ebony*, **23**, 4 (February 1968), 35.

17. Excerpt from notes and discussion and reports of workshops of National Association of Afro-American Educators, Chicago, 1968. [Mimeographed.]

18. An example of this attitude was contained in the report of the President's civil disorders commission (Kerner Commission). "The Black Power advocates of today consciously feel that they are the most militant group in the Negro protest movement. Yet they have retreated from a direct confrontation with American society on the issue of integration and, by preaching separatism, unconsciously function as an accommodation to white racism" (*Report of the National Advisory Commission on Civil Disorders*, New York: E. P. Dutton, 1968, p. 235).

19. Cook County Department of Public Aid, *The Challenge of Change*, (annual report), Chicago, 1967, p. 11.

IMPERATIVES IN
URBAN EDUCATION

Donald H. Smith

The great American Dream of free public education for all children to the upper limits of their potential has never materialized. And for the disadvantaged minorities, Negroes, Mexicans, Puerto Ricans, Amerindians, and poor Southern whites, American public education has been pitifully ineffectual. Judged by almost any critical factor—number of dropouts, level of achievement, number of college entrants, type and duration of employment, and lifestyle—the schools have failed the dispossessed minority pupils.

Two recent works, *Our Children Are Dying* by Nat Hentoff and *Death at an Early Age* by Jonathan Kozol, attest to the shocking and inhumane waste of Negro pupils in the New York and Boston public schools respectively. The

Donald H. Smith, "Imperatives in Urban Education." A paper presented to the Annual Meeting of the American Association of Colleges for Teacher Education at Chicago, Feb. 15, 1968. Excerpts of this paper were published as "Changing Controls in Ghetto Schools," *Phi Delta Kappa*, **49** (April 1968), 451–452. Reprinted with permission of the author and publisher.

picture in Chicago, Los Angeles, and our other large cities is no less bleak. So distressing is the plight of poor kids in our schools that Edgar Friedenberg was compelled to write for *Saturday Review* an article entitled "Requiem for the Urban School." Friedenberg concludes that:

> Improvement in the urban schools will come when—and only when—the residents whose children attend those schools demand and get enough political power either to destroy and replace the present school bureaucracy or to impress upon it that they can no longer be patronized.[1]

The schools have failed and their society's agents, the teachers, have failed and those who have trained the teachers have also failed. Only if we can recognize the magnitude of our failure and its price—hungry, angry, bitter citizens whose lowly state threatens the security of all—can we then begin to reverse the tide.

Too often so-called experts on the disadvantaged child—and disadvantaged means Negro to most to them—place the burden of education on the shoulders of the children and their parents. Since it is well known that most disadvantaged children come from homes that are economically and educationally deprived, it is presumed that however dedicated and talented the teacher may be the cause is hopeless—witness *Up the Down Staircase*. Only a supergod, Phi Beta Kappa—perhaps "Sir Poitier"—can teach the unteachable.

Such mushy thinking has gotten us in the fix we're in now: the collapse of the urban school.

I reject the thesis that the fault lies within the ghetto; and neither does it lie within the stars. *The fault lies within the larger society that fails to acknowledge the existence of black people, and subsequently trains teachers and constructs curricula and materials for a presumably monolithic white middle-class society.*

Teachers have failed because, for the most part they don't know anything about, care little about and have not been trained to teach their black and brown pupils.

These children are no longer only a part of, but have in fact *become*, the urban school population. Negro pupils are in the majority in 12 of our largest cities and are better than 40 percent of the population in at least five other large cities. Add to this total the Mexicans and the Puerto Ricans, and the revelation is that the white child is the urban minority. The new teacher training curricula are going to have to face up squarely to this hard racial fact and to other hard facts if we are to save the one institution that has within it the potential to save our nation.

These are critical times, times when men young and old, liberal and conservative, black and white must talk and must listen.

Let us consider together five imperative issues in urban education.

Certainly these are not the only significant issues, but I make no effort to touch all bases.

Imperative Number One is *the need to change the attitudes and expectations of teachers of disadvantaged youth.*

A number of years ago when I was a guidance counselor in an inner city high school I suggested to the valedictorian that he apply to Harvard. Inner-city admissions to the Ivy League are few—male valedictorians at inner-city high schools are also few. Yet even though he had achieved the distinction of leading his class in scholarship, this Negro youngster could not conceive of his applying to Harvard. The idea was even more implausible to the white scholarship counselor at the high school, who did everything to discourage the boy. True, he was a brilliant student in math and science but surely his college board scores in the language arts were to low for him to consider a first-rate university.

The combination of the student's poor self-image and its re-enforcement by his white counselor were difficult to overcome, but after much persistence and pressure, I finally succeeded in getting our valedictorian to apply. The April rejection slip he received seemed to indicate that he and the scholarship counselor were right. But on the day the rejection notice came, I received a call from Harvard's Director of Admissions. He had detected something about my letter of recommendation that indicated my understanding of this boy. The Harvard official went on to explain that in spite of his low language scores, and in spite of this year's rejection, he was the kind of boy that Harvard wanted. Would he consider enrolling in an Eastern prep school for a year? Perhaps a scholarship could be arranged. If not, Harvard would be his anonymous benefactor. This young man did attend that prep school for a year and he graduated from Harvard last June. Last summer he worked as a teacher of hard-core dropouts, and now he is back at Harvard, in law school.

I have talked to teachers and children in Harlem, in Watts, in Alabama, and Georgia and Mississippi and in many other parts of the nation, and while I have found some superior teaching in almost every school I've visited, I have generally been appalled by the pervasive discouragement and low levels of expectation which are held by most teachers for poor children, particularly black ones.

A few decades ago a brilliant young boy attended an East Lansing, Michigan high school, the only Negro in his class. In his autobiography he wrote about his English teacher who would daily give words of encouragement to the class, urging them to go on to college, to make something of themselves. One day the boy confided to his teacher that he, too, had been inspired and that he hoped some day to become a lawyer. The boy was crushed when his teacher advised him to forget law and become a plumber or carpenter. Circumstances determined that this boy would not finish high school and, hence, enter any profession. But one can only wonder what contribution he might have made to all Americans had Malcolm "X" been encouraged to realize his dreams. Perhaps he might have lived to be appointed to the Supreme Court.

Of great irony was the teacher's advice to become a plumber or a carpenter, when the reality is that it is easier for a Negro lad to get into law school than into plumbers' or carpenters' unions.

It is a moot point whether teachers and counselors discourage black children because of bigotry or out of some misguided paternalism, which is, itself a form of racism. But as long as school personnel continue to have dual punishment and reward systems, and dual levels of expectation, they will continue to maim poor children psychologically and deprive them of their opportunity to enter and flourish in the mainstream of a land of plenty.

Unfortunately, it is not only in the area of college and vocational guidance that teacher attitudes and expectations hurt children, but also right within the instructional setting the behavior of teachers can mediate the achievement of pupils.

Worthy of our consideration is the very important research of Robert Rosenthal and Lenore Jacobson[2] which clearly indicates the critical relationship between teacher expectations and pupil achievement. Rosenthal and Jacobson found that experimenters working with rats which they have been led to believe were dull had little success in teaching them, but working with rats which were allegedly bright, they had significant success. Rosenthal and Jacobson concluded that:

> Regardless of whether the rat's task was to learn a maze or the appropriate responses in a Skinnnr box, the results were the same. Rats who were believed by their experimenters to be brighter showed learning which was significantly superior to the learning by rats whose experimenters believed them to be dull.

But rats are not children, so Rosenthal and Jacobson moved their experiment into a school of the South San Francisco Unified School District. They administered to all of the children of the Oak School a test which they called the "Harvard Test of Inflected Acquisition", actually a standardized intelligence test, generally non-verbal, the Flanagan Tests of General Ability.

Based not upon test results, but upon random selection, twenty per cent of the children in each classroom were "identified" to their teachers as pupils whose test results indicated they were intellectual bloomers who would undergo significant learning spurts during that year. Once again the Mertonian self-fulfilling prophecy was confirmed: Children designated as spurters did show greater intellectual gains than children not so designated. This was true of children of high intellectual ability as well as children of lower ability. Because their teachers had been conned into believing that some children were going to bloom, their own behavior toward and perceptions of those children serve as mediating factors that helped to make the learning spurts possible.

If we are going to begin to put an end to the human waste in our schools then imperative number one is to change teachers' perceptions of and consequent behavior toward pupils they have formerly believed are racially and intellectually inferior. And this imperative leads to imperative number two.

Imperative Number Two is *the need for drastic changes in the training of teachers*. Teachers are frightened and frustrated as they attempt each day to confront what is for most of them the urban ordeal. My own experience as a new teacher was common to the experiences of many teachers. The educational training that I had received as an undergraduate, and even later as a graduate student, was in no way related to the problems I encountered in the schools and to the needs of my pupils. For the most part—and surely there are a few notable exceptions—teacher training for urban schools has been and is irrelevant. Except for rare instances, it has not begun to address itself to the kinds of information and experiences young people need to develop appropriate attitudes to teach successfully in the ghetto.

No engineering school in the country would attempt to teach its students to build bridges without first attempting to teach the concept of what a bridge is and such factors as how bridges differ in structure and purpose. Further, the would-be bridge builder would have to know something about soil dynamics, the nature of the neighborhood, to determine whether or not or how his structure could be supported at the desired location.

No medical school would attempt to teach surgery or dermatology without first teaching the anatomy of the whole body and the functions of various organs.

Yet schools of education send their products into Spanish Harlem or Lawndale or Watts with no knowledge of the nature of the children, no knowledge of the neighborhood and the community residents, and no appreciation for the culture of those communities. It is amazing that any excellent teaching occurs. When it does it is as a result of on-the-job training come by through a rat in the maze, hit and miss procedure. Schools of education must cease attempting to prepare teachers for a monolithic white school which does not exist in the heart of the interior, if it exists anywhere.

The proper study for inner-city teachers is the inner city. To teach Negro, Mexican, Puerto Rican, Amerindian, and poor Southern white children, a teacher will have to be taught, herself, the history and culture of Negroes, Spanish-speaking, American Indians and Southern white migrant children. Teachers must be taught the anthro-sociopsychological factors related to poverty, racism, and oppression. And they will need to know the idiom of the black ghettos and the Southern Mountains, and the Spanish of El Barrio. Further, teachers in training should, early in their undergraduate years, be exposed to a variety of experiences which will help them to understand the lifestyle and coping mechanisms imposed by social and economic exclusion.

Hopefully, through early contacts with children of poverty and through formal study of their history and culture, teacher cadets will learn not only about the needs of the children and their communities, but also they will gain insights into themselves, their stereotypes and biases and into how their behavior affects the lives of children entrusted to them.

Just how we convince colleges and universities to re-order their teacher-training curricula and practices is difficult to know. Even if a significant number of the great teacher-producing institutions were to decide tomorrow to bring their training programs into consonance with pressing urban needs, they would be hard-put, indeed, to get their faculties to step to a new drummer or to acquire faculty with the new visions. Perhaps it is just this type of dilemma which has induced the U.S. Office of Education to initiate the Triple T Project (Training the Teachers of Teachers).

At the Center for Inner City Studies we don't pretend that we have all the religion, but we are attempting, on the graduate level, to provide the kind of urban immersion that I am advocating. A few of our recent graduates have already been hired by Teacher Corps and universities to give some direction.

Imperative Number Two urges radical change in the training of teachers and other school personnel to satisfy both the needs of the children and of the teachers themselves.

The Third Imperative is *the need for curriculum change within the schools*. Many researchers have documented the psychic damage which racism has done to young Negro children. Exposed to a society which postulates and which reinforces an image of inferiority through the mass media and through the assignment of a second-class lifestyle to black people, little children of color and older ones doubt themselves, and frequently reject themselves and others like them. School curriculum will have to be restructured to be responsive to the affective as well as the cognitive needs of disadvantaged pupils.

Curriculum is defined here as any experiences which help children to learn and which help pupils to develop qualities of self-actualization.

Courses will have to be instituted into public school curricula which will re-order reality for black children, and for that matter, white children, too. Black and Spanish-speaking children must be taught their heritage, and they must be encouraged to take great pride in that heritage. I will leave to the historians whether, for example, Afro-American history ought to be taught separately or as part of the general American history, from which it is presently absent. My concern is that all children be informed that the miraculous achievements of Dr. Christian Barnard were, in some measure, made possible by the work of a black man, Dr. Daniel Hale Williams who in 1893 performed the first successful heart surgery in America. A single achievement, however great, would not be so significant in the history of civilization which has witnessed many great achievements. But what is significant, however, is that black people have made countless contributions to mankind, which have been deliberately omitted from world and American history. If black people really knew the truth about themselves and their magnificent accomplishments, they would soon discontinue the self-abnegation which has characterized the black experience in America.

But black and other exploited poor need more than their history. Self-acceptance and racial pride are important affective development. But what of cognitions? Black people will need specific weapons to fight back against oppression and exploitation. They need economics and they need politics. Who controls the ghetto? Why are rents disproportionately higher in the black belt? Why are food prices higher and meat inferior at white-owned black stores than at white-owned white stores? Why do drugstores in the ghetto charge more, sometimes 100% more for medicines? And what about auto dealers? Why do the poor pay more? Why do the black poor pay the most? How can poor people develop and martial economic and political forces to control their own destinies? These and others are the burning questions for which curriculum and instruction must provide some answers.

For example, mathematics can be taught in terms of budgets, interest rates, insurance payments and the like. The sciences can be taught with respect to the ghetto's needs: the biology of reproduction, the chemistry of foods and medicines and so on.

Language arts and social studies should also serve the community's culture and its needs. In this regard James Baldwin, Martin Luther King, and Malcolm "X" are more important than Shakespeare and Melville. Charles Drew, the discoverer of blood plasma is more important to black people than Enrico Fermi. And the biography of Frederick Douglass is more significant than the biography of George Washington. I am not suggesting that a sonnet of Shelly should never find its way into the black school, or that the discoveries of Steinmetz and Edison are not important for all science students, but I am clearly and strongly advocating that the genuine accomplishments of distinguished black men are of greater importance to the intellectual development of black children.

Schools must stop preparing Afro-Americans for menial jobs and minor roles in the social order. The task of curriculum and instruction in the black community is to prepare black pupils to celebrate themselves and to help them discover the wherewithal and the methodology to begin to enjoy the fruits of an affluent nation, heretofore available only to whites and a few hand-picked blacks.

Imperative Number Four is *the need to change controls in the urban schools*. The subject of control has become a topic of concern in many quarters. For instance, the Coleman Report of *Equality of Educational Opportunity* talks about a sense of control as one of the important variables that determine Negro achievement.[3] The Coleman Report postulates that a Negro pupil's sense of control is heightened as the proportion of white pupils in his environment is increased. Increasing the control factor, Coleman and associates contend, increases achievement. Yet, the same Coleman Report also claims that while achievement increases in the integrated school, the self-concept of Negro pupils is diminished.[4] More attention to this in a moment.

Other voices than Coleman's are speaking of control, *actual* rather than a *sense* of control. Black people all over America are demanding that they be self-determining by controlling all factors in the ghetto: The economy, the politics, the schools, everything.

Returning to the Coleman Report, I am not surprised that young black children feel a sense of diminished self-esteem in integrated schools. Picture yourself being bussed across town to the white school. Obviously your school wasn't good enough for you to learn there, or for white children to come and join you. So for your own good you had to be herded off on buses to the good school. Once there you might have to wade through jeering pickets to reach the building. Or if not that, then you encounter hostile teachers, some overtly, some subtly so. Most white students will ignore you, a few well meaning ones will patronize you. Under such circumstances I find highly questionable Professor Coleman's assertion that black pupils do, indeed, achieve more because of a newly acquired sense of control. I would assert that a more logical explanation for increased achievement is a combination of the following:

1. The schools to which the black pupils were bussed are middle-class white schools where there is considerable academic press. White middle-class parents demand that teachers teach. They accept no nonsense about missing library books and cognitive deficits.

2. Faculties in those schools are stable. They are permanent rather than substitutes. Children in those schools expect and have continuity. They have the same teachers everyday, unlike children in the ghetto who may have as many as ten or more teachers in a single term.

3. Negro pupils learn because of the above factors and because the teachers expect their pupils to learn, and teach accordingly. I cannot understand how Negroes could feel a greater sense of control, when as even Professor Coleman reveals their self-esteem is lessened in the white school.

Because the control factor is alleged to be critical, and I believe that it is, let us look at the matter of control in terms of the ghetto school. It is hardly conceivable that any but a few children could feel a sense of control in the black school where the principal is white, the assistant principal and the counselors are white, the school engineer is white, the window washers are white and if the windows get broken the glaziers are white. And so is the superintendent of schools, even in Washington, D.C. It is virtually impossible for black pupils or black teachers to feel a sense of potency when from the top of the school system right to the boiler room, they are administered, supervised and manipulated by white people. This pattern of white dominance of black welfare and black interests is omni-present and pervasive in all areas of the black existence.

Of special interest is the finding of the Report, *Racial Isolation in the Public Schools* that no known compensatory education program has been successful in increasing the achievement of Negro pupils.[5] Assess that finding against the fact that at a recent national meeting of all the State ESEA Title I Directors, there was not a single Negro in the group. Further, at a recent meeting held in Washington, which was comprised of over six hundred NDEA and Experienced Teacher Fellowship Program directors there were not more than twenty-five Negroes among the six hundred. It is little wonder that compensatory programs designed and administered by white people conducted in black schools run by white people have yielded few positive results for black children.

Carrying the analysis a step further, one is hard-pressed to find black and brown decision makers in the U.S. Office of Education, which commissions, approves, and dispenses funds for these programs.

I am sure there are hundreds of reasons why white people are in complete control of the education of twenty-two or more million blacks. These reasons range from arguments of longevity, color-blindness, professional territoriality, and "Divine Right of Kings," to the simple equation: "We've got you outnumbered."

It would be futile for me to enumerate and attempt to answer all of these questions. I would simply submit that there are a few reasons which are superordinate and are more compelling reasons why substantial changes must be made in this self-defeating structure.

First, the urban schools are in shambles as black students are struggling and fighting to live. They are being cheated and they know it, but they have no sense of control and no socially approved means of self-determination. Therefore some of them find other sources of potency, other ways to confront a dehumanizing, oppressive system: Hurling bottled fire, smashing windows, stealing cars, looting.

I would prefer and I think you would prefer to have these angry, abused young people find their power and their self-esteem by flexing their muscles and developing their manhood in the determination and direction of their own destinies. Through their own black symbols of authority, real ones, not white-appointed Uncle Toms, they will have available more positive channels for self-actualization.

Second, white people have already demonstrated their inadequacy or their unwillingness to provide quality education for black people. Joseph Alsop has written that if the worst racist in America set out to design a structure which would keep the Negro enchained, he could do no better than to use the present public education system.[6]

Third, as evidenced by the two-year controversy at IS 201, black people are becoming determined that they will run their own schools, and they are determined that teachers and administrators will be held accountable to black communities. As black communities stiffen, fewer and fewer white people will be permitted to have authoritative positions in those communities.

Therefore, it is my contention that the survival of the urban schools is dependent upon the willingness of the educational establishment to change the control factors in all aspects of urban education, from the U.S. Office of Education right down to the pre-schools. Enlightened self-interest would seem to dictate this.

The Fifth and final Imperative is *the upgrading of the black schools.*

Even if integration were a desirable goal, though a growing number of black people believe it is not, its achievement does not seem likely in the immediate future. The masses of black children cannot wait until the millennium for their equal educational opportunities. We must, therefore, make it possible for quality education to take place in the black school.

Yet, if the teachers who work in the black school, the children who attend it and the community perceive it as an inferior school, then it is, in fact, an inferior school.

We must change the black school's ethos. This can be done by staffing it with teachers who have been trained to understand and respect black and brown people; by administering it with black and brown people who are accountable to the pupils and their community; and by re-ordering curriculum and instruction to meet the real not imaginary needs of the pupils. Finally, though I have not listed adequate financing as an imperative, it nonetheless is. However, I have limited my discussion to those factors which do not involve substantial additional expenditures, but which call instead for changes in attitudes, assumptions and structures. Unquestionably, the demands that Negroes are placing upon society for changes in all institutions, particularly the schools, can result in all Americans being the beneficiaries.

If, somehow, we can sense the urgency of abandoning a public school that never worked; if we can change curriculum and materials so radically that all children can identify with the curriculum because it is relevant to their needs; if we can train teachers to understand and love most of their children—

irrespective of race or class—; if we can change the symbols of control, then perhaps there is some hope for the American school.

If we cannot bring about these changes which beg to be made, there is little hope for the schools or for the nation.

NOTES

1. Edgar Friedenberg, "Requiem for the Urban School," *Saturday Review* (Nov. 18, 1967).

2. Robert Rosenthal and Lenore Jacobson, "Self-Fulfilling Prophecies in the Classroom; Teachers' Expectations as Unintended Determinants of Pupils' Intellectual Competence." A paper presented at the American Psychological Association, Washington, D.C., September, 1967.

3. *Equality of Educational Opportunity*, Washington, D.C.: U.S. Government Printing Office, 1966.

4. *Ibid.*, p. 323.

5. U.S. Commission on Civil Rights, *Racial Isolation in the Public Schools*, Washington, D.C.: U.S. Government Printing Office, 1967, Chapter 4.

6. Joseph Alsop, "No More Nonsense About Ghetto Education," *New Republic* (July 22, 1967).

DISCUSSION QUESTIONS

1. Joyce contends that the melting pot concept has failed in American society. Do you agree or disagree? Explain.

2. According to Howard, culturally different children "have much to teach America, especially about the nature of freedom." What lessons about freedom can society learn from our oppressed minority groups?

3. What contributions might the humanities make to the education of poor children?

4. McIntosh accuses the public school of promoting an "uncritical acceptance" of our political institutions. Is this accusation justified? If so, how might the social studies help make children social critics and agents of change?

5. What specific contributions can the social studies make to the liberation of blacks and other oppressed groups?

6. Hamilton argues that the conception of a *legitimate* education for black children must be determined by the black community and not by educational experts. How does this argument conflict with our traditional

assumptions about the role of the professional educator? How might this conflict be resolved?

7. Smith, in the final selection in this chapter, contends that minority group pupils frequently fail to learn because we lack a *commitment* to educate them. How can teachers develop such a commitment?

8. What changes does Smith feel are essential if urban schools are to be successful? How might we bring about these changes?

SUGGESTED READINGS

Baldwin, James, "A Talk To Teachers," *Saturday Review* pp. 42–44, 60 ff., December 21, 1963

Carmichael, Stokely, and Charles V. Hamilton, *Black Power: The Politics of Liberation in America.* New York: Vintage Books, 1967

Clark, Kenneth B., "Alternative Public School Systems," *Harvard Educational Review*, **38**, 100–113, 1968

Fantini, Mario D., and Milton A. Young, *Designing Education For Tomorrow's Cities.* New York: Holt, Rinehart and Winston, 1970

Frost, Joe L., and Glenn R. Hawkes (Editors), *The Disadvantaged Child: Issues and Innovations, Second Edition.* Boston: Houghton Mifflin, 1970

Gittell, Marilyn, and Alan G. Hevesi (Editors), *The Politics of Urban Education.* New York: Frederick A. Praeger, 1969

Green, Robert L., *Racial Crisis in American Education.* Chicago: Follett Educational Corporation, 1969

Herndon, James, *The Way It Spozed To Be.* New York: Bantam Books, 1968

Jarolimek, John (Editor), "The Elementary School: Focus on the Culturally Different," *Social Education*, **33**, 61–82, 1969. [Articles by Edward G. Ponder, James A. Banks, Robert V. Dumont, Jr., Richard D. Arnold, and Richard Wisniewski.]

King, Martin L., Jr., *Where Do We Go From Here: Chaos or Community?* New York: Bantam Books, 1968

Kohl, Herbert R., *The Open Classroom: A Practical Guide To A New Way of Teaching.* New York: Vintage Books, 1969

Kontos, Peter G., and James J. Murphy, *Teaching Urban Youth: A Source Book for Urban Education.* New York: John Wiley & Sons, 1967

Passow, A. Harry, *Education in Depressed Areas.* New York: Teachers College Press, 1963

Selakovich, Daniel, *Social Studies for the Disadvantaged.* New York: Holt, Rinehart and Winston, 1970

Stone, James G., and Frederick W. Schneider, *Teaching in the Inner City: A Book of Readings*. New York: Thomas Y. Crowell Company, 1970

Toffler, Alvin (Editor), *The Schoolhouse in the City*. New York: Frederick A. Praeger, 1968

Trubowitz, Sidney, *A Handbook for Teaching in the Ghetto School*. Chicago: Quadrangle Books, 1968

Webster, Staten W. (Editor), *The Disadvantaged Learner: Knowing, Understanding, Educating*. San Francisco: Chandler Publishing Company, 1966. [Also available in three separate volumes.]

Webster, Staten W., "Social Studies for Disadvantaged Students," in Staten G. Webster (Editor), *The Disadvantaged Learner: Knowing, Understanding, Educating*, pp. 586–594. San Francisco: Chandler Publishing Company, 1966

ABCDE7987654321